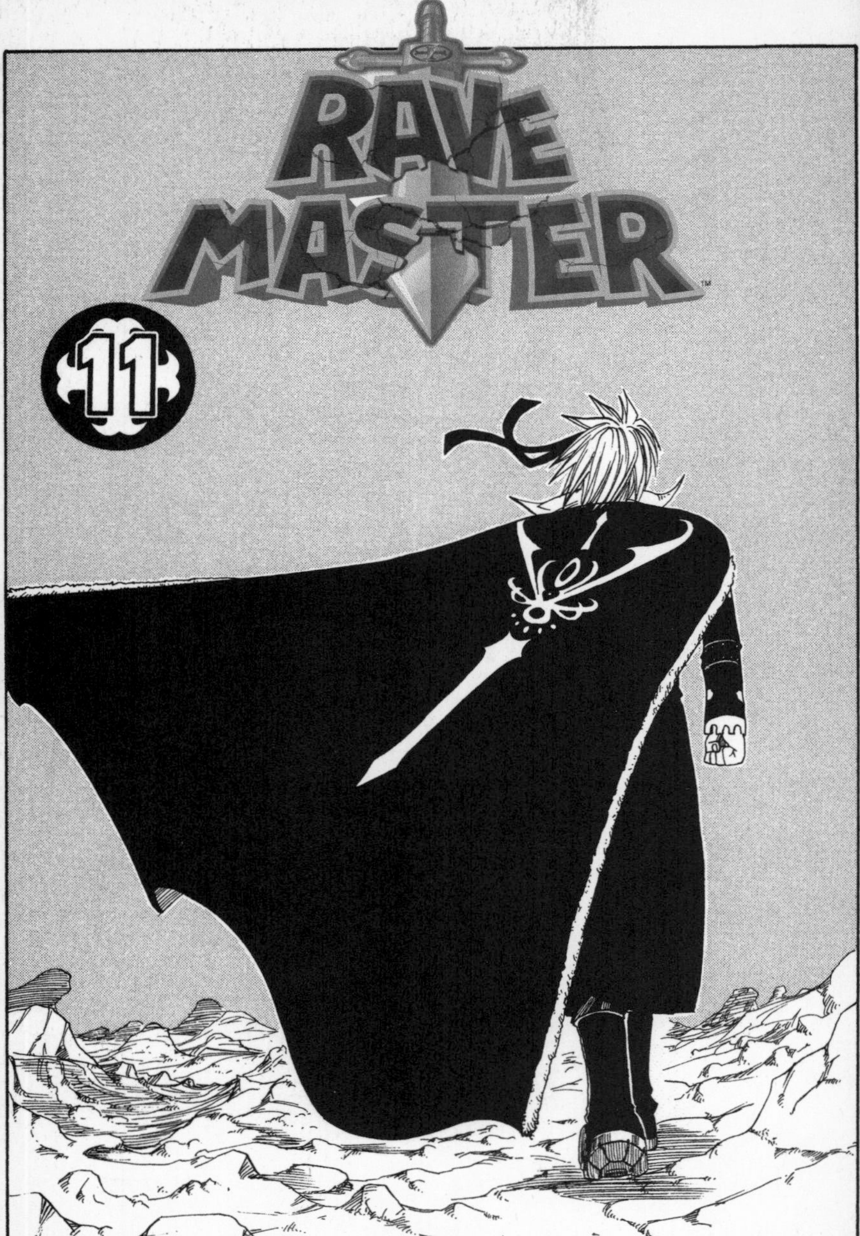
RAVE MASTER™
11

Rave Master Vol. 11

created by Hiro Mashima

Translation - Jeremiah Bourque
Retouch and Lettering - Marnie Echols and Louis Csontos
Graphic Designer - Vicente Rivera, Jr.
Cover Design - Raymond Makowski

Editor - Jake Forbes
Digital Imaging Manager - Chris Buford
Pre-Press Manager - Antonio DePietro
Production Managers - Jennifer Miller and Mutsumi Miyazaki
Art Director - Matt Alford
Managing Editor - Jill Freshney
VP of Production - Ron Klamert
President and C.O.O. - John Parker
Publisher and C.E.O. - Stuart Levy

A 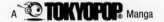 Manga

TOKYOPOP Inc.
5900 Wilshire Blvd. Suite 2000
Los Angeles, CA 90036

E-mail: info@TOKYOPOP.com
Come visit us online at www.TOKYOPOP.com

ISBN: 1-59182-521-0

First TOKYOPOP printing: October 2004
10 9 8 7 6 5 4 3 2 1
Printed in the USA

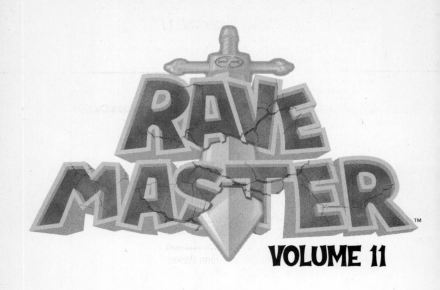

VOLUME 11

Story and Art by
HIRO MASHIMA

NORTHWEST

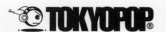

HAMBURG // LONDON // LOS ANGELES // TOKYO

THE STORY SO FAR...

Demon Card lies in shambles, its leader dead, its agents gathered up by the **Imperial Army.** As the Empire attempts to restore order, various criminal syndicates, such as the Doryu Ghost Attack Squad, seek to fill the void left by DC's demise. Meanwhile, Haru Glory and his friends continue their quest to find the remaining two Rave Stones and unlock **Star Memory.** In order to fund their search, Haru teamed up with **Ruby,** a penguin-like billionaire with a good heart and a love of rare and unique items. Their next stop is **Symphonia,** the birthplace of Rave, which was destroyed 51 years ago in the Overdrive. But to get there, the gang must first past through the infamous **Death Storm.**

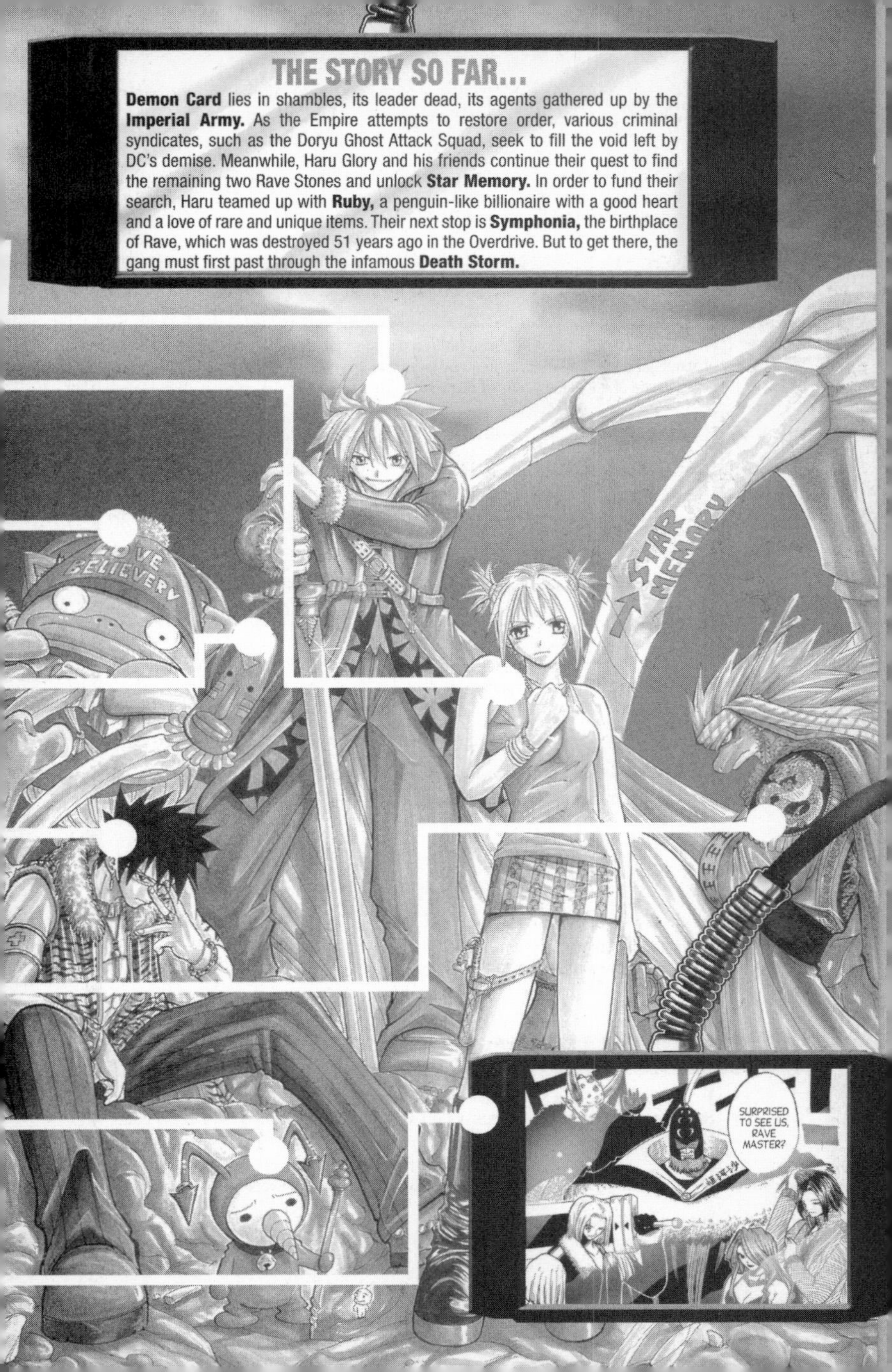
STAR MEMORY
LOVE BELIEVER
SURPRISED TO SEE US, RAVE MASTER?

THE RAVE MASTER CREW

HARU GLORY

A small-town boy turned savior of the world. As the **Rave Master** (the only one capable of using the holy weapon RAVE), Haru set forth to find the missing Rave Stones and defeat Demon Card. He fights with the **Ten Powers Sword,** a weapon that takes on different forms at his command. With Demon Card seemingly out of the way, Haru now seeks the remaining two Rave Stones in order to open the way to Star Memory.

ELIE

The girl without memories. Elie joined Haru on his quest when he promised to help her find out about her past. She's cute, spunky and loves gambling and shopping in equal measures. Locked inside of her is the power of **Etherion.**

RUBY

A "penguin-type" senteniod, Ruby loves rare and unusual items. After Haru saved him from Pumpkin Doryu's gang, Ruby agreed to sponsor Haru's team in their search for the ultimate rare treasures: the Rave Stones!

GRIFFON KATO (GRIFF)

Griff is a loyal friend, even if he is a bit of a coward. His rubbery body can stretch and change shape as needed. Griff's two greatest pleasures in life are mapmaking and peeping on Elie.

MUSICA

A **"Silverclaimer"** (an alchemist who can shape silver at will) and a former street punk who made good. He joined Haru for the adventure, but now that Demon Card is defeated, does he have any reason to stick around?

LET

A member of the Dragon race, he was formerly a member of the Demon Card's Five Palace Guardians. He was so impressed by Haru's fighting skills and pureness of heart that he made a truce with the Rave Master.

PLUE

The **Rave Bearer,** Plue is the faithful companion to the Rave Master. In addition to being Haru's guide, Plue also has powers of his own. When he's not getting Haru into or out of trouble, Plue can be found enjoying a sucker, his favorite treat.

THE ORACION SIX

Demon Card's six generals. Haru defeated Shuda after finding the Rave of Wisdom. The other five generals were presumed dead after King destroyed Demon Card Headquarters.

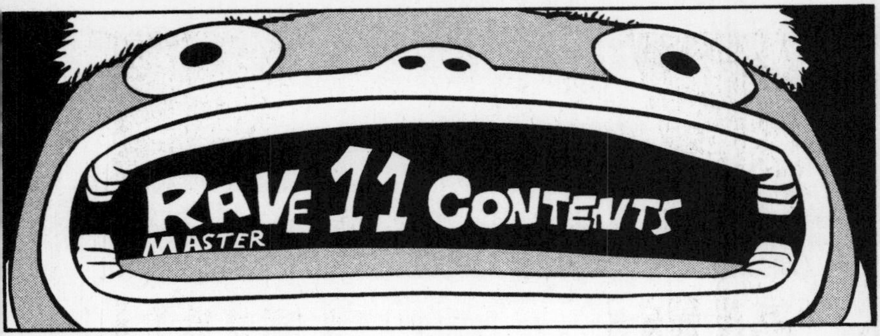
RAVE MASTER 11 CONTENTS

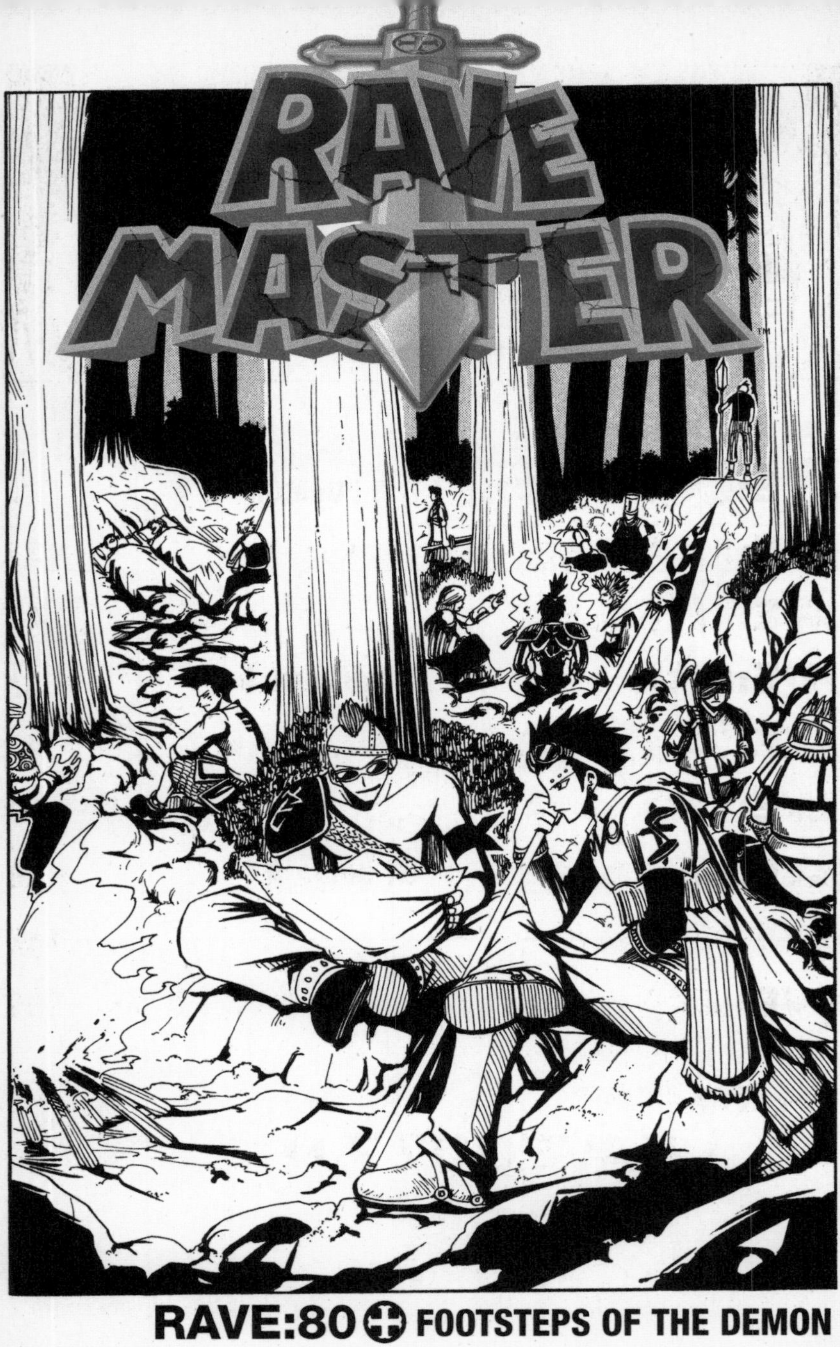
RAVE MASTER

RAVE:80 ✠ FOOTSTEPS OF THE DEMON

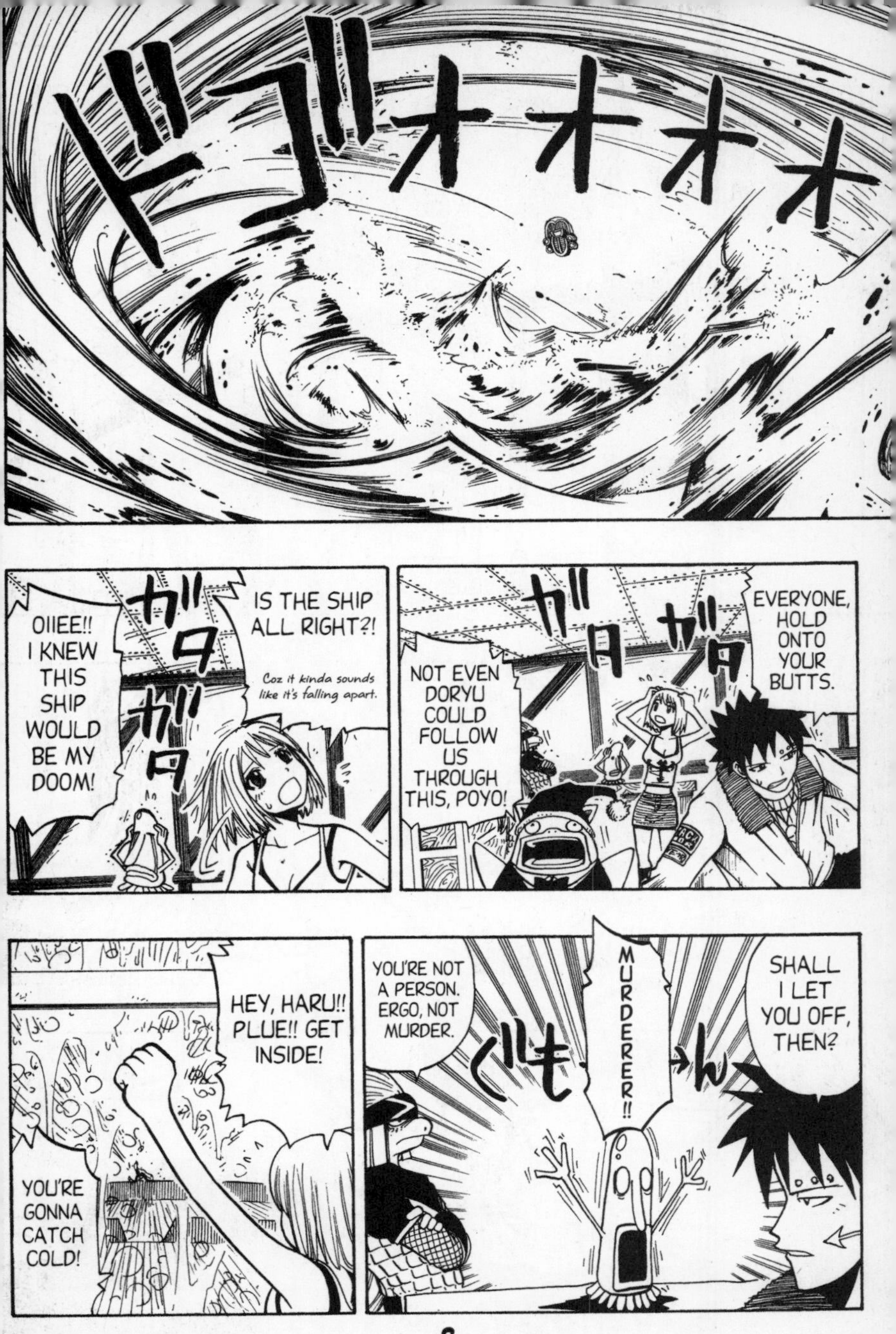
ドゴオオオ
EVERYONE, HOLD ONTO YOUR BUTTS.
ガタ ガタ
NOT EVEN DORYU COULD FOLLOW US THROUGH THIS, POYO!
IS THE SHIP ALL RIGHT?!
Coz it kinda sounds like it's falling apart.
ガタガタ
OIIEE!! I KNEW THIS SHIP WOULD BE MY DOOM!
SHALL I LET YOU OFF, THEN?
MURDERER!!
YOU'RE NOT A PERSON. ERGO, NOT MURDER.
ぐもーん
HEY, HARU!! PLUE!! GET INSIDE!
YOU'RE GONNA CATCH COLD!

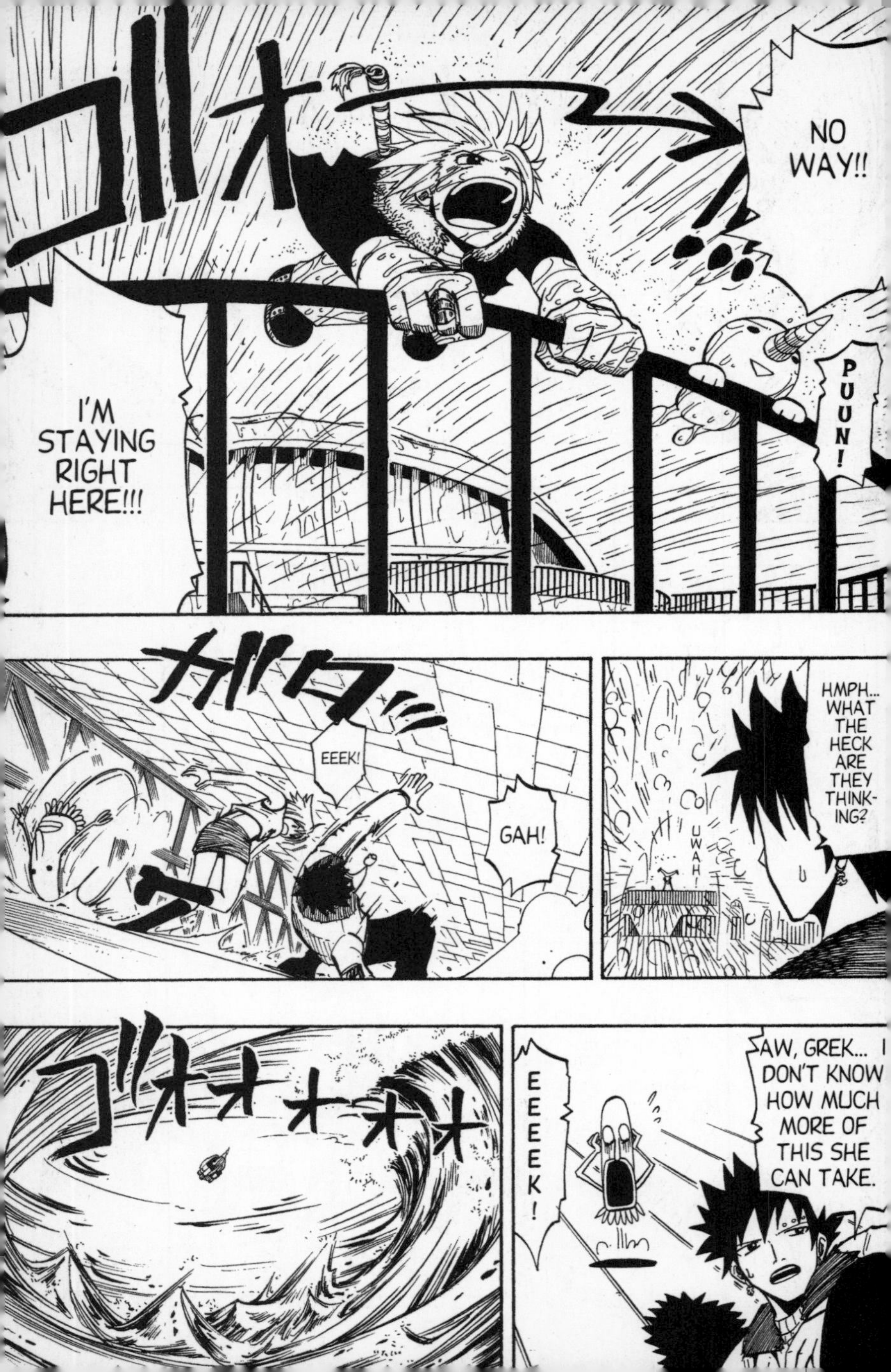

NO WAY!!
PUUN!
I'M STAYING RIGHT HERE!!!
HMPH... WHAT THE HECK ARE THEY THINKING?
UWAH!
EEEK!
GAH!
AW, GREK... I DON'T KNOW HOW MUCH MORE OF THIS SHE CAN TAKE.
EEEEK!

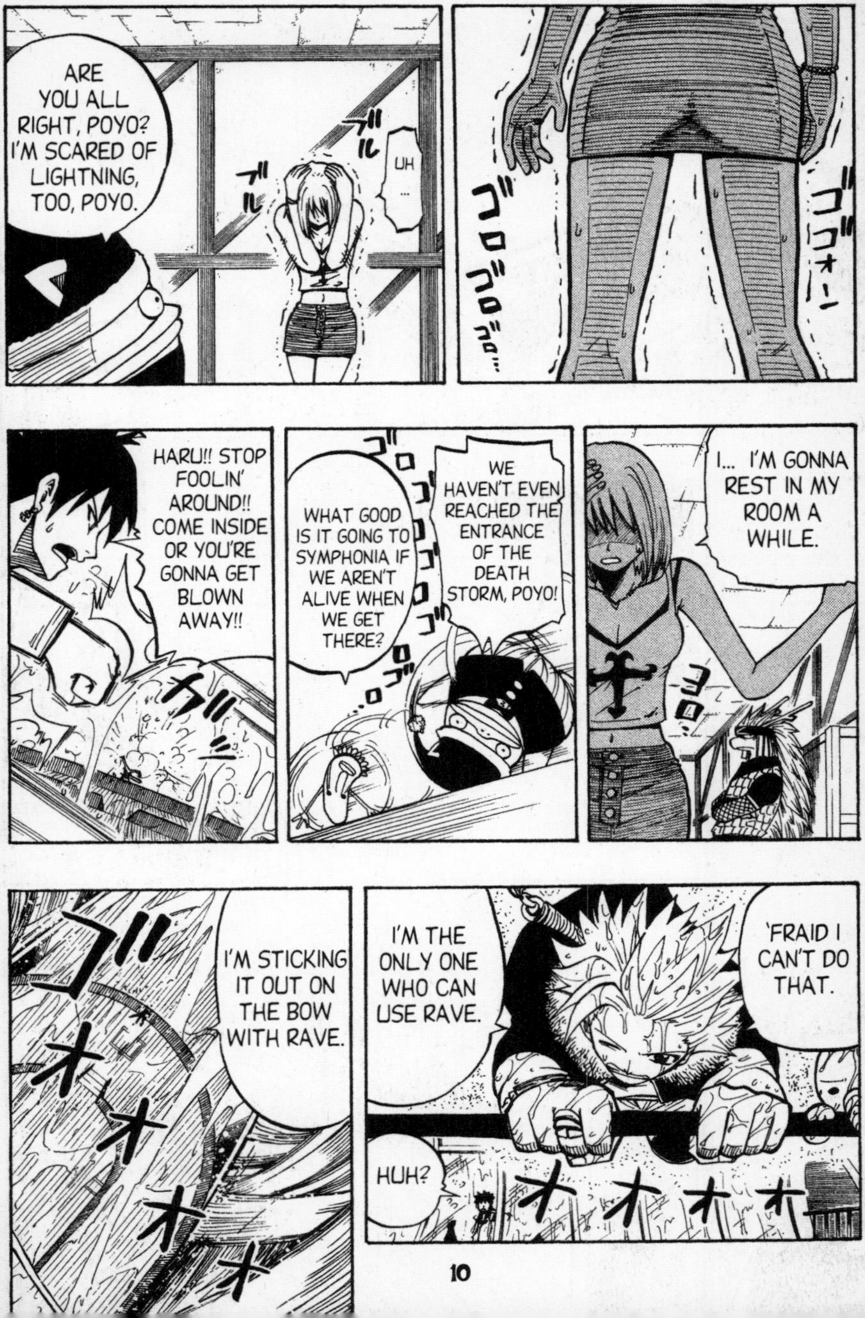
UH ...
ARE YOU ALL RIGHT, POYO? I'M SCARED OF LIGHTNING, TOO, POYO.
I... I'M GONNA REST IN MY ROOM A WHILE.
WE HAVEN'T EVEN REACHED THE ENTRANCE OF THE DEATH STORM, POYO!
WHAT GOOD IS IT GOING TO SYMPHONIA IF WE AREN'T ALIVE WHEN WE GET THERE?
HARU!! STOP FOOLIN' AROUND!! COME INSIDE OR YOU'RE GONNA GET BLOWN AWAY!!
'FRAID I CAN'T DO THAT.
I'M THE ONLY ONE WHO CAN USE RAVE.
HUH?
I'M STICKING IT OUT ON THE BOW WITH RAVE.

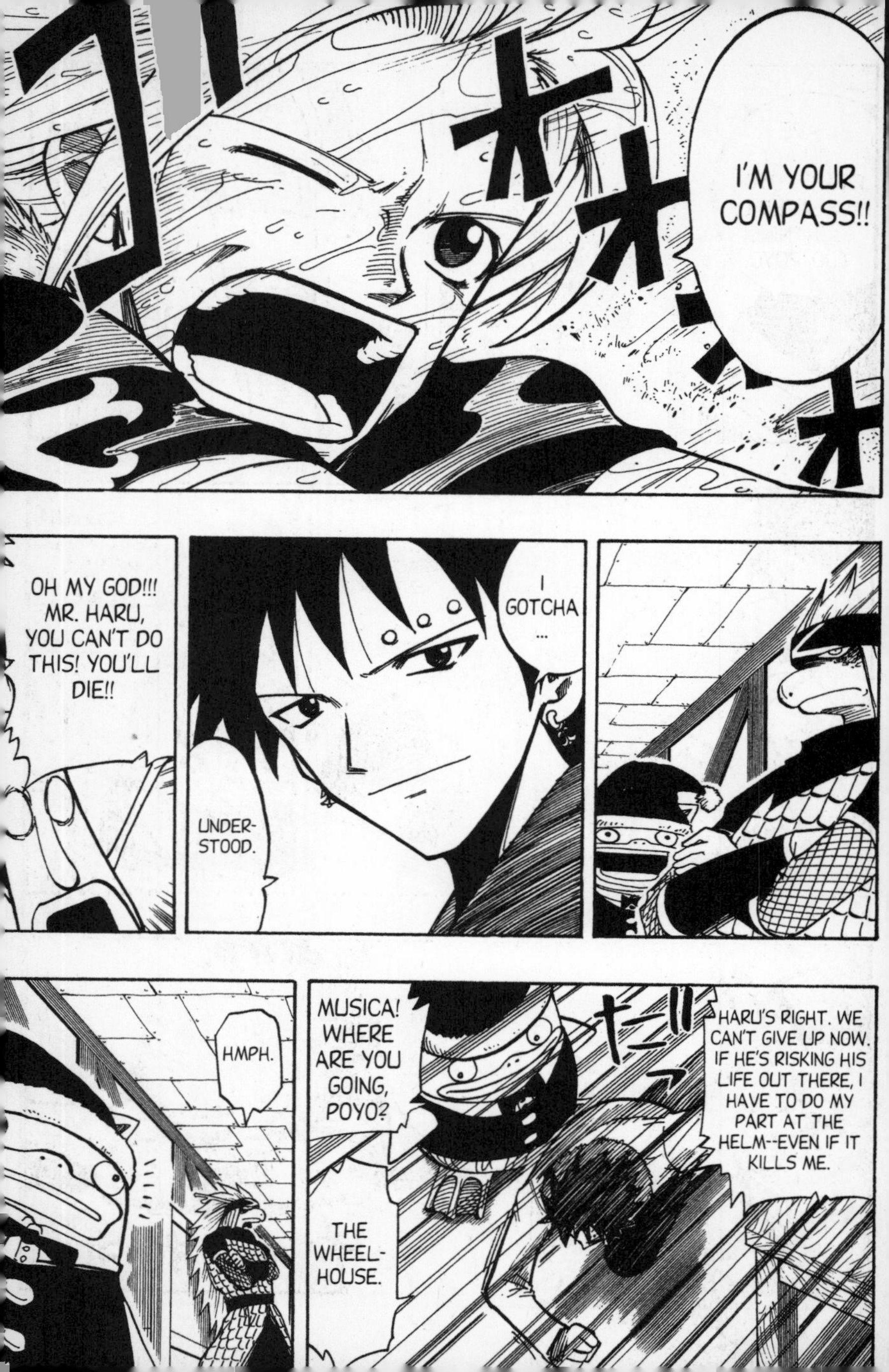
I'M YOUR COMPASS!!
I GOTCHA ...
UNDERSTOOD.
OH MY GOD!!! MR. HARU, YOU CAN'T DO THIS! YOU'LL DIE!!
MUSICA! WHERE ARE YOU GOING, POYO?
THE WHEEL-HOUSE.
HARU'S RIGHT. WE CAN'T GIVE UP NOW. IF HE'S RISKING HIS LIFE OUT THERE, I HAVE TO DO MY PART AT THE HELM--EVEN IF IT KILLS ME.
HMPH.

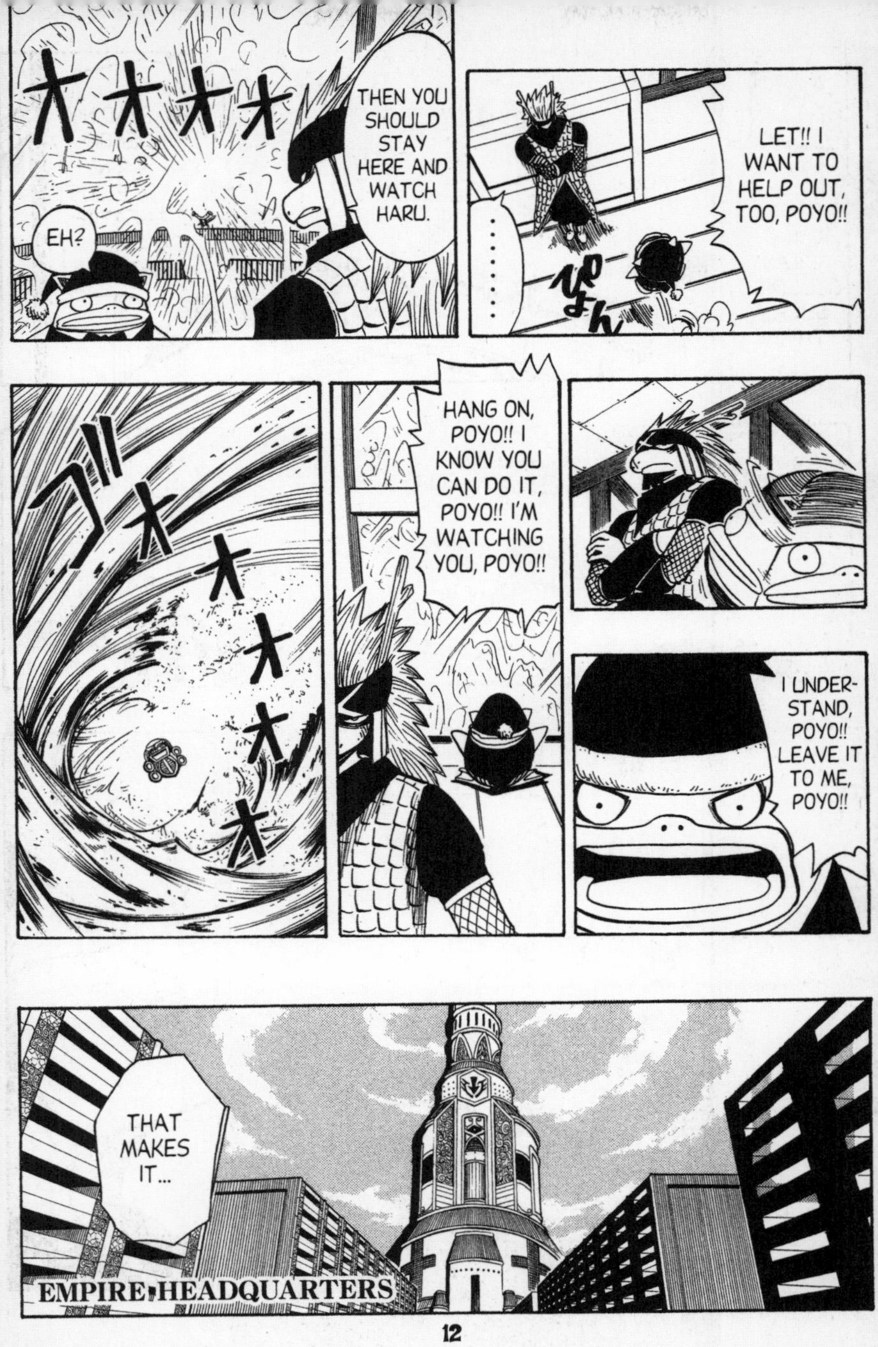

LET!! I WANT TO HELP OUT, TOO, POYO!!
...
ぴょん
THEN YOU SHOULD STAY HERE AND WATCH HARU.
オオオオ
EH?
I UNDER-STAND, POYO!! LEAVE IT TO ME, POYO!!
HANG ON, POYO!! I KNOW YOU CAN DO IT, POYO!! I'M WATCHING YOU, POYO!!
ゴオオオオオ
THAT MAKES IT...
EMPIRE HEADQUARTERS

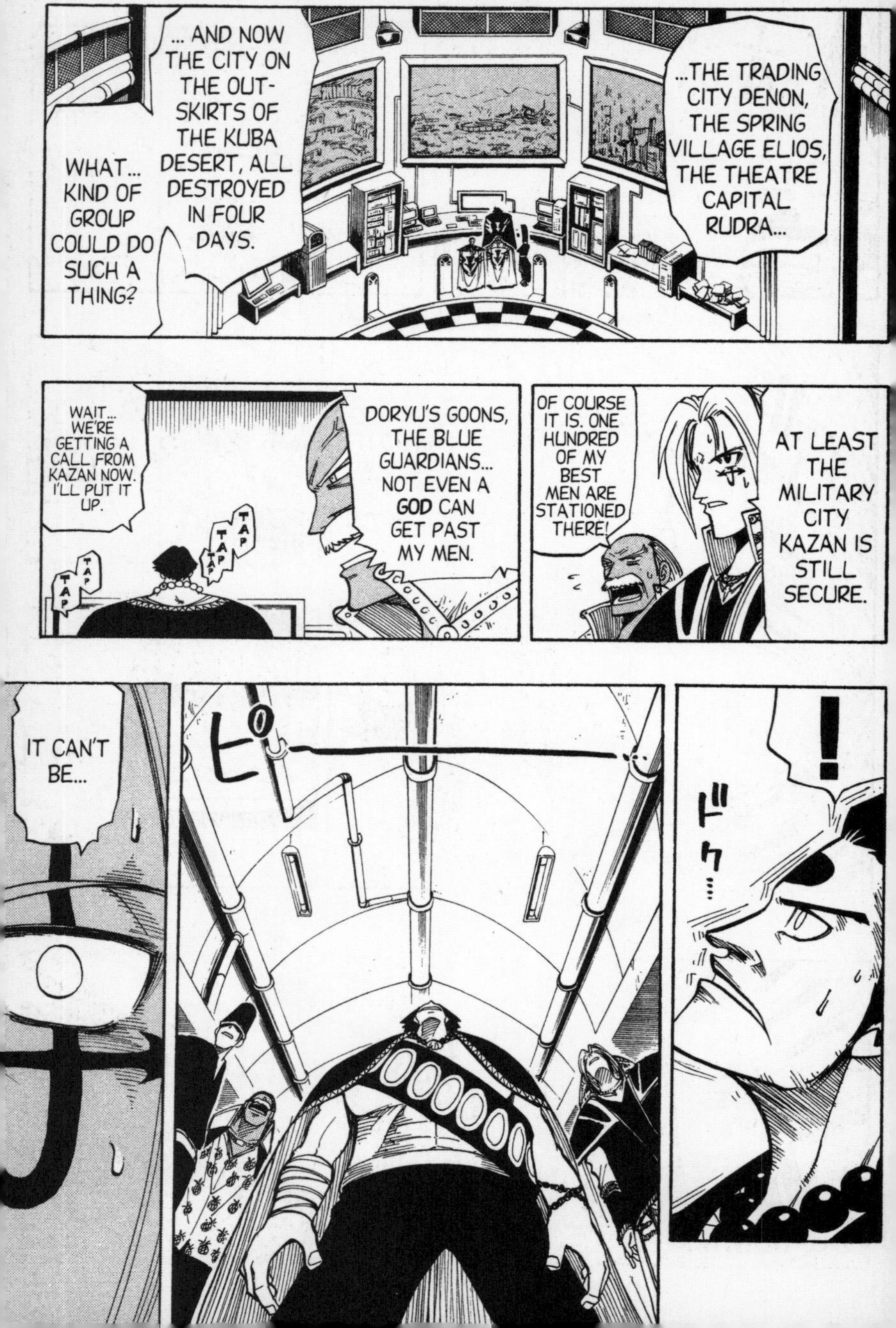
...THE TRADING CITY DENON, THE SPRING VILLAGE ELIOS, THE THEATRE CAPITAL RUDRA...
... AND NOW THE CITY ON THE OUT-SKIRTS OF THE KUBA DESERT, ALL DESTROYED IN FOUR DAYS.
WHAT... KIND OF GROUP COULD DO SUCH A THING?
AT LEAST THE MILITARY CITY KAZAN IS STILL SECURE.
OF COURSE IT IS. ONE HUNDRED OF MY BEST MEN ARE STATIONED THERE!
DORYU'S GOONS, THE BLUE GUARDIANS... NOT EVEN A **GOD** CAN GET PAST MY MEN.
TAP TAP
TAP TAP
WAIT... WE'RE GETTING A CALL FROM KAZAN NOW. I'LL PUT IT UP.
!
ドク…
ピー
IT CAN'T BE...

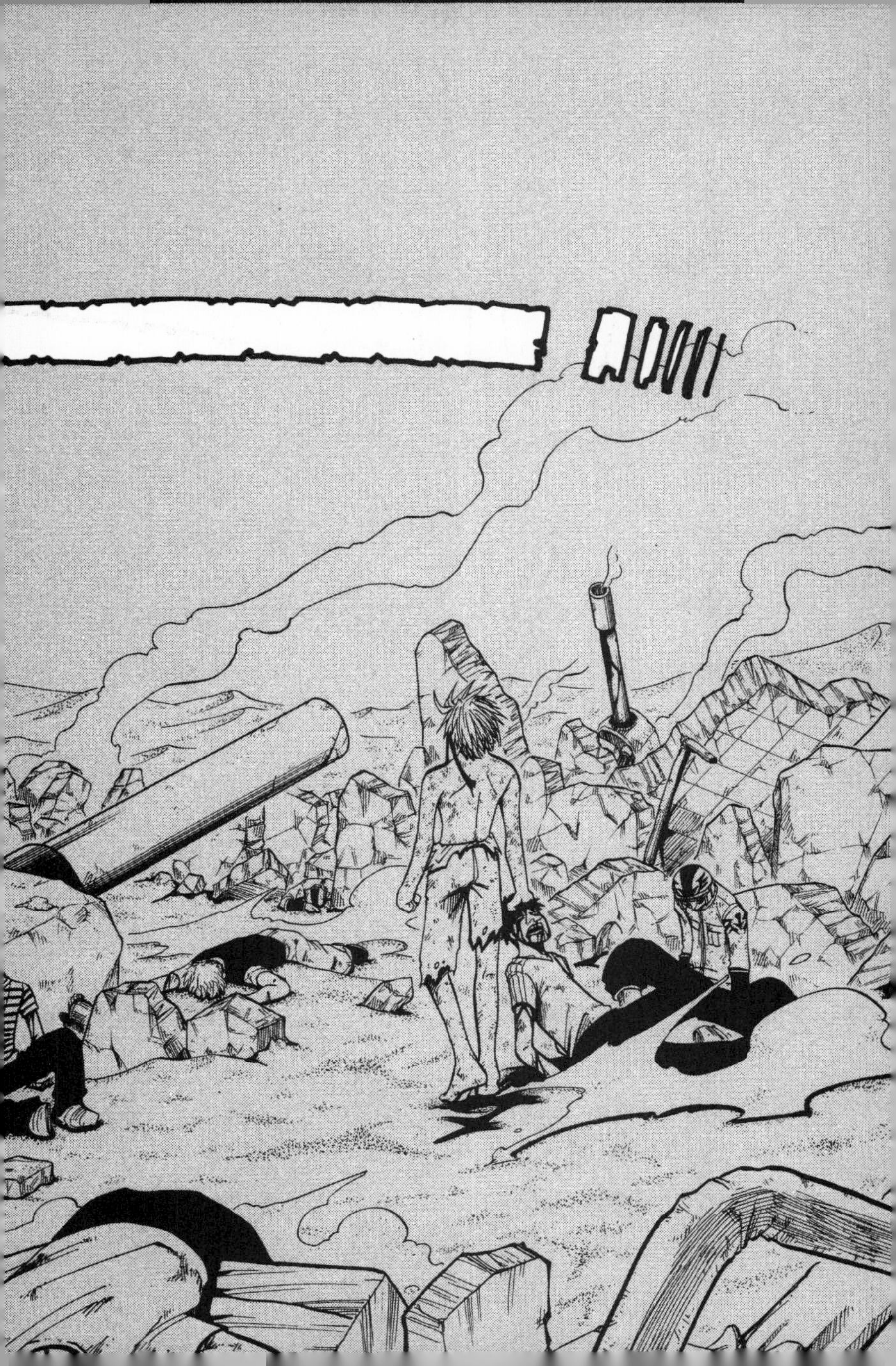

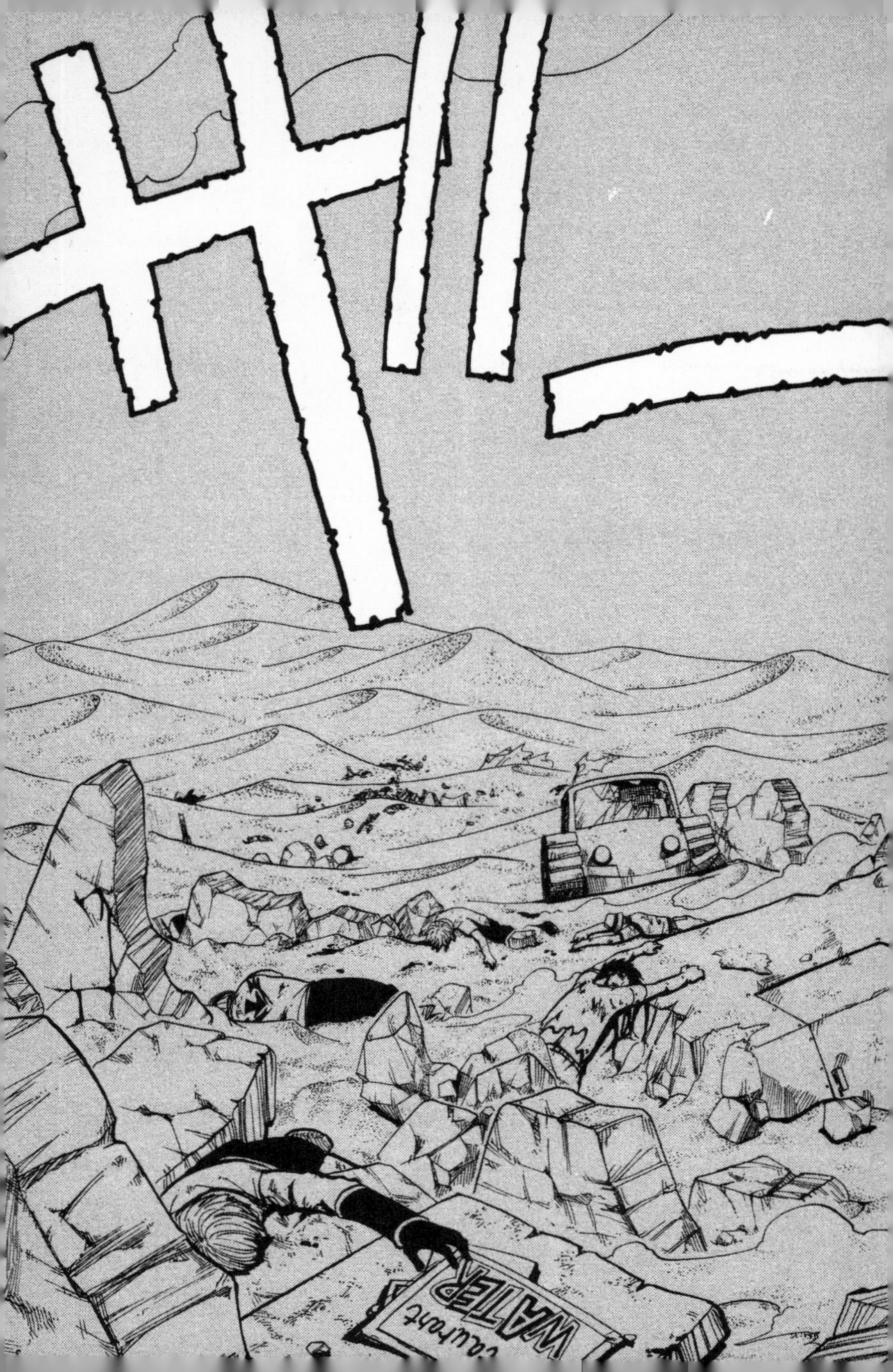
ザー
WATER
taurant

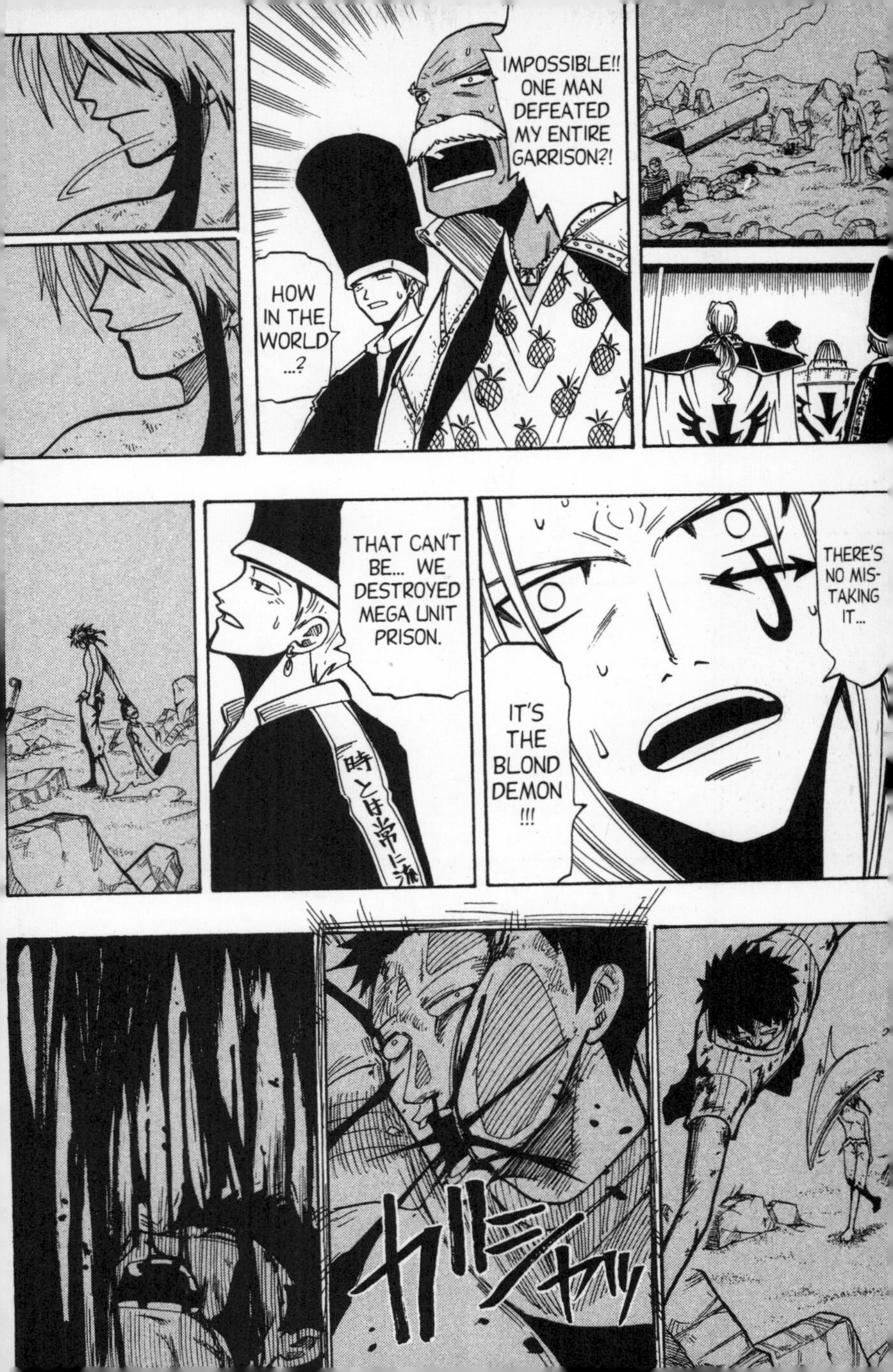
IMPOSSIBLE!! ONE MAN DEFEATED MY ENTIRE GARRISON?!
HOW IN THE WORLD ...?
THERE'S NO MISTAKING IT...
IT'S THE BLOND DEMON!!!
THAT CAN'T BE... WE DESTROYED MEGA UNIT PRISON.

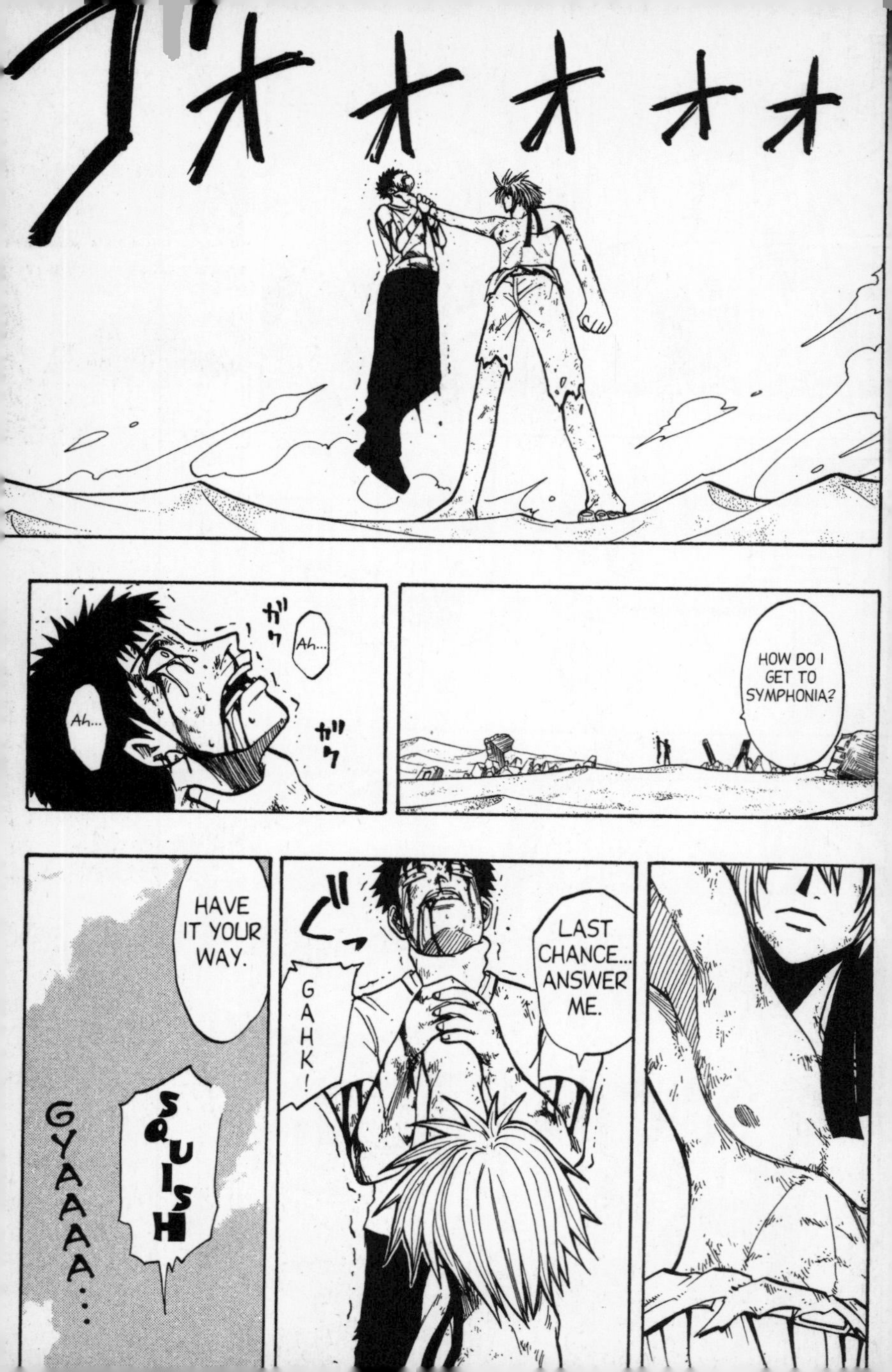
ゴオオオオオ
HOW DO I GET TO SYMPHONIA?
ガク
Ah...
Ah...
ガク
LAST CHANCE... ANSWER ME.
ぐっ
GAHK!
HAVE IT YOUR WAY.
SQUISH
GYAAAA...

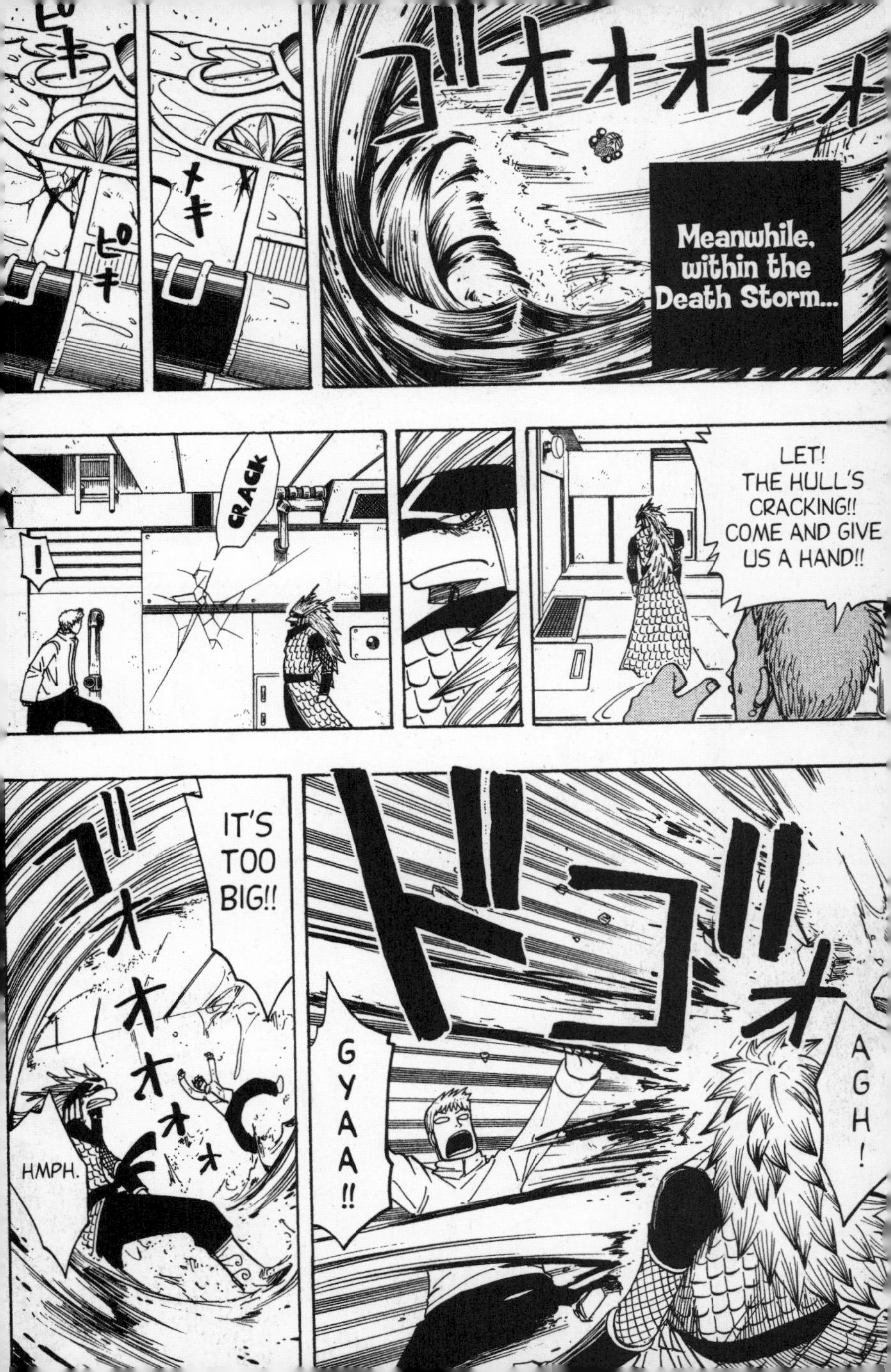
ゴオオオオオ
Meanwhile, within the Death Storm...
ピキ
メキ
ピキ
LET! THE HULL'S CRACKING!! COME AND GIVE US A HAND!!
CRACK
!
ドゴオ
AGH!
GYAA!!
IT'S TOO BIG!!
ゴオオオオ
HMPH.

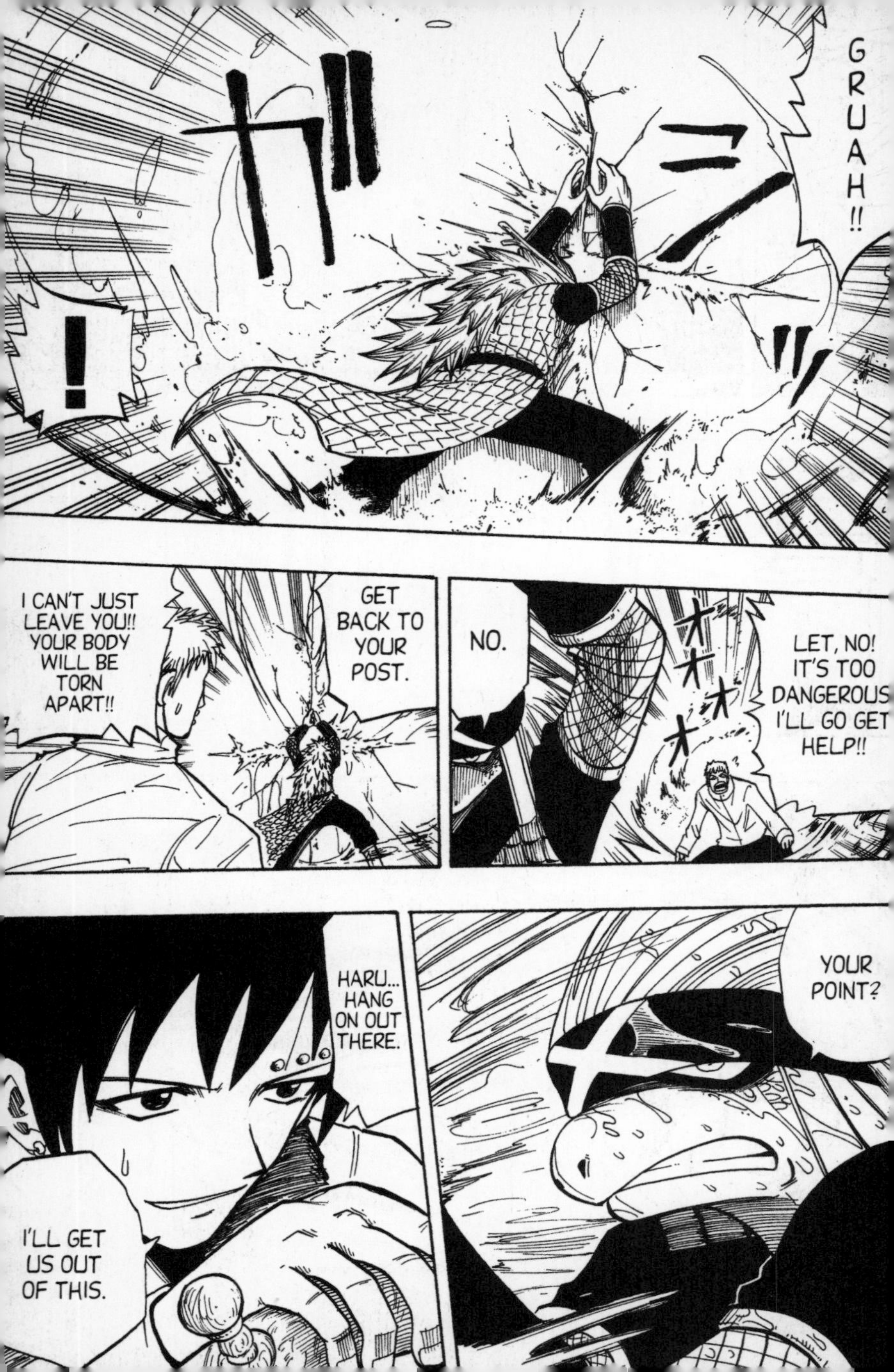
GRUAH!!
!
LET, NO! IT'S TOO DANGEROUS I'LL GO GET HELP!!
NO.
GET BACK TO YOUR POST.
I CAN'T JUST LEAVE YOU!! YOUR BODY WILL BE TORN APART!!
YOUR POINT?
HARU... HANG ON OUT THERE.
I'LL GET US OUT OF THIS.

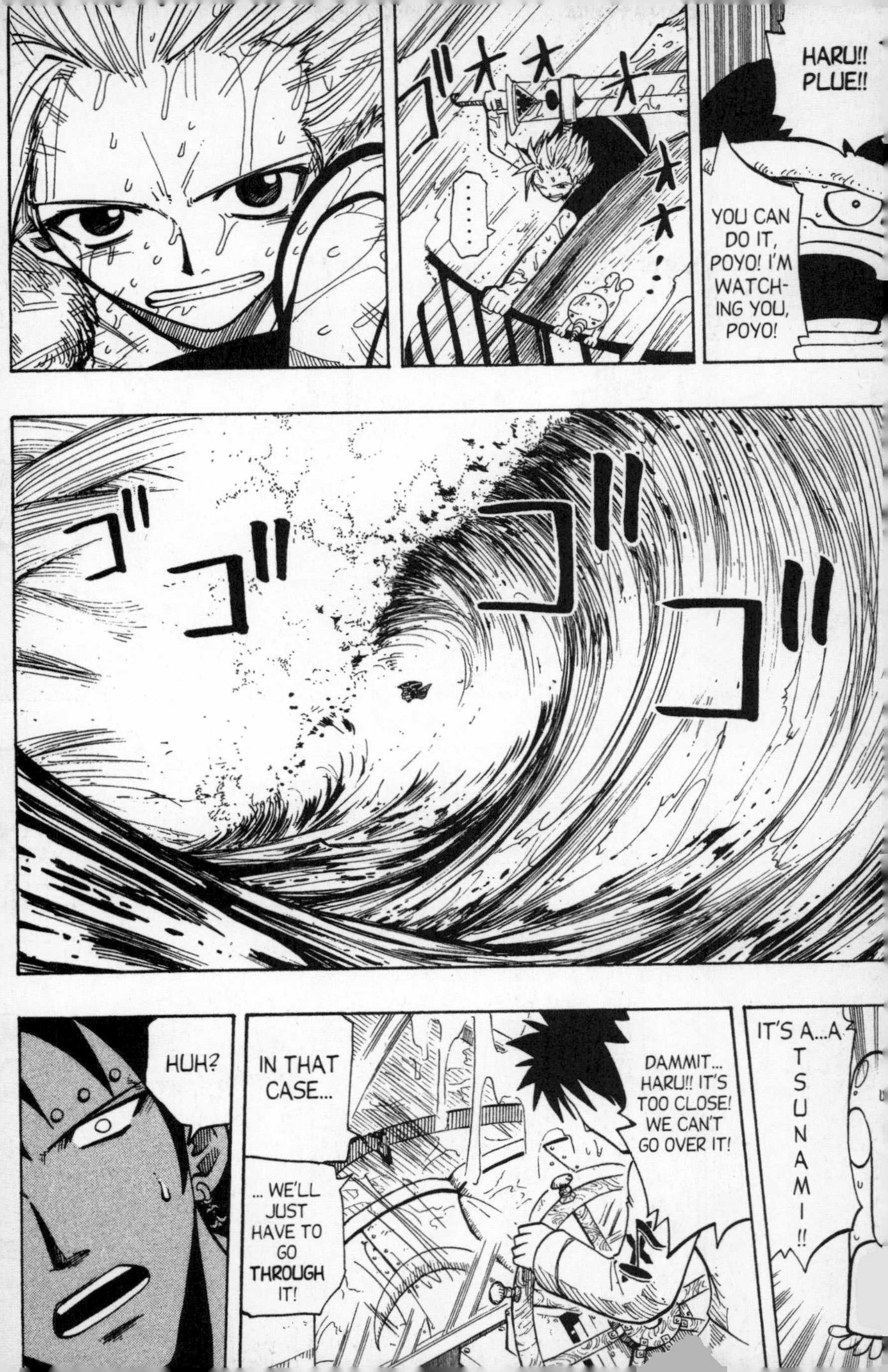
HARU!! PLUE!!
YOU CAN DO IT, POYO! I'M WATCHING-ING YOU, POYO!
......
ゴゴゴゴ
IT'S A...A TSUNAMI!!
DAMMIT... HARU!! IT'S TOO CLOSE! WE CAN'T GO OVER IT!
IN THAT CASE...
... WE'LL JUST HAVE TO GO **THROUGH** IT!
HUH?

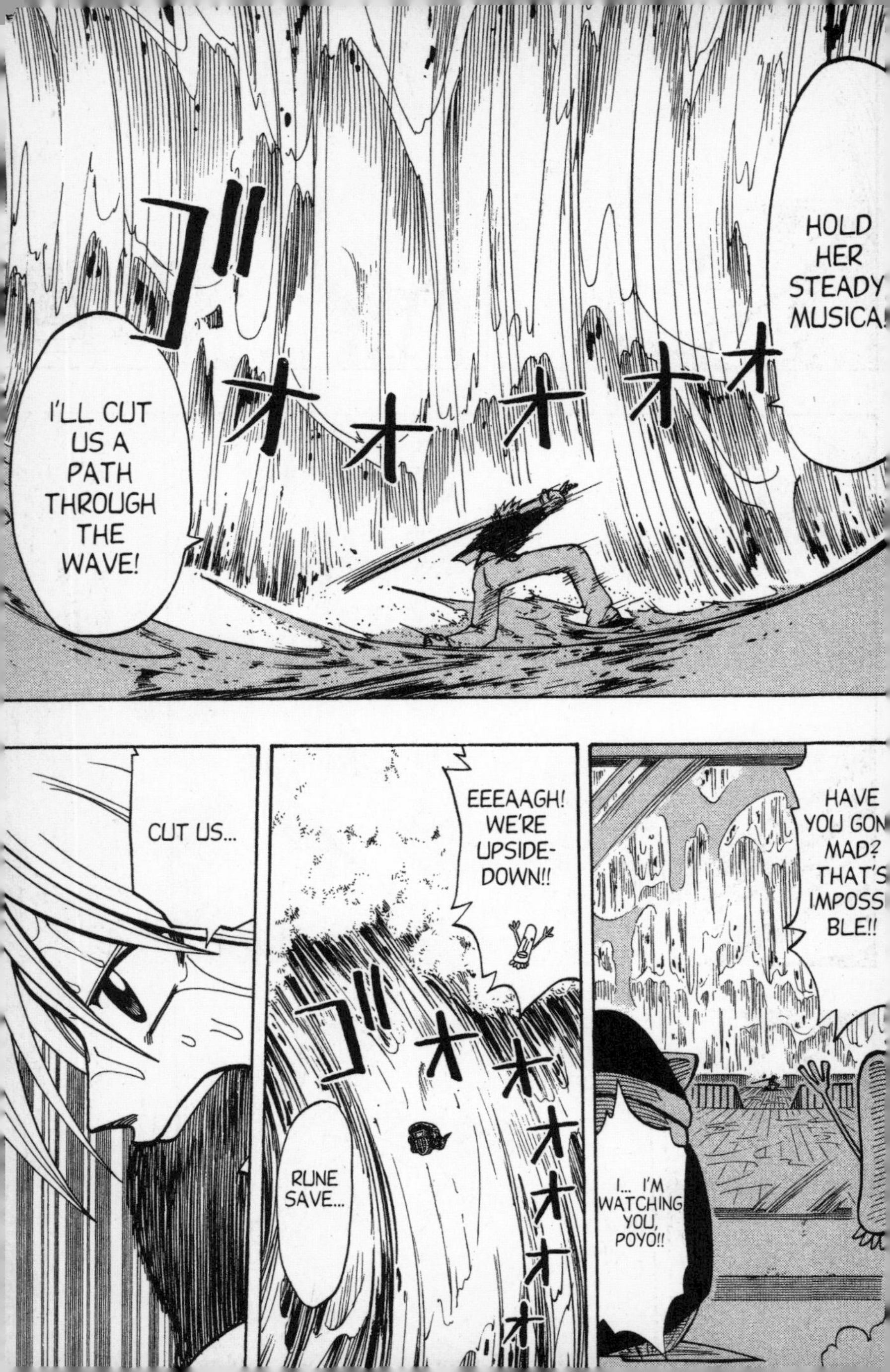
HOLD HER STEADY MUSICA!
ゴオオオオオ
I'LL CUT US A PATH THROUGH THE WAVE!
HAVE YOU GON MAD? THAT'S IMPOSS BLE!!
I... I'M WATCHING YOU, POYO!!
EEEAAGH! WE'RE UPSIDE-DOWN!!
ゴオオオオオオ
RUNE SAVE...
CUT US...

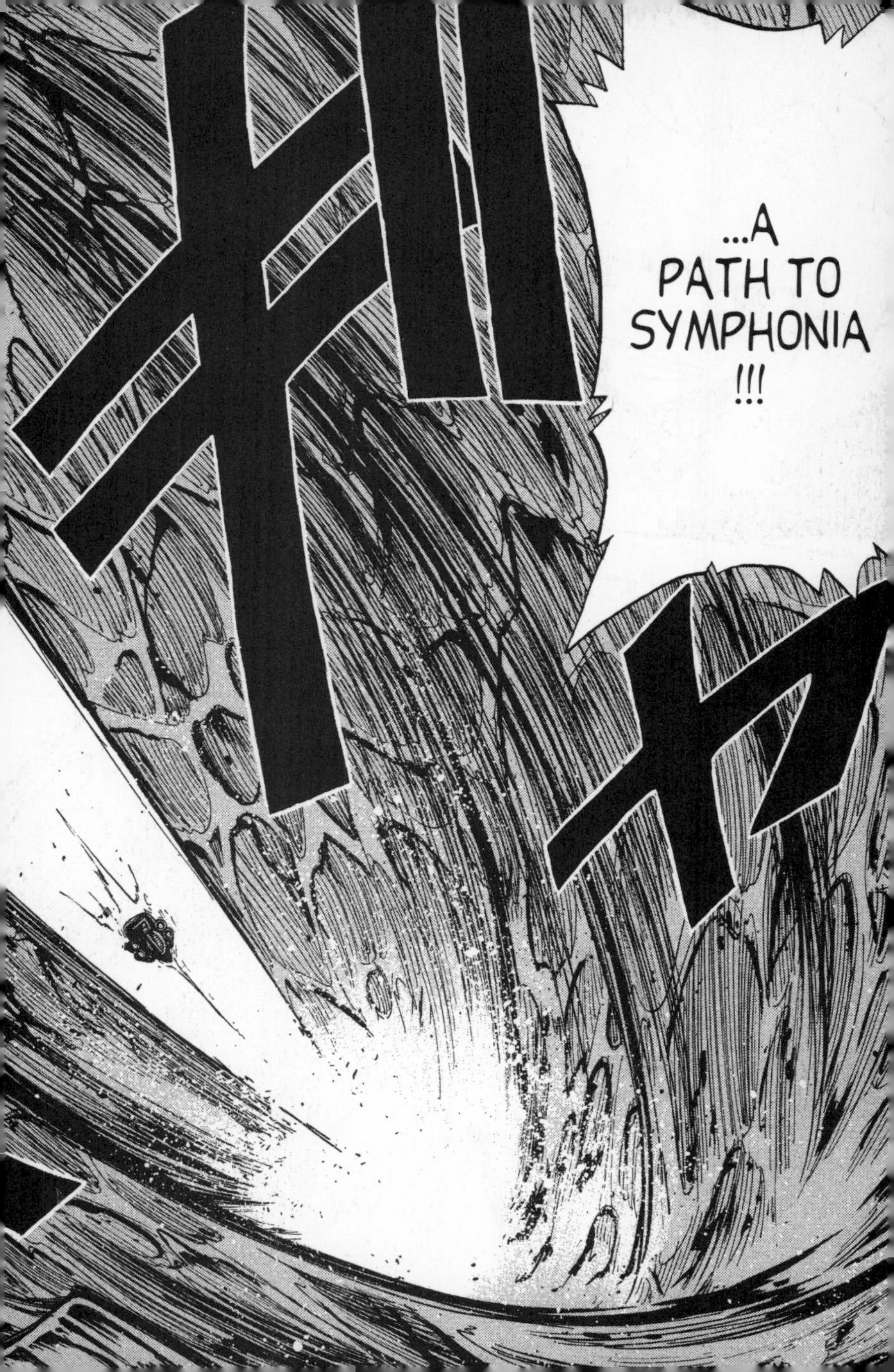
...A PATH TO SYMPHONIA !!!

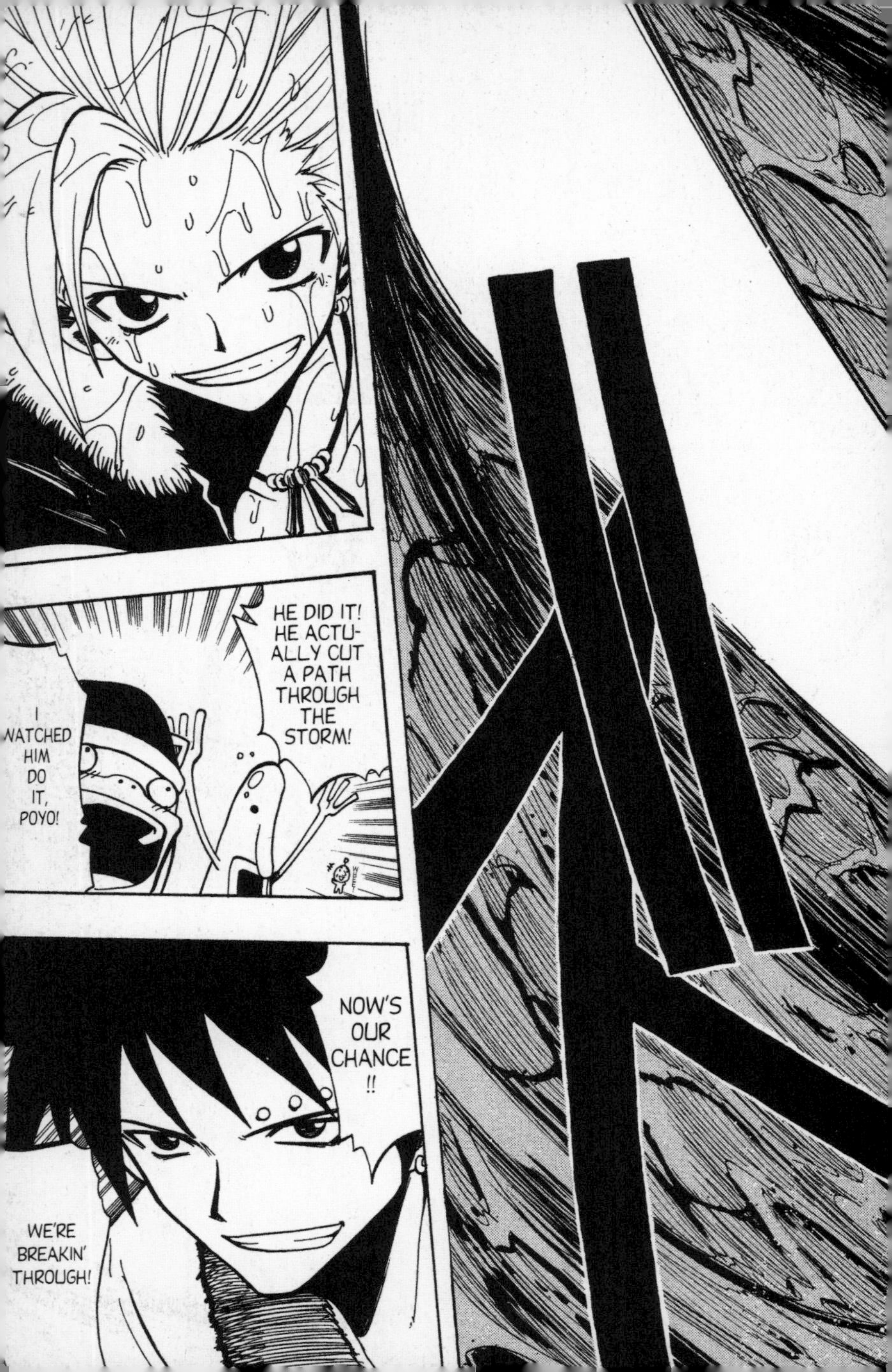
HE DID IT! HE ACTUALLY CUT A PATH THROUGH THE STORM!
I WATCHED HIM DO IT, POYO!
NOW'S OUR CHANCE!!
WE'RE BREAKIN' THROUGH!

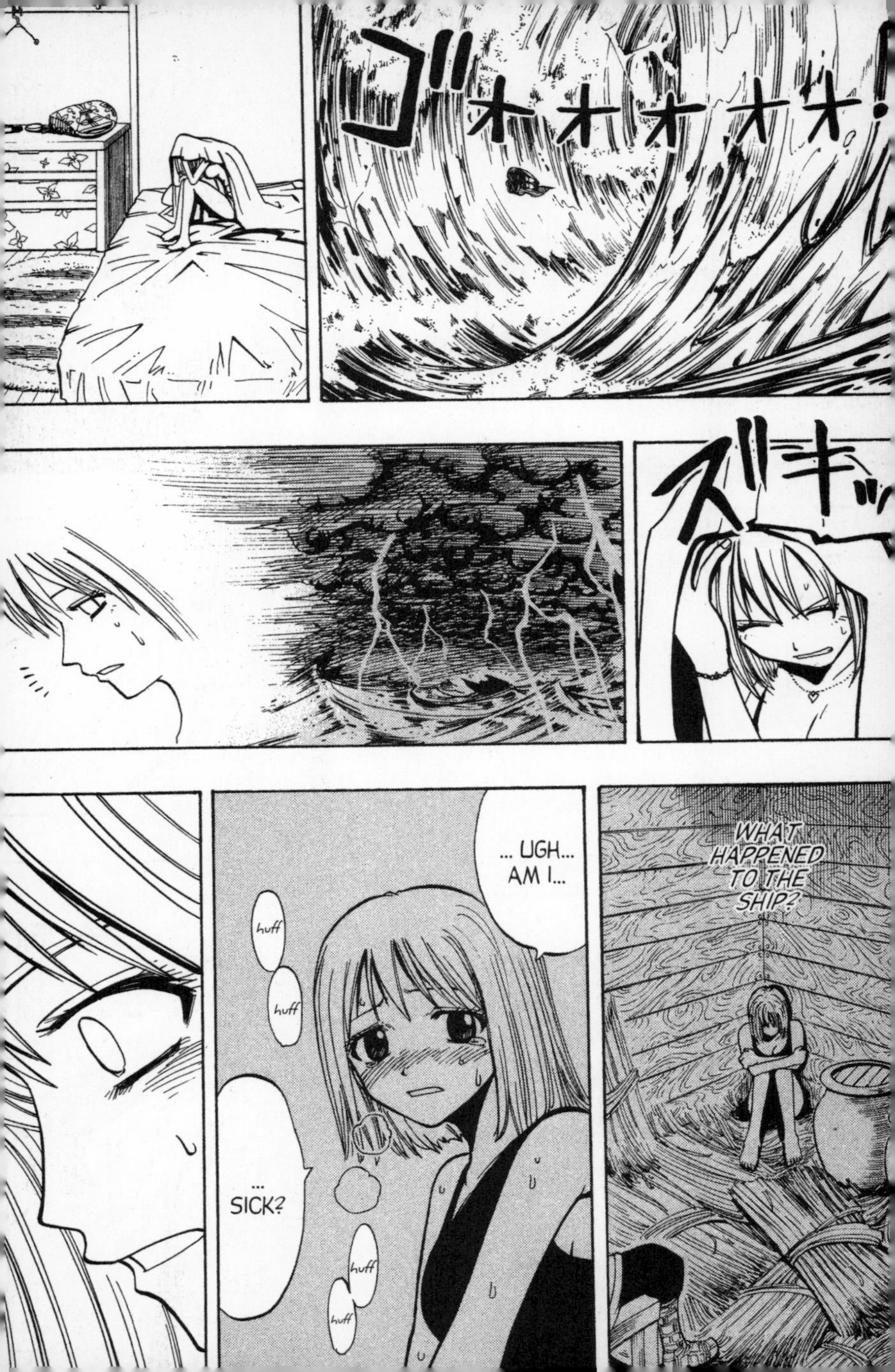
ゴオオオオオ！
ズキッ
WHAT HAPPENED TO THE SHIP?
... UGH... AM I...
huff
huff
... SICK?
huff
huff

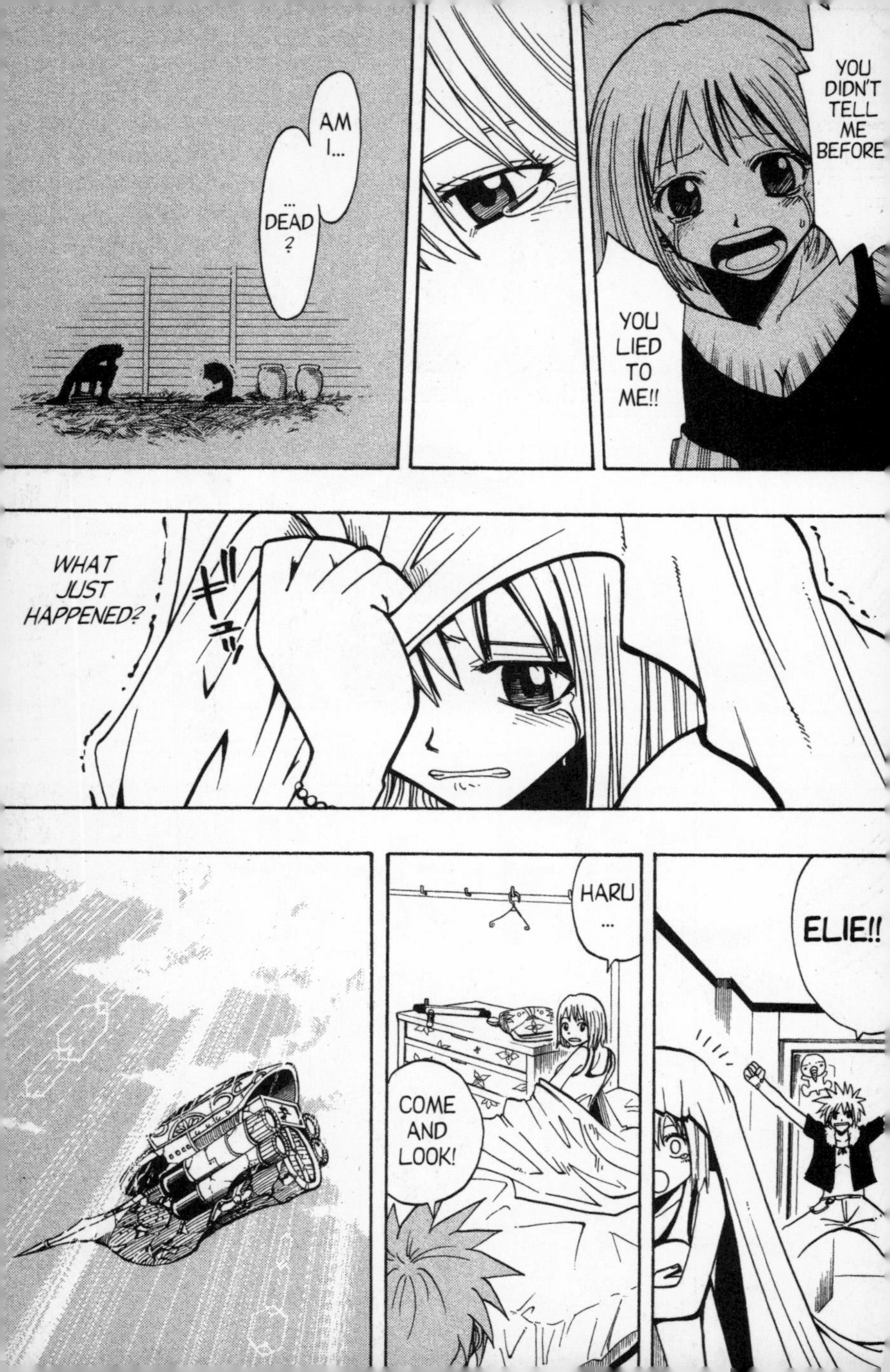
YOU DIDN'T TELL ME BEFORE
YOU LIED TO ME!!
AM I...
...DEAD?
WHAT JUST HAPPENED?
ELIE!!
HARU...
COME AND LOOK!

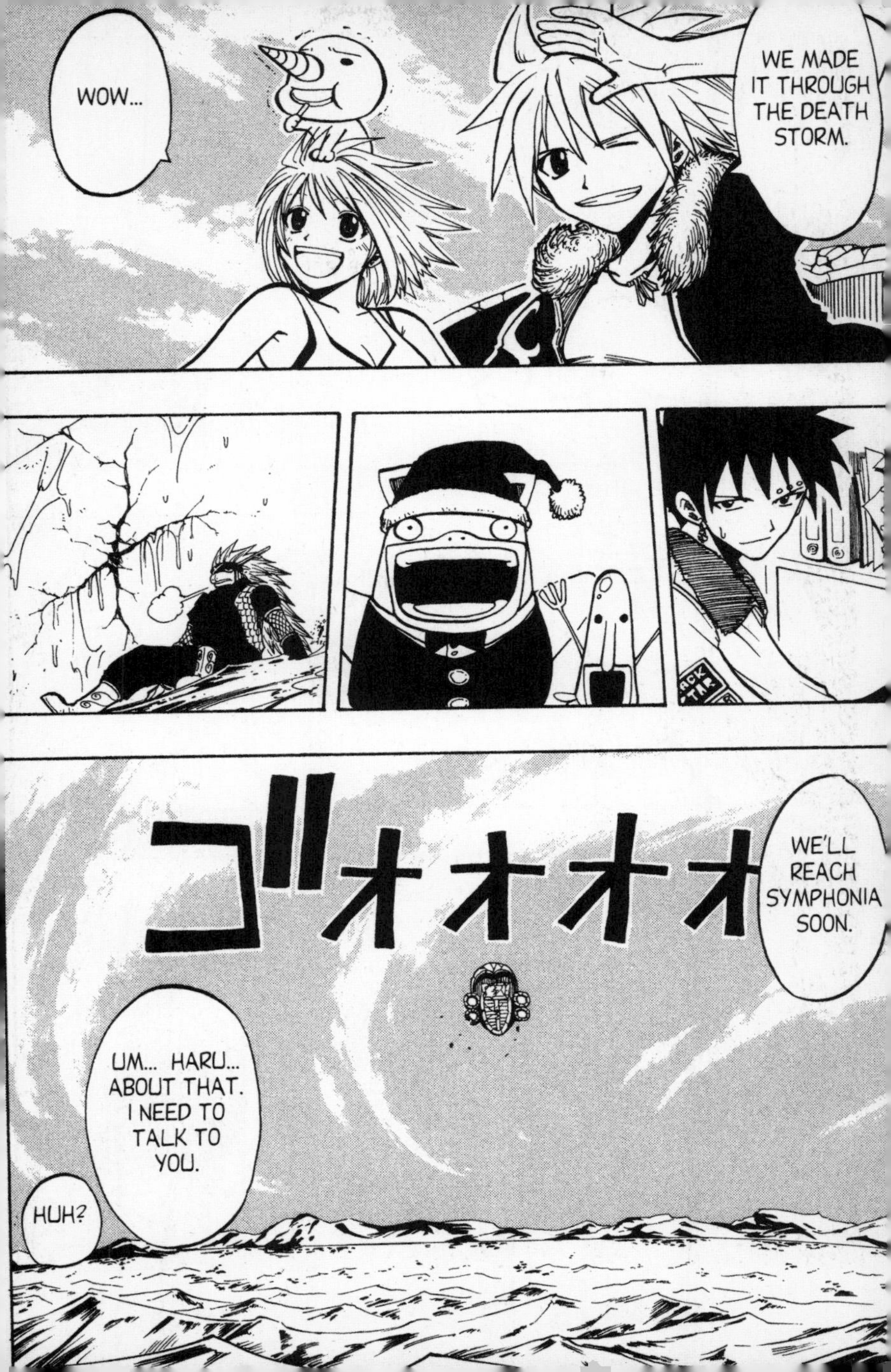
WE MADE IT THROUGH THE DEATH STORM.
WOW...
WE'LL REACH SYMPHONIA SOON.
ゴオオオ
UM... HARU... ABOUT THAT. I NEED TO TALK TO YOU.
HUH?

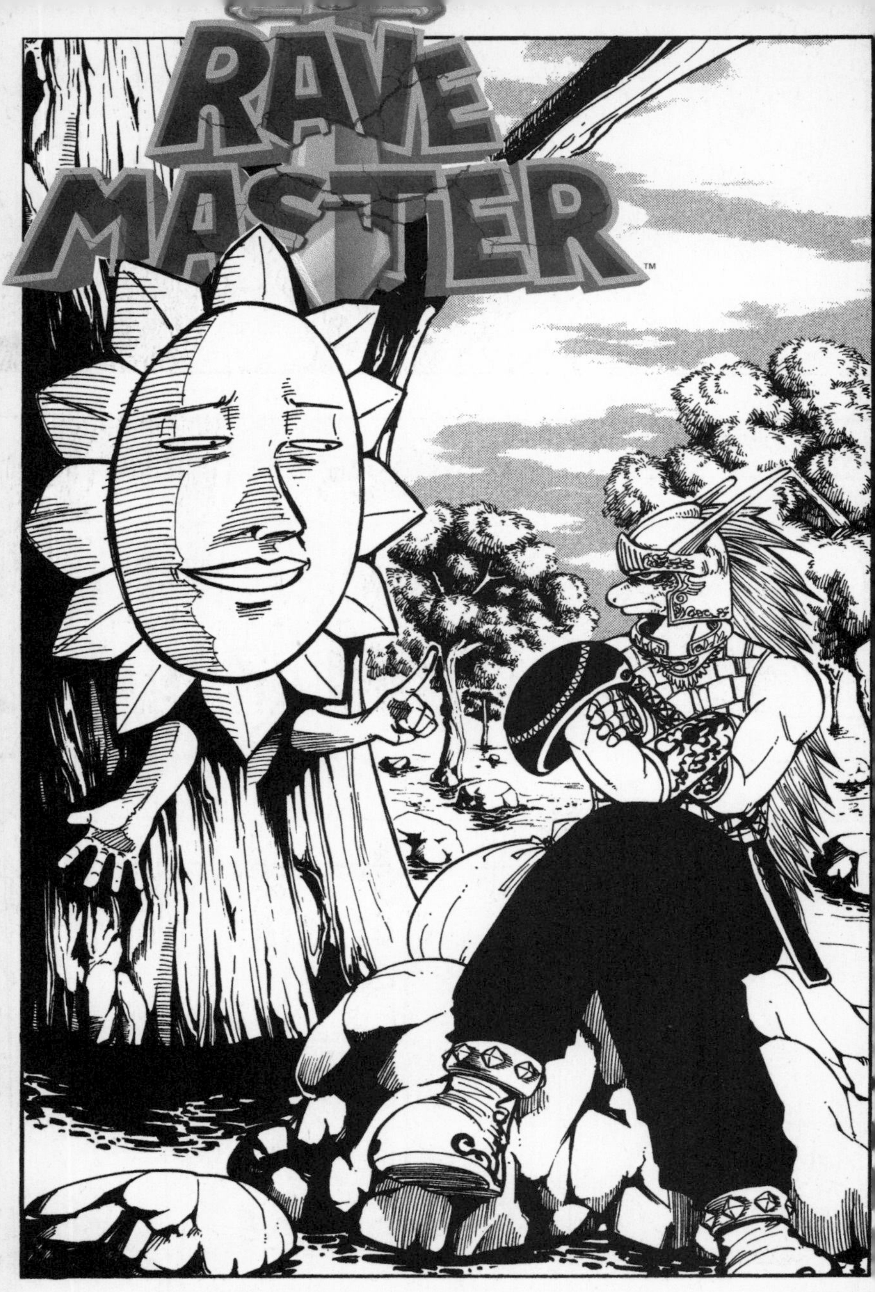
RAVE MASTER™

RAVE:81 ✠ THE VOICE OF SYMPHONIA

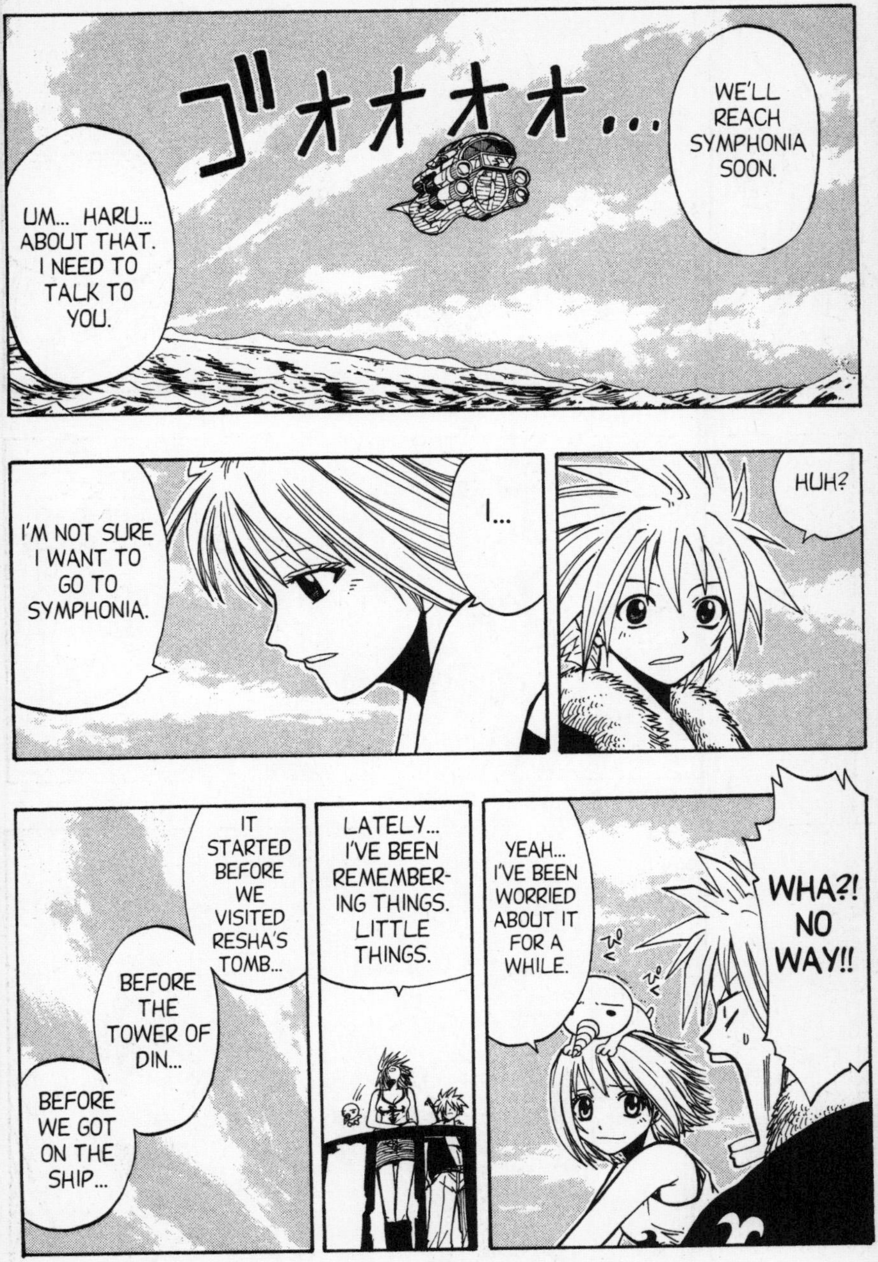
WE'LL REACH SYMPHONIA SOON.
ゴオオオオ...
UM... HARU... ABOUT THAT. I NEED TO TALK TO YOU.
HUH?
I...
I'M NOT SURE I WANT TO GO TO SYMPHONIA.
WHA?! NO WAY!!
YEAH... I'VE BEEN WORRIED ABOUT IT FOR A WHILE.
LATELY... I'VE BEEN REMEMBER-ING THINGS. LITTLE THINGS.
IT STARTED BEFORE WE VISITED RESHA'S TOMB...
BEFORE THE TOWER OF DIN...
BEFORE WE GOT ON THE SHIP...

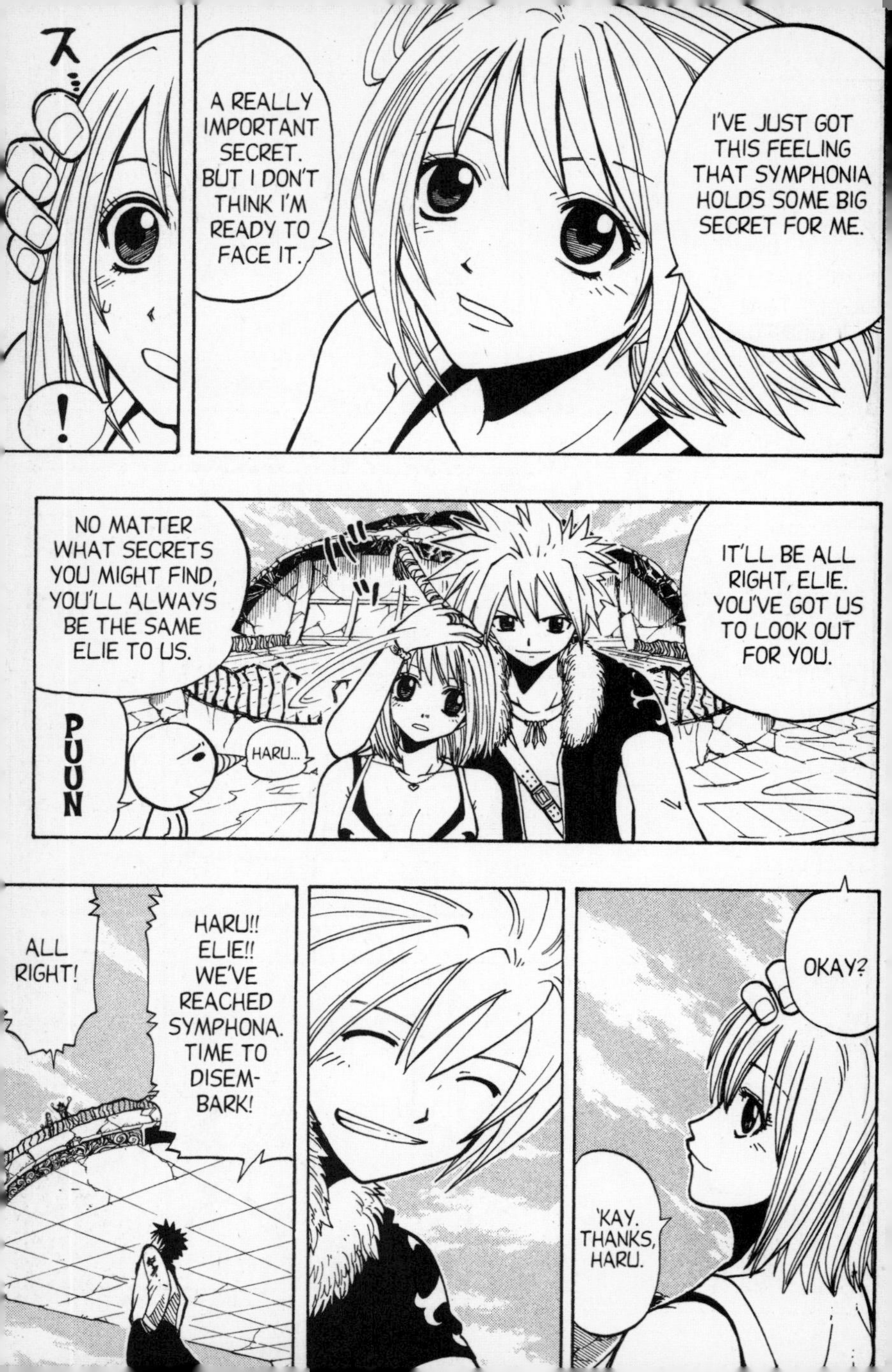
I'VE JUST GOT THIS FEELING THAT SYMPHONIA HOLDS SOME BIG SECRET FOR ME.
A REALLY IMPORTANT SECRET. BUT I DON'T THINK I'M READY TO FACE IT.
ス
!
IT'LL BE ALL RIGHT, ELIE. YOU'VE GOT US TO LOOK OUT FOR YOU.
NO MATTER WHAT SECRETS YOU MIGHT FIND, YOU'LL ALWAYS BE THE SAME ELIE TO US.
HARU...
PUUN
OKAY?
'KAY. THANKS, HARU.
HARU!! ELIE!! WE'VE REACHED SYMPHONA. TIME TO DISEMBARK!
ALL RIGHT!

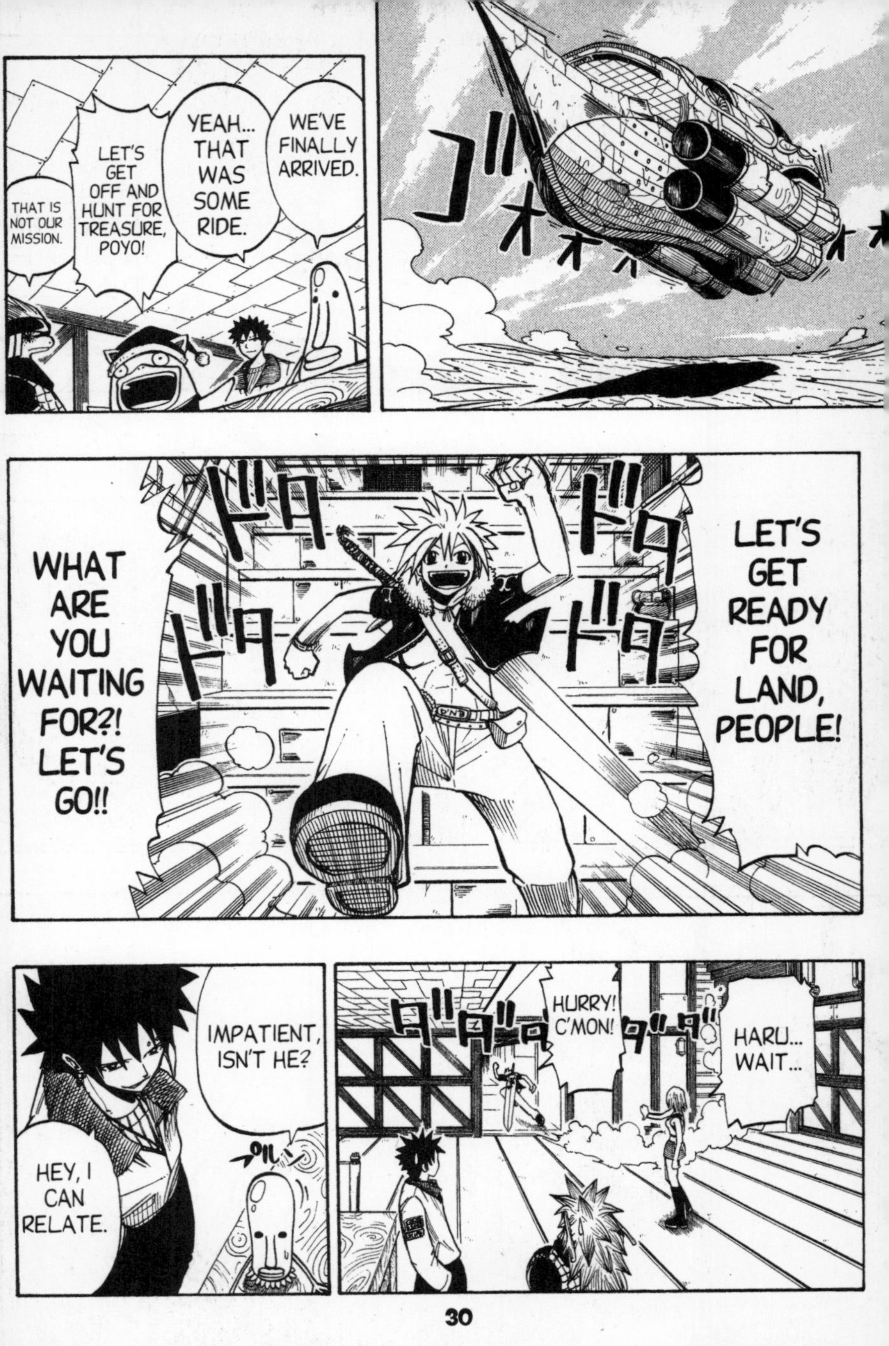
WE'VE FINALLY ARRIVED.
YEAH... THAT WAS SOME RIDE.
LET'S GET OFF AND HUNT FOR TREASURE, POYO!
THAT IS NOT OUR MISSION.
LET'S GET READY FOR LAND, PEOPLE!
ドタドタ
ドタドタ
WHAT ARE YOU WAITING FOR?! LET'S GO!!
HARU... WAIT...
HURRY! C'MON!
IMPATIENT, ISN'T HE?
HEY, I CAN RELATE.

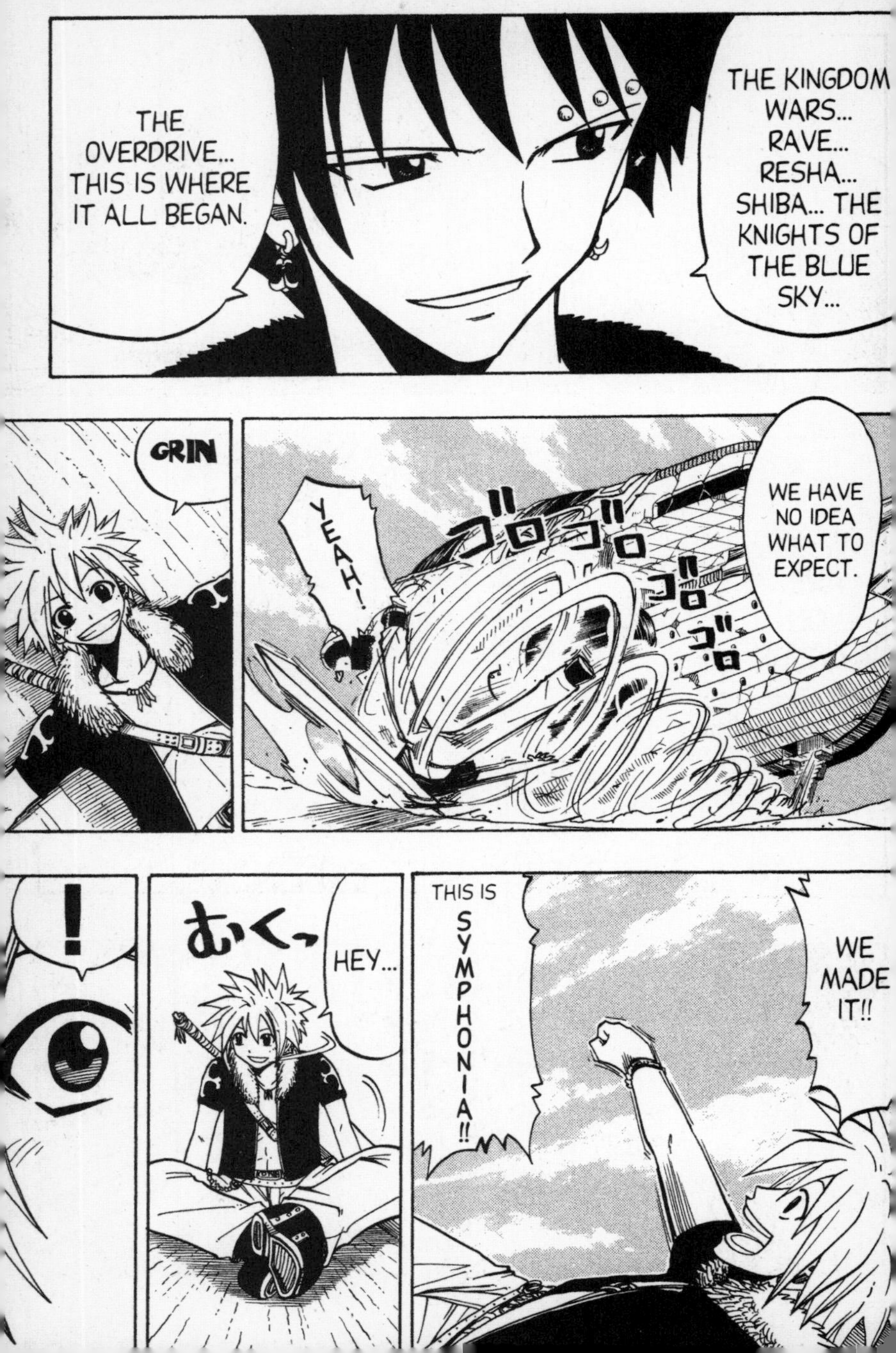
THE KINGDOM WARS... RAVE... RESHA... SHIBA... THE KNIGHTS OF THE BLUE SKY...
THE OVERDRIVE... THIS IS WHERE IT ALL BEGAN.
WE HAVE NO IDEA WHAT TO EXPECT.
ゴロゴロ
ゴロゴロ
YEAH!
GRIN
WE MADE IT!!
THIS IS SYMPHONIA!!
HEY...
むくっ
!

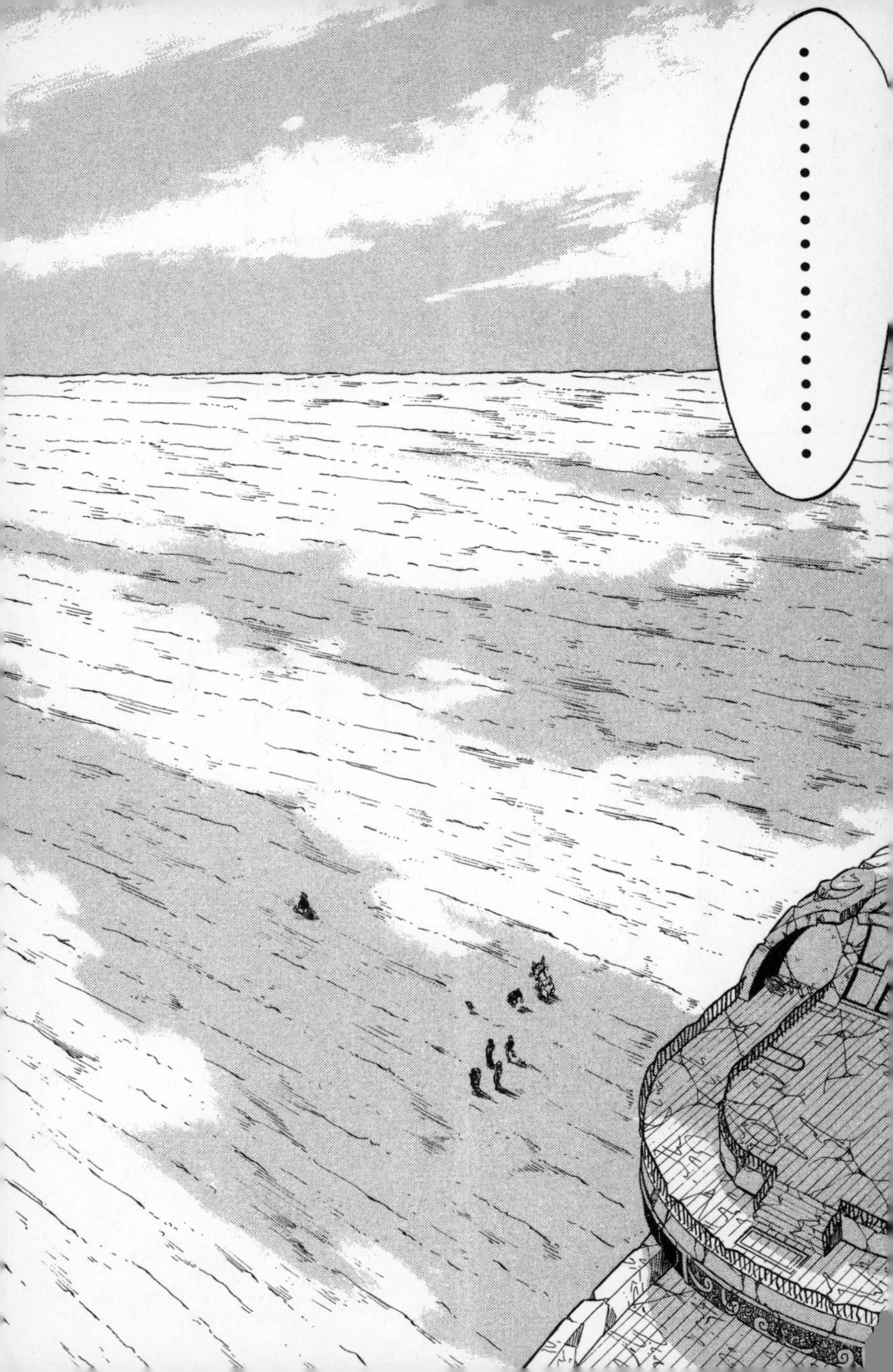

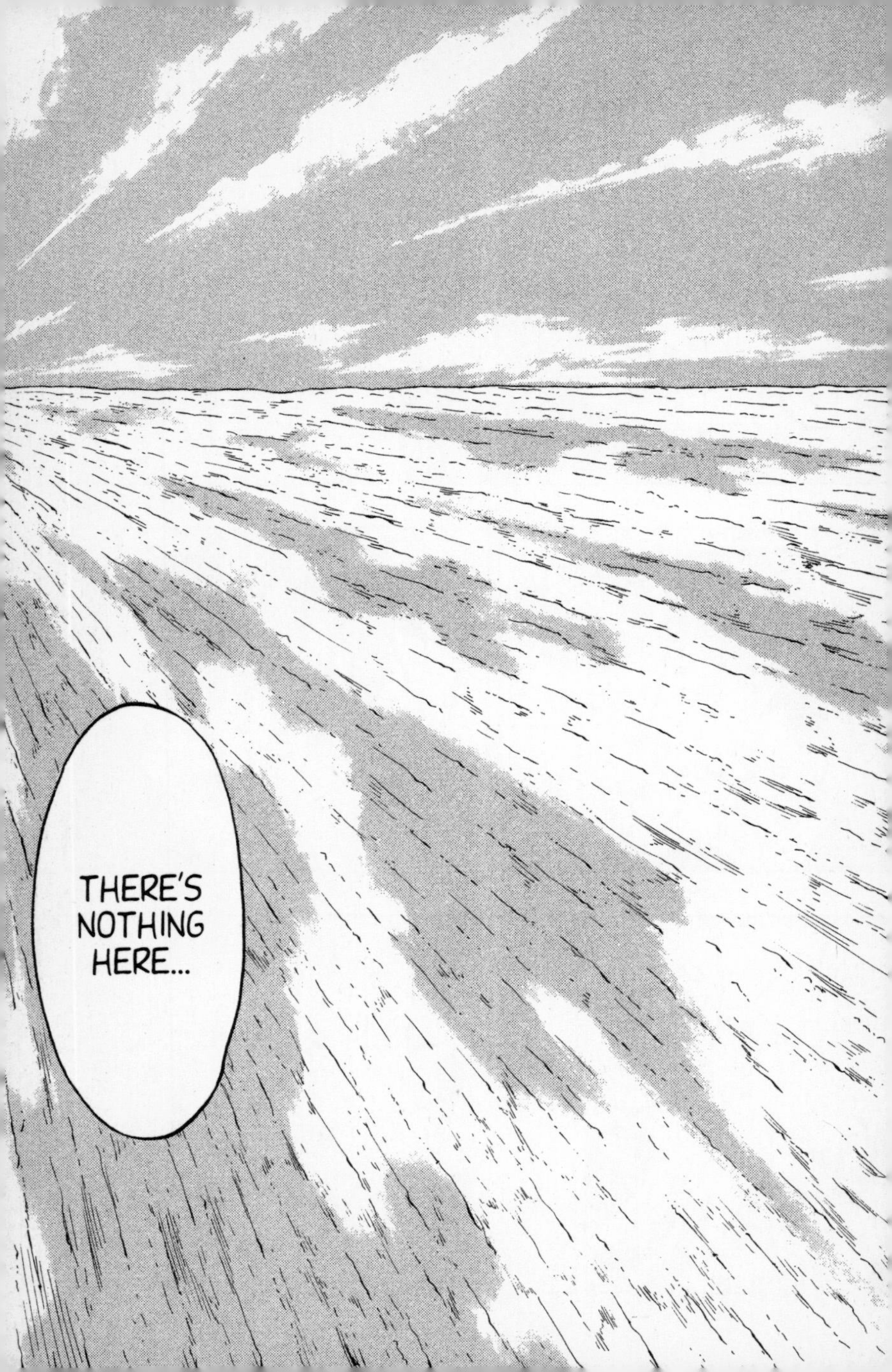
THERE'S NOTHING HERE...

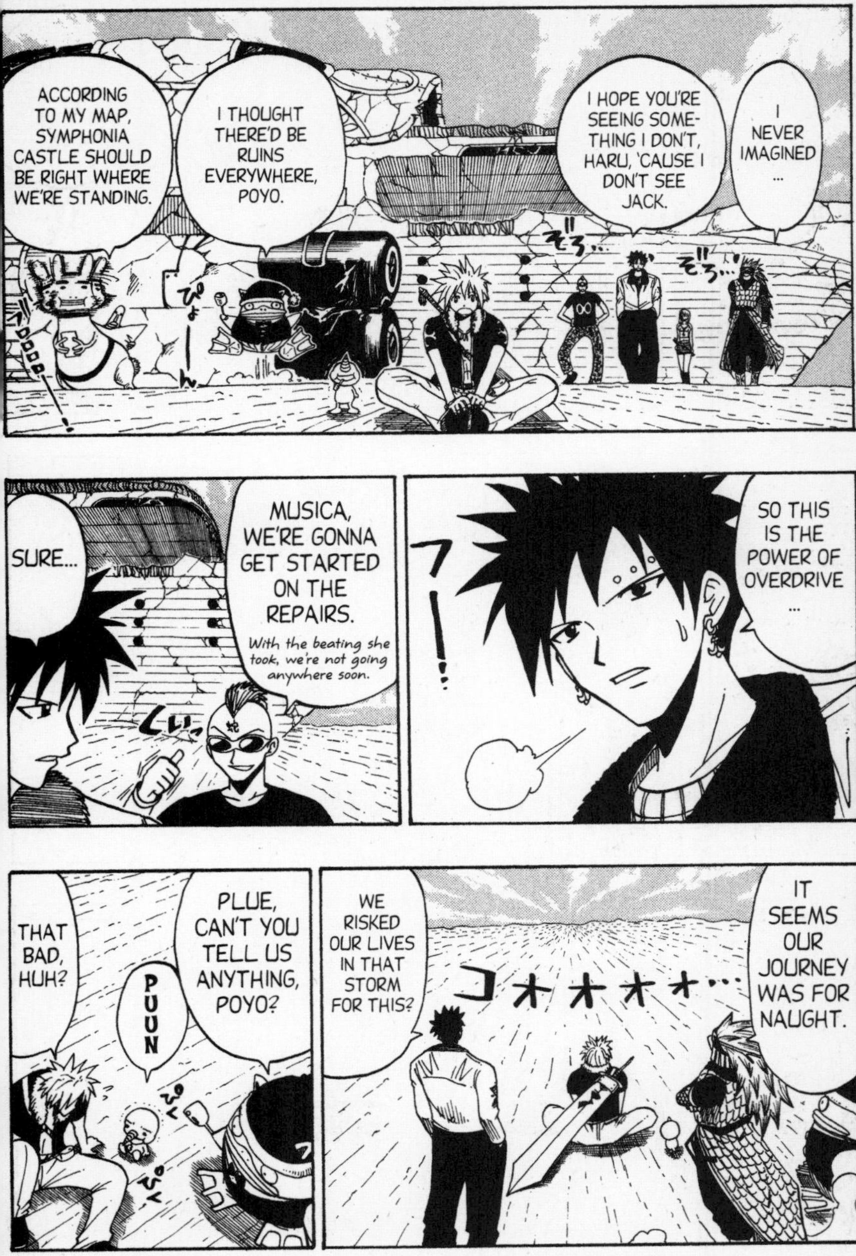
I NEVER IMAGINED ...
I HOPE YOU'RE SEEING SOME-THING I DON'T, HARU, 'CAUSE I DON'T SEE JACK.
I THOUGHT THERE'D BE RUINS EVERYWHERE, POYO.
ACCORDING TO MY MAP, SYMPHONIA CASTLE SHOULD BE RIGHT WHERE WE'RE STANDING.
SO THIS IS THE POWER OF OVERDRIVE ...
MUSICA, WE'RE GONNA GET STARTED ON THE REPAIRS.
With the beating she took, we're not going anywhere soon.
SURE...
IT SEEMS OUR JOURNEY WAS FOR NAUGHT.
コオオオオ…
WE RISKED OUR LIVES IN THAT STORM FOR THIS?
PLUE, CAN'T YOU TELL US ANYTHING, POYO?
PUUN
THAT BAD, HUH?

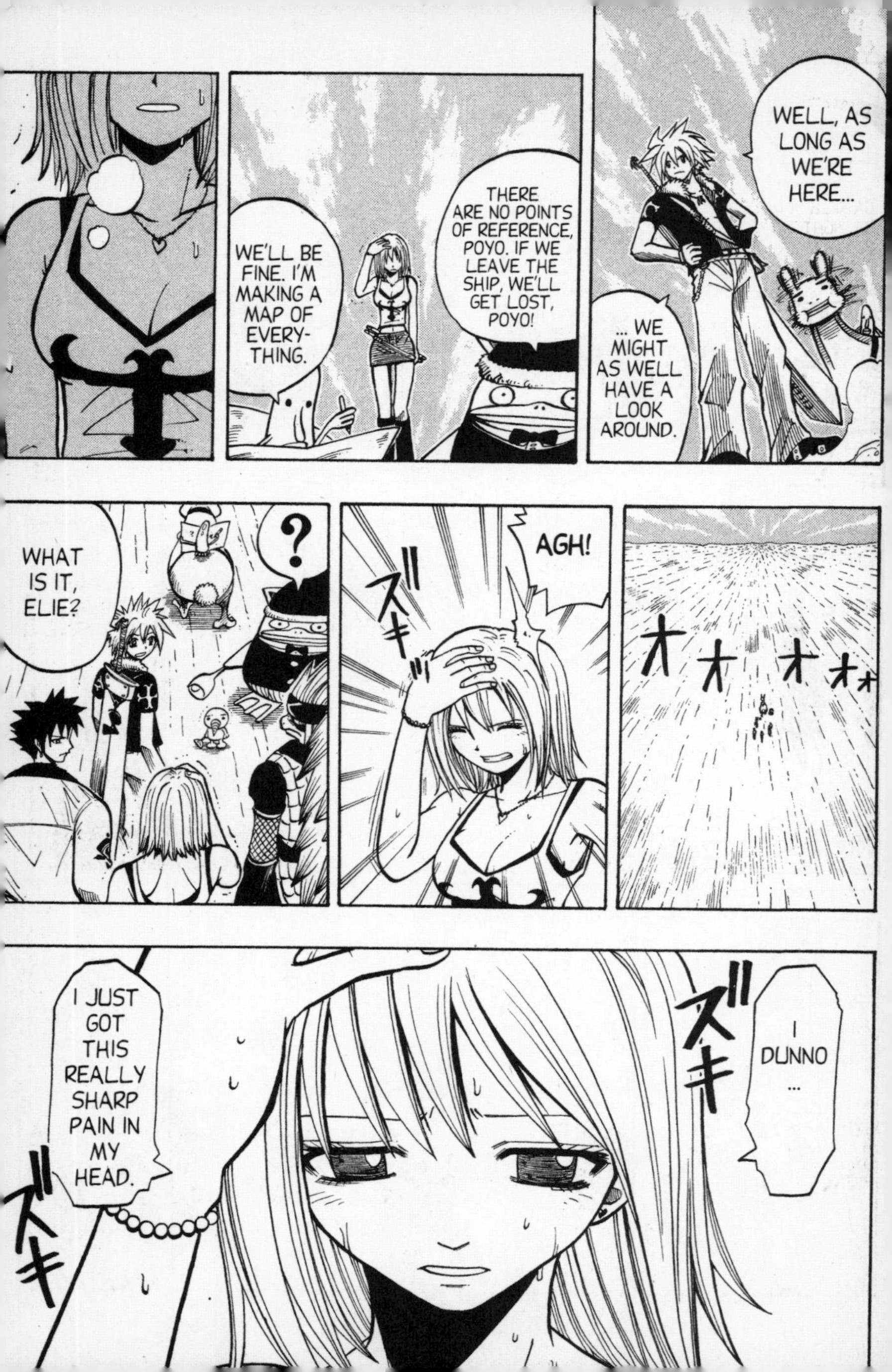
WELL, AS LONG AS WE'RE HERE...
... WE MIGHT AS WELL HAVE A LOOK AROUND.
THERE ARE NO POINTS OF REFERENCE, POYO. IF WE LEAVE THE SHIP, WE'LL GET LOST, POYO!
WE'LL BE FINE. I'M MAKING A MAP OF EVERYTHING.
オオオオ
AGH!
ズキ
?
WHAT IS IT, ELIE?
ズキ
I DUNNO ...
I JUST GOT THIS REALLY SHARP PAIN IN MY HEAD.
ズキ

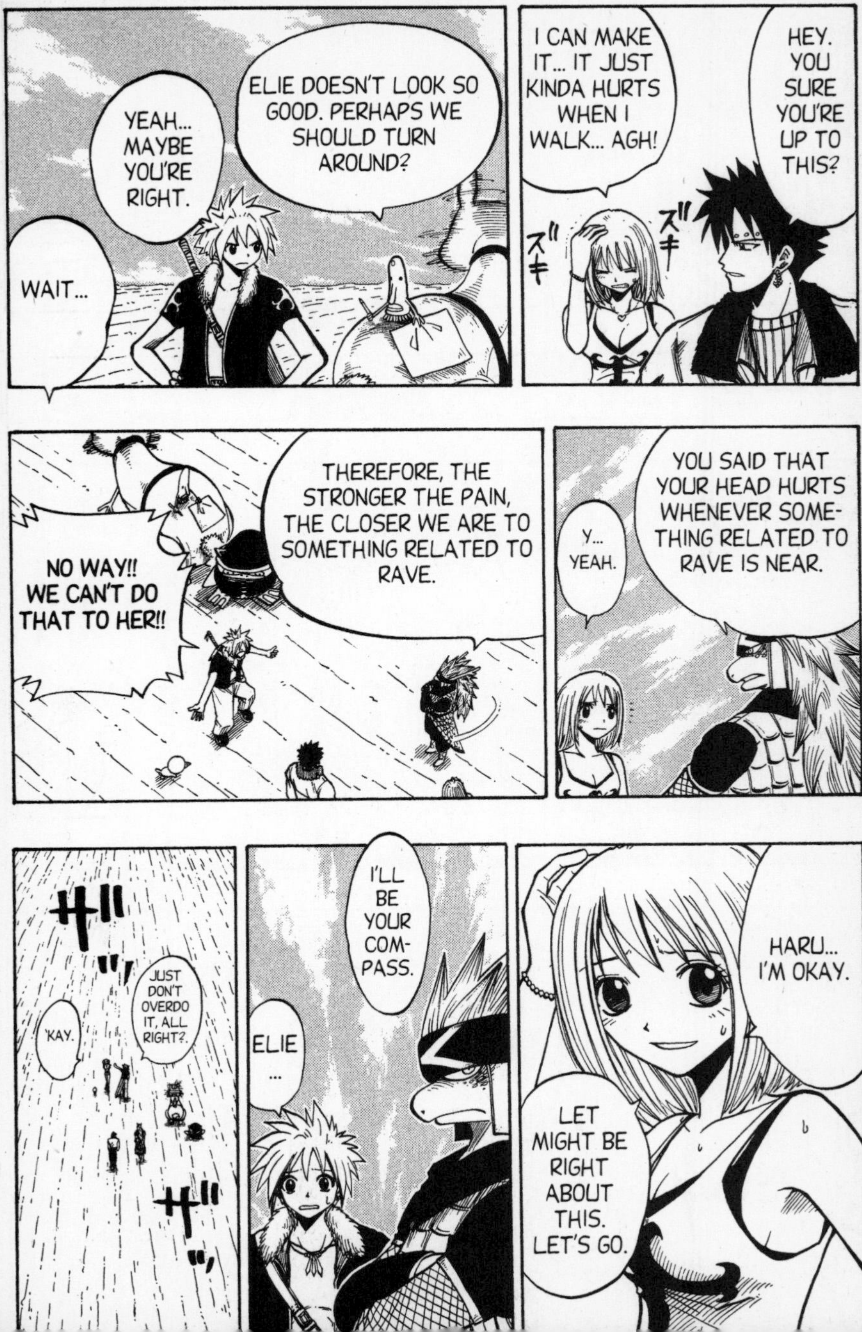
HEY. YOU SURE YOU'RE UP TO THIS?
I CAN MAKE IT... IT JUST KINDA HURTS WHEN I WALK... AGH!
ズキ
ズキ
ELIE DOESN'T LOOK SO GOOD. PERHAPS WE SHOULD TURN AROUND?
YEAH... MAYBE YOU'RE RIGHT.
WAIT...
YOU SAID THAT YOUR HEAD HURTS WHENEVER SOME-THING RELATED TO RAVE IS NEAR.
Y... YEAH.
THEREFORE, THE STRONGER THE PAIN, THE CLOSER WE ARE TO SOMETHING RELATED TO RAVE.
NO WAY!! WE CAN'T DO THAT TO HER!!
HARU... I'M OKAY.
LET MIGHT BE RIGHT ABOUT THIS. LET'S GO.
I'LL BE YOUR COM-PASS.
ELIE ...
JUST DON'T OVERDO IT, ALL RIGHT?.
'KAY.

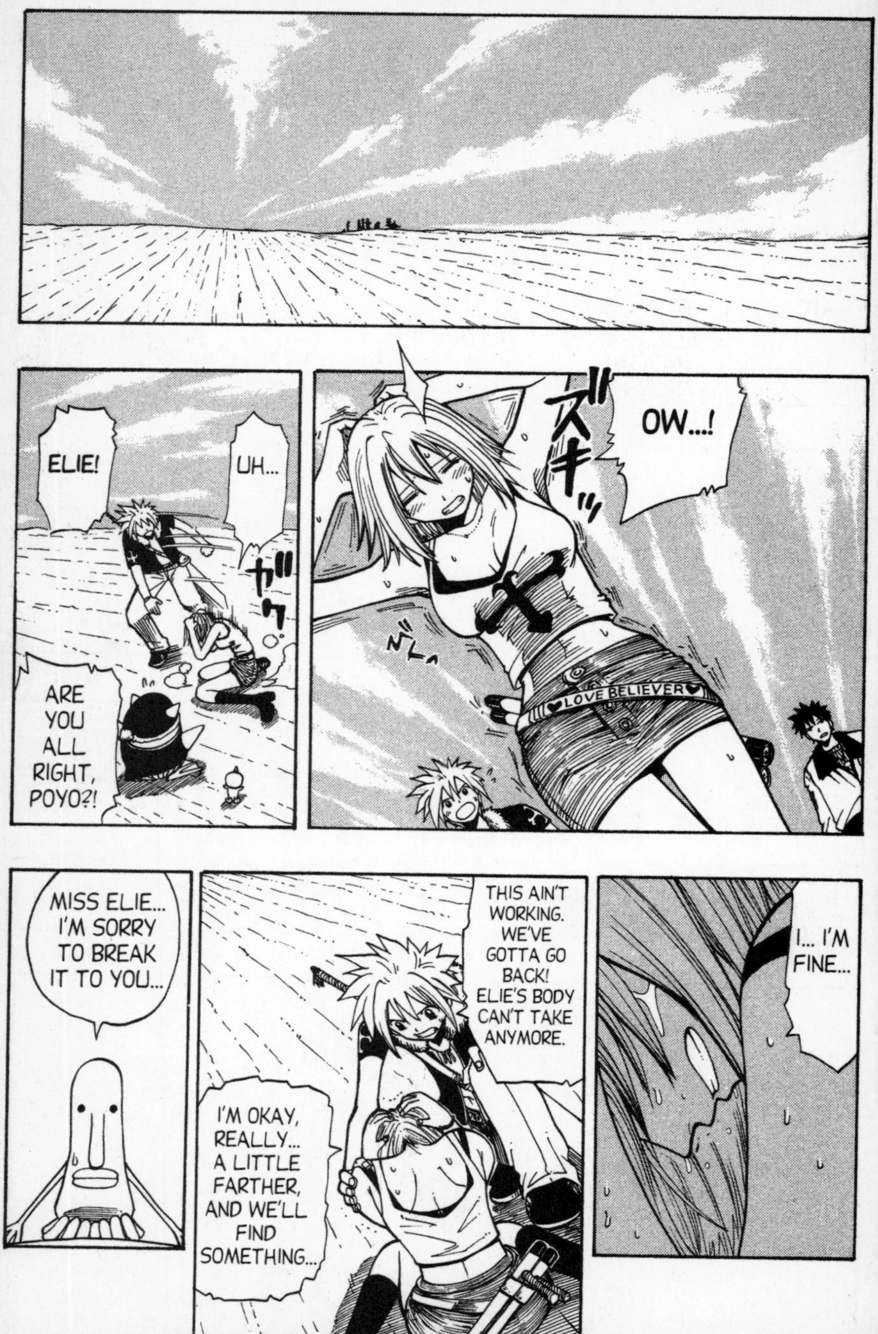
ズキッ
OW...!
♥LOVE BELIEVER♥
UH...
ELIE!
ガク
ARE YOU ALL RIGHT, POYO?!
I... I'M FINE...
THIS AIN'T WORKING. WE'VE GOTTA GO BACK! ELIE'S BODY CAN'T TAKE ANYMORE.
I'M OKAY, REALLY... A LITTLE FARTHER, AND WE'LL FIND SOMETHING...
MISS ELIE... I'M SORRY TO BREAK IT TO YOU...

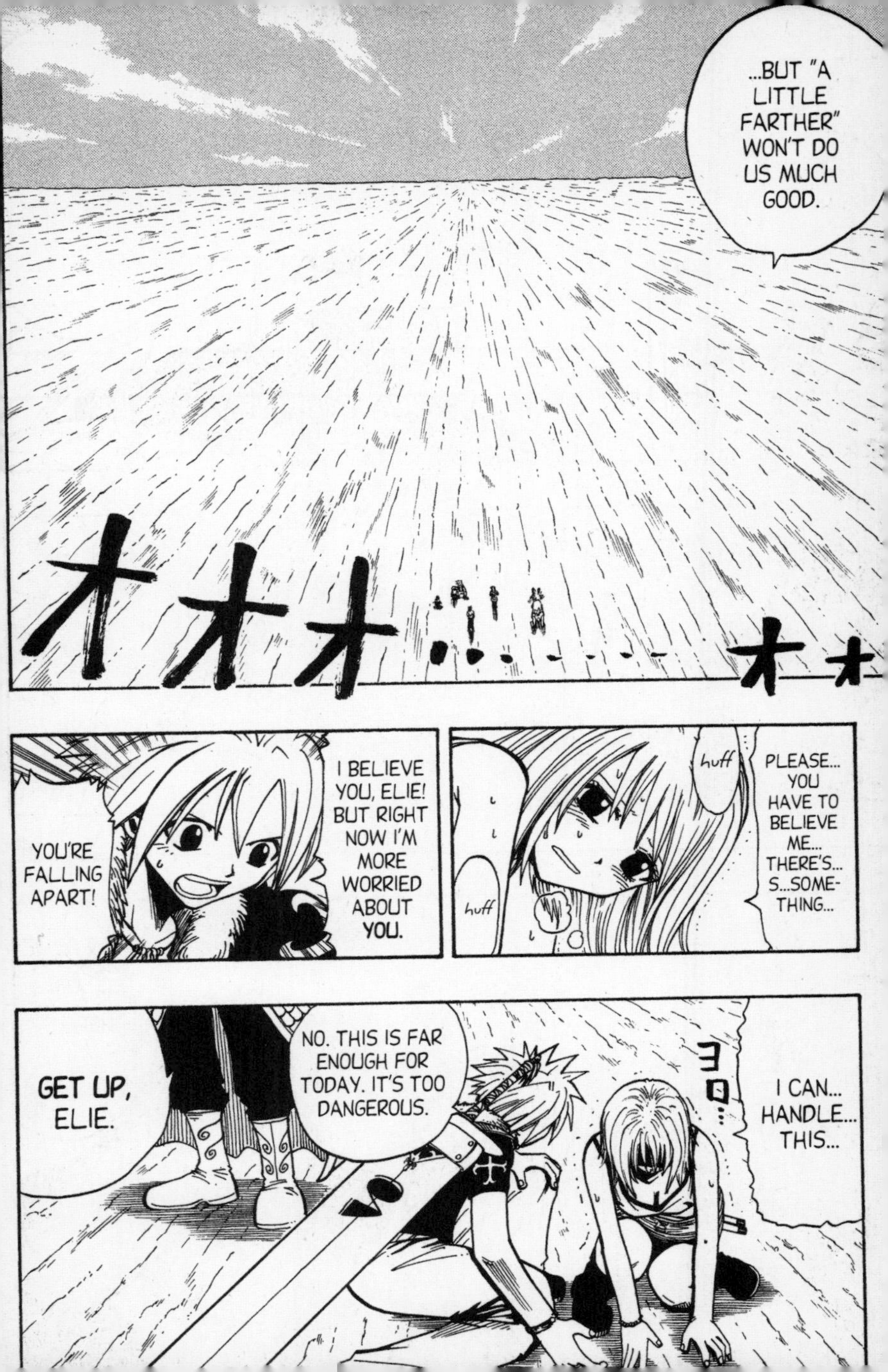
...BUT "A LITTLE FARTHER" WON'T DO US MUCH GOOD.
オオオ…………オオ
huff
PLEASE... YOU HAVE TO BELIEVE ME... THERE'S... S...SOME-THING...
huff
I BELIEVE YOU, ELIE! BUT RIGHT NOW I'M MORE WORRIED ABOUT **YOU.**
YOU'RE FALLING APART!
I CAN... HANDLE... THIS...
ヨロ…
NO. THIS IS FAR ENOUGH FOR TODAY. IT'S TOO DANGEROUS.
GET UP, ELIE.

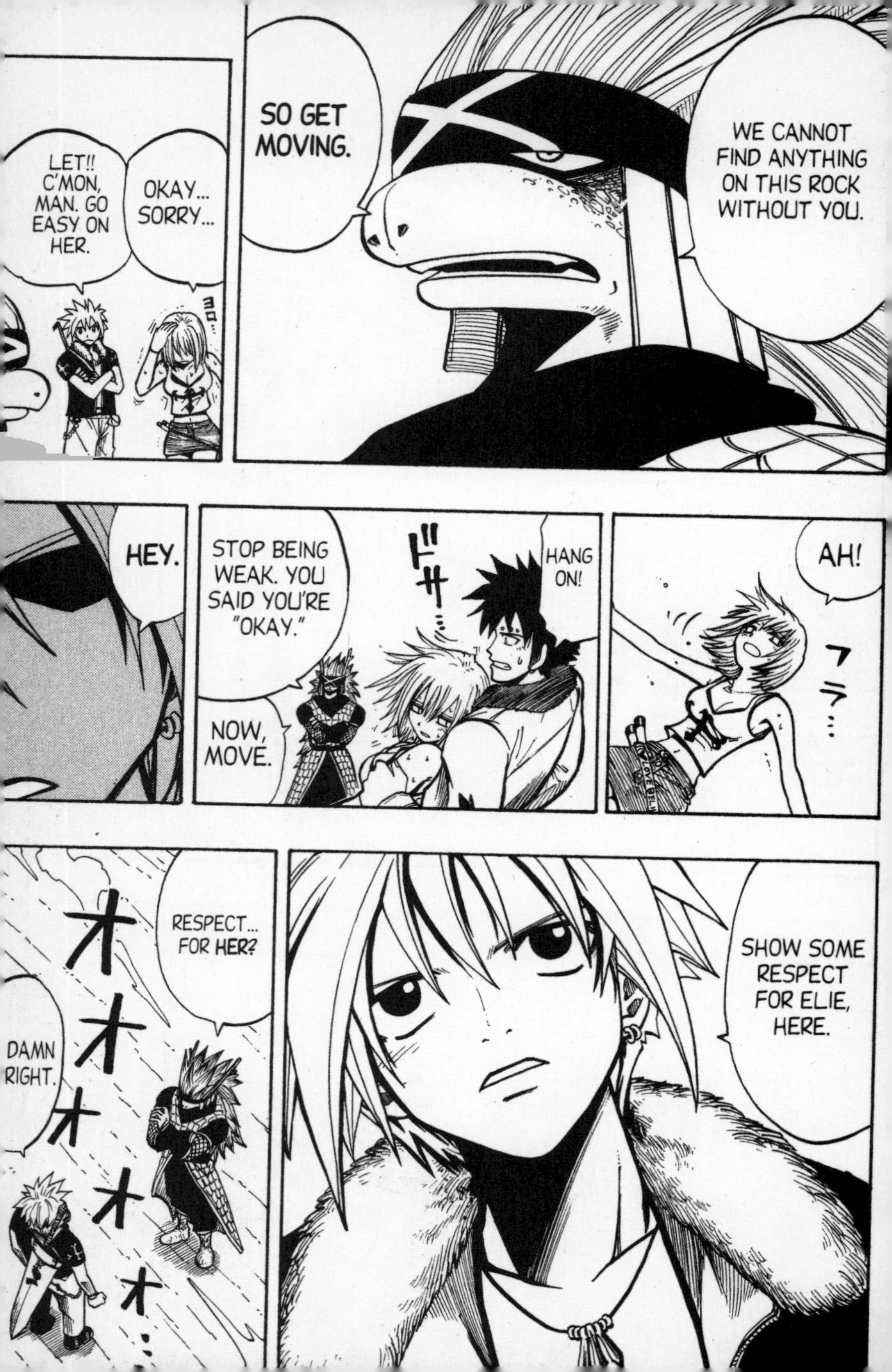
WE CANNOT FIND ANYTHING ON THIS ROCK WITHOUT YOU.
SO GET MOVING.
OKAY... SORRY...
ヨロ…
LET!! C'MON, MAN. GO EASY ON HER.
AH!
フラ…
HANG ON!
ドサ…
STOP BEING WEAK. YOU SAID YOU'RE "OKAY."
NOW, MOVE.
HEY.
SHOW SOME RESPECT FOR ELIE, HERE.
RESPECT... FOR HER?
オオオオオ…
DAMN RIGHT.

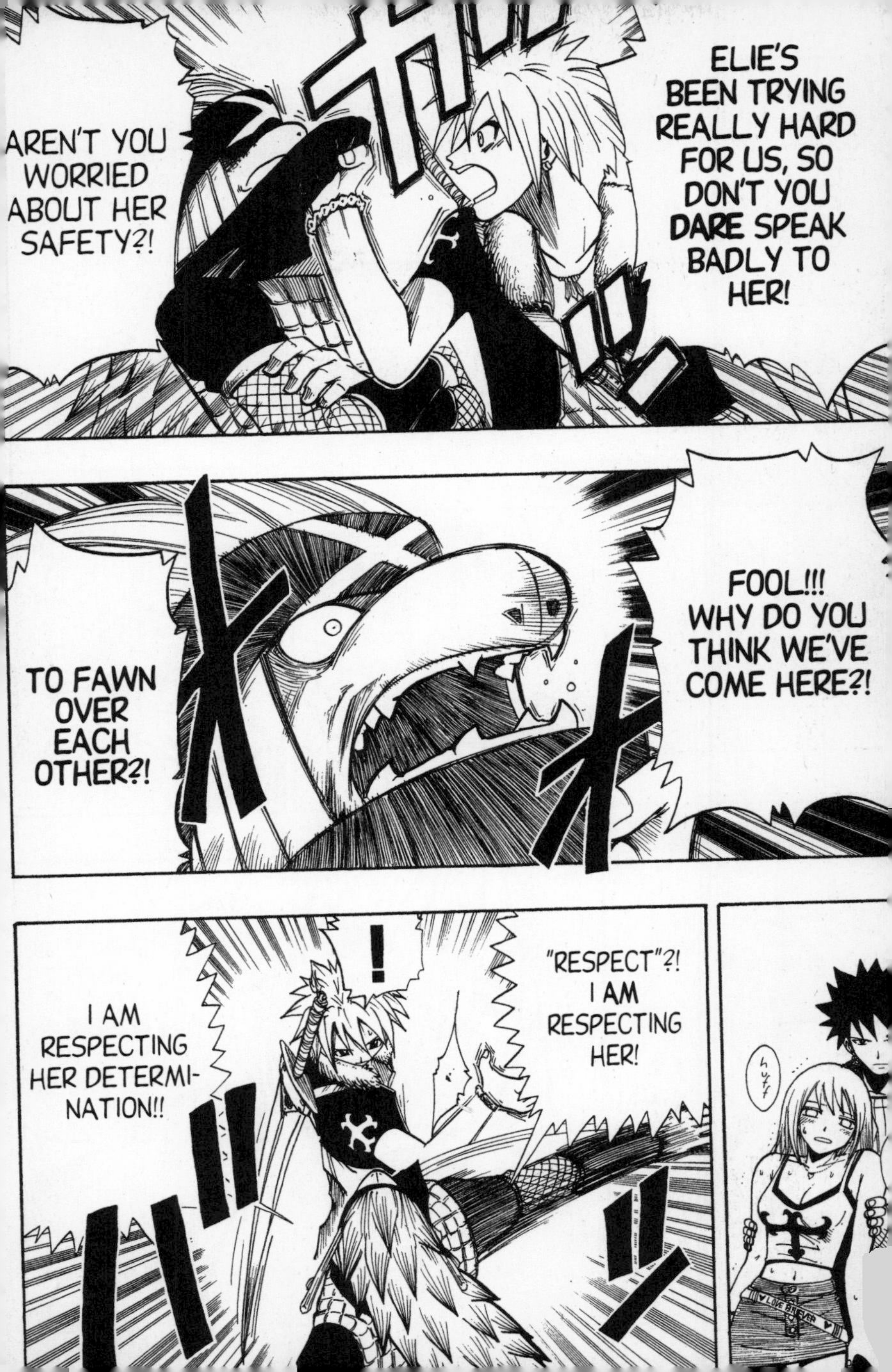
ELIE'S BEEN TRYING REALLY HARD FOR US, SO DON'T YOU DARE SPEAK BADLY TO HER!
AREN'T YOU WORRIED ABOUT HER SAFETY?!
FOOL!!! WHY DO YOU THINK WE'VE COME HERE?!
TO FAWN OVER EACH OTHER?!
huff
!
"RESPECT"?! I AM RESPECTING HER!
I AM RESPECTING HER DETERMI-NATION!!

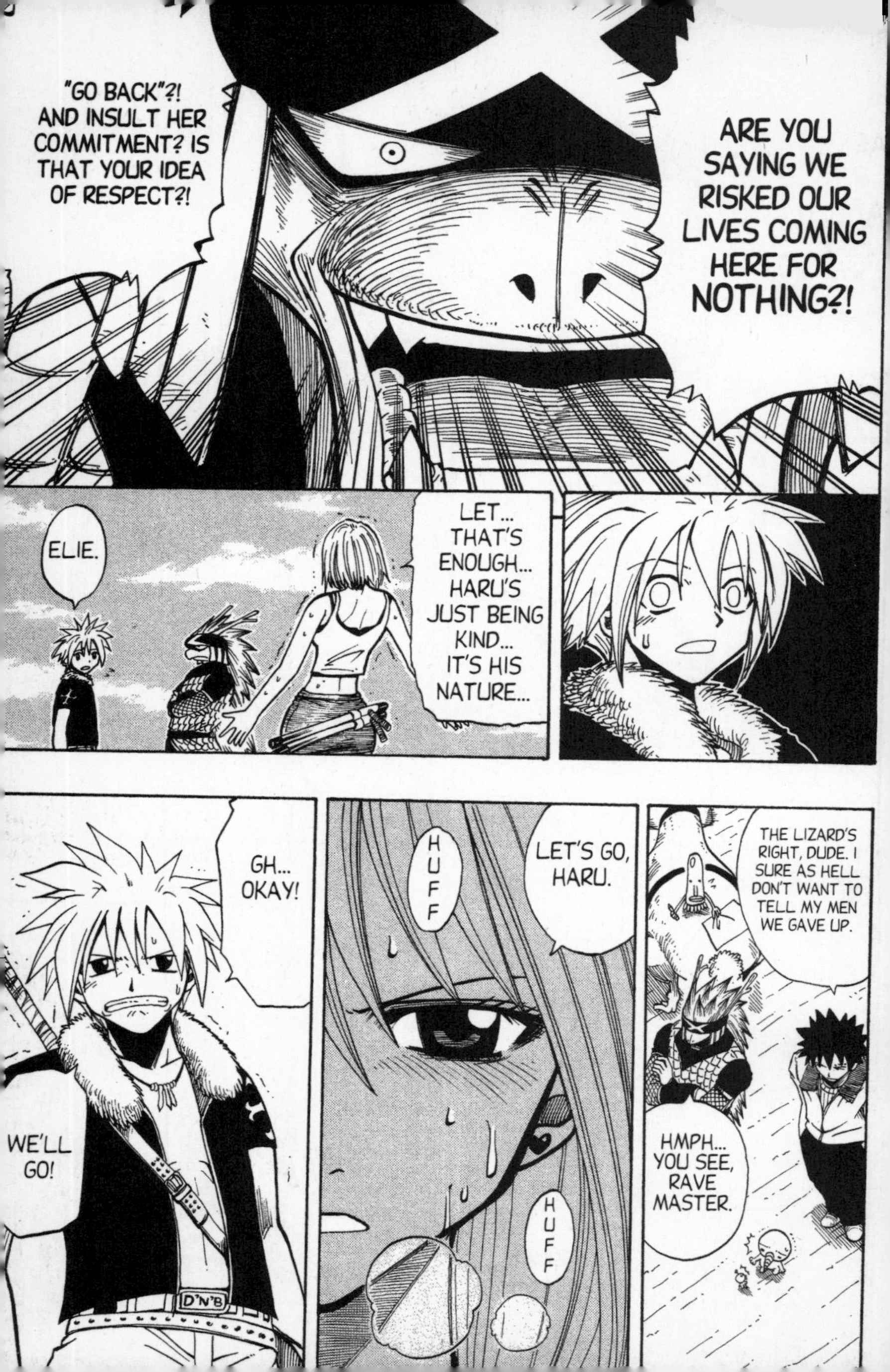
ARE YOU SAYING WE RISKED OUR LIVES COMING HERE FOR NOTHING?!
"GO BACK"?! AND INSULT HER COMMITMENT? IS THAT YOUR IDEA OF RESPECT?!
LET... THAT'S ENOUGH... HARU'S JUST BEING KIND... IT'S HIS NATURE...
ELIE.
THE LIZARD'S RIGHT, DUDE. I SURE AS HELL DON'T WANT TO TELL MY MEN WE GAVE UP.
HMPH... YOU SEE, RAVE MASTER.
LET'S GO, HARU.
HUFF
HUFF
GH... OKAY!
WE'LL GO!
D'N'B

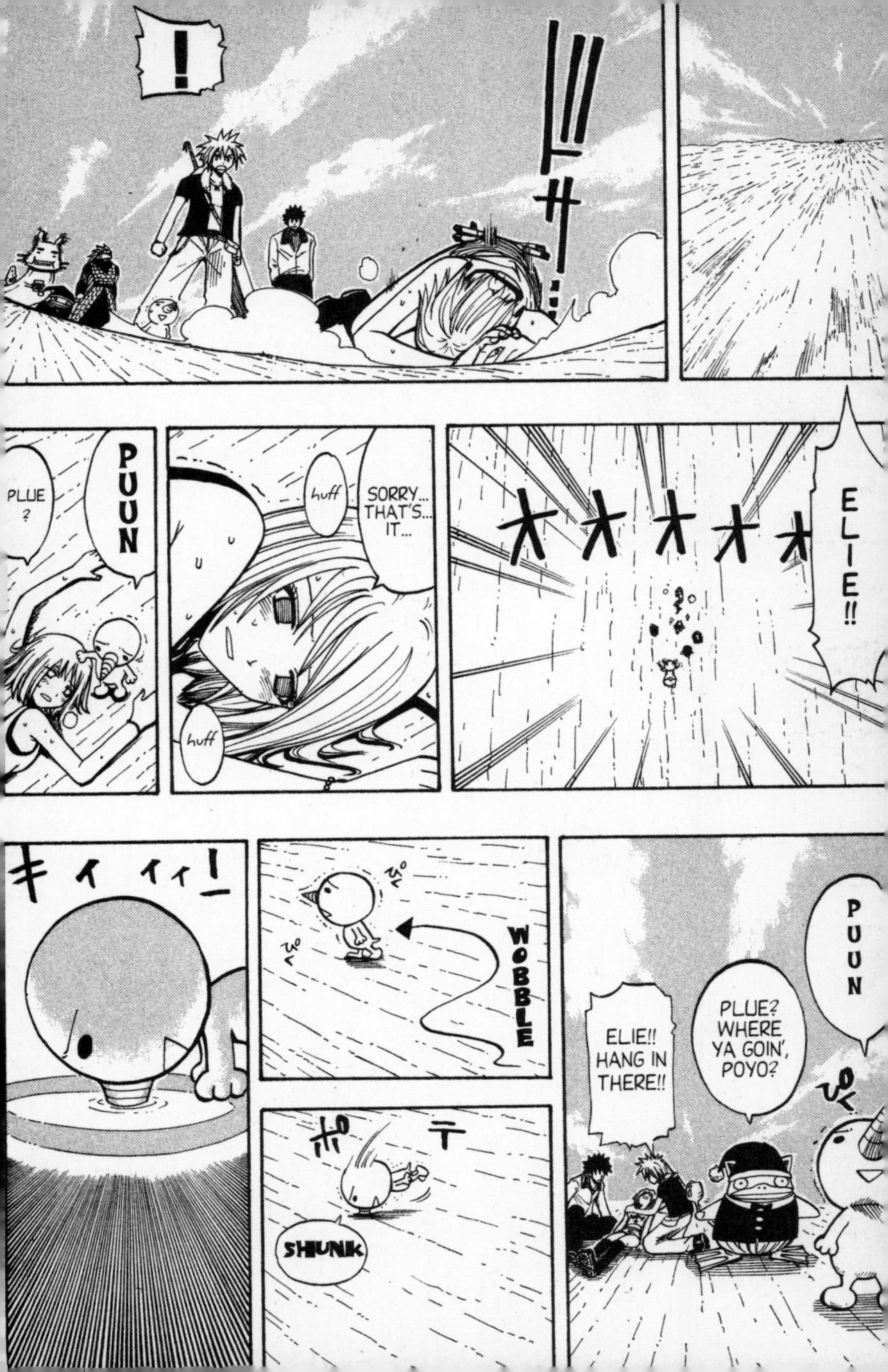

!
ELIE!!
SORRY... THAT'S... IT...
huff
huff
PUUN
PLUE?
PUUN
PLUE? WHERE YA GOIN', POYO?
ELIE!! HANG IN THERE!!
WOBBLE
SHUNK

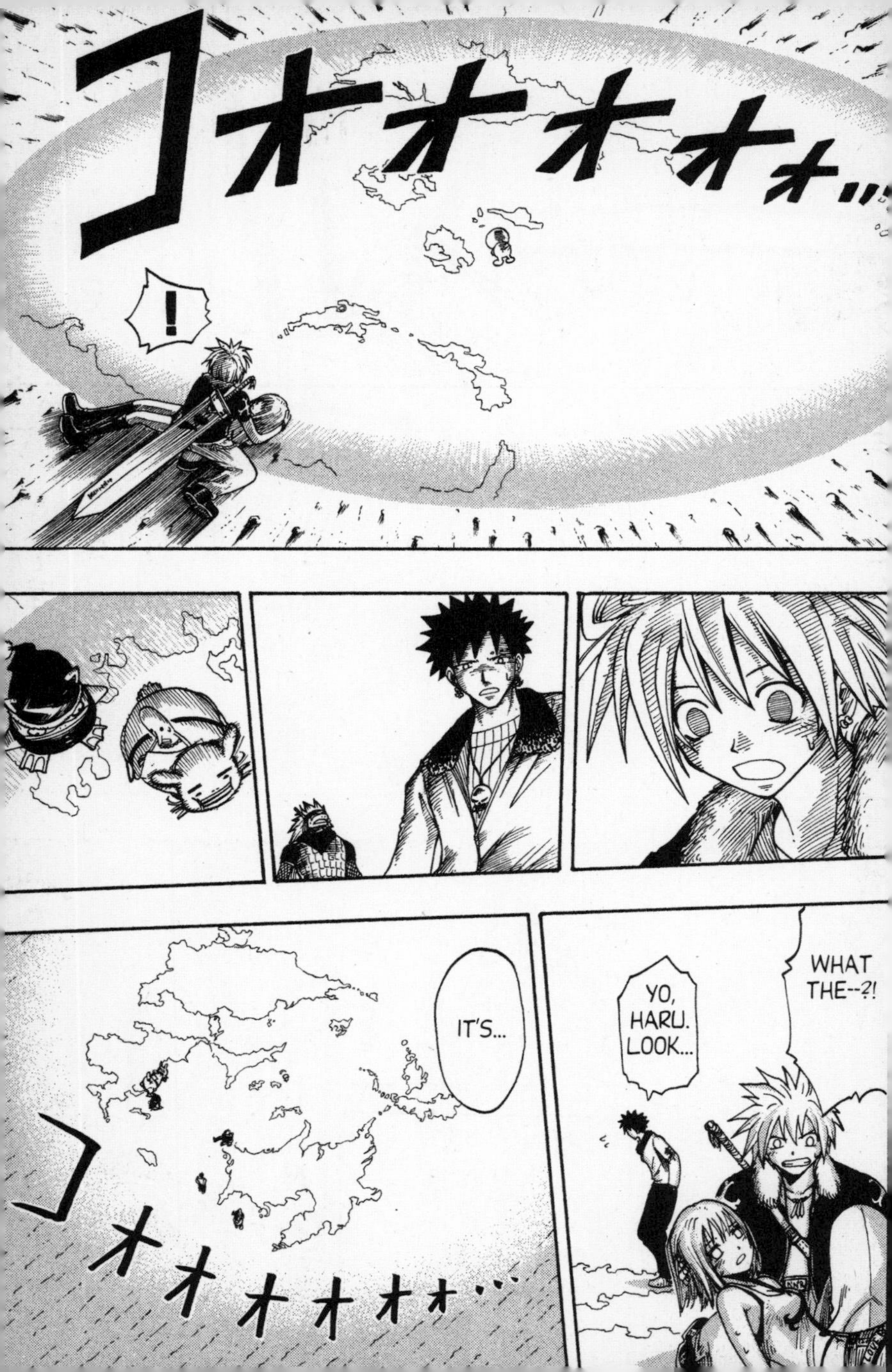
コオオオオォ…
!
WHAT THE--?!
YO, HARU. LOOK...
IT'S...
コオオオオオォ…

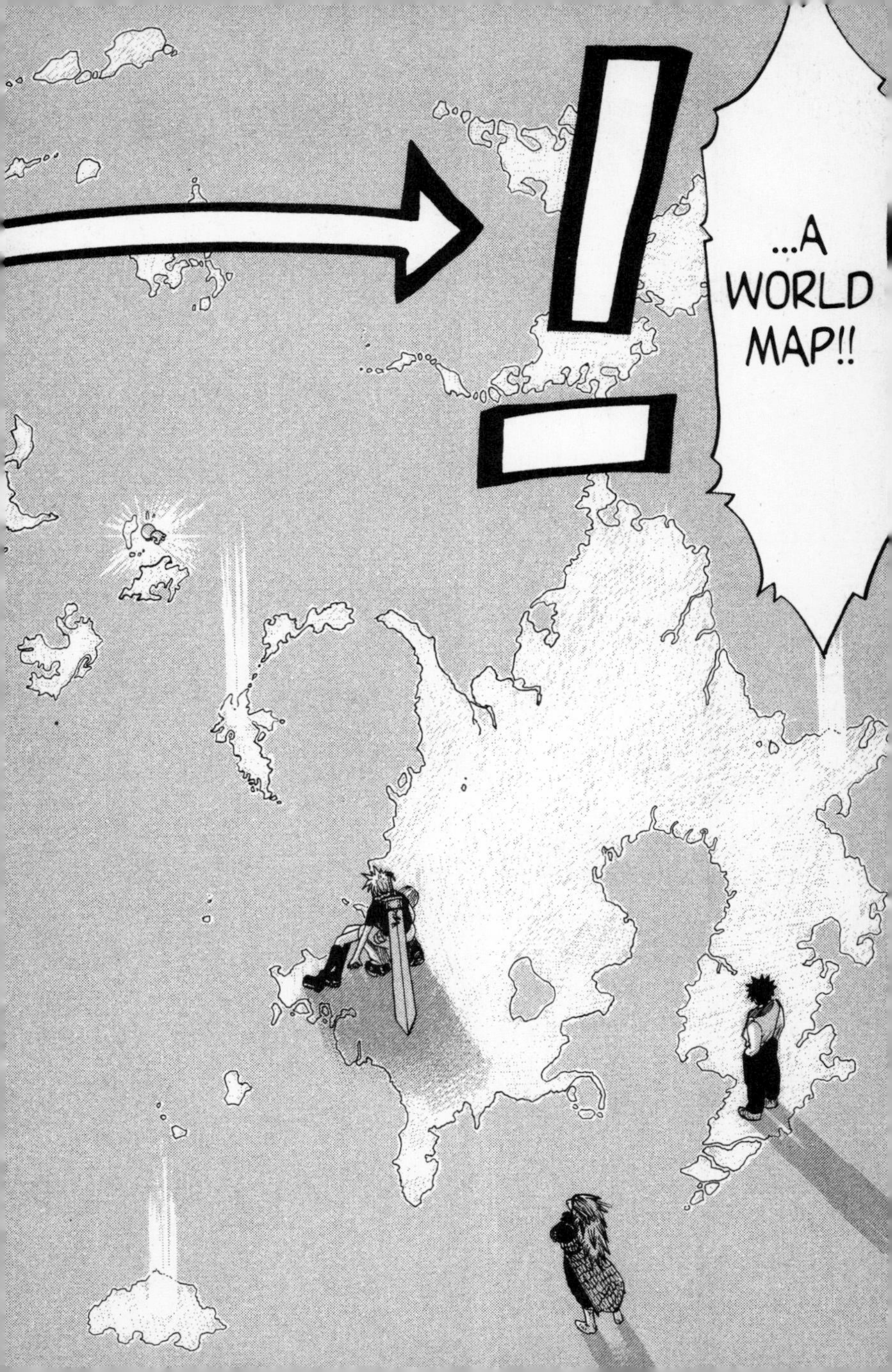
!
...A WORLD MAP!!

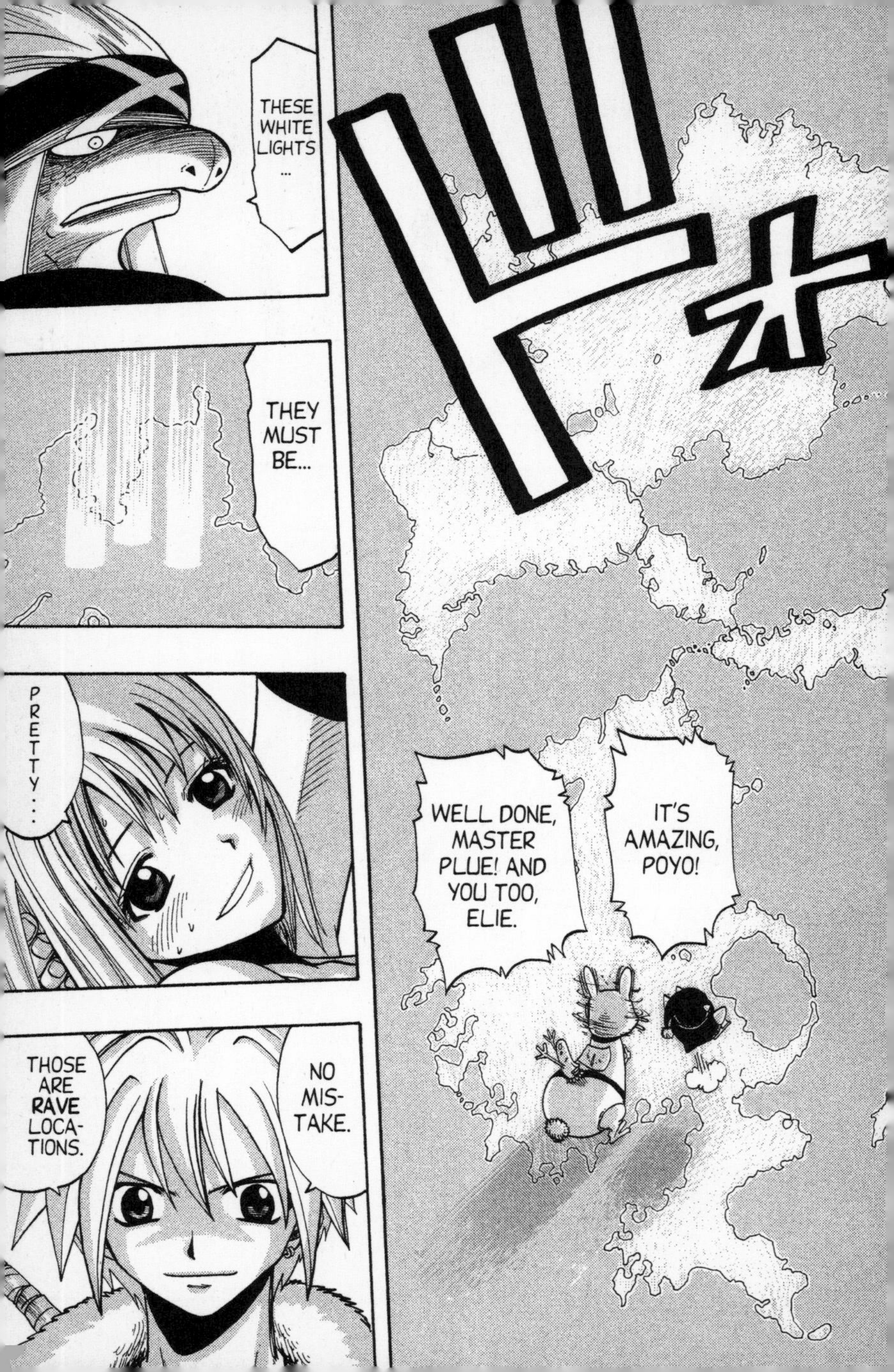
ドッ
IT'S AMAZING, POYO!
WELL DONE, MASTER PLUE! AND YOU TOO, ELIE.
THESE WHITE LIGHTS ...
THEY MUST BE...
PRETTY...
NO MISTAKE.
THOSE ARE **RAVE** LOCATIONS.

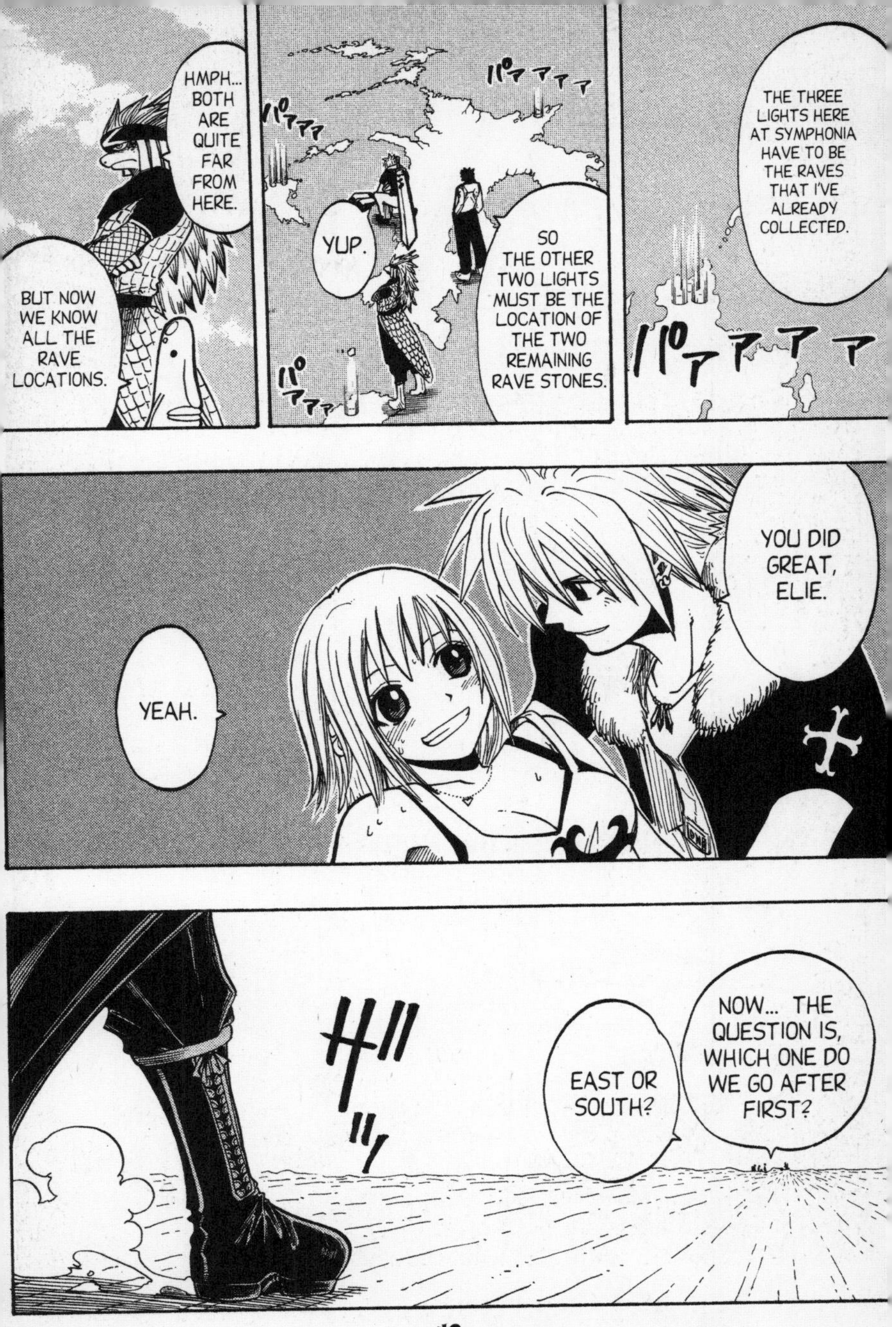
THE THREE LIGHTS HERE AT SYMPHONIA HAVE TO BE THE RAVES THAT I'VE ALREADY COLLECTED.
パアアアア
SO THE OTHER TWO LIGHTS MUST BE THE LOCATION OF THE TWO REMAINING RAVE STONES.
YUP.
HMPH... BOTH ARE QUITE FAR FROM HERE.
BUT NOW WE KNOW ALL THE RAVE LOCATIONS.
YOU DID GREAT, ELIE.
YEAH.
NOW... THE QUESTION IS, WHICH ONE DO WE GO AFTER FIRST?
EAST OR SOUTH?

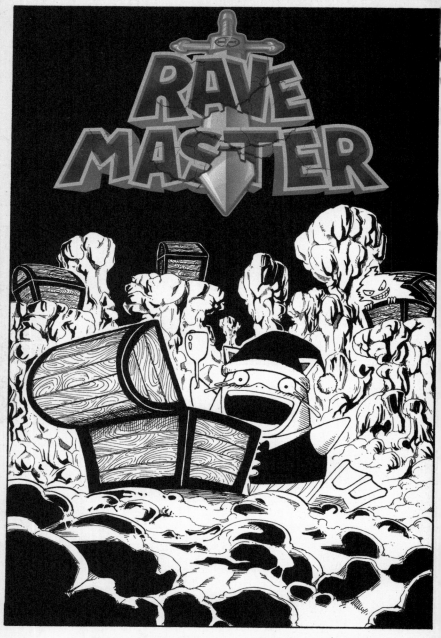

RAVE:82 ✛ TOWARDS THE VORTEX OF CHAOS

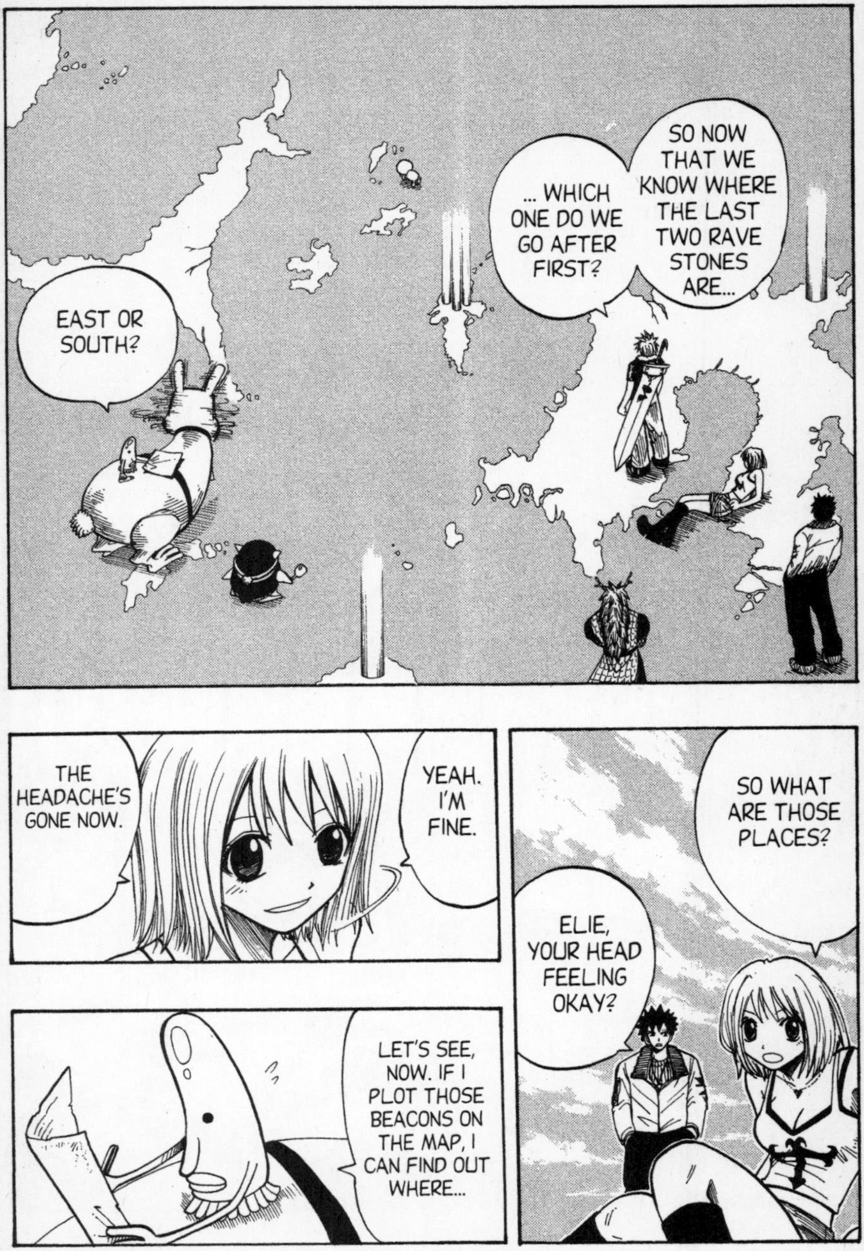
SO NOW THAT WE KNOW WHERE THE LAST TWO RAVE STONES ARE...
... WHICH ONE DO WE GO AFTER FIRST?
EAST OR SOUTH?
SO WHAT ARE THOSE PLACES?
ELIE, YOUR HEAD FEELING OKAY?
YEAH. I'M FINE.
THE HEADACHE'S GONE NOW.
LET'S SEE, NOW. IF I PLOT THOSE BEACONS ON THE MAP, I CAN FIND OUT WHERE...

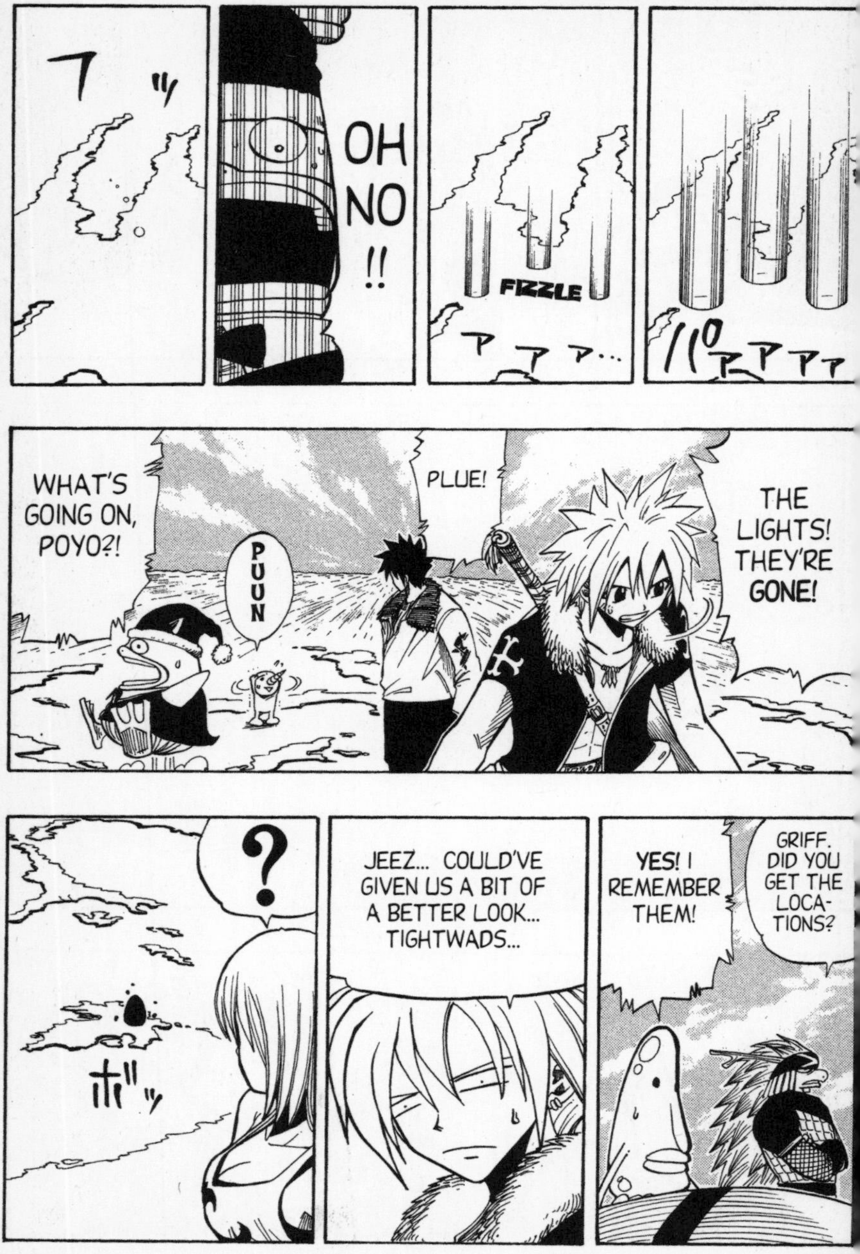
FIZZLE
OH NO !!
THE LIGHTS! THEY'RE GONE!
PLUE!
PUUN
WHAT'S GOING ON, POYO?!
GRIFF. DID YOU GET THE LOCA-TIONS?
YES! I REMEMBER THEM!
JEEZ... COULD'VE GIVEN US A BIT OF A BETTER LOOK... TIGHTWADS...
?

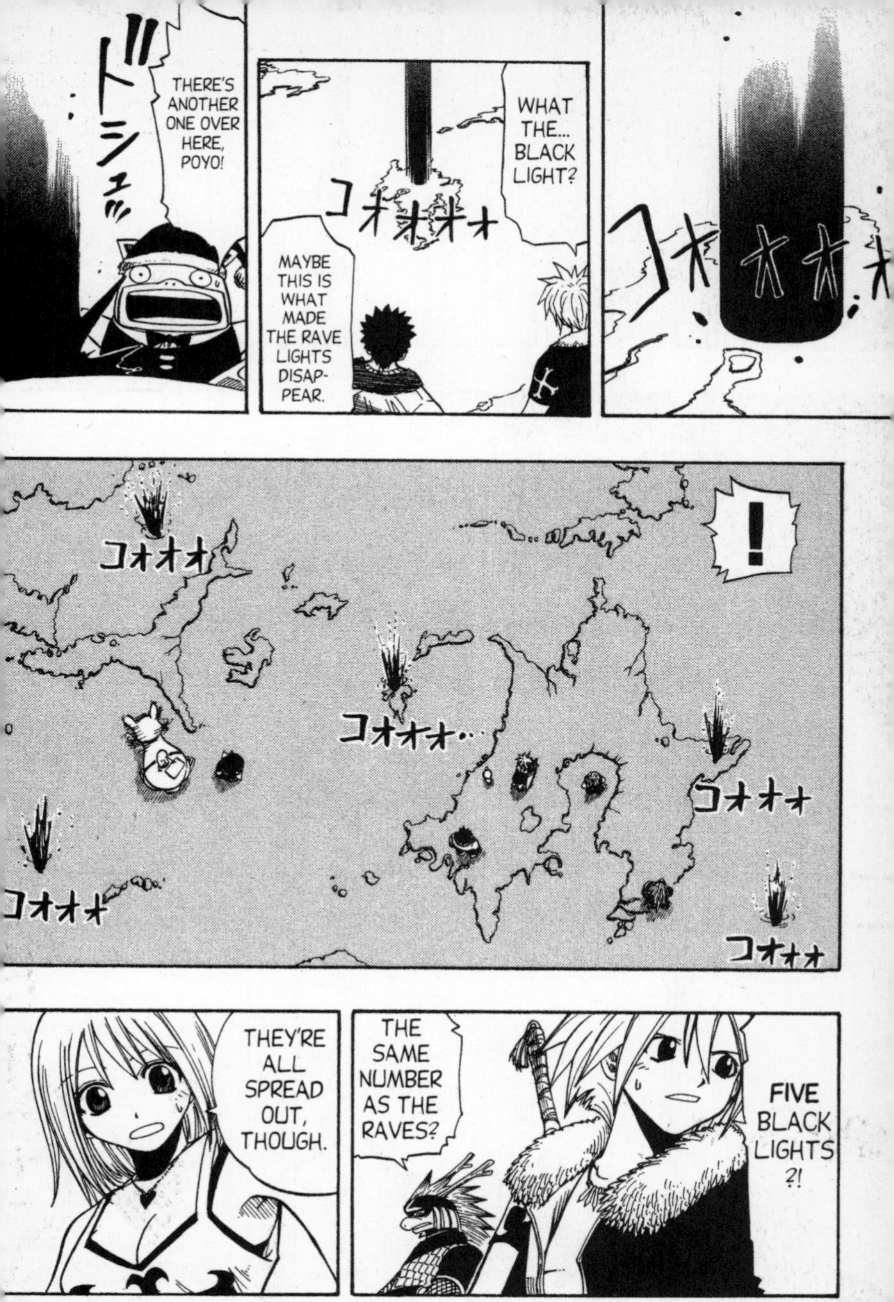

コォォォォ
WHAT THE... BLACK LIGHT?
コォォォォォ
MAYBE THIS IS WHAT MADE THE RAVE LIGHTS DISAPPEAR.
ドシュッ
THERE'S ANOTHER ONE OVER HERE, POYO!
!
コォォォ
コォォォ...
コォォォ
コォォォ
コォォォ
FIVE BLACK LIGHTS?!
THE SAME NUMBER AS THE RAVES?
THEY'RE ALL SPREAD OUT, THOUGH.

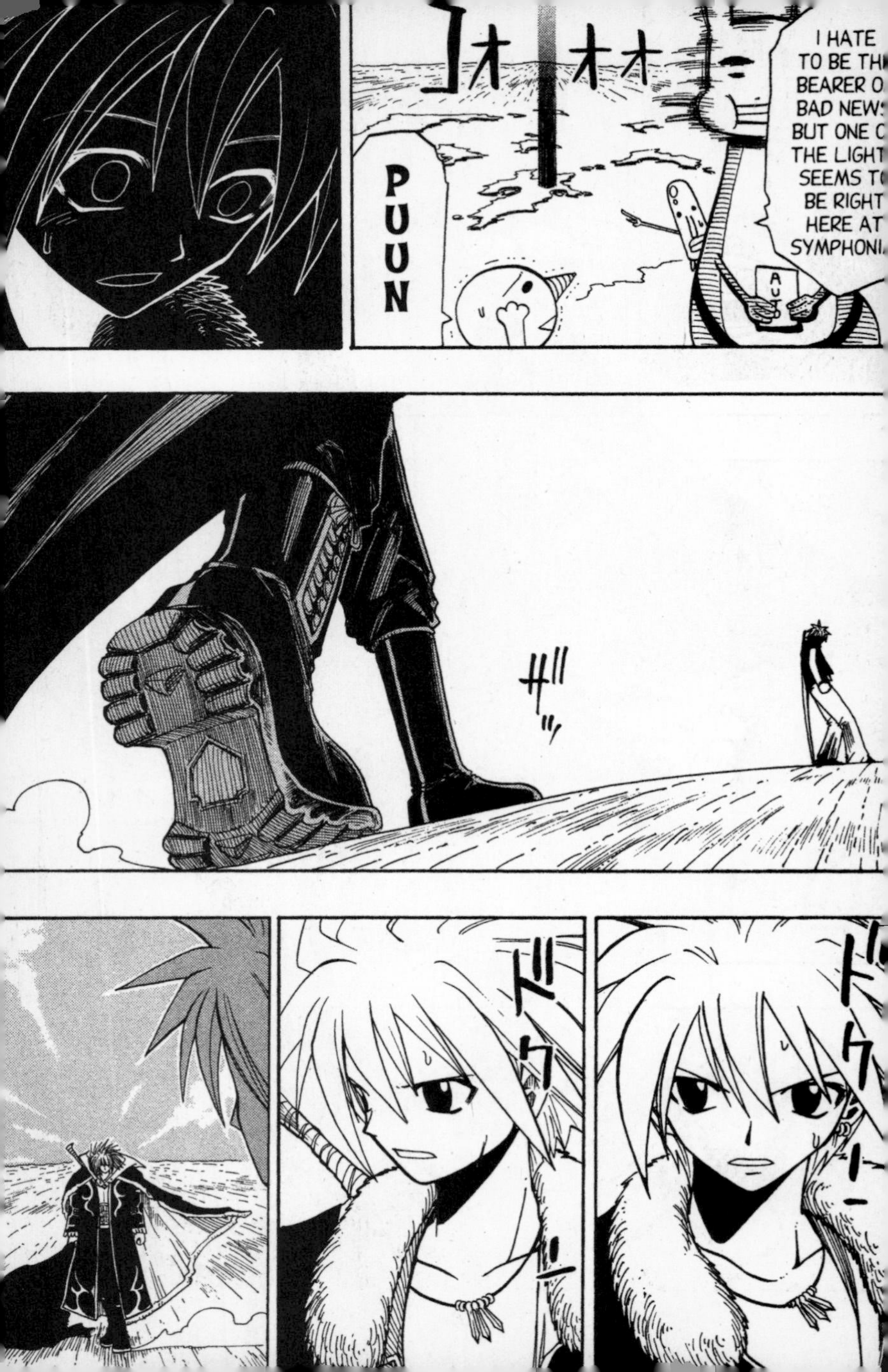
I HATE TO BE TH BEARER O BAD NEWS BUT ONE O THE LIGHT SEEMS T BE RIGHT HERE AT SYMPHONI
PUUN

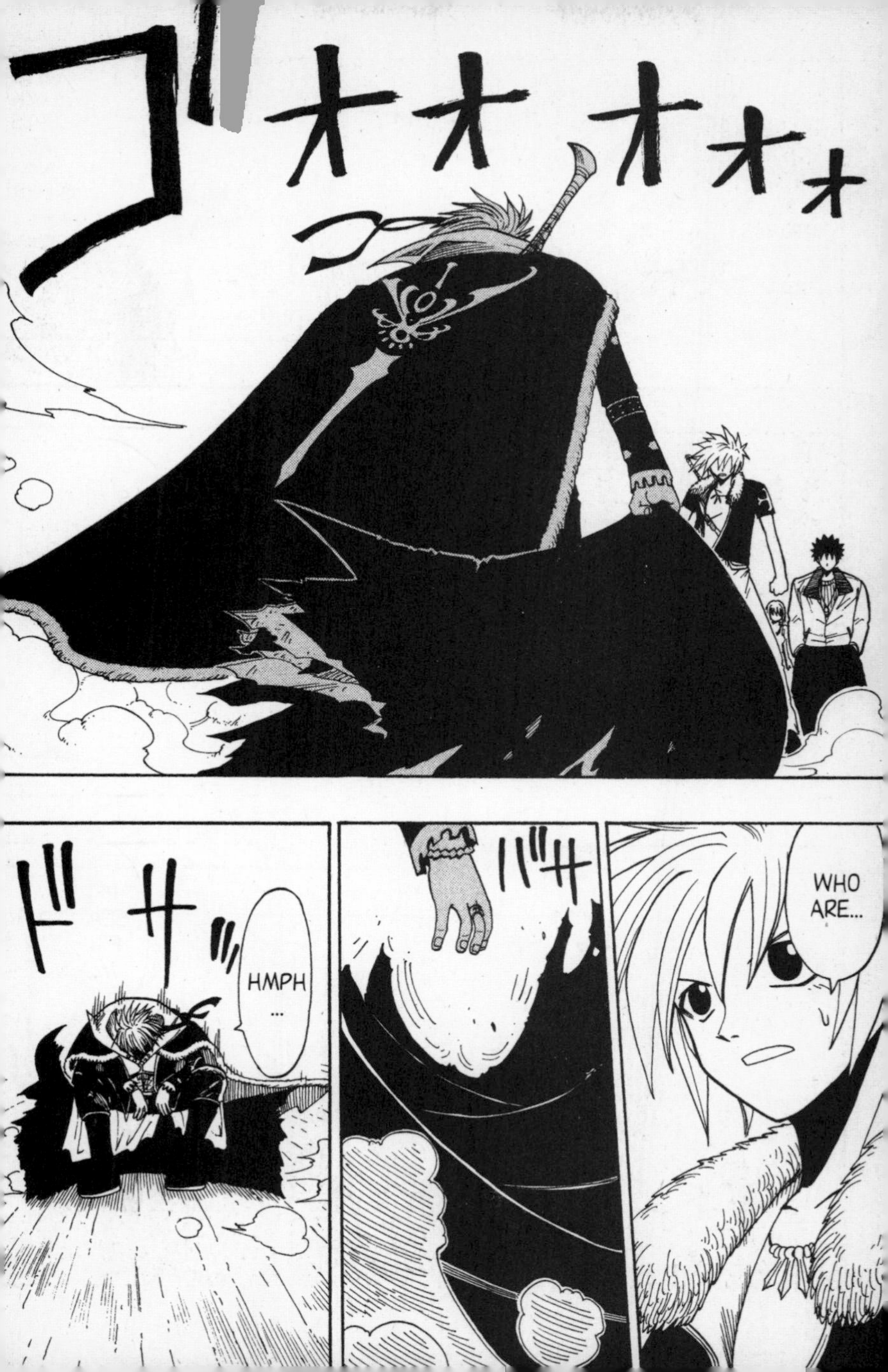
ゴオオオオォ
WHO ARE...
バサ
ドサ
HMPH ...

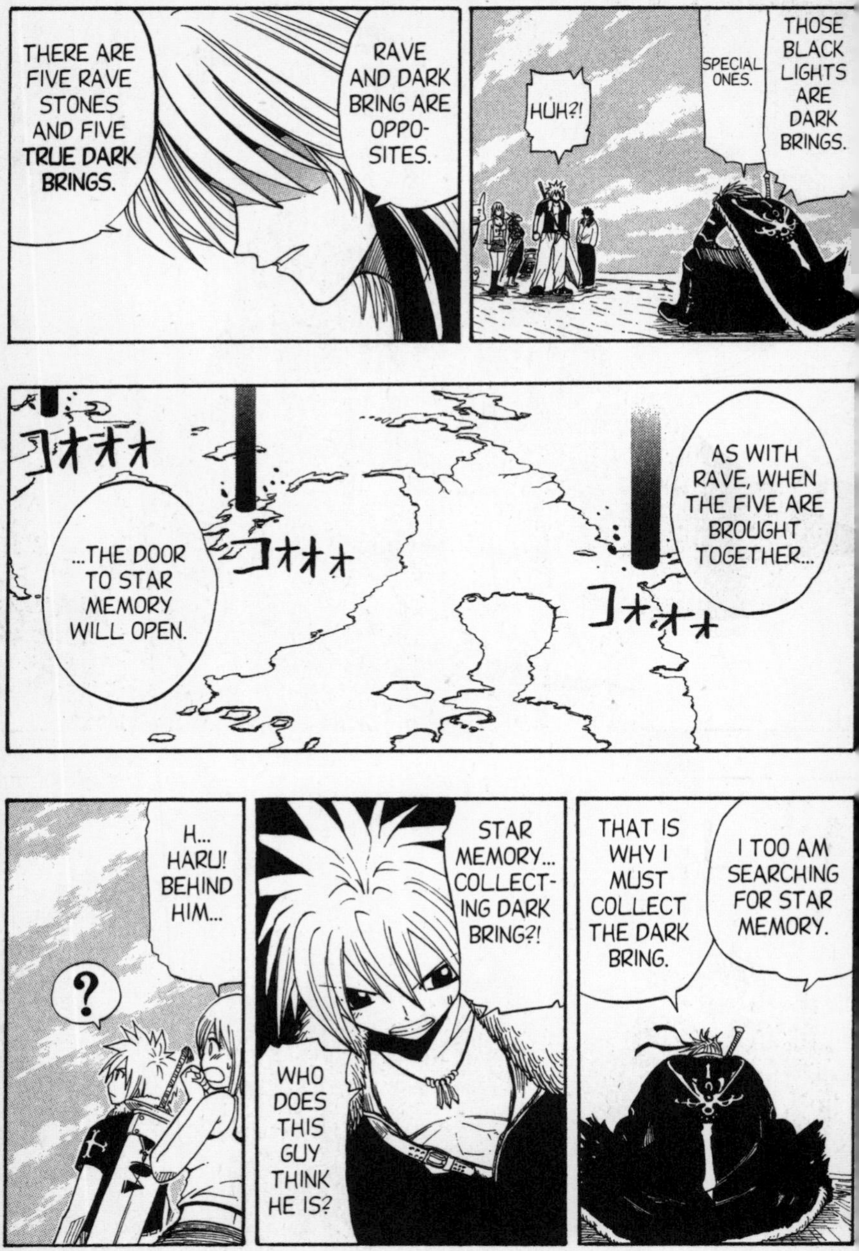
THOSE BLACK LIGHTS ARE DARK BRINGS.
SPECIAL ONES.
HUH?!
RAVE AND DARK BRING ARE OPPOSITES.
THERE ARE FIVE RAVE STONES AND FIVE TRUE DARK BRINGS.
AS WITH RAVE, WHEN THE FIVE ARE BROUGHT TOGETHER...
コオオオ
コオオオ
コオオオ
...THE DOOR TO STAR MEMORY WILL OPEN.
I TOO AM SEARCHING FOR STAR MEMORY.
THAT IS WHY I MUST COLLECT THE DARK BRING.
STAR MEMORY... COLLECTING DARK BRING?!
WHO DOES THIS GUY THINK HE IS?
H... HARU! BEHIND HIM...
?

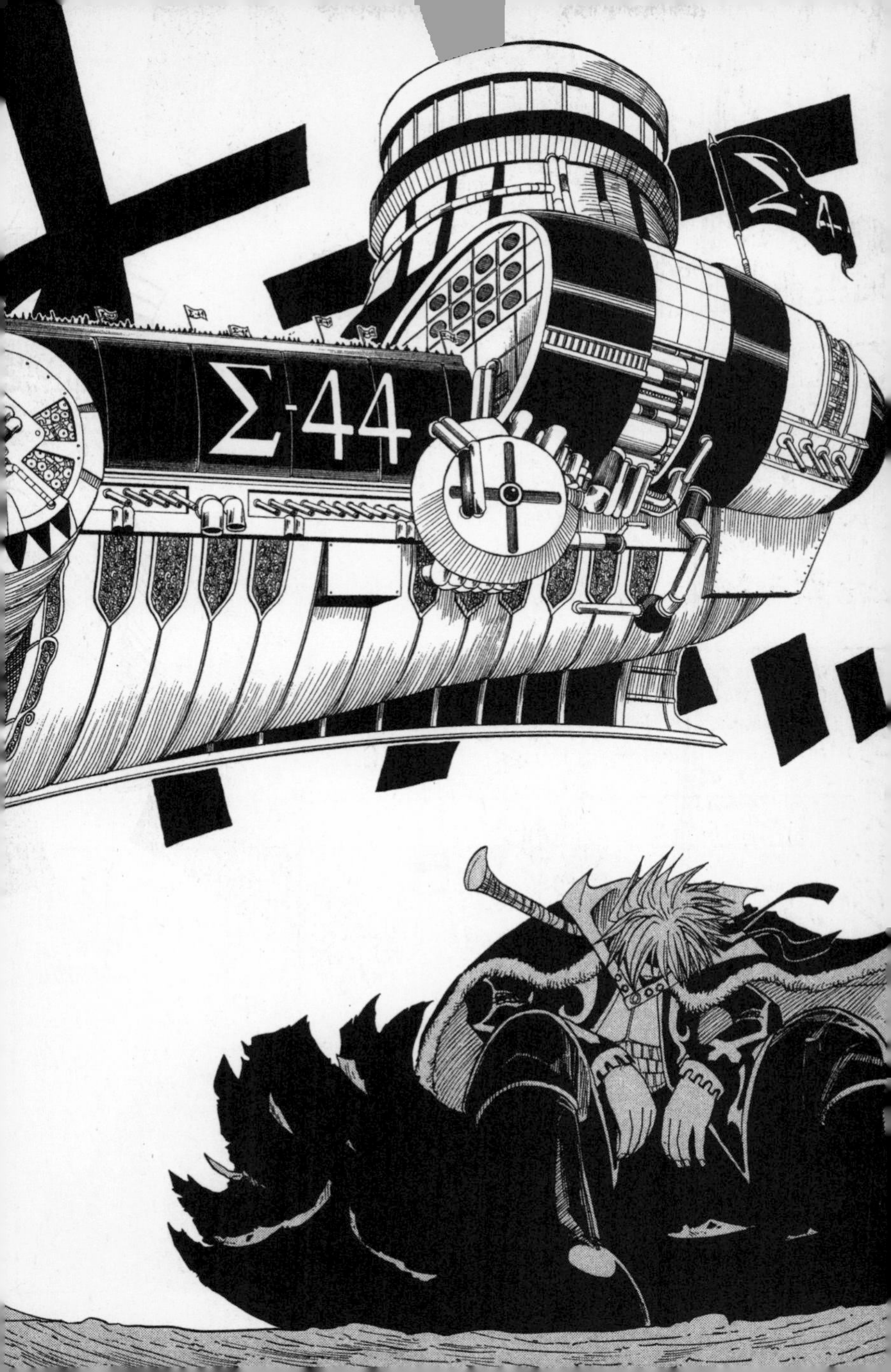
Σ-44

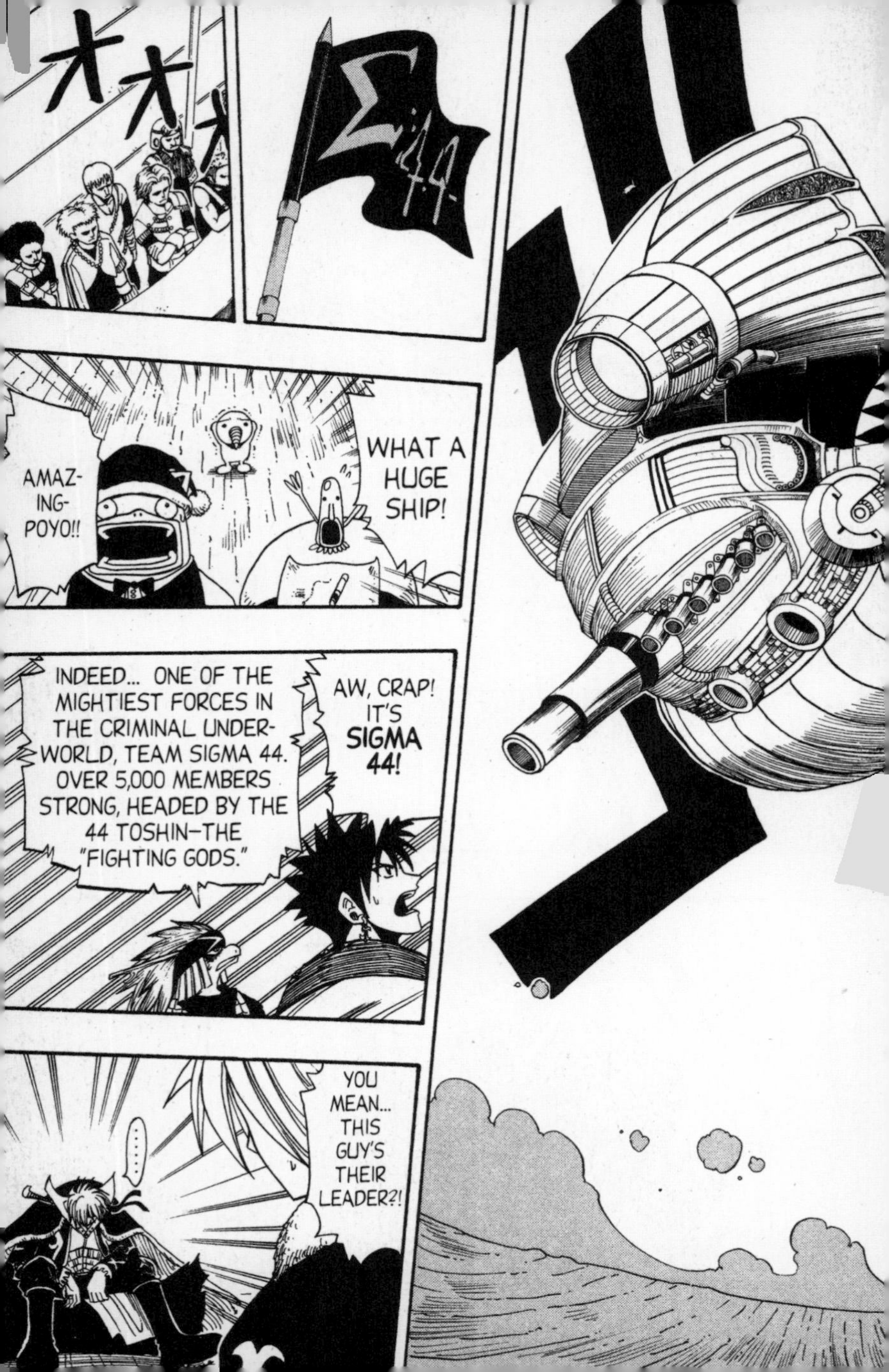

オオオ
WHAT A HUGE SHIP!
AMAZ-ING-POYO!!
AW, CRAP! IT'S **SIGMA 44!**
INDEED... ONE OF THE MIGHTIEST FORCES IN THE CRIMINAL UNDER-WORLD, TEAM SIGMA 44. OVER 5,000 MEMBERS STRONG, HEADED BY THE 44 TOSHIN—THE "FIGHTING GODS."
YOU MEAN... THIS GUY'S THEIR LEADER?!
......

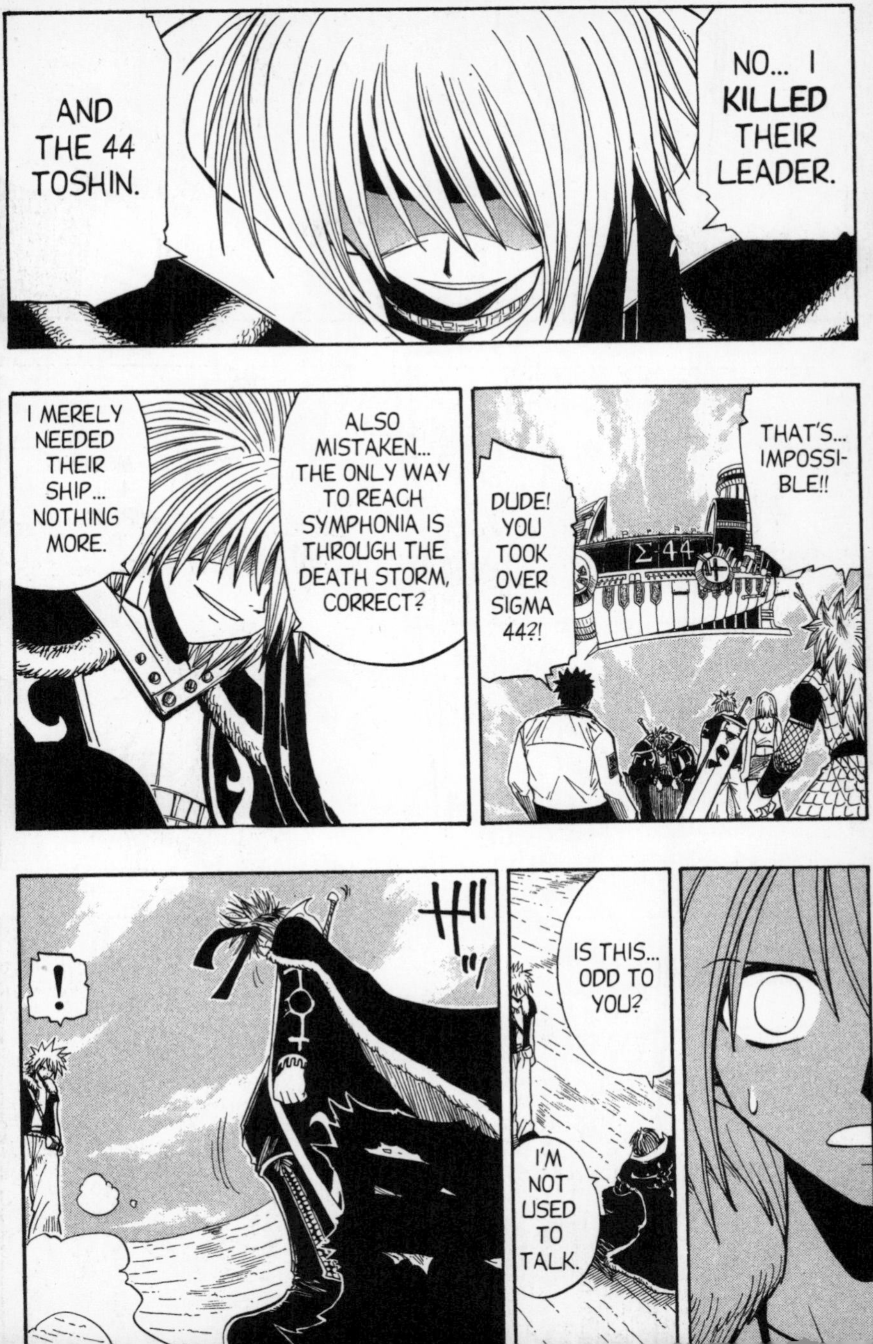
NO... I KILLED THEIR LEADER.
AND THE 44 TOSHIN.
THAT'S... IMPOSSI-BLE!!
DUDE! YOU TOOK OVER SIGMA 44?!
ALSO MISTAKEN... THE ONLY WAY TO REACH SYMPHONIA IS THROUGH THE DEATH STORM, CORRECT?
I MERELY NEEDED THEIR SHIP... NOTHING MORE.
IS THIS... ODD TO YOU?
I'M NOT USED TO TALK.
!

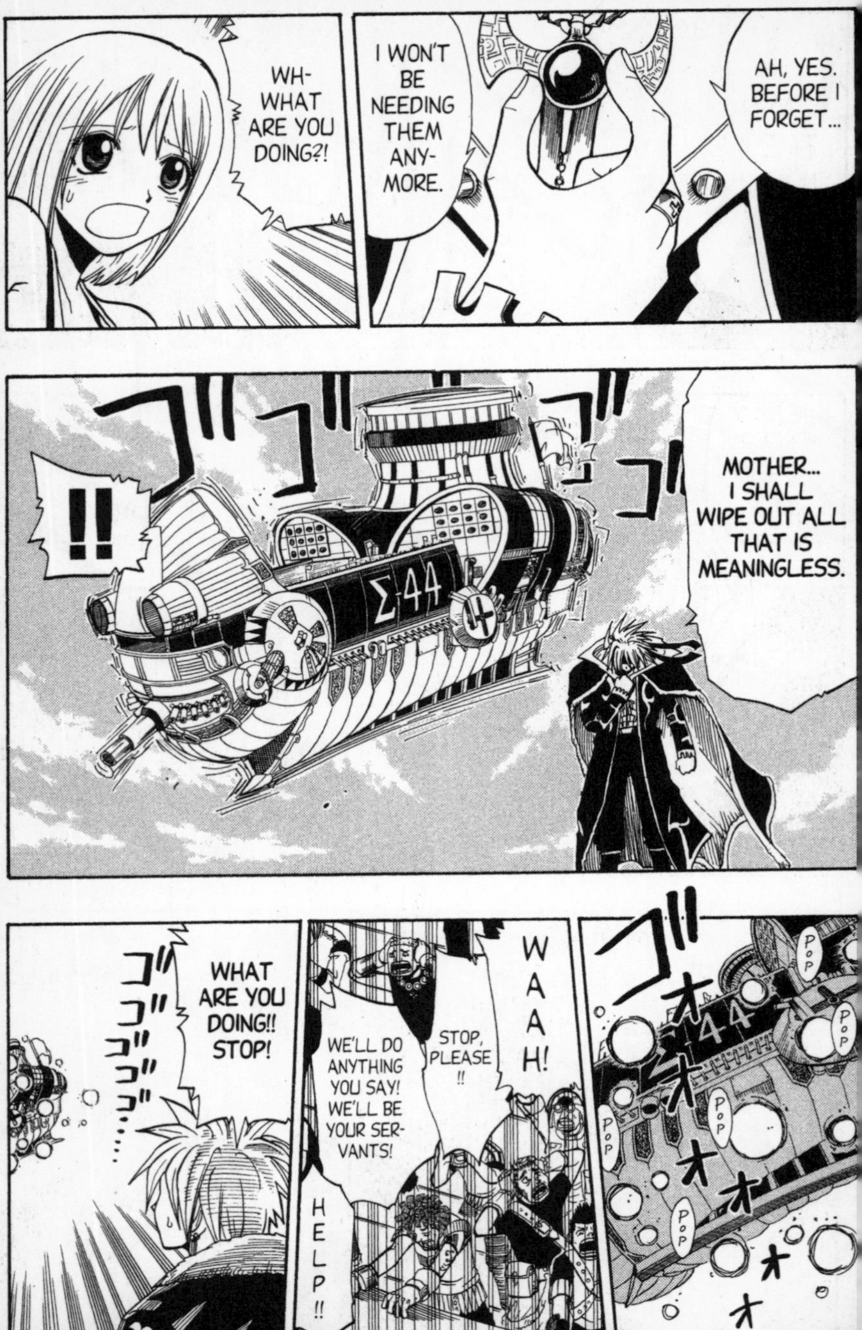
AH, YES. BEFORE I FORGET...
I WON'T BE NEEDING THEM ANYMORE.
WH- WHAT ARE YOU DOING?!
MOTHER... I SHALL WIPE OUT ALL THAT IS MEANINGLESS.
!!
PoP
PoP
PoP
PoP
PoP
PoP
WAAAH!
STOP, PLEASE!!
WE'LL DO ANYTHING YOU SAY! WE'LL BE YOUR SERVANTS!
HELP!!
WHAT ARE YOU DOING!! STOP!

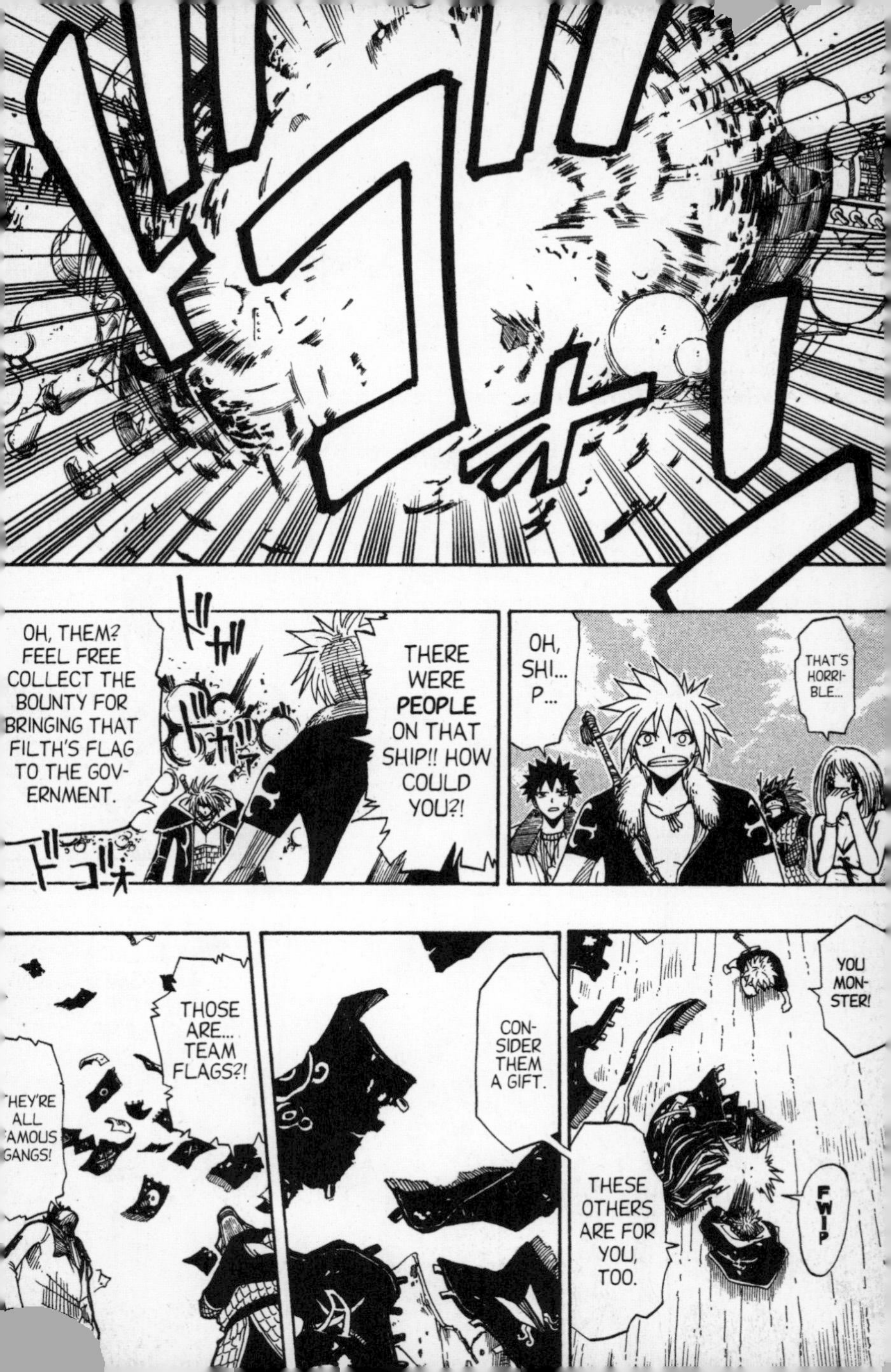
THAT'S HORRI-BLE...
OH, SHI... P...
THERE WERE PEOPLE ON THAT SHIP!! HOW COULD YOU?!
OH, THEM? FEEL FREE COLLECT THE BOUNTY FOR BRINGING THAT FILTH'S FLAG TO THE GOV-ERNMENT.
YOU MON-STER!
FWIP
THESE OTHERS ARE FOR YOU, TOO.
CON-SIDER THEM A GIFT.
THOSE ARE... TEAM FLAGS?!
HEY'RE ALL AMOUS GANGS!

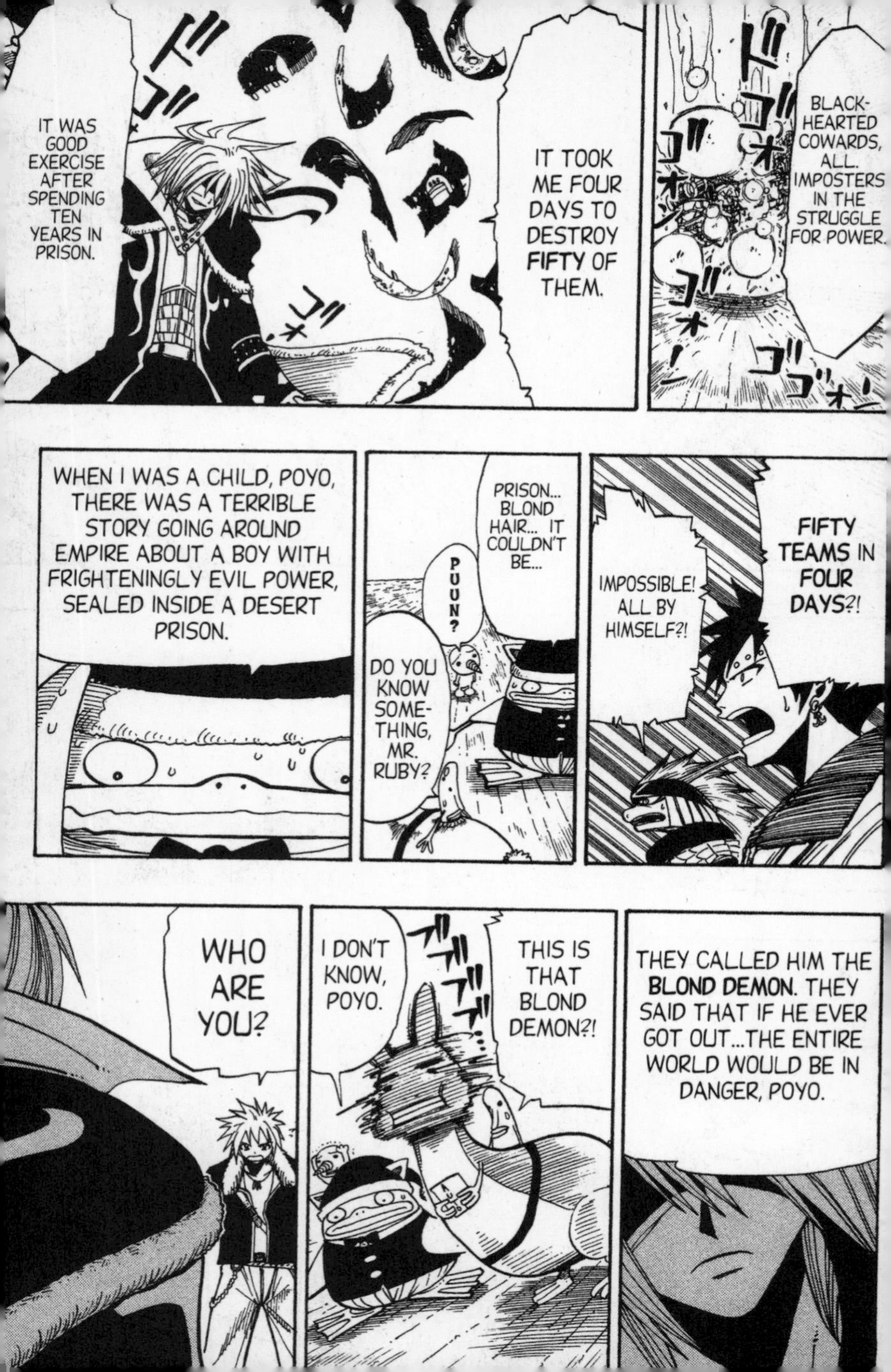
BLACK-HEARTED COWARDS, ALL. IMPOSTERS IN THE STRUGGLE FOR POWER.
IT TOOK ME FOUR DAYS TO DESTROY FIFTY OF THEM.
IT WAS GOOD EXERCISE AFTER SPENDING TEN YEARS IN PRISON.
FIFTY TEAMS IN FOUR DAYS?!
IMPOSSIBLE! ALL BY HIMSELF?!
PRISON... BLOND HAIR... IT COULDN'T BE...
PUUN?
DO YOU KNOW SOMETHING, MR. RUBY?
WHEN I WAS A CHILD, POYO, THERE WAS A TERRIBLE STORY GOING AROUND EMPIRE ABOUT A BOY WITH FRIGHTENINGLY EVIL POWER, SEALED INSIDE A DESERT PRISON.
THEY CALLED HIM THE BLOND DEMON. THEY SAID THAT IF HE EVER GOT OUT...THE ENTIRE WORLD WOULD BE IN DANGER, POYO.
THIS IS THAT BLOND DEMON?!
I DON'T KNOW, POYO.
WHO ARE YOU?

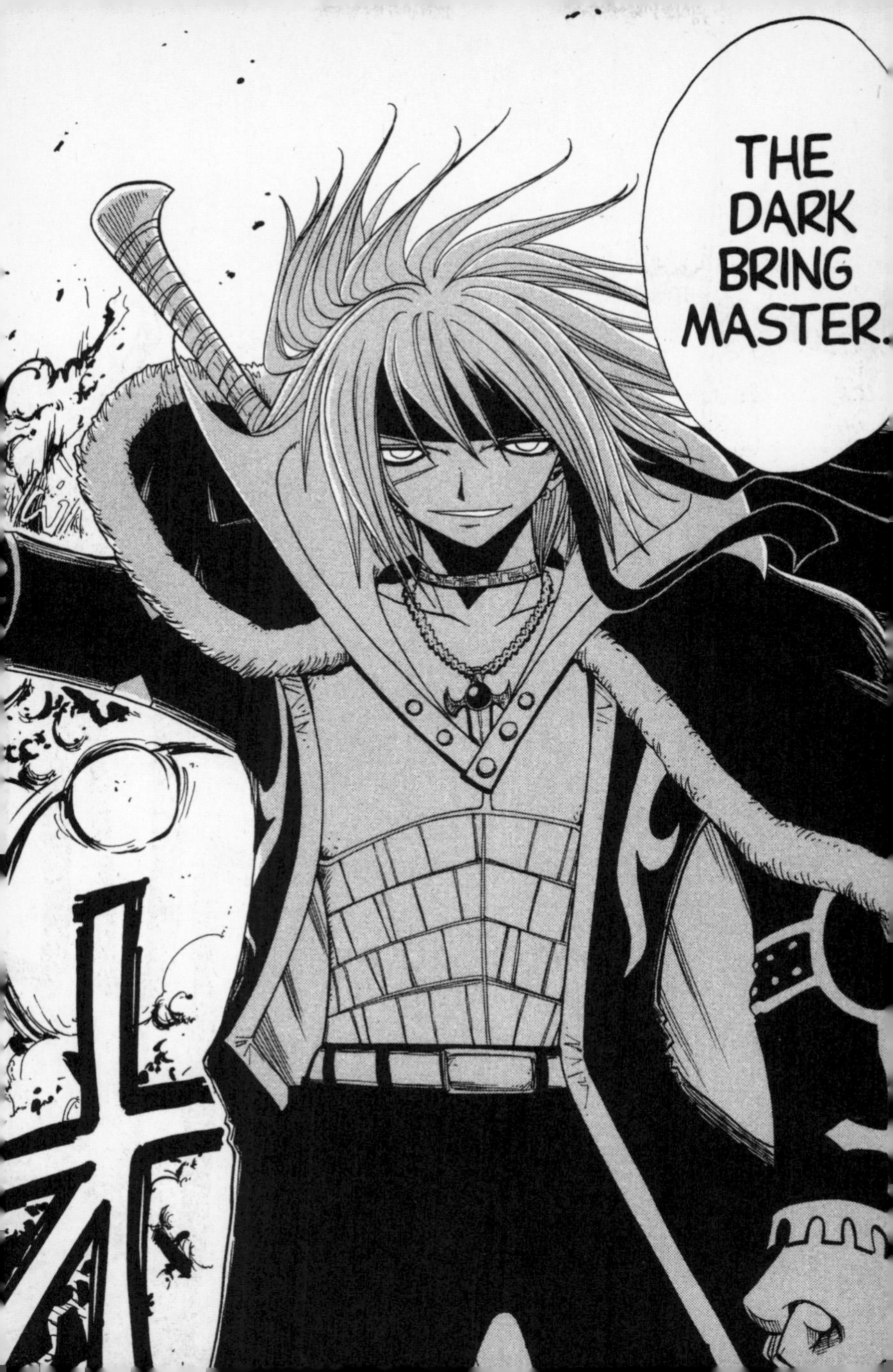
THE DARK BRING MASTER.

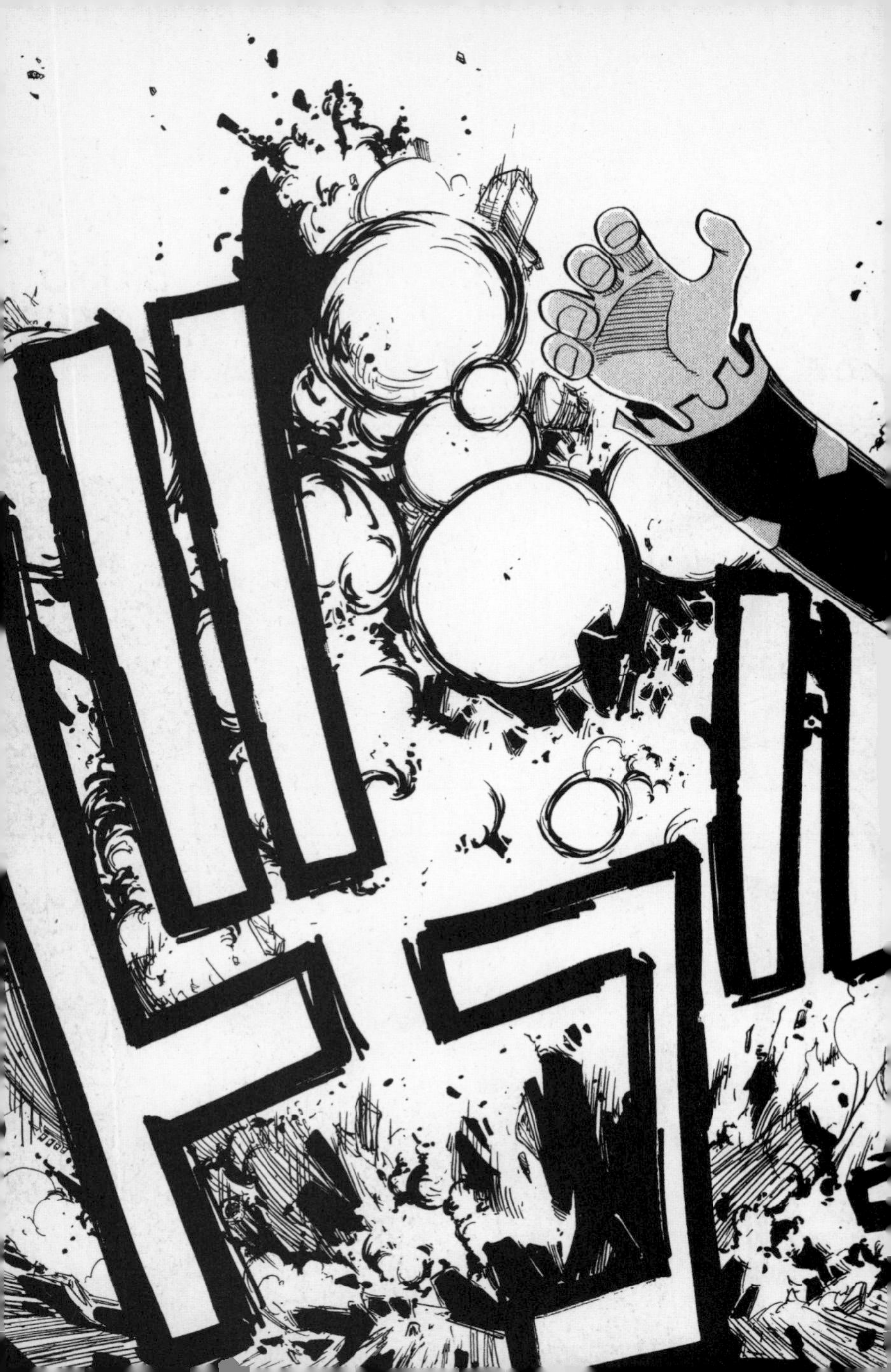

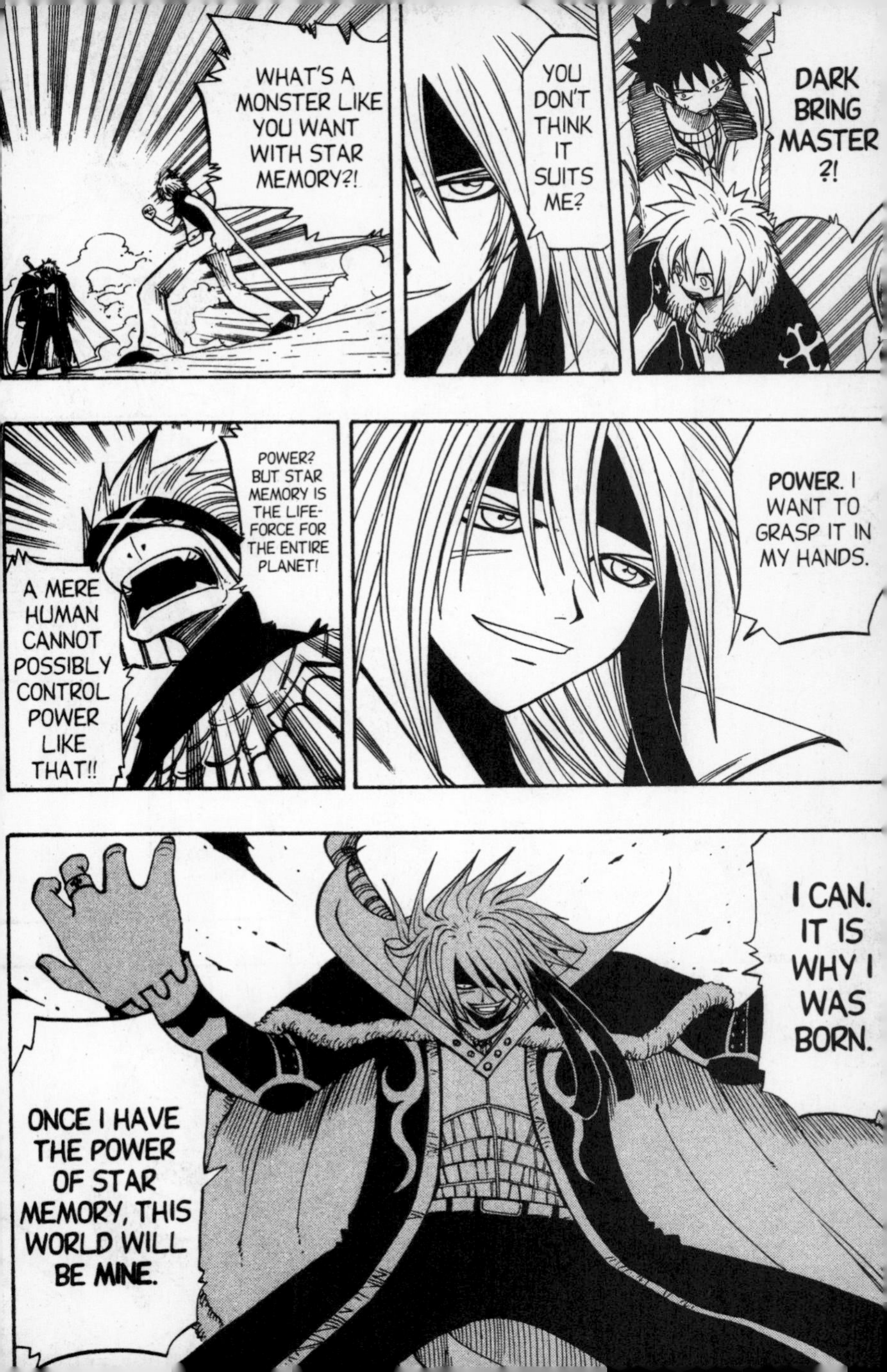
DARK BRING MASTER?!
YOU DON'T THINK IT SUITS ME?
WHAT'S A MONSTER LIKE YOU WANT WITH STAR MEMORY?!
POWER. I WANT TO GRASP IT IN MY HANDS.
POWER? BUT STAR MEMORY IS THE LIFE-FORCE FOR THE ENTIRE PLANET!
A MERE HUMAN CANNOT POSSIBLY CONTROL POWER LIKE THAT!!
I CAN. IT IS WHY I WAS BORN.
ONCE I HAVE THE POWER OF STAR MEMORY, THIS WORLD WILL BE MINE.

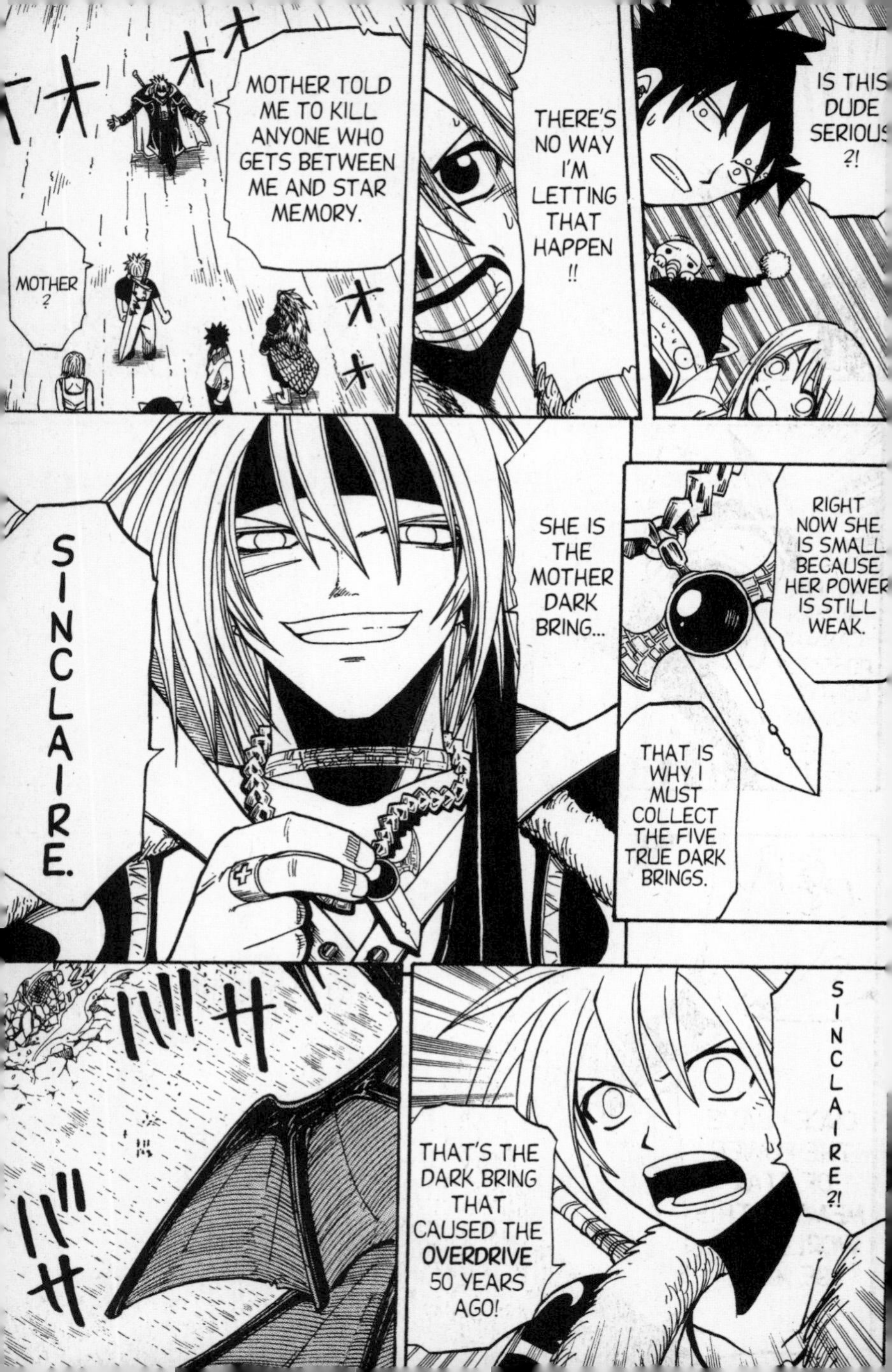
IS THIS DUDE SERIOUS ?!
THERE'S NO WAY I'M LETTING THAT HAPPEN !!
MOTHER TOLD ME TO KILL ANYONE WHO GETS BETWEEN ME AND STAR MEMORY.
MOTHER ?
RIGHT NOW SHE IS SMALL BECAUSE HER POWER IS STILL WEAK.
THAT IS WHY I MUST COLLECT THE FIVE TRUE DARK BRINGS.
SHE IS THE MOTHER DARK BRING...
SINCLAIRE.
SINCLAIRE ?!
THAT'S THE DARK BRING THAT CAUSED THE **OVERDRIVE** 50 YEARS AGO!

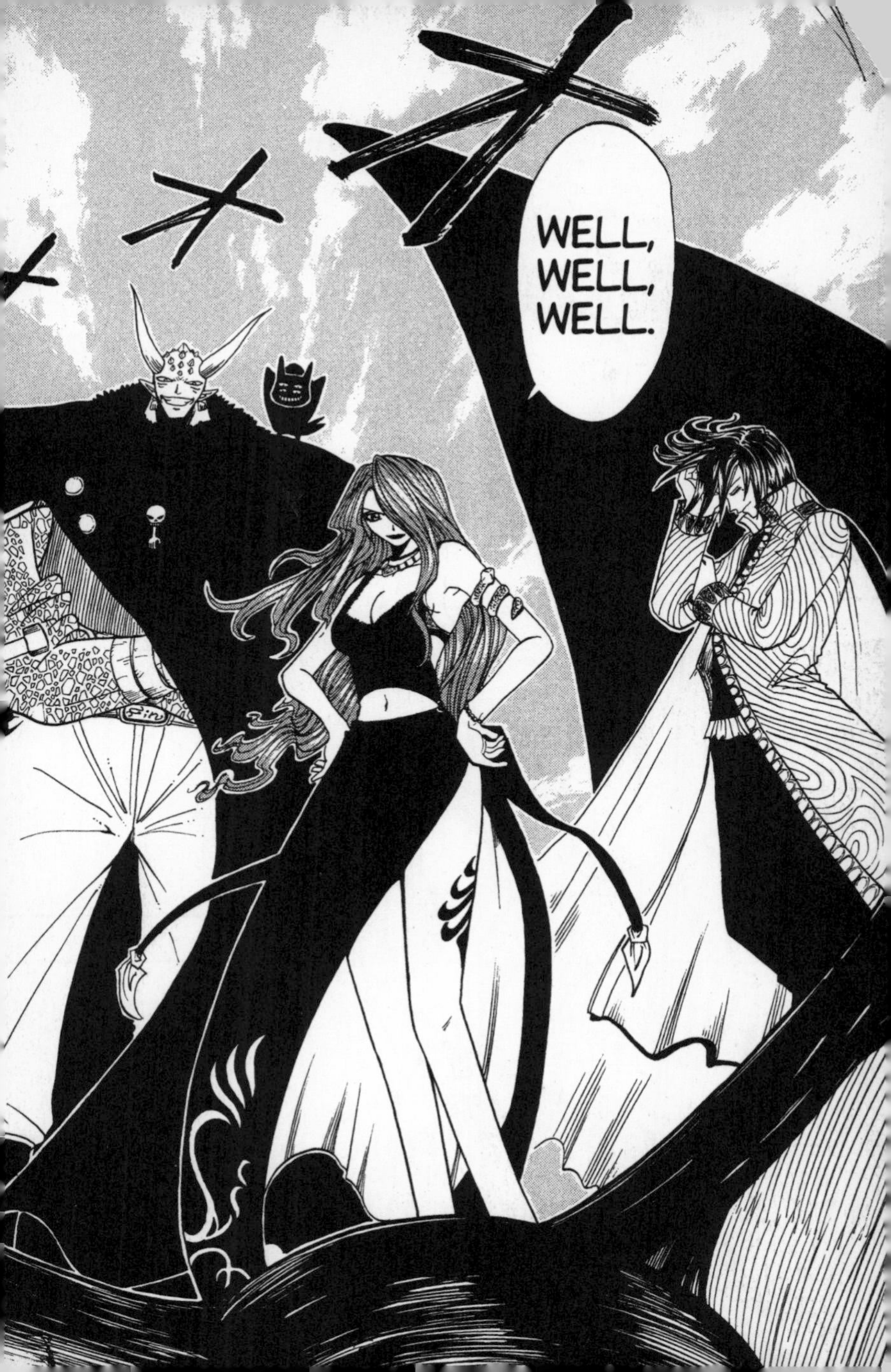
WELL, WELL, WELL.

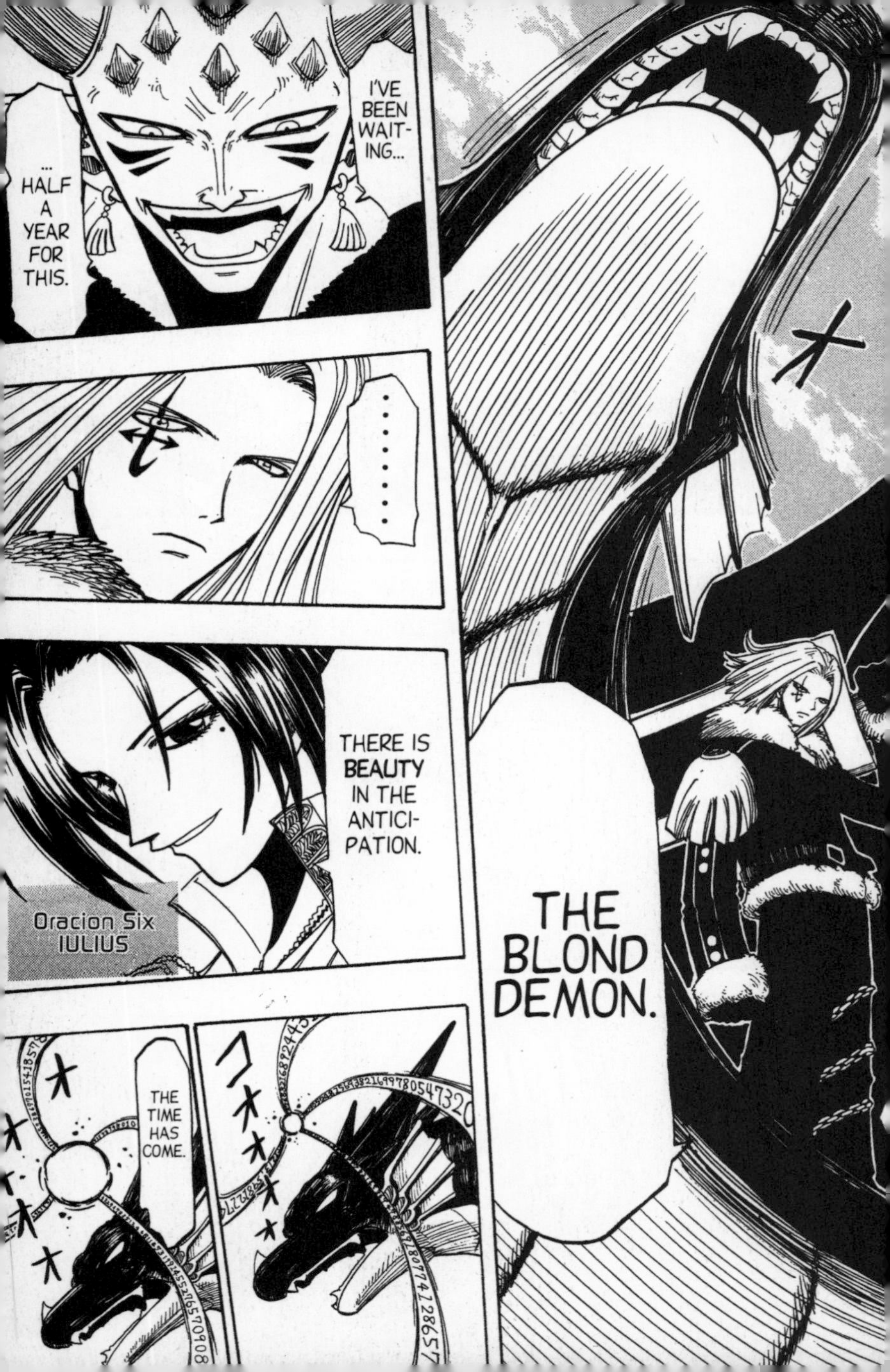
THE BLOND DEMON.
I'VE BEEN WAITING...
... HALF A YEAR FOR THIS.
......
THERE IS **BEAUTY** IN THE ANTICIPATION.
Oracion Six IULIUS
THE TIME HAS COME.

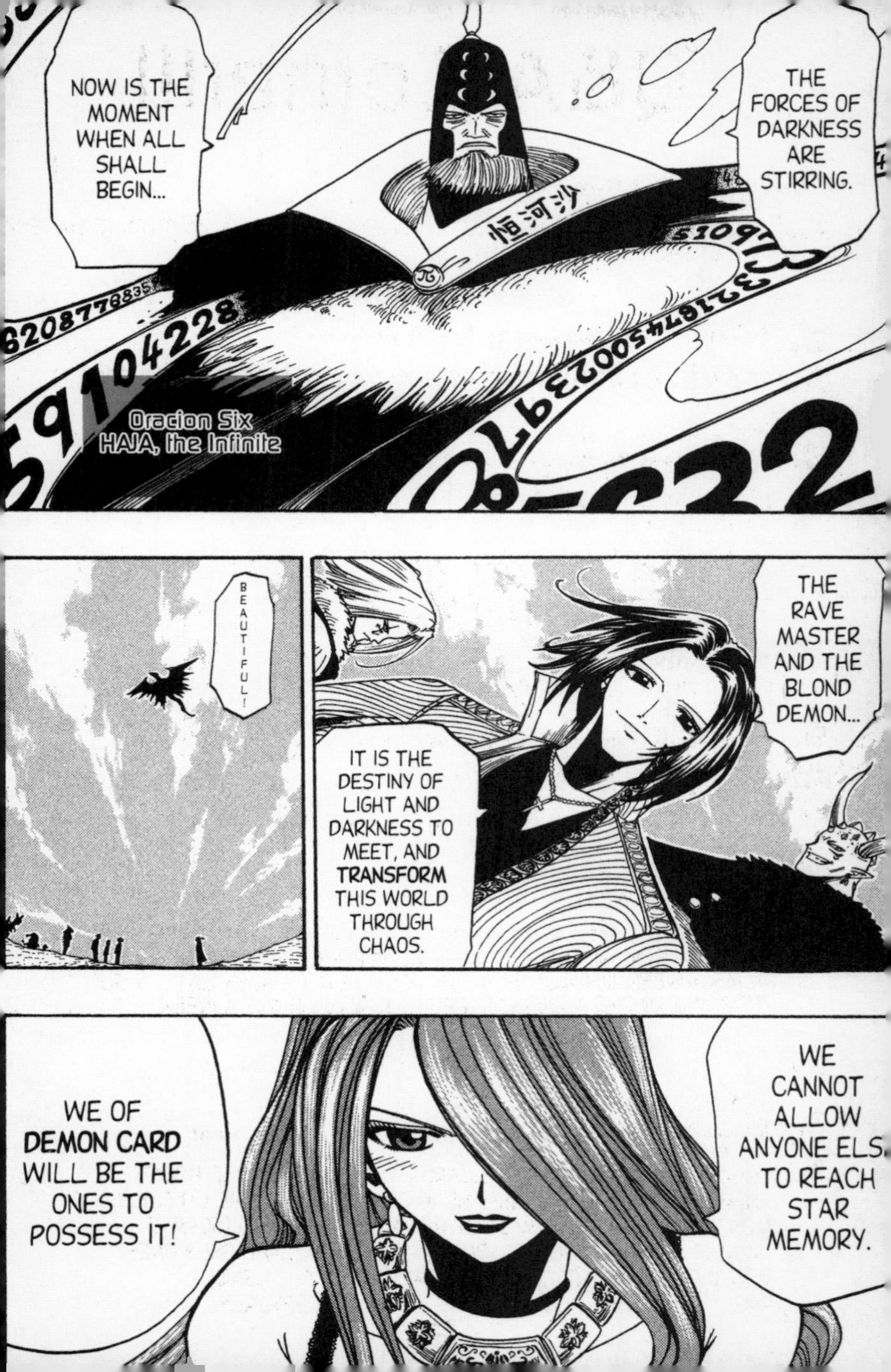
THE FORCES OF DARKNESS ARE STIRRING.
NOW IS THE MOMENT WHEN ALL SHALL BEGIN...
恒河沙
Oracion Six HAJA, the Infinite
THE RAVE MASTER AND THE BLOND DEMON...
IT IS THE DESTINY OF LIGHT AND DARKNESS TO MEET, AND **TRANSFORM** THIS WORLD THROUGH CHAOS.
BEAUTIFUL!
WE CANNOT ALLOW ANYONE ELS TO REACH STAR MEMORY.
WE OF **DEMON CARD** WILL BE THE ONES TO POSSESS IT!

Q&A Corner!!!

Q. Tell us Elie's three sizes!

A. SURE!! THIS GETS ASKED A LOT.. I HAVEN'T ACTUALLY WRITTEN IT, HAVE I? WELL, SHE'S 38-23-34.

Q. What's Ruby supposed to be? A penguin?

A. HE'S ACTUALLY "SENTENOID, PENGUIN-TYPE" BUT PENGUIN'S CLOSE ENOUGH.

Q. I can't find all the Number Men in Knights of Kingdom...

A. OK!! ALL WILL BE REVEALED.
1-> P14 FRAME 7
2-> P23 BOTTOM
3-> P26 PANEL 3, UPPER LEFT
4-> P35 PANEL 1
5-> P25 PANEL 1 UNDER SHIBU'S FEET
6-> P37 PANEL 1, LEFT
7-> P35 PANEL 8, UPPER LEFT
8-> P17 PANEL 2, UPPER RIGHT

Q. How much fan mail do you get in a week?

A. TONS. BUT I READ THEM ALL. SEND MORE ANYTIME!! IT'S GREAT ENCOURAGEMENT.

Q. You wrote that you like movies, but how many do you see?

A. I LIKE MOVIES, BUT I'M NOT A TRUE FILM FANATIC--THAT HONOR IS RESERVED FOR MY OLDER BROTHER. I SEE ABOUT THREE OR FOUR FILMS A WEEK, USUALLY ON DVD, BUT I'VE BEEN BUSY LATELY SO IT'S DOWN TO ONE A WEEK. I SEE A MINIMUM OF ONE A WEEK.

Q. Why do you hate caterpillars? I think they're neat.

A. THERE USED TO BE CATERPILLARS IN MY FAMILY'S OLD HOUSE. THERE WERE LOTS OF TREES NEAR OUT BACK AND THE LITTLE MONSTERS WOULD CRAWL OUT OF THERE IN DROVES (SCARY!). I WAS A LATCHKEY KID, SO WHEN I CAME HOME, THE ONLY ONES WAITING FOR ME WERE THE CATERPILLARS!! THEY SAID "WELCOME BACK!" I COULDN'T GO IN!! I WAS A CRYBABY.

RAVE:83 ✚ PREDESTINED ENCOUNTER

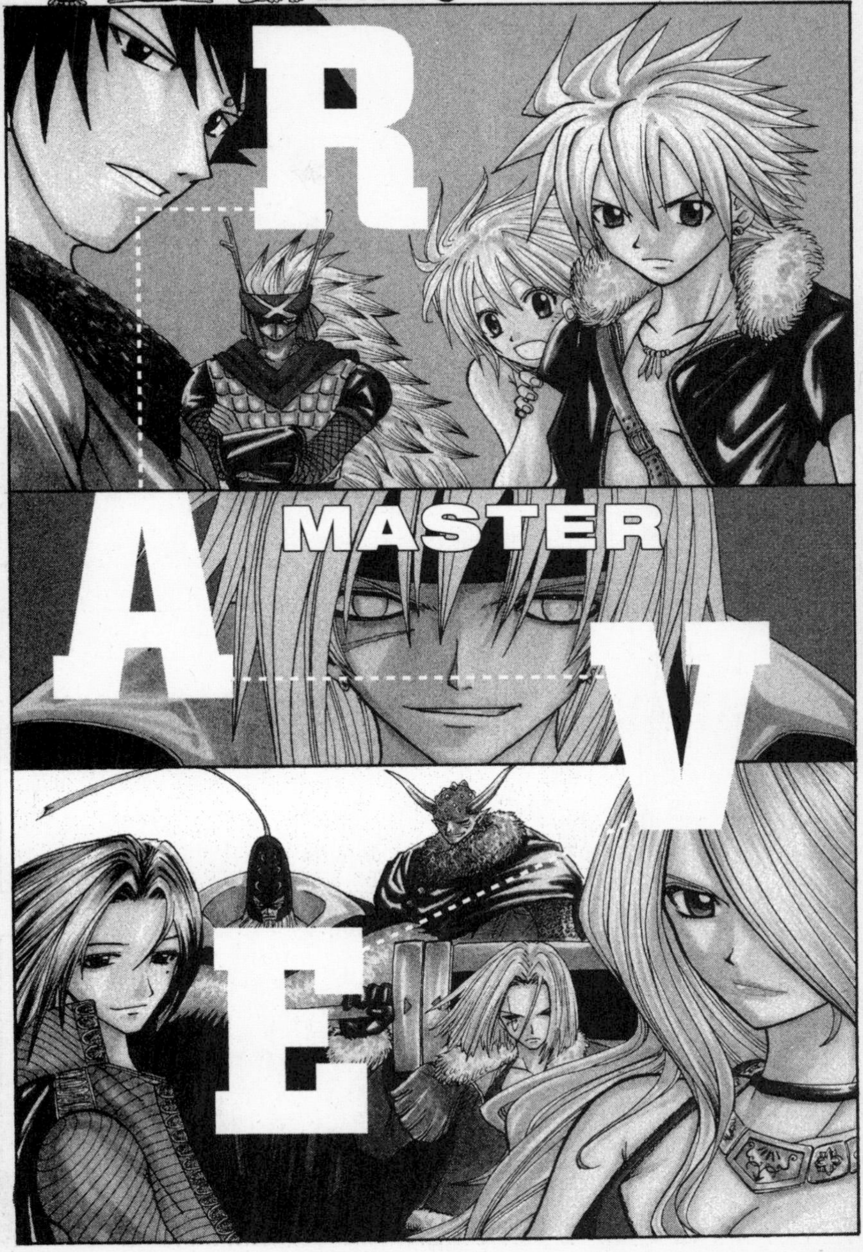
RAVE MASTER

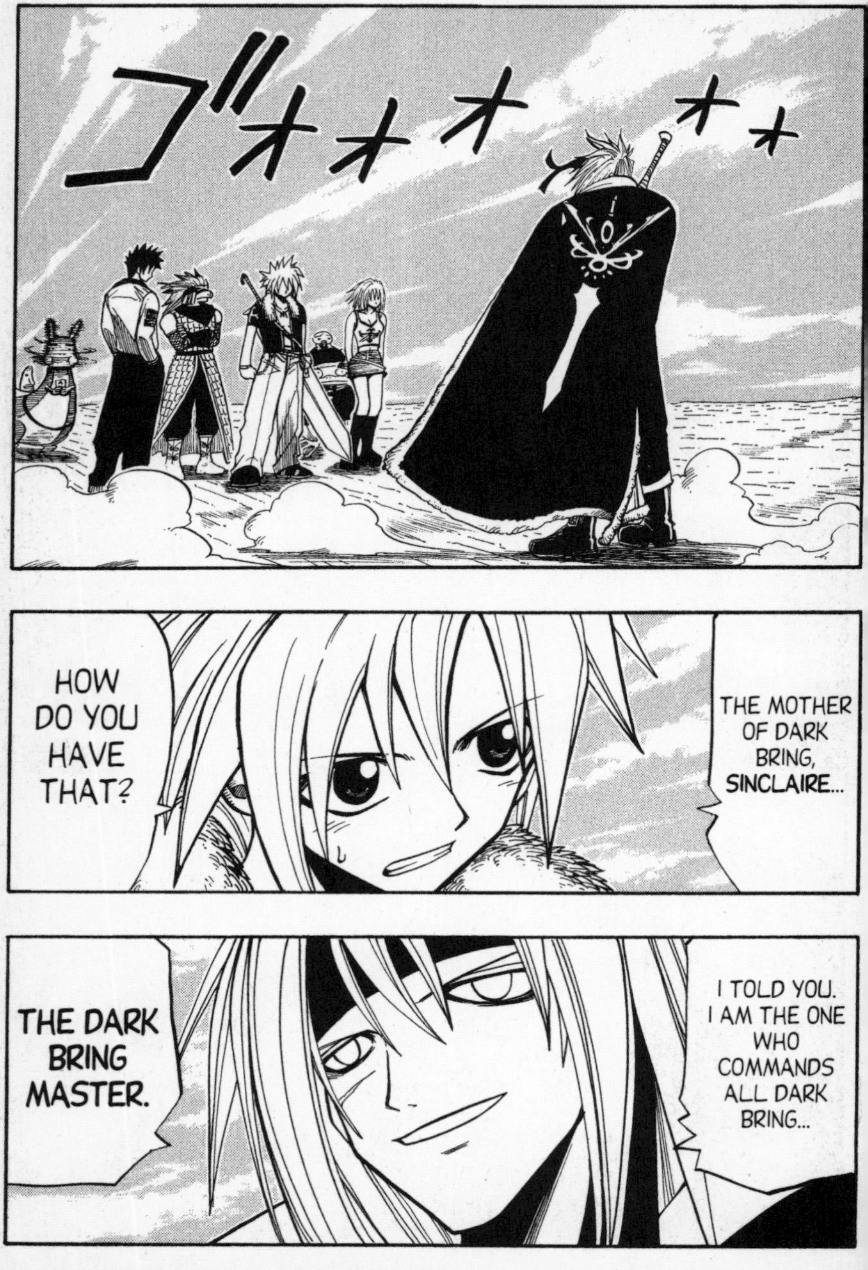
ゴオオオオオ
THE MOTHER OF DARK BRING, SINCLAIRE...
HOW DO YOU HAVE THAT?
I TOLD YOU. I AM THE ONE WHO COMMANDS ALL DARK BRING...
THE DARK BRING MASTER.

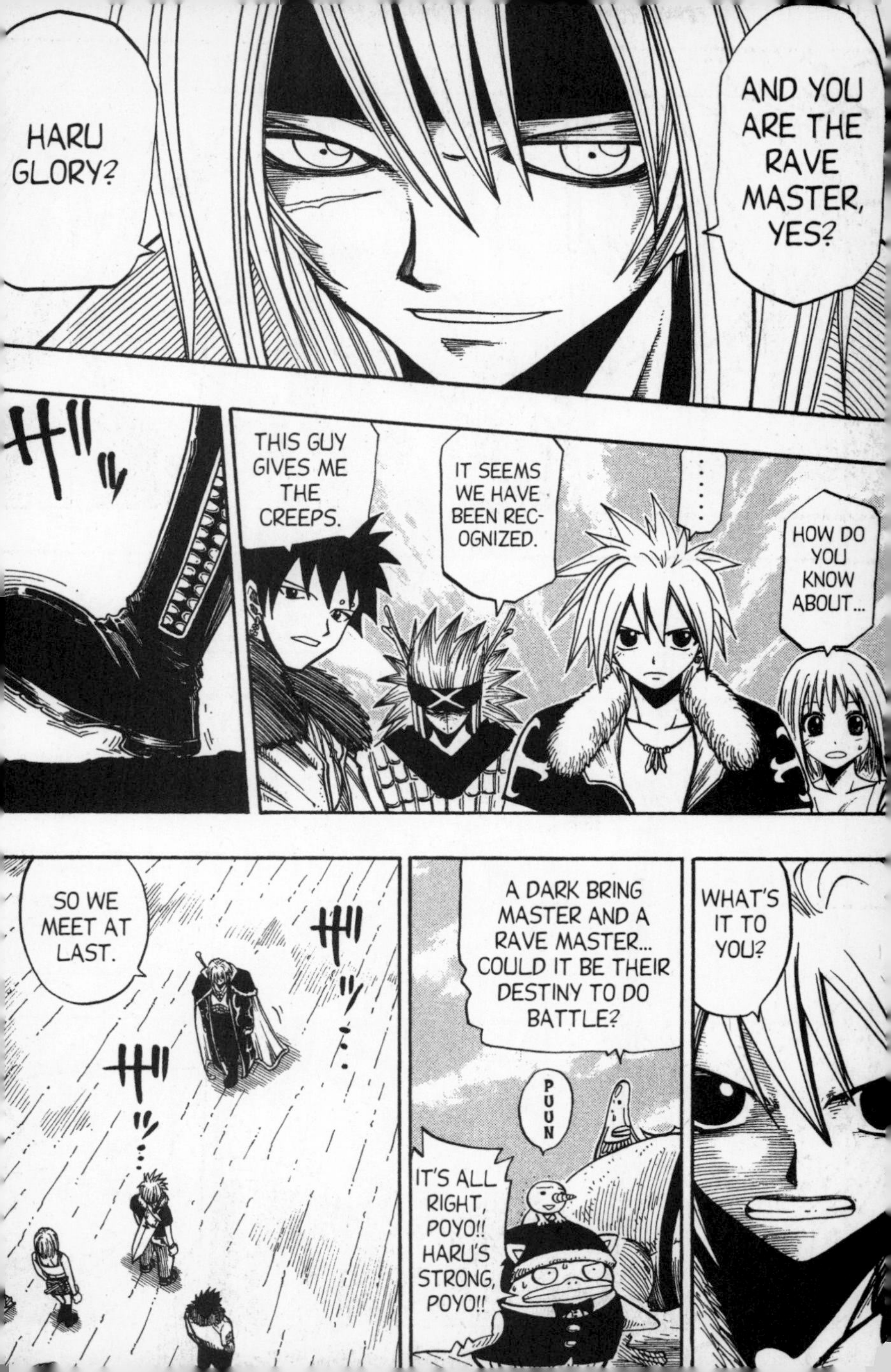
AND YOU ARE THE RAVE MASTER, YES?
HARU GLORY?
HOW DO YOU KNOW ABOUT...
......
IT SEEMS WE HAVE BEEN RECOGNIZED.
THIS GUY GIVES ME THE CREEPS.
WHAT'S IT TO YOU?
A DARK BRING MASTER AND A RAVE MASTER... COULD IT BE THEIR DESTINY TO DO BATTLE?
PUUN
IT'S ALL RIGHT, POYO!! HARU'S STRONG, POYO!!
SO WE MEET AT LAST.

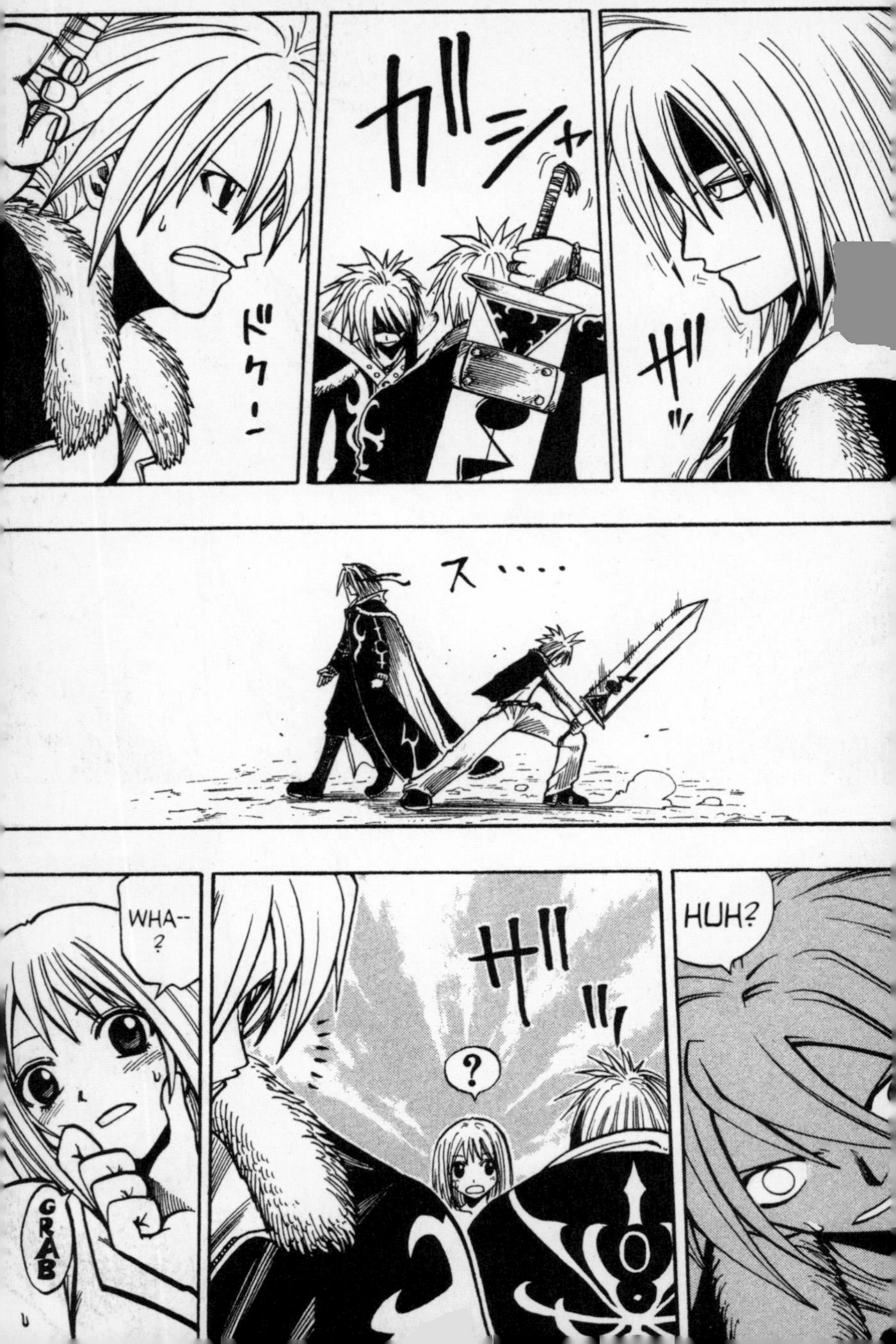

ザッ
ガシャ
ドクン
ス…
HUH?
ザッ
?
WHA--?
GRAB

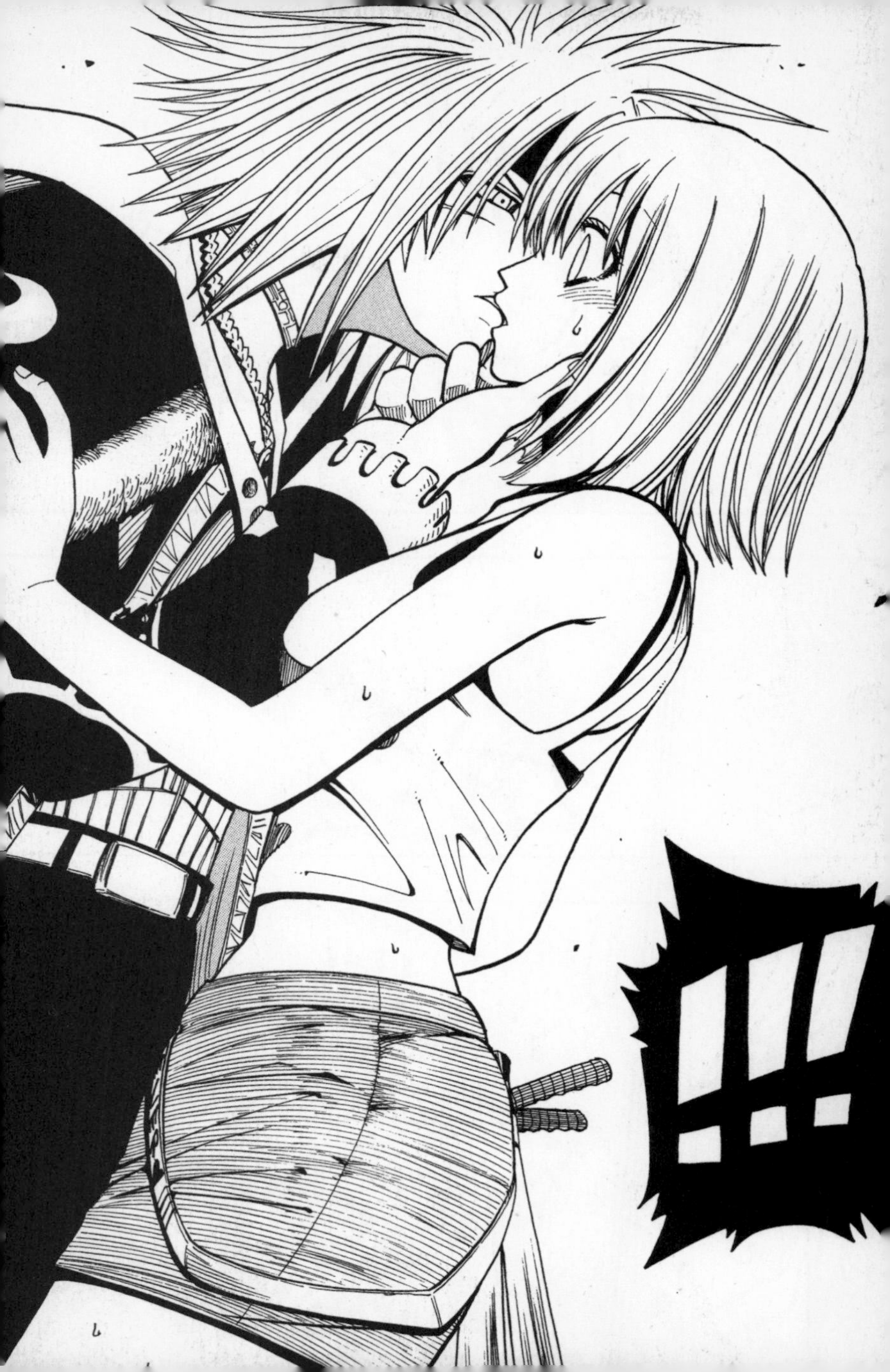
!!!

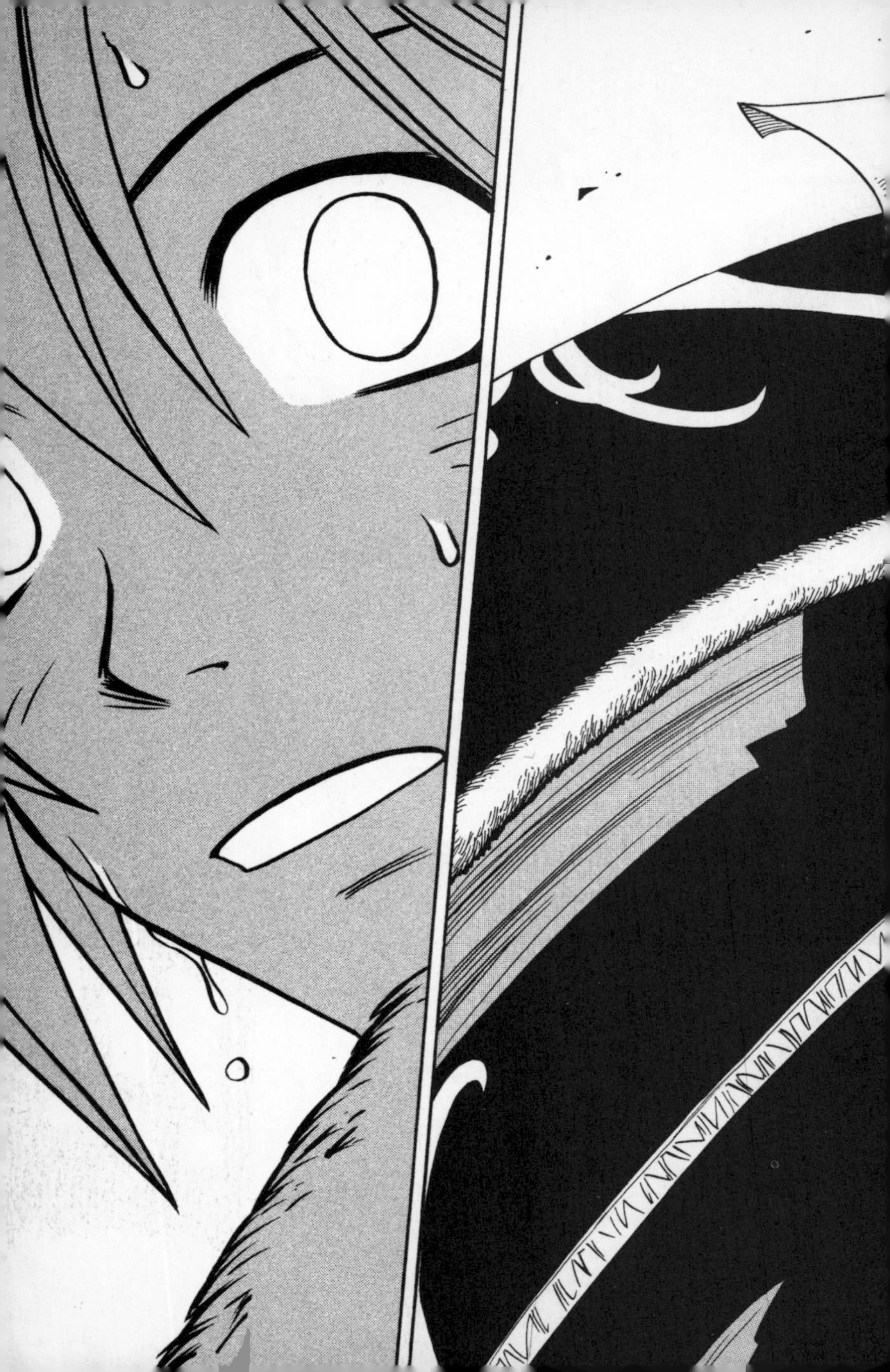

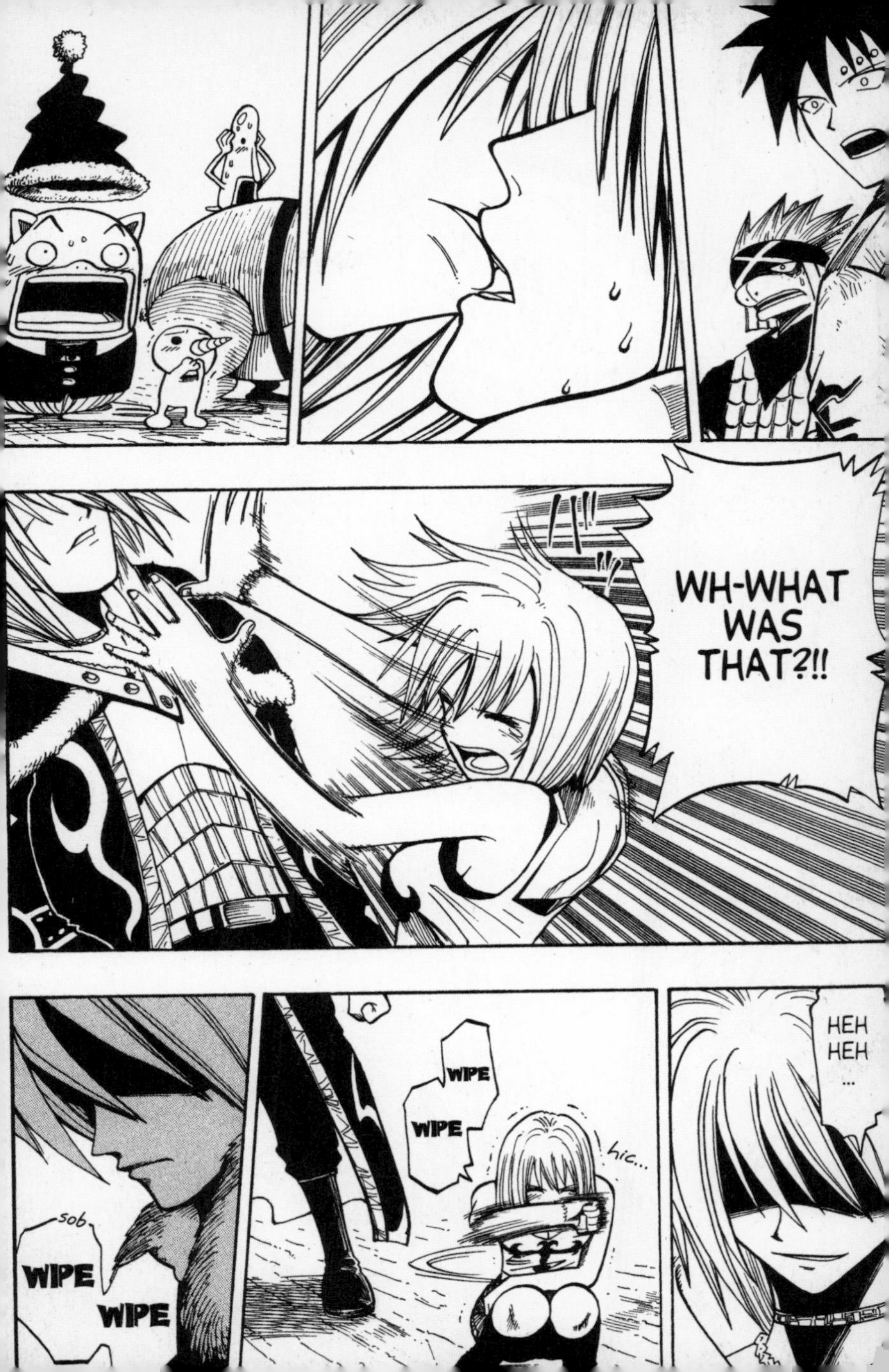
WH-WHAT WAS THAT?!!
HEH HEH ...
WIPE
WIPE
hic...
sob
WIPE
WIPE

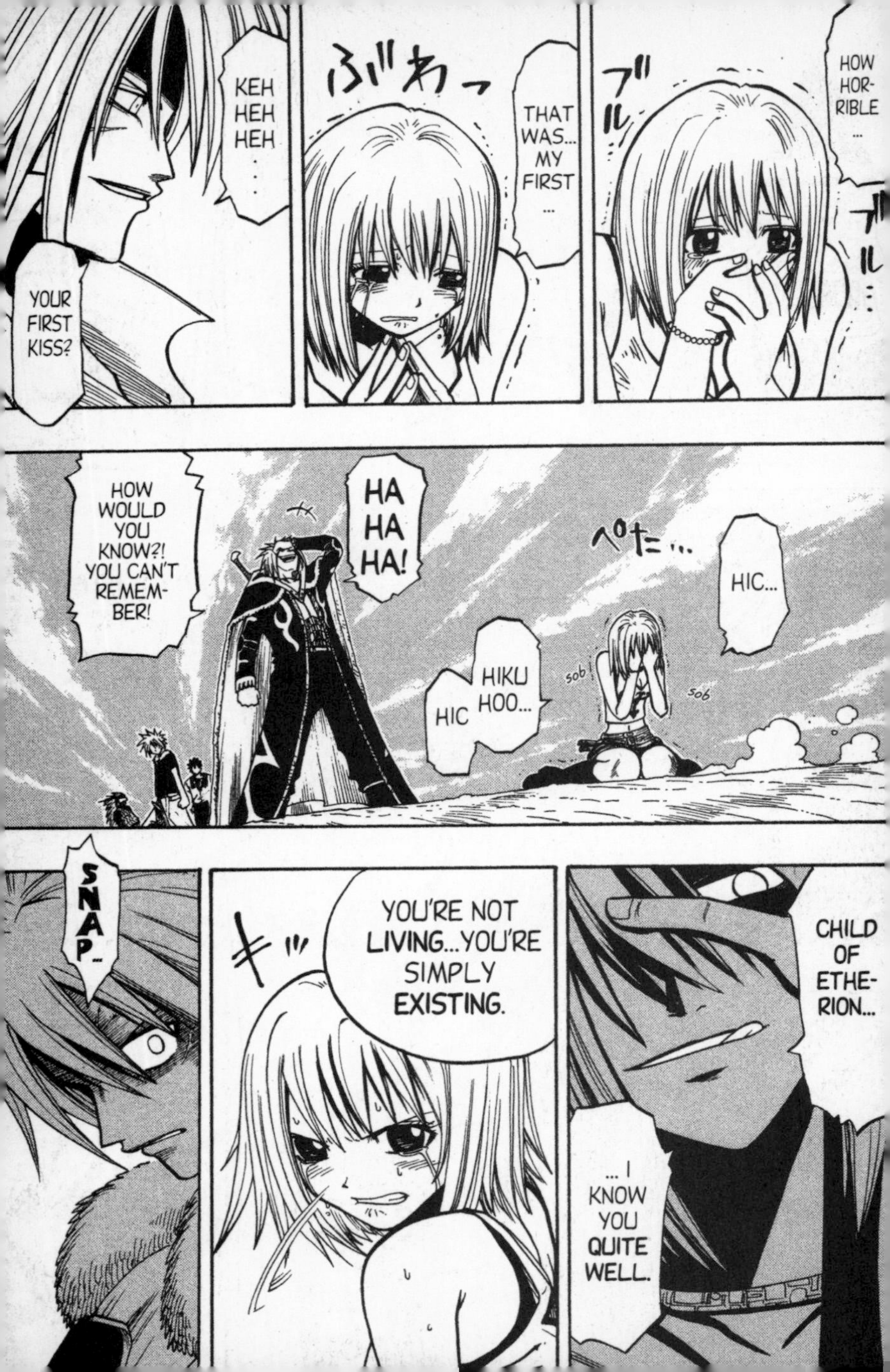
HOW HORRIBLE...
ブル
ブル...
ぶわっ
THAT WAS... MY FIRST...
KEH HEH HEH...
YOUR FIRST KISS?
ぺた...
HIC...
sob
sob
HA HA HA!
HIKU HOO...
HIC
HOW WOULD YOU KNOW?! YOU CAN'T REMEMBER!
CHILD OF ETHERION...
...I KNOW YOU QUITE WELL.
キッ
YOU'RE NOT LIVING...YOU'RE SIMPLY EXISTING.
SNAP...

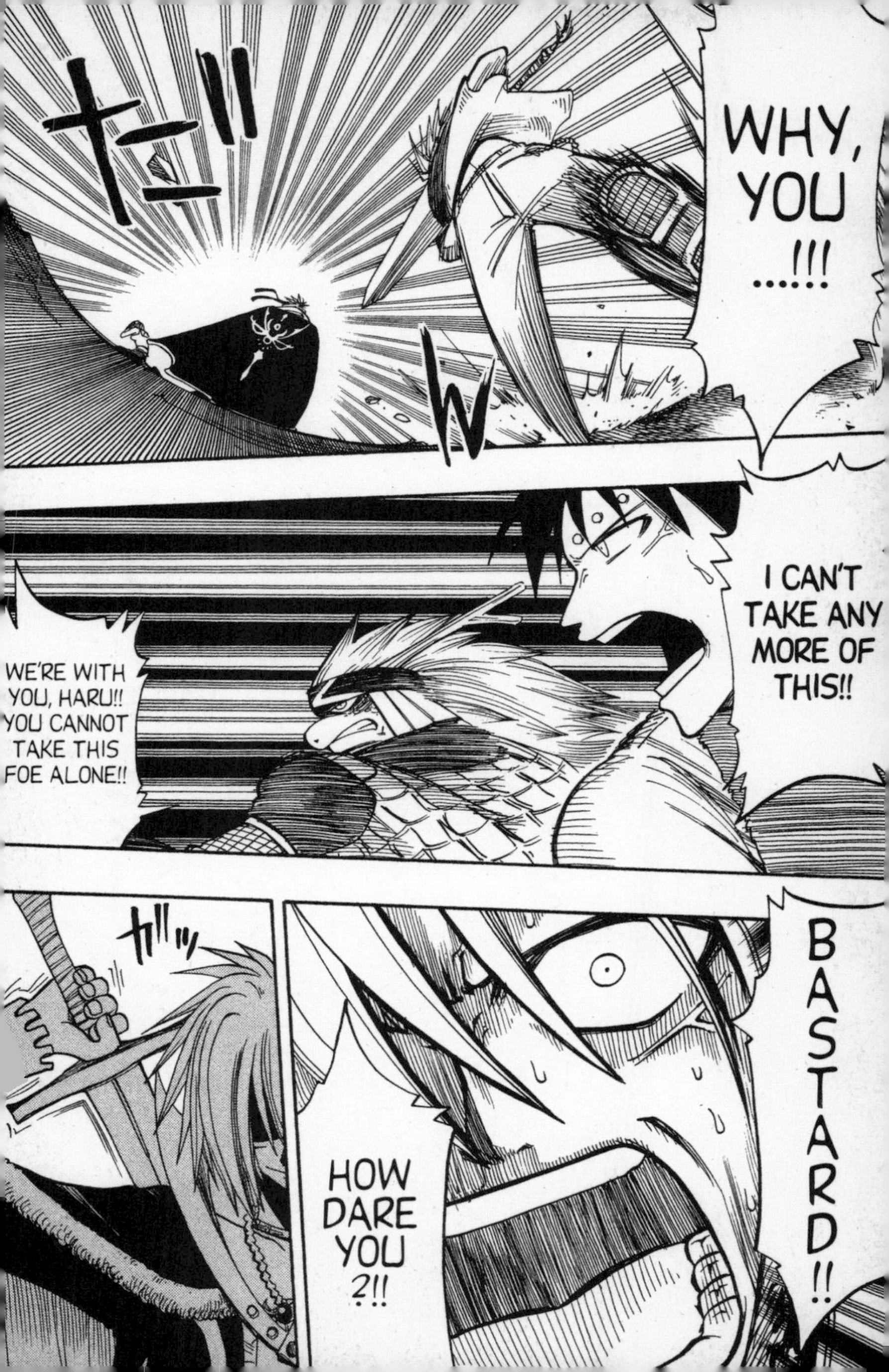
WHY, YOU ....!!!
I CAN'T TAKE ANY MORE OF THIS!!
WE'RE WITH YOU, HARU!! YOU CANNOT TAKE THIS FOE ALONE!!
BASTARD!!
HOW DARE YOU ?!!

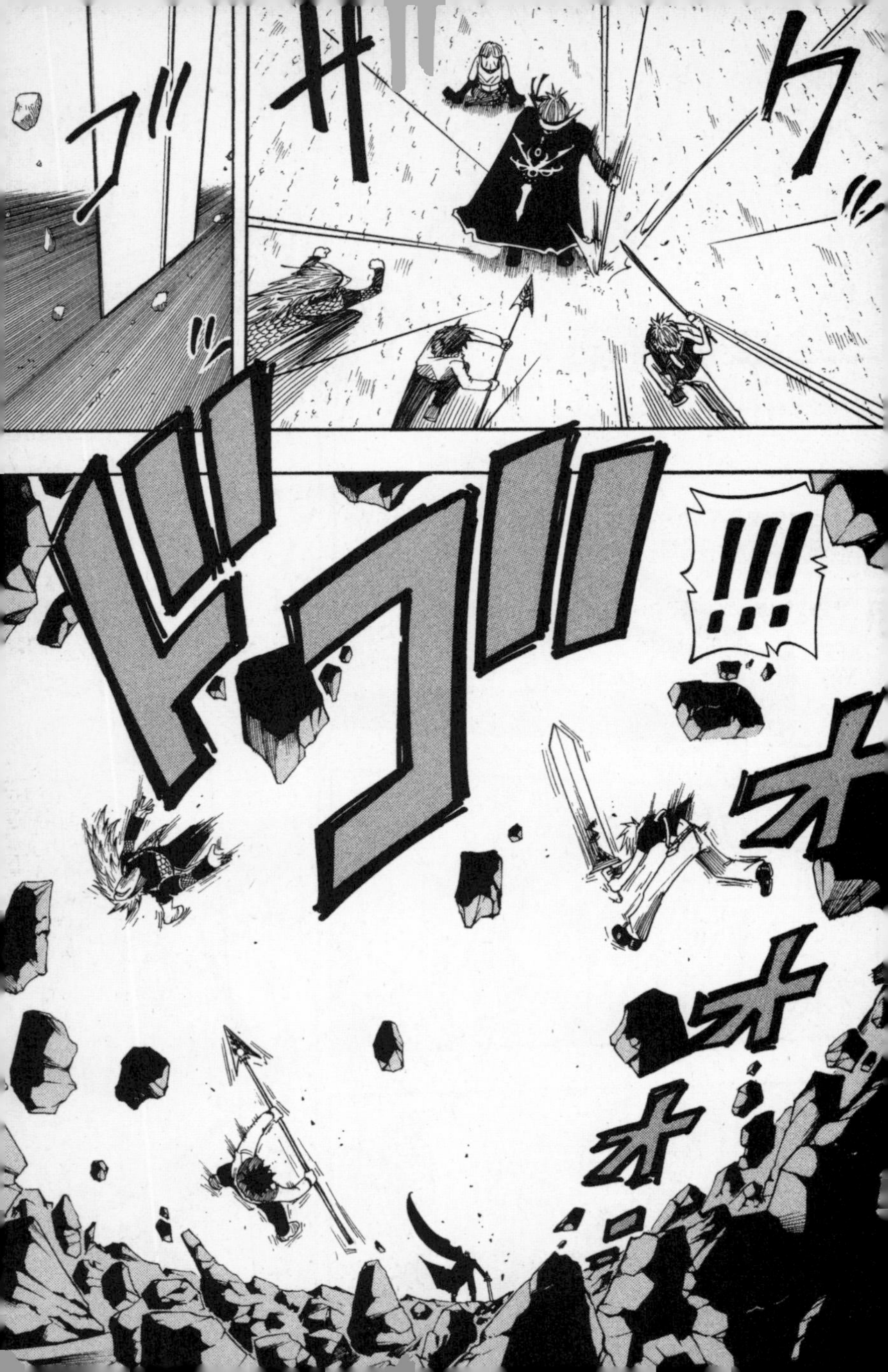
ザク
ブッ
!!!
ドゴオオオ

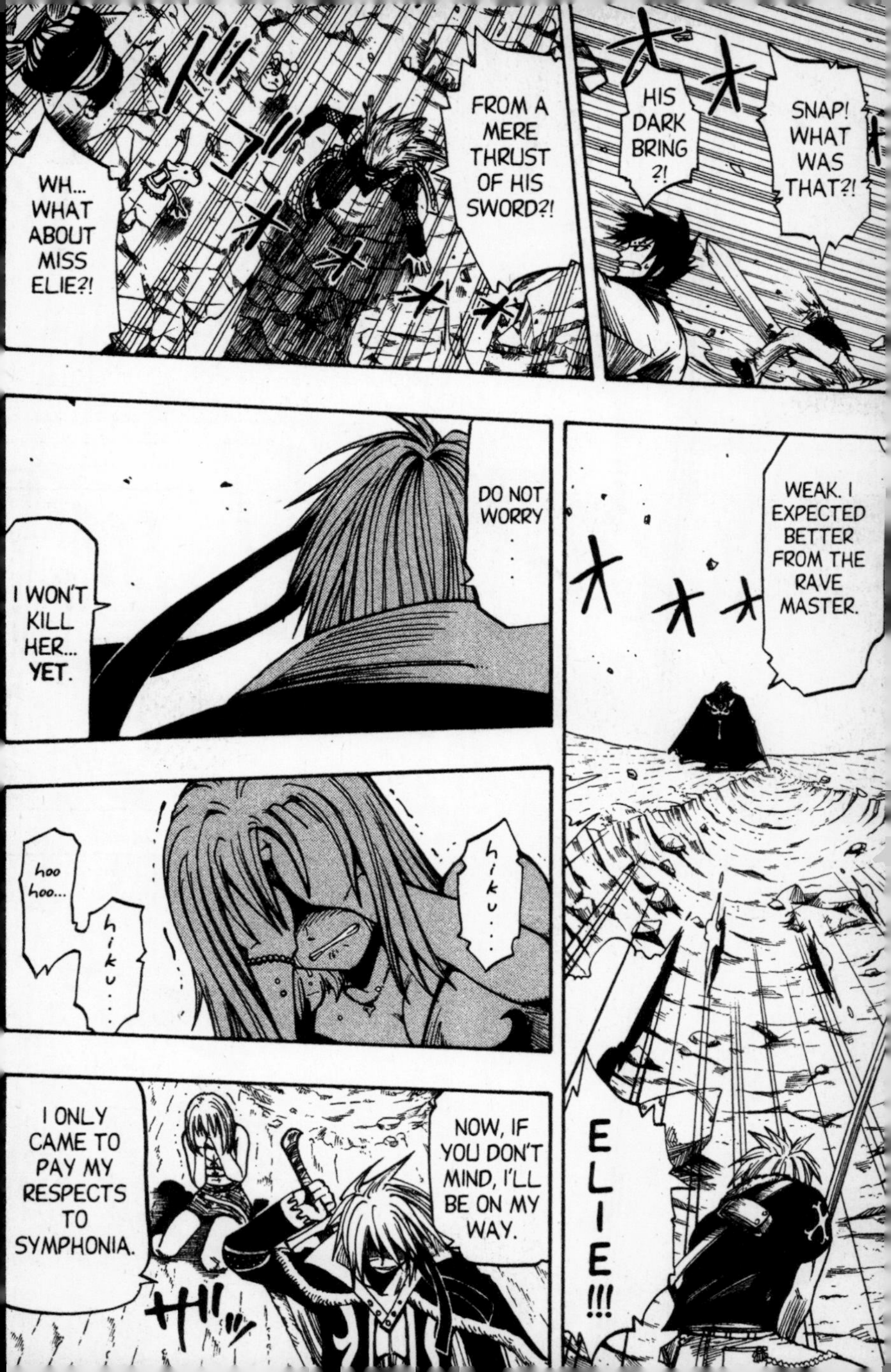
SNAP! WHAT WAS THAT?!
HIS DARK BRING?!
FROM A MERE THRUST OF HIS SWORD?!
WH... WHAT ABOUT MISS ELIE?!
WEAK. I EXPECTED BETTER FROM THE RAVE MASTER.
ELIE!!!
DO NOT WORRY...
I WON'T KILL HER... YET.
hiku...
hoo hoo...
hiku...
NOW, IF YOU DON'T MIND, I'LL BE ON MY WAY.
I ONLY CAME TO PAY MY RESPECTS TO SYMPHONIA.

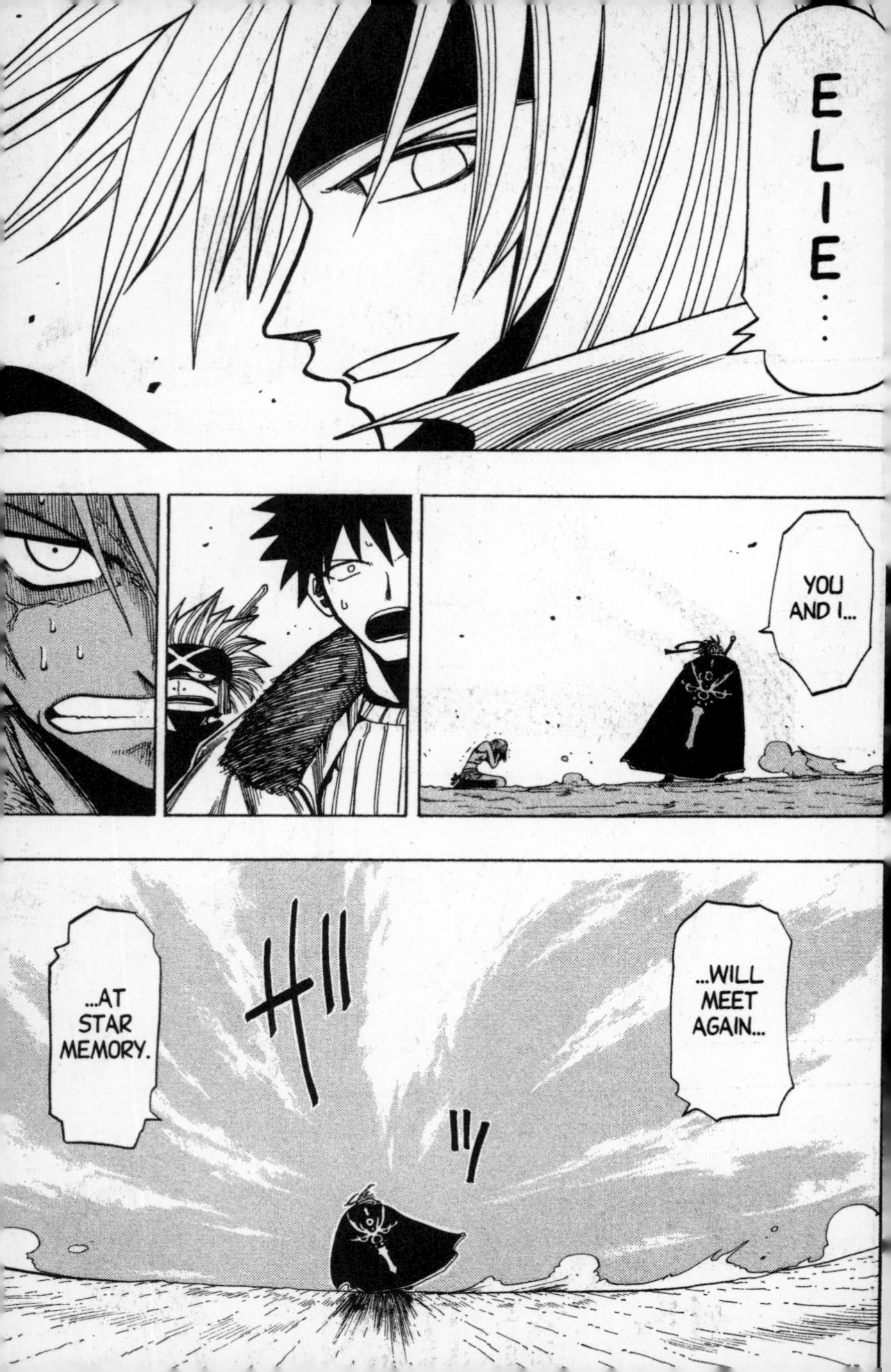
ELIE...
YOU AND I...
...WILL MEET AGAIN...
...AT STAR MEMORY.

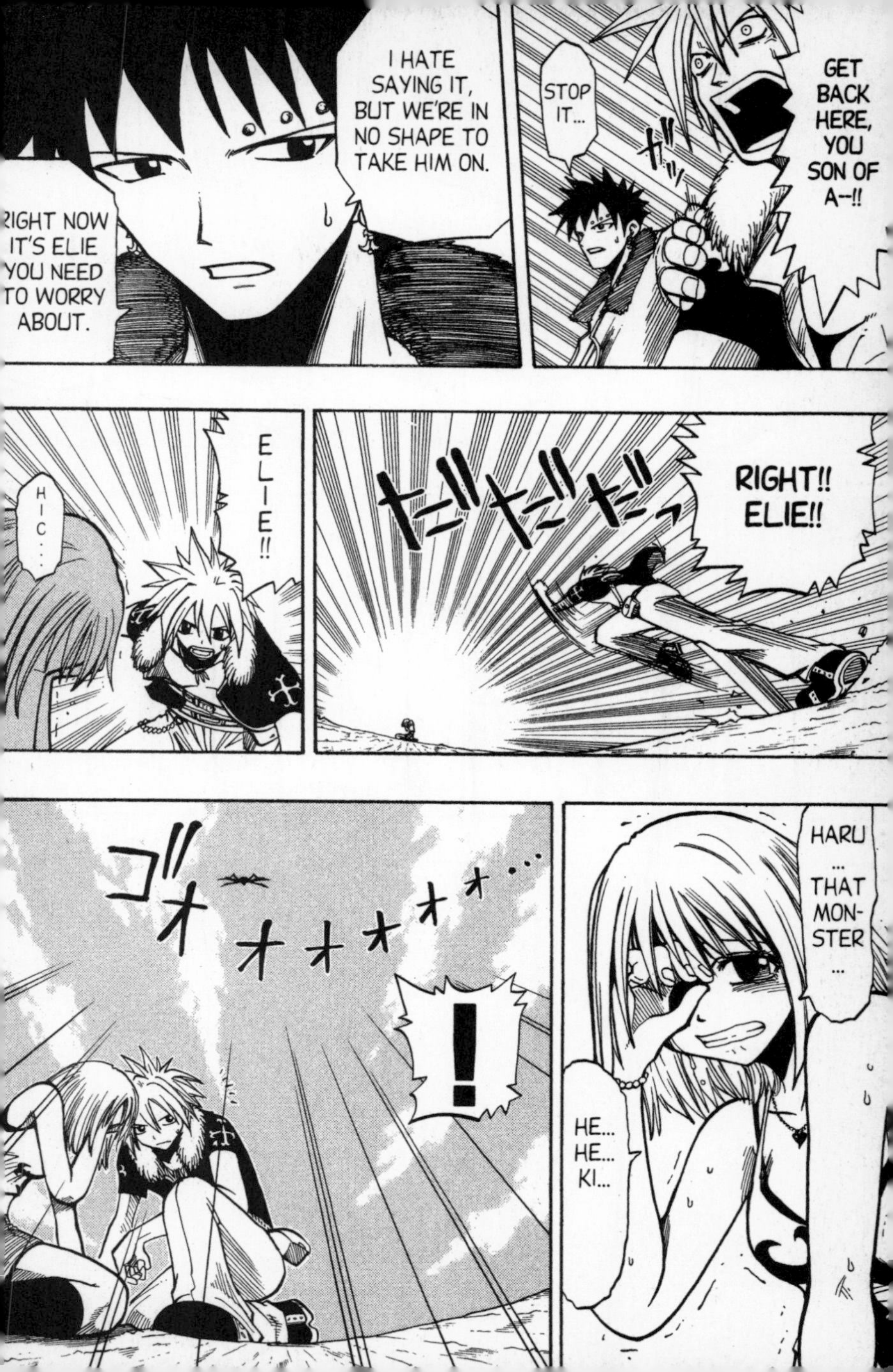
GET BACK HERE, YOU SON OF A--!!
STOP IT...
I HATE SAYING IT, BUT WE'RE IN NO SHAPE TO TAKE HIM ON.
RIGHT NOW IT'S ELIE YOU NEED TO WORRY ABOUT.
RIGHT!! ELIE!!
ELIE!!
HIC...
HARU ... THAT MONSTER ...
HE... HE... KI...
!

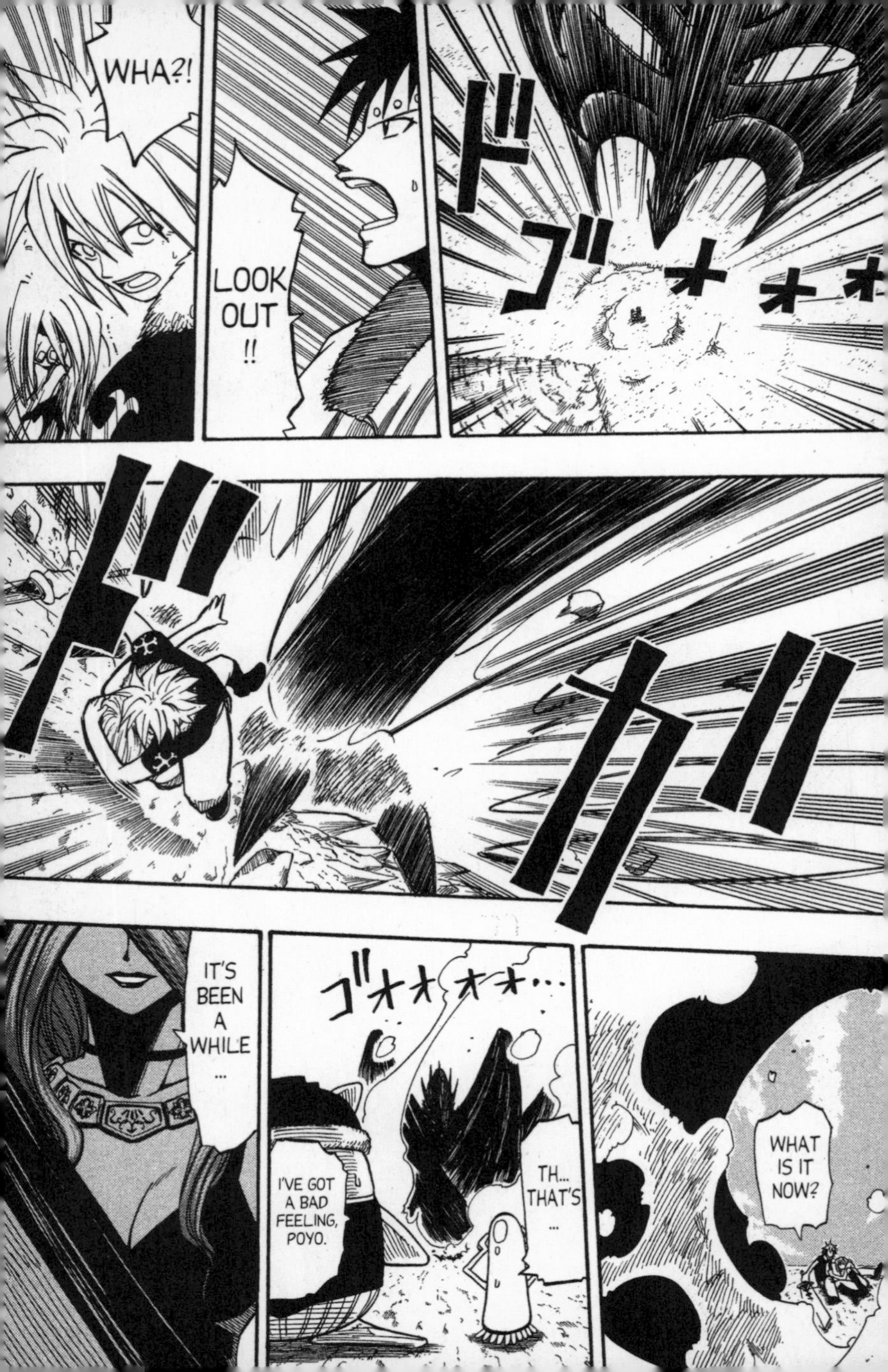
ドゴオォォ
LOOK OUT !!
WHA?!
WHAT IS IT NOW?
ゴォォォォォ…
TH... THAT'S ...
I'VE GOT A BAD FEELING, POYO.
IT'S BEEN A WHILE ...

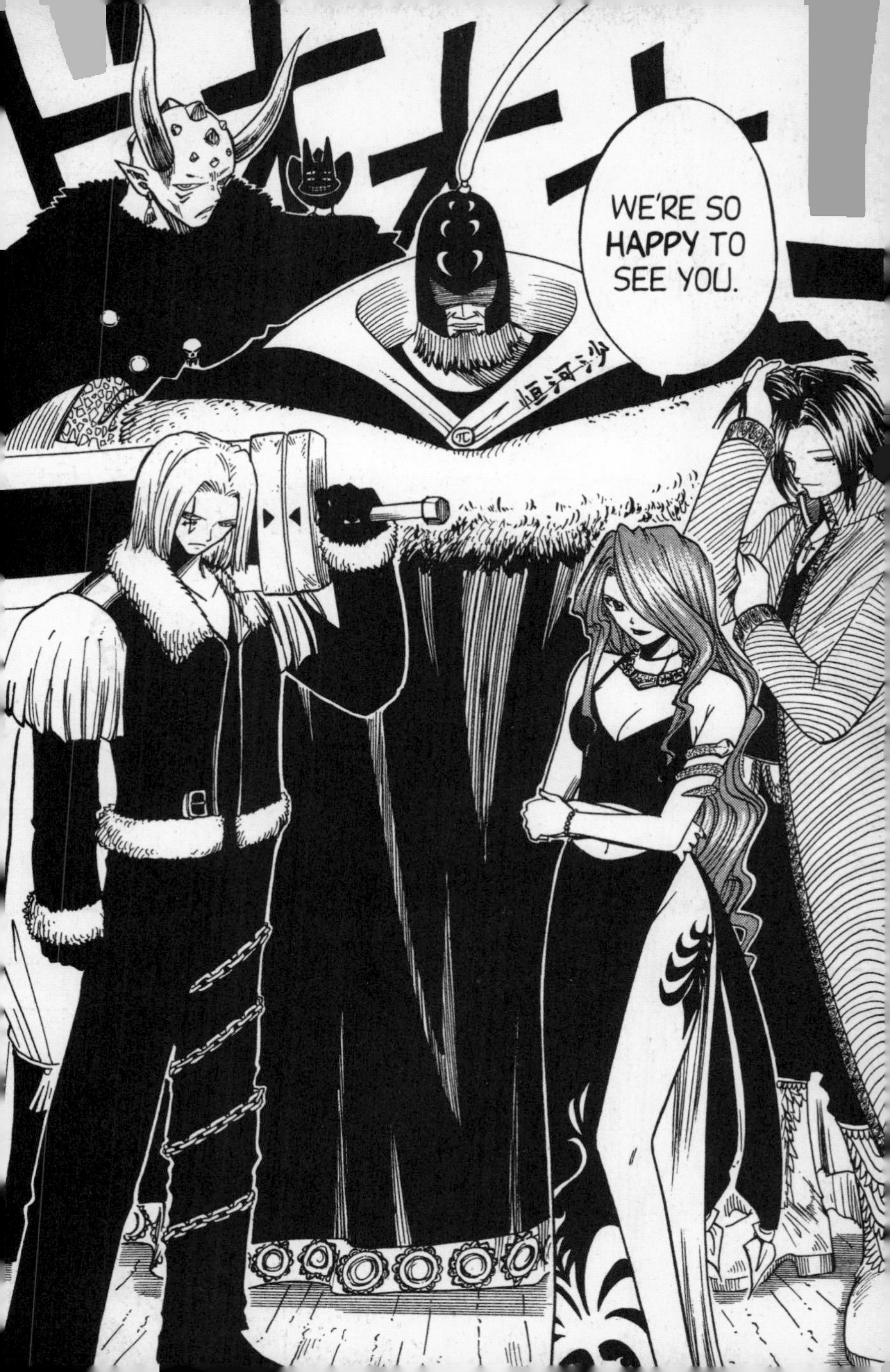
WE'RE SO HAPPY TO SEE YOU.

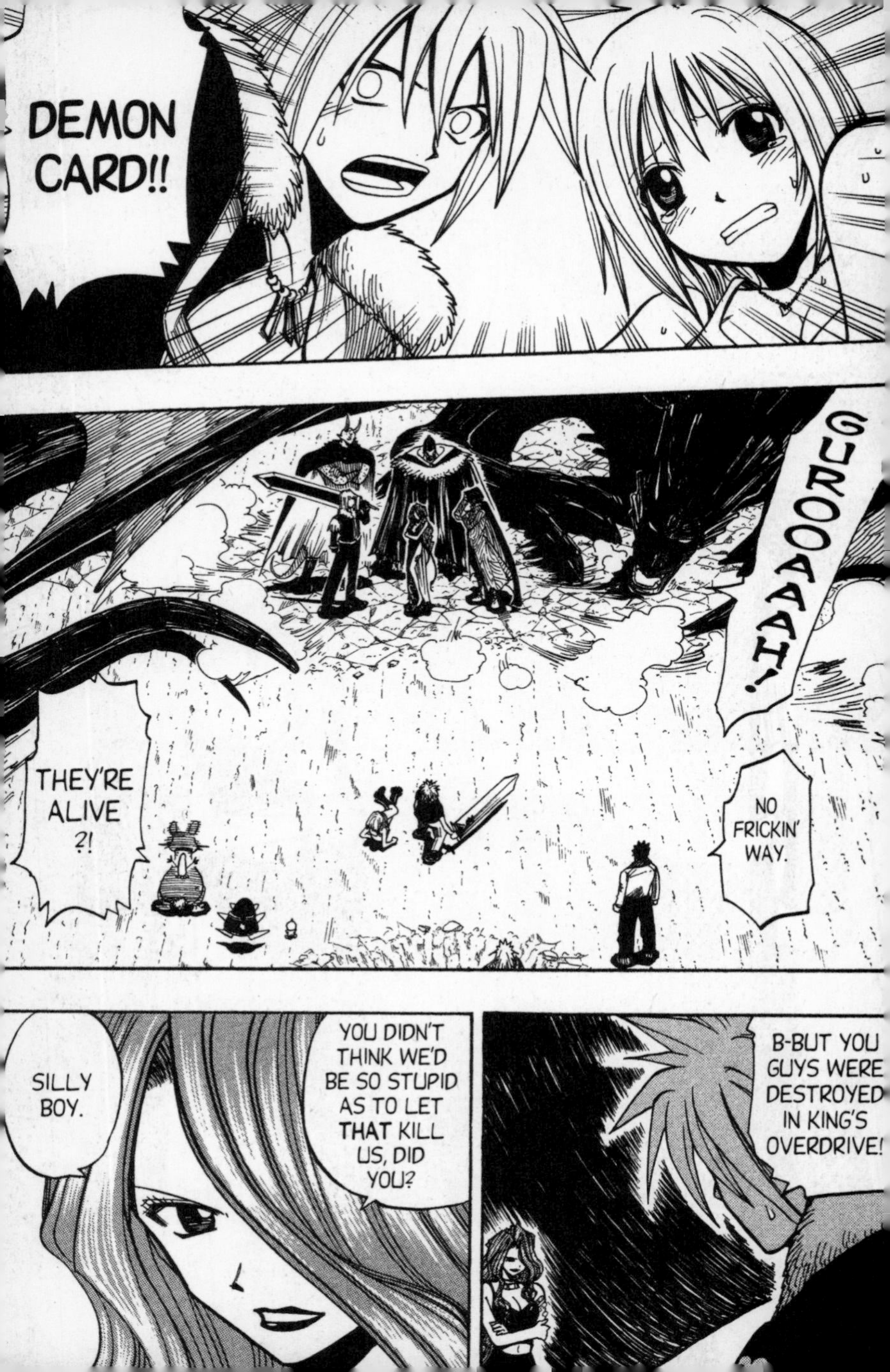
DEMON CARD!!
GUROOOAAAH!
NO FRICKIN' WAY.
THEY'RE ALIVE ?!
B-BUT YOU GUYS WERE DESTROYED IN KING'S OVERDRIVE!
YOU DIDN'T THINK WE'D BE SO STUPID AS TO LET THAT KILL US, DID YOU?
SILLY BOY.

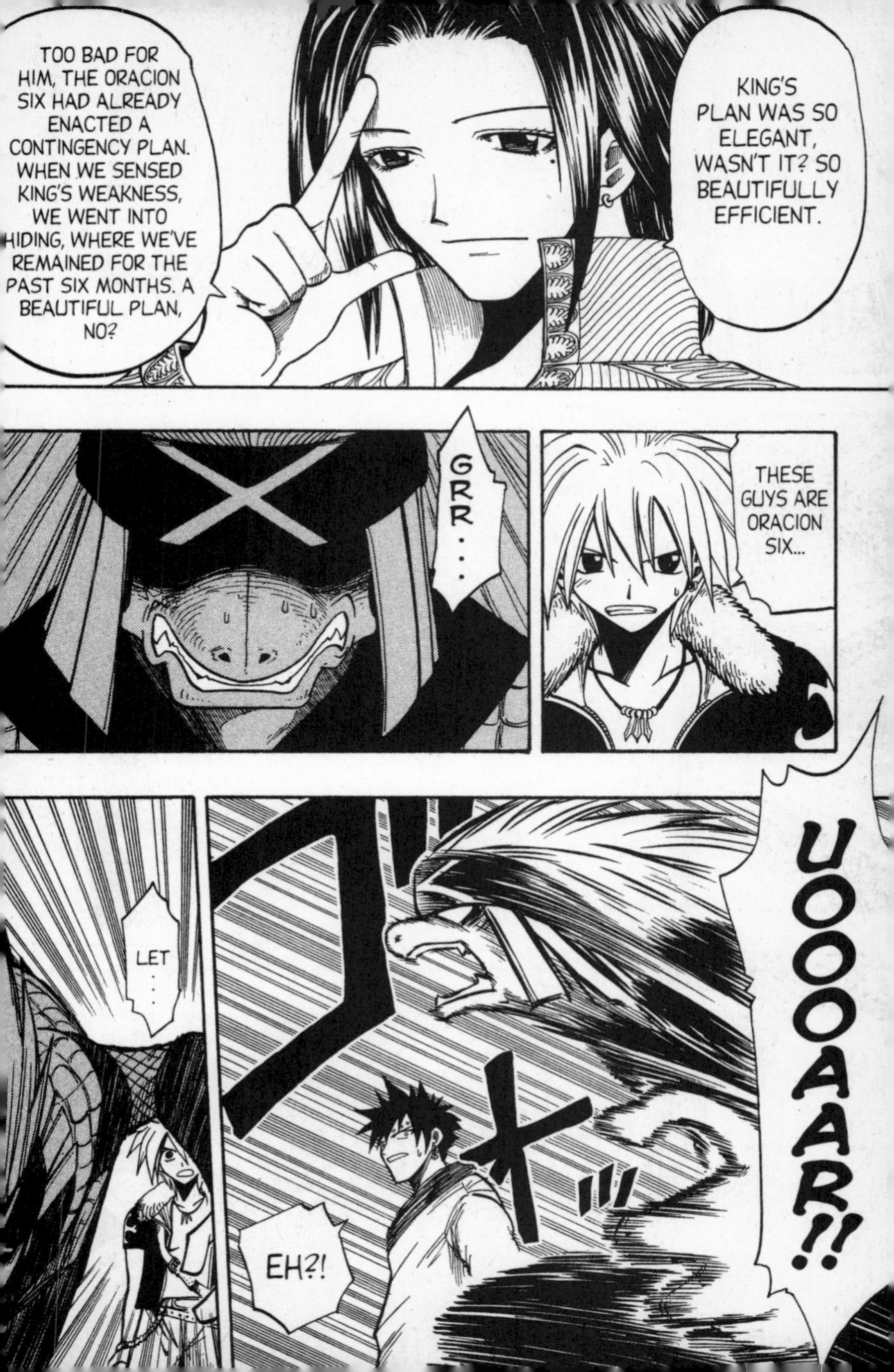
KING'S PLAN WAS SO ELEGANT, WASN'T IT? SO BEAUTIFULLY EFFICIENT.
TOO BAD FOR HIM, THE ORACION SIX HAD ALREADY ENACTED A CONTINGENCY PLAN. WHEN WE SENSED KING'S WEAKNESS, WE WENT INTO HIDING, WHERE WE'VE REMAINED FOR THE PAST SIX MONTHS. A BEAUTIFUL PLAN, NO?
THESE GUYS ARE ORACION SIX...
GRR...
UOOOOAAR?!!
EH?!
LET...

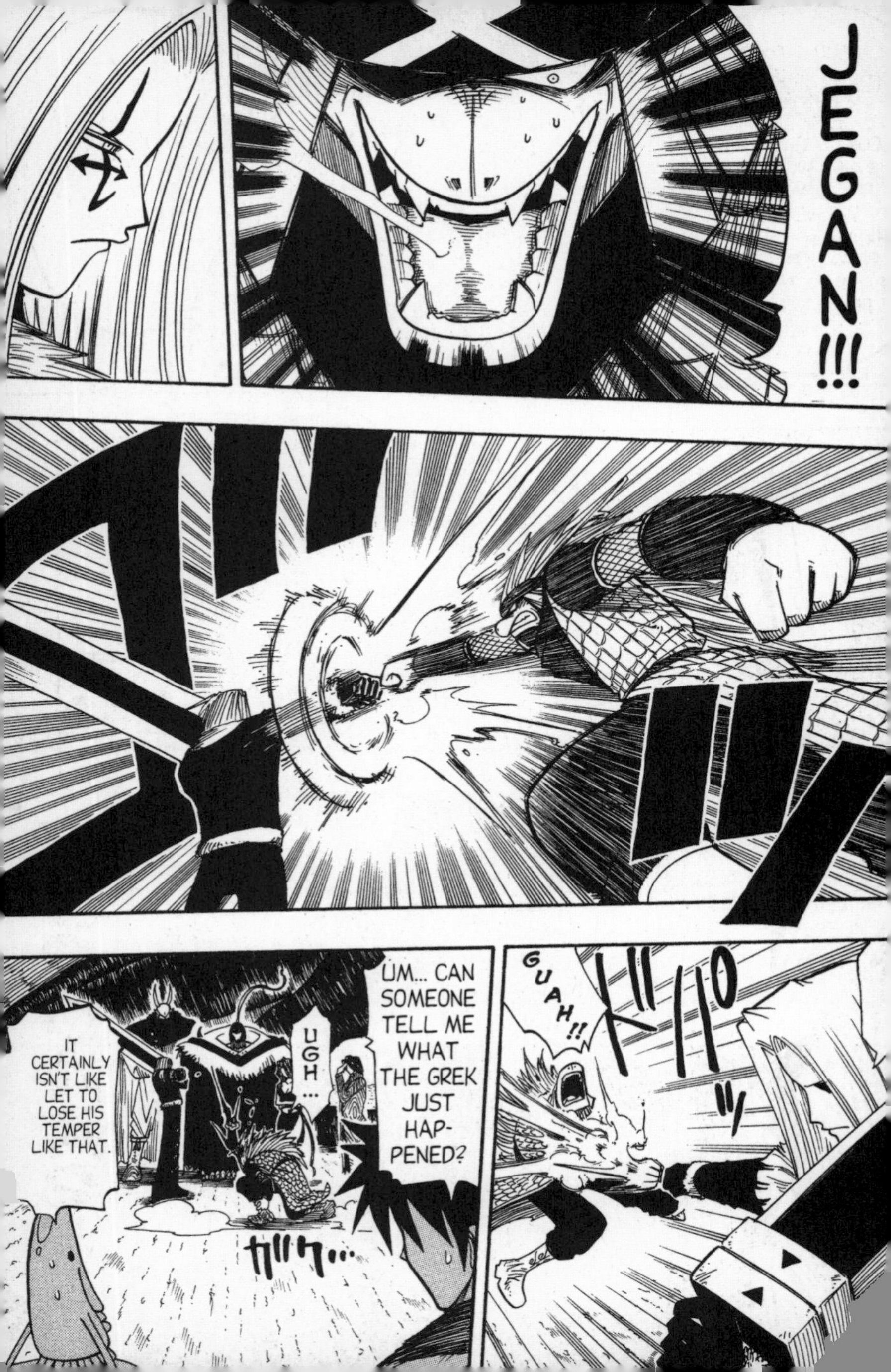
JEGAN!!!
GUAH!!
UM... CAN SOMEONE TELL ME WHAT THE GREK JUST HAP-PENED?
UGH...
IT CERTAINLY ISN'T LIKE LET TO LOSE HIS TEMPER LIKE THAT.

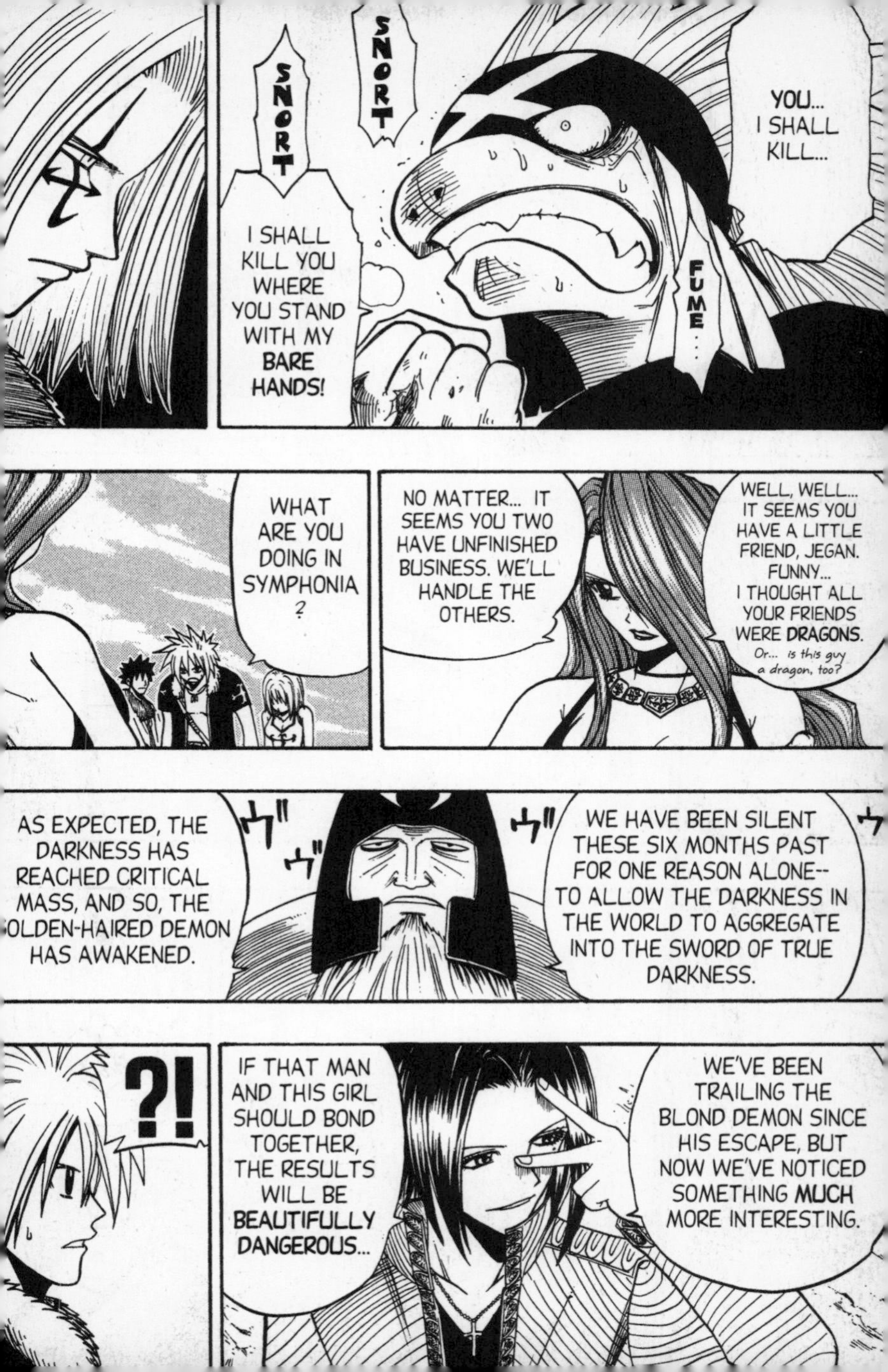
YOU... I SHALL KILL...
FUME...
SNORT
SNORT
I SHALL KILL YOU WHERE YOU STAND WITH MY BARE HANDS!
WELL, WELL... IT SEEMS YOU HAVE A LITTLE FRIEND, JEGAN. FUNNY... I THOUGHT ALL YOUR FRIENDS WERE DRAGONS.
Or... is this guy a dragon, too?
NO MATTER... IT SEEMS YOU TWO HAVE UNFINISHED BUSINESS. WE'LL HANDLE THE OTHERS.
WHAT ARE YOU DOING IN SYMPHONIA?
WE HAVE BEEN SILENT THESE SIX MONTHS PAST FOR ONE REASON ALONE-- TO ALLOW THE DARKNESS IN THE WORLD TO AGGREGATE INTO THE SWORD OF TRUE DARKNESS.
AS EXPECTED, THE DARKNESS HAS REACHED CRITICAL MASS, AND SO, THE OLDEN-HAIRED DEMON HAS AWAKENED.
WE'VE BEEN TRAILING THE BLOND DEMON SINCE HIS ESCAPE, BUT NOW WE'VE NOTICED SOMETHING MUCH MORE INTERESTING.
IF THAT MAN AND THIS GIRL SHOULD BOND TOGETHER, THE RESULTS WILL BE BEAUTIFULLY DANGEROUS...
?!

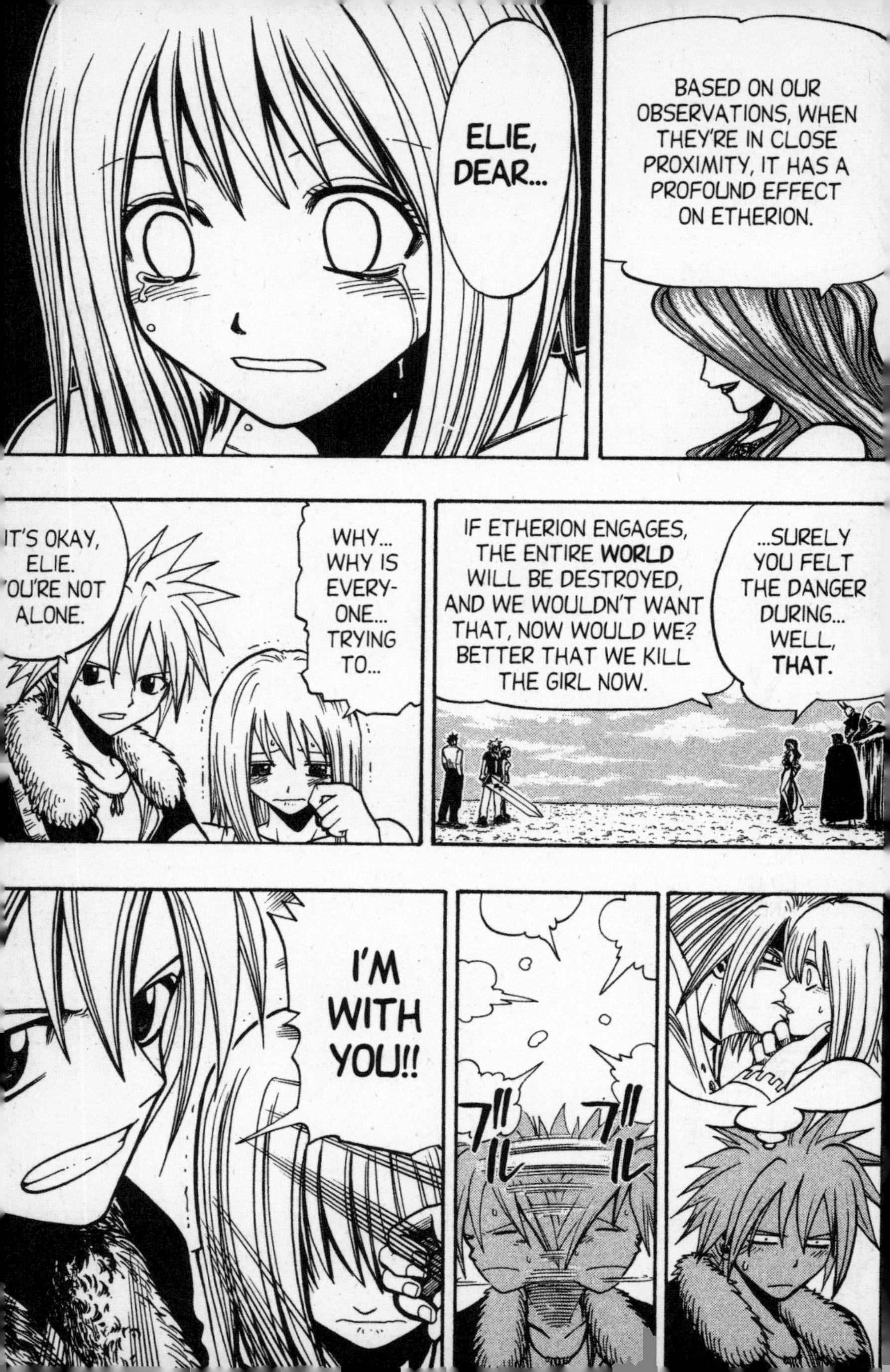
BASED ON OUR OBSERVATIONS, WHEN THEY'RE IN CLOSE PROXIMITY, IT HAS A PROFOUND EFFECT ON ETHERION.
ELIE, DEAR...
...SURELY YOU FELT THE DANGER DURING... WELL, THAT.
IF ETHERION ENGAGES, THE ENTIRE WORLD WILL BE DESTROYED, AND WE WOULDN'T WANT THAT, NOW WOULD WE? BETTER THAT WE KILL THE GIRL NOW.
WHY... WHY IS EVERY-ONE... TRYING TO...
IT'S OKAY, ELIE. OU'RE NOT ALONE.
ブル
ブル
I'M WITH YOU!!

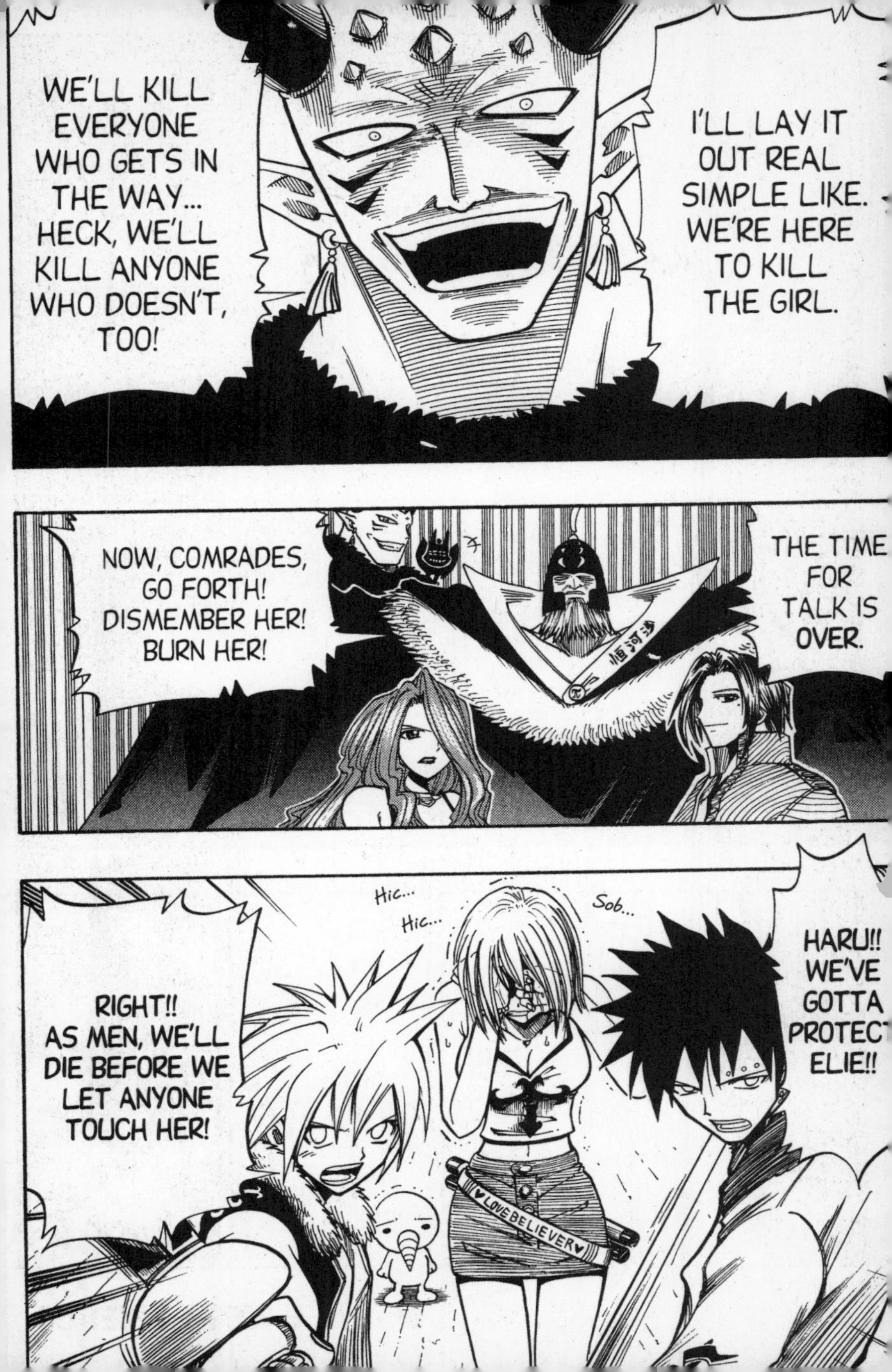
I'LL LAY IT OUT REAL SIMPLE LIKE. WE'RE HERE TO KILL THE GIRL.
WE'LL KILL EVERYONE WHO GETS IN THE WAY... HECK, WE'LL KILL ANYONE WHO DOESN'T, TOO!
THE TIME FOR TALK IS OVER.
NOW, COMRADES, GO FORTH! DISMEMBER HER! BURN HER!
HARU!! WE'VE GOTTA PROTECT ELIE!!
Sob...
Hic...
Hic...
LOVE BELIEVER
RIGHT!! AS MEN, WE'LL DIE BEFORE WE LET ANYONE TOUCH HER!

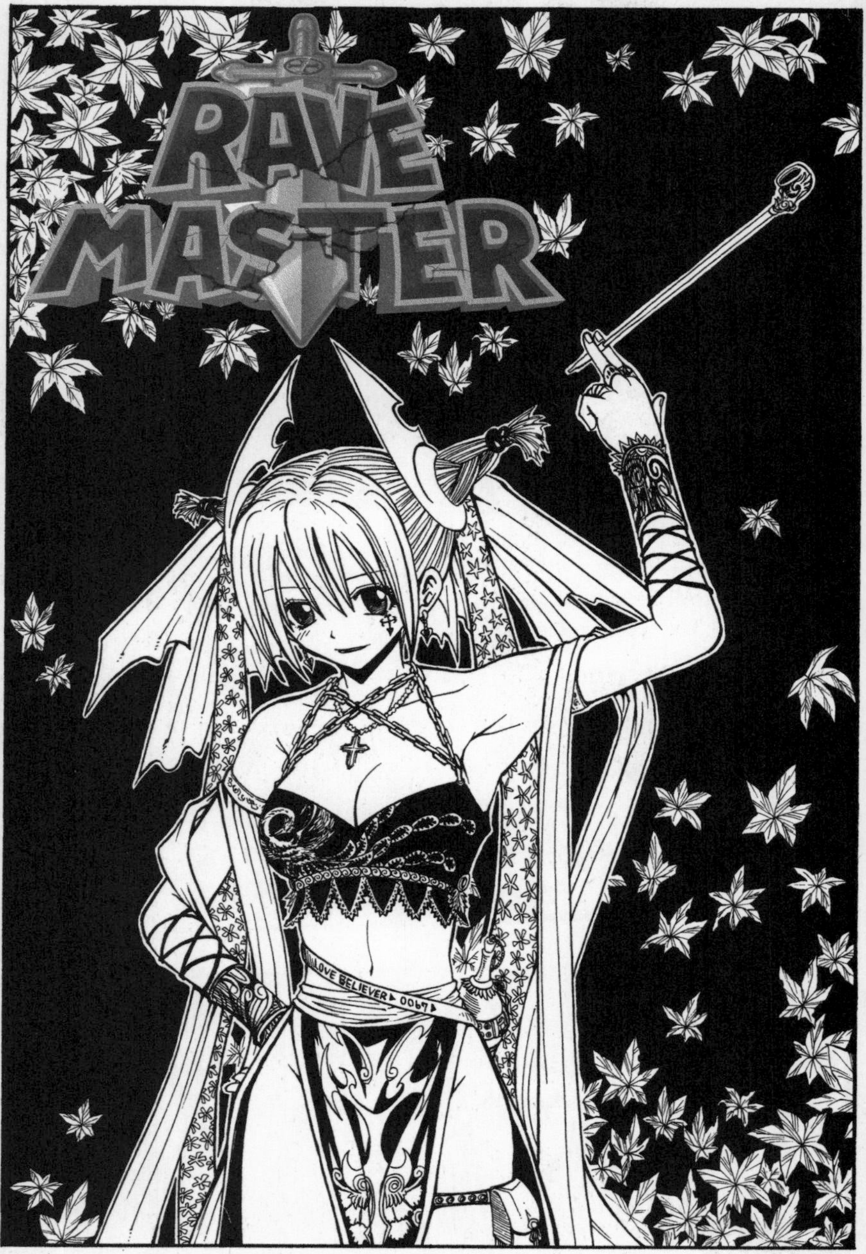
RAVE MASTER
LOVE BELIEVER ▸ 0067 ▸

RAVE:84 ✠ BECAUSE WE'RE FRIENDS

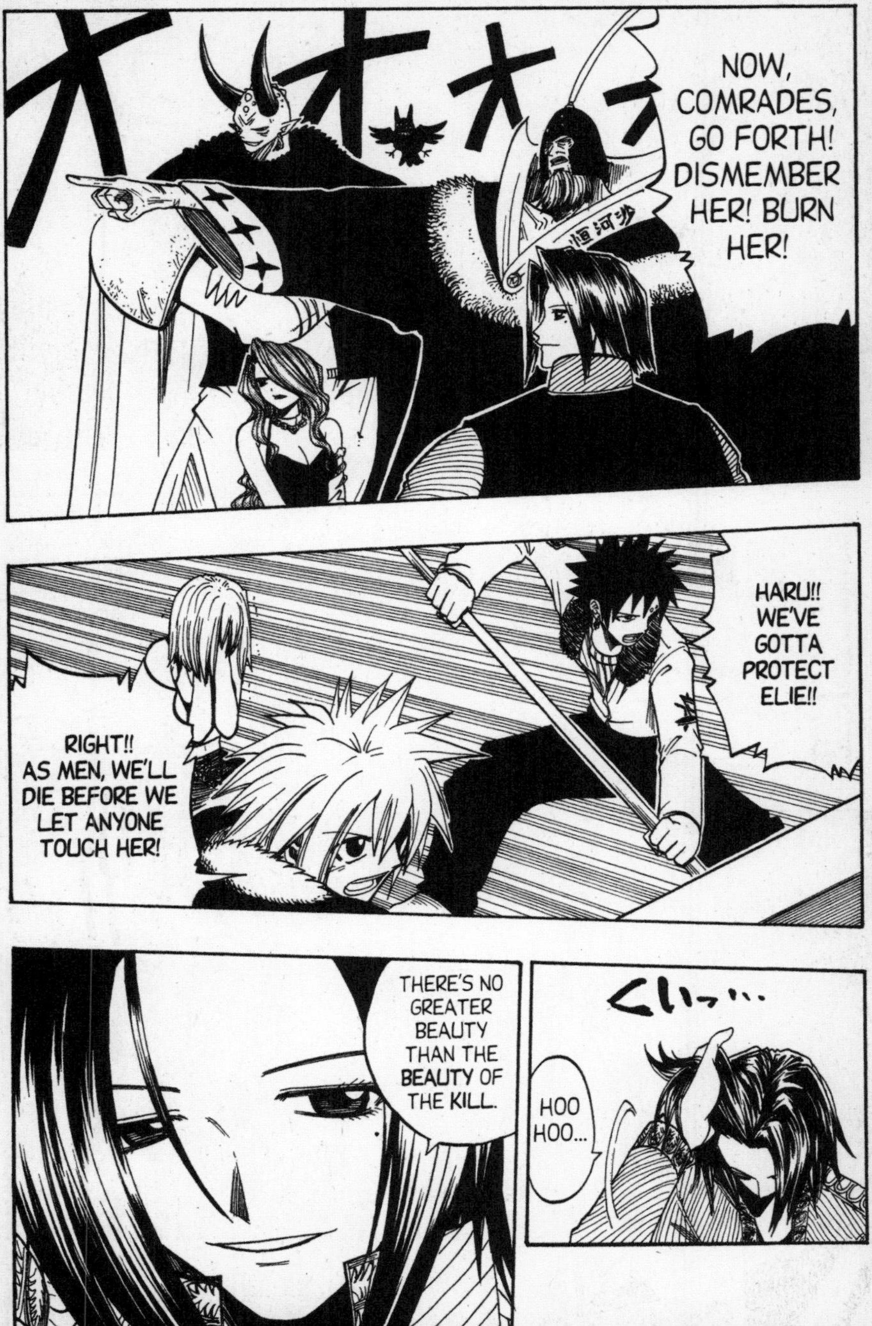
オオオォ
NOW, COMRADES, GO FORTH! DISMEMBER HER! BURN HER!
HARU!! WE'VE GOTTA PROTECT ELIE!!
RIGHT!! AS MEN, WE'LL DIE BEFORE WE LET ANYONE TOUCH HER!
くいっ...
HOO HOO...
THERE'S NO GREATER BEAUTY THAN THE BEAUTY OF THE KILL.

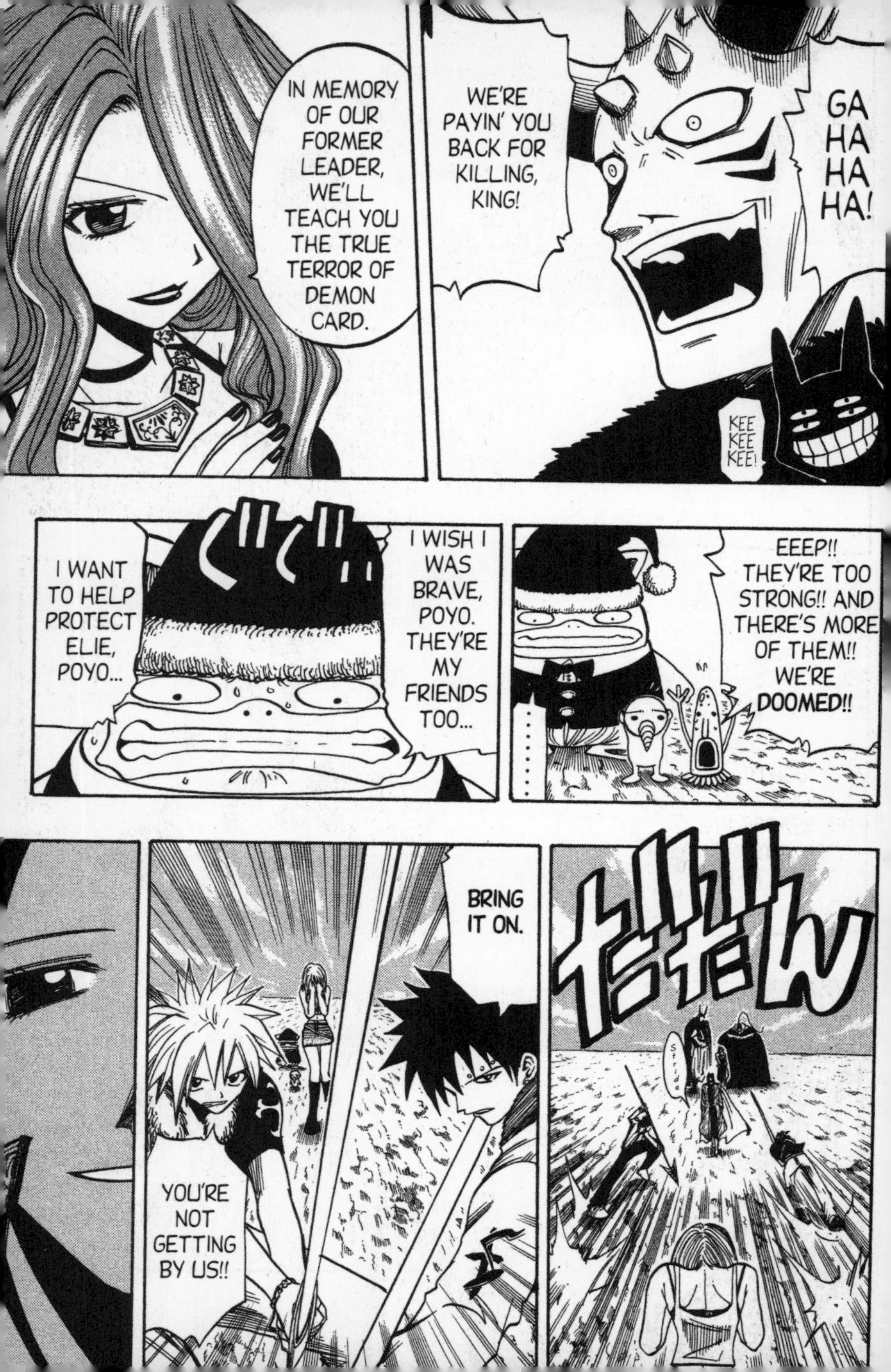
GA HA HA HA!
WE'RE PAYIN' YOU BACK FOR KILLING, KING!
KEE KEE KEE!
IN MEMORY OF OUR FORMER LEADER, WE'LL TEACH YOU THE TRUE TERROR OF DEMON CARD.
EEEP!! THEY'RE TOO STRONG!! AND THERE'S MORE OF THEM!! WE'RE **DOOMED**!!
I WISH I WAS BRAVE, POYO. THEY'RE MY FRIENDS TOO...
I WANT TO HELP PROTECT ELIE, POYO...
stride
BRING IT ON.
YOU'RE NOT GETTING BY US!!

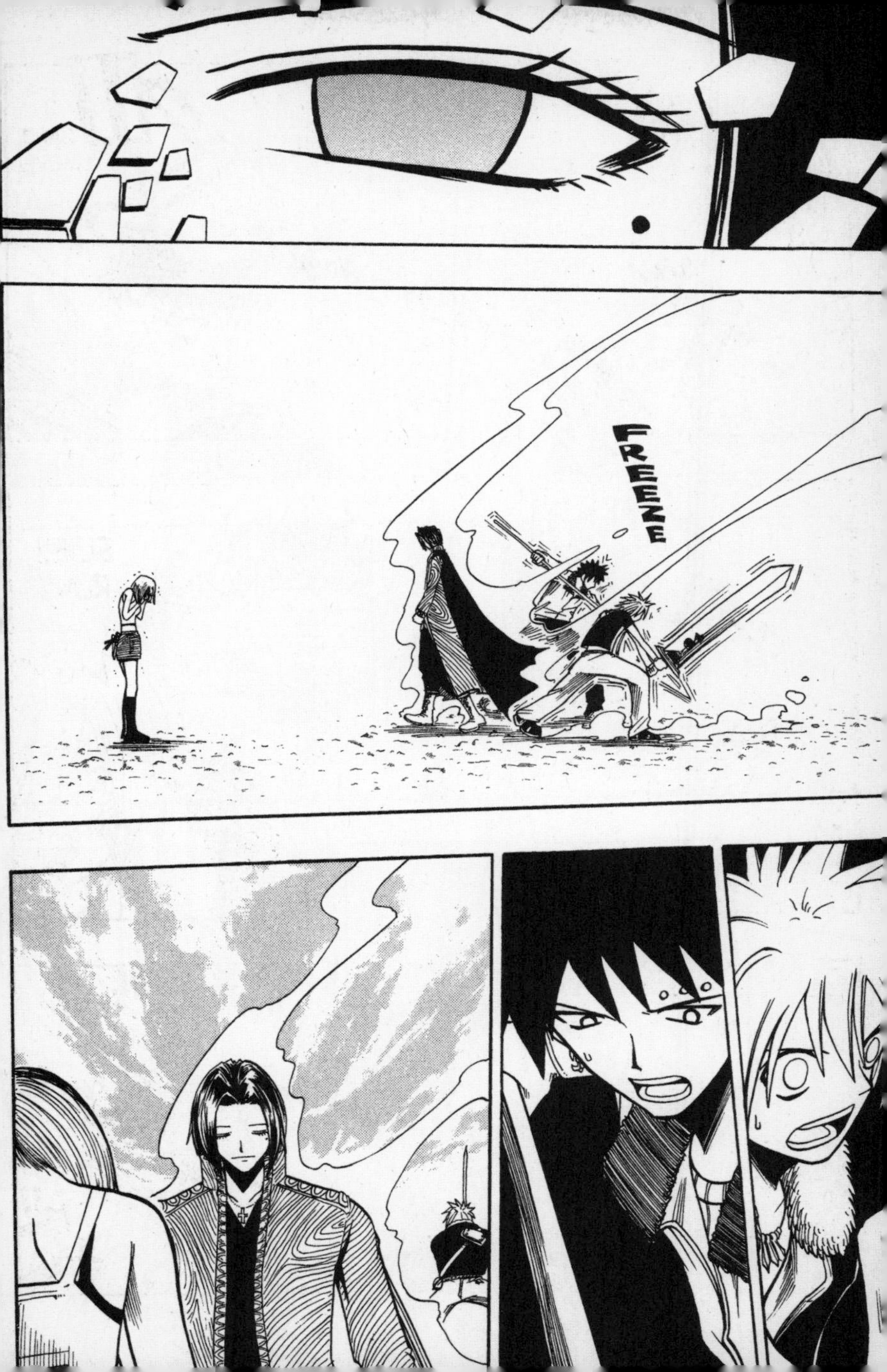
FREEZE

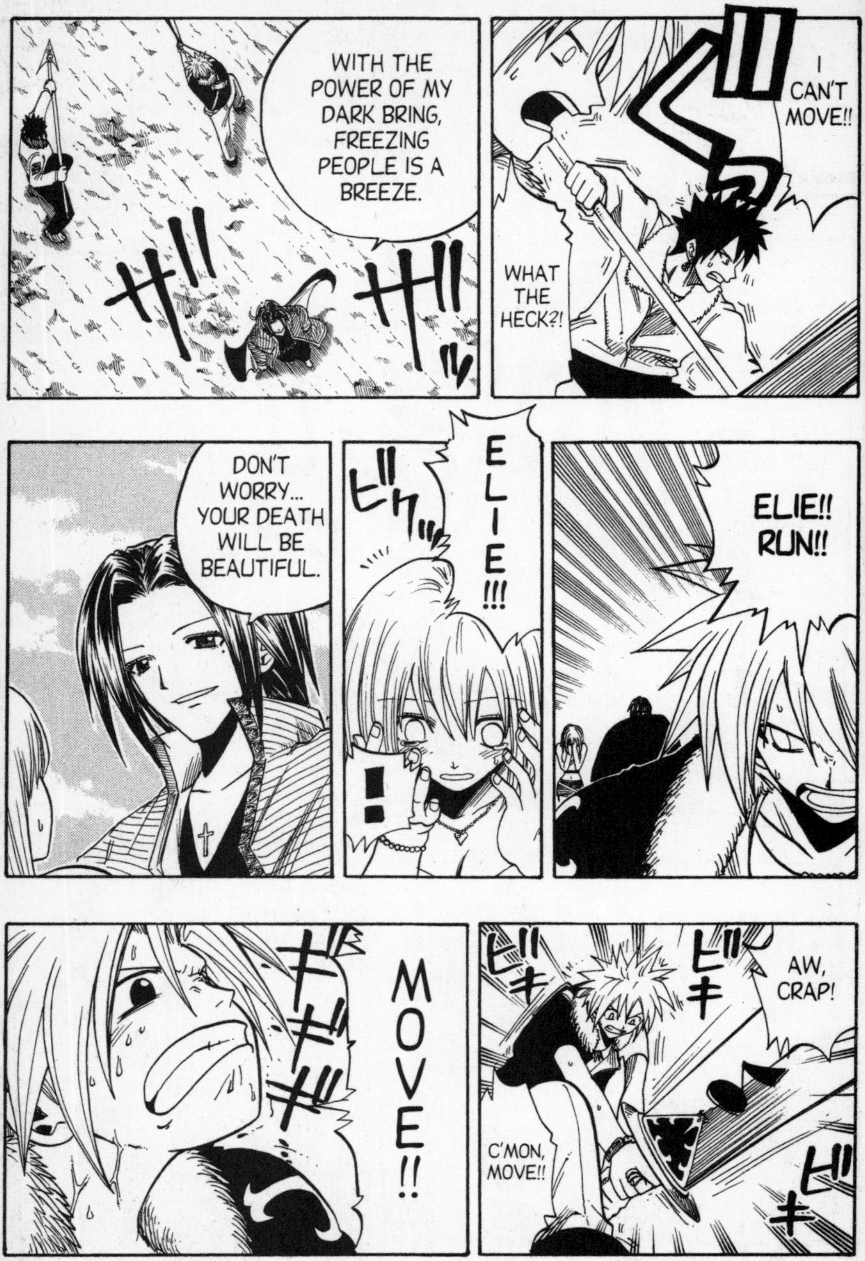
I CAN'T MOVE!!
WHAT THE HECK?!
WITH THE POWER OF MY DARK BRING, FREEZING PEOPLE IS A BREEZE.
ELIE!! RUN!!
ELIE!!!
DON'T WORRY... YOUR DEATH WILL BE BEAUTIFUL.
AW, CRAP!
C'MON, MOVE!!
MOVE!!

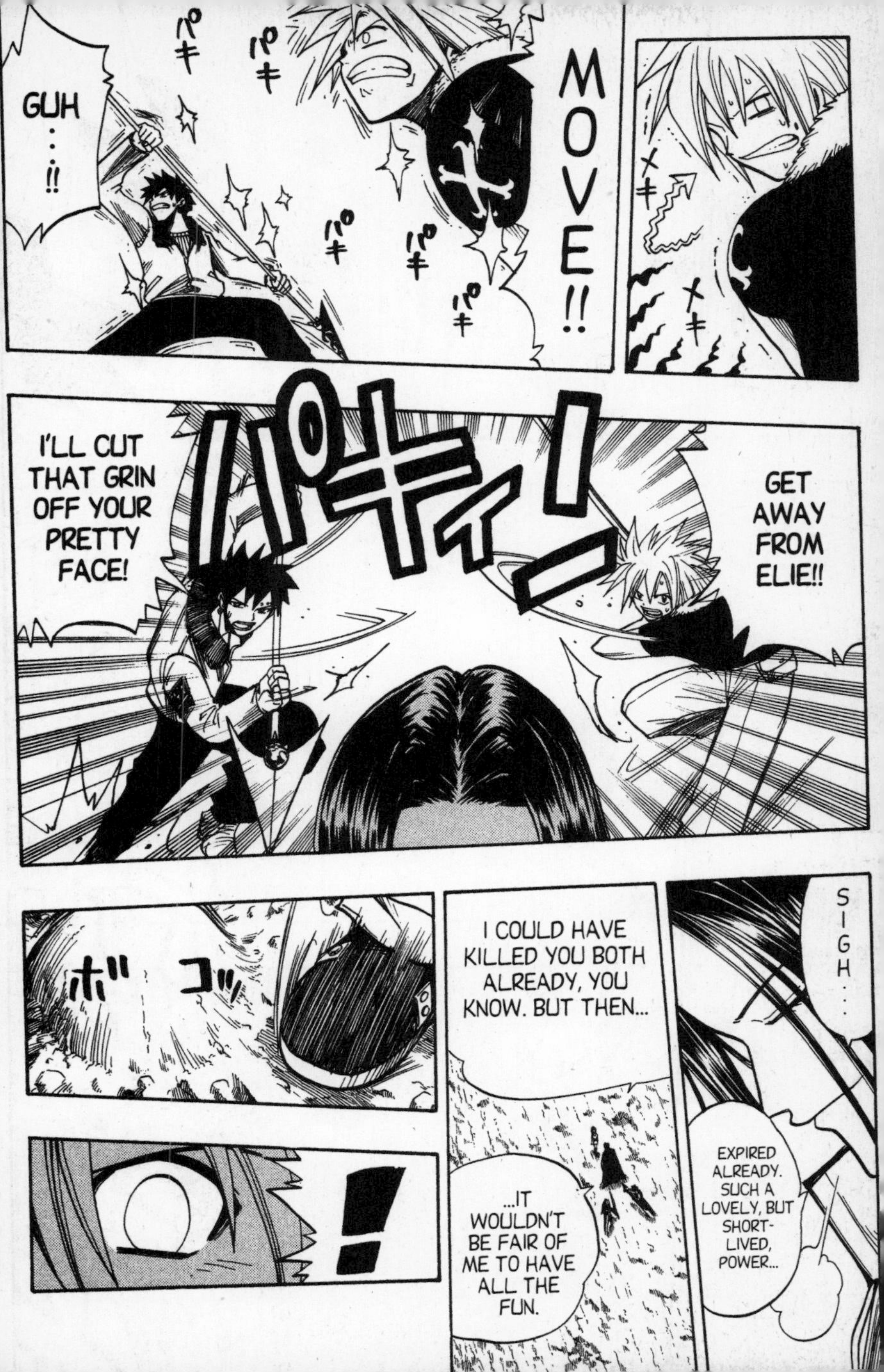
メキ
メキ
MOVE!!
パキ
パキ
パキ
パキ
パキ
GUH...!!
GET AWAY FROM ELIE!!
パキィーン
I'LL CUT THAT GRIN OFF YOUR PRETTY FACE!
SIGH...
EXPIRED ALREADY. SUCH A LOVELY, BUT SHORT-LIVED, POWER...
I COULD HAVE KILLED YOU BOTH ALREADY, YOU KNOW. BUT THEN...
...IT WOULDN'T BE FAIR OF ME TO HAVE ALL THE FUN.
ボコッ
!

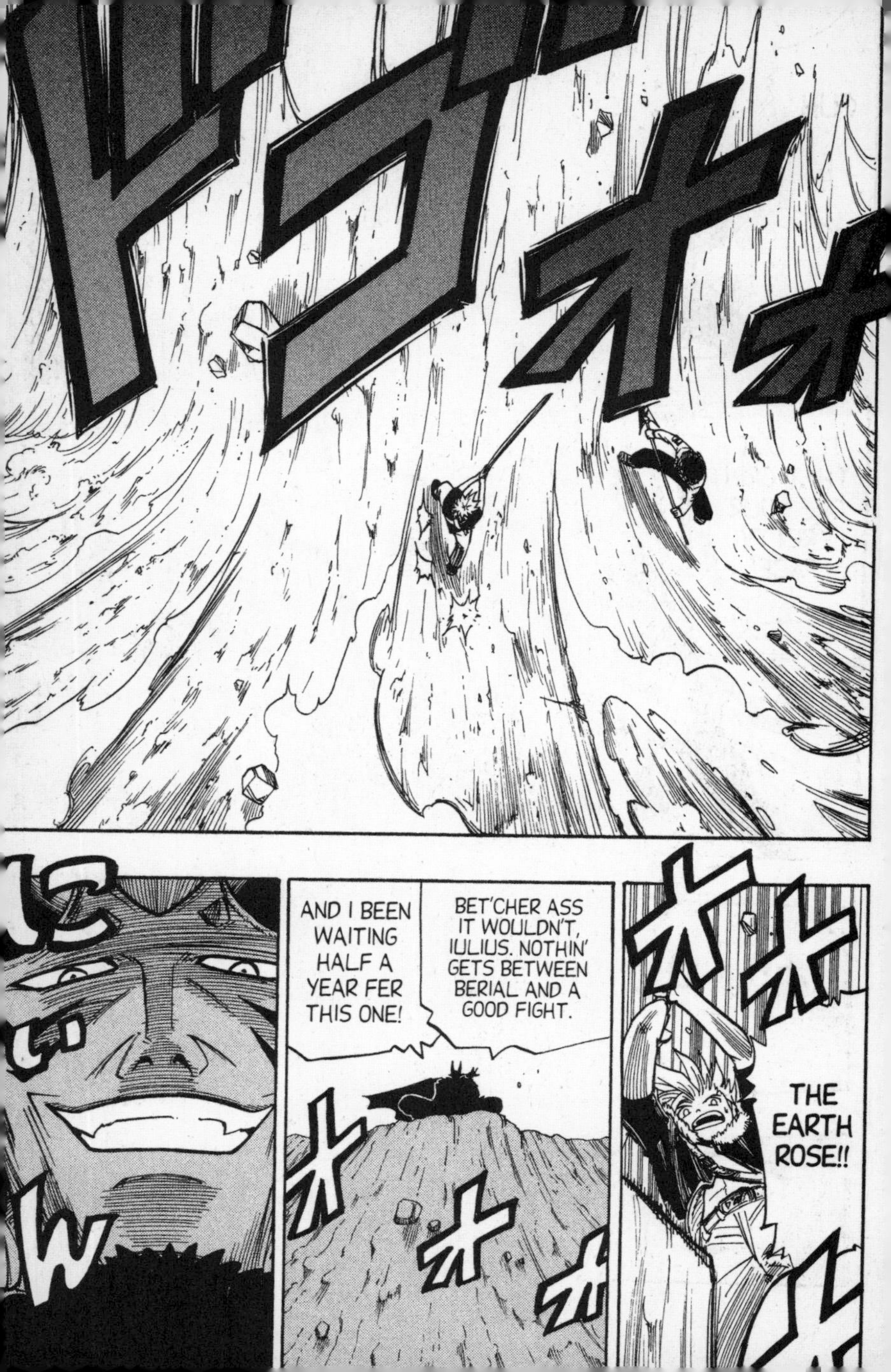
THE EARTH ROSE!!
BET'CHER ASS IT WOULDN'T, IULIUS. NOTHIN' GETS BETWEEN BERIAL AND A GOOD FIGHT.
AND I BEEN WAITING HALF A YEAR FER THIS ONE!

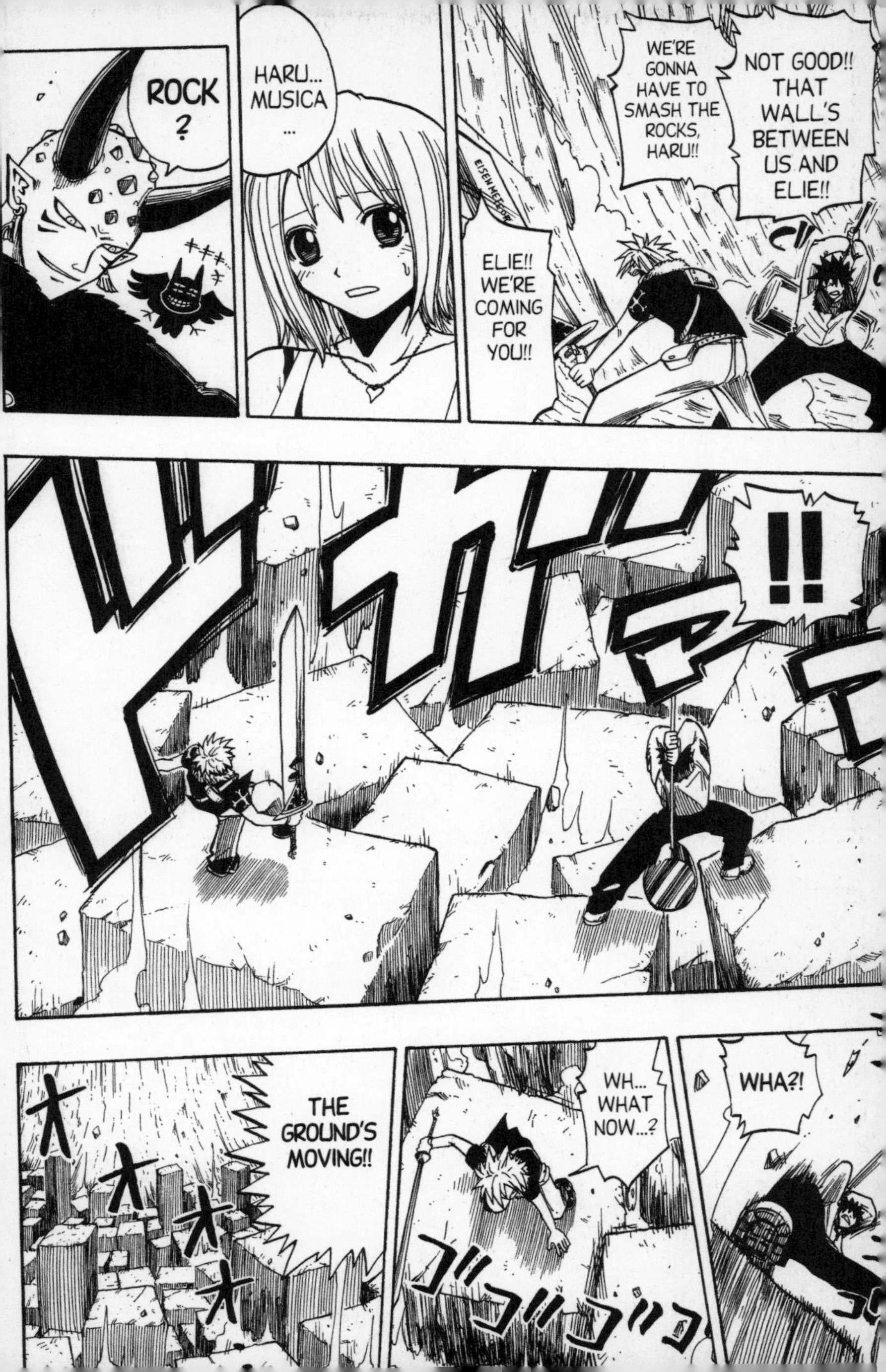
NOT GOOD!! THAT WALL'S BETWEEN US AND ELIE!!
WE'RE GONNA HAVE TO SMASH THE ROCKS, HARU!!
ELIE!! WE'RE COMING FOR YOU!!
HARU... MUSICA ...
ROCK ?
!!
WHA?!
WH... WHAT NOW...?
THE GROUND'S MOVING!!

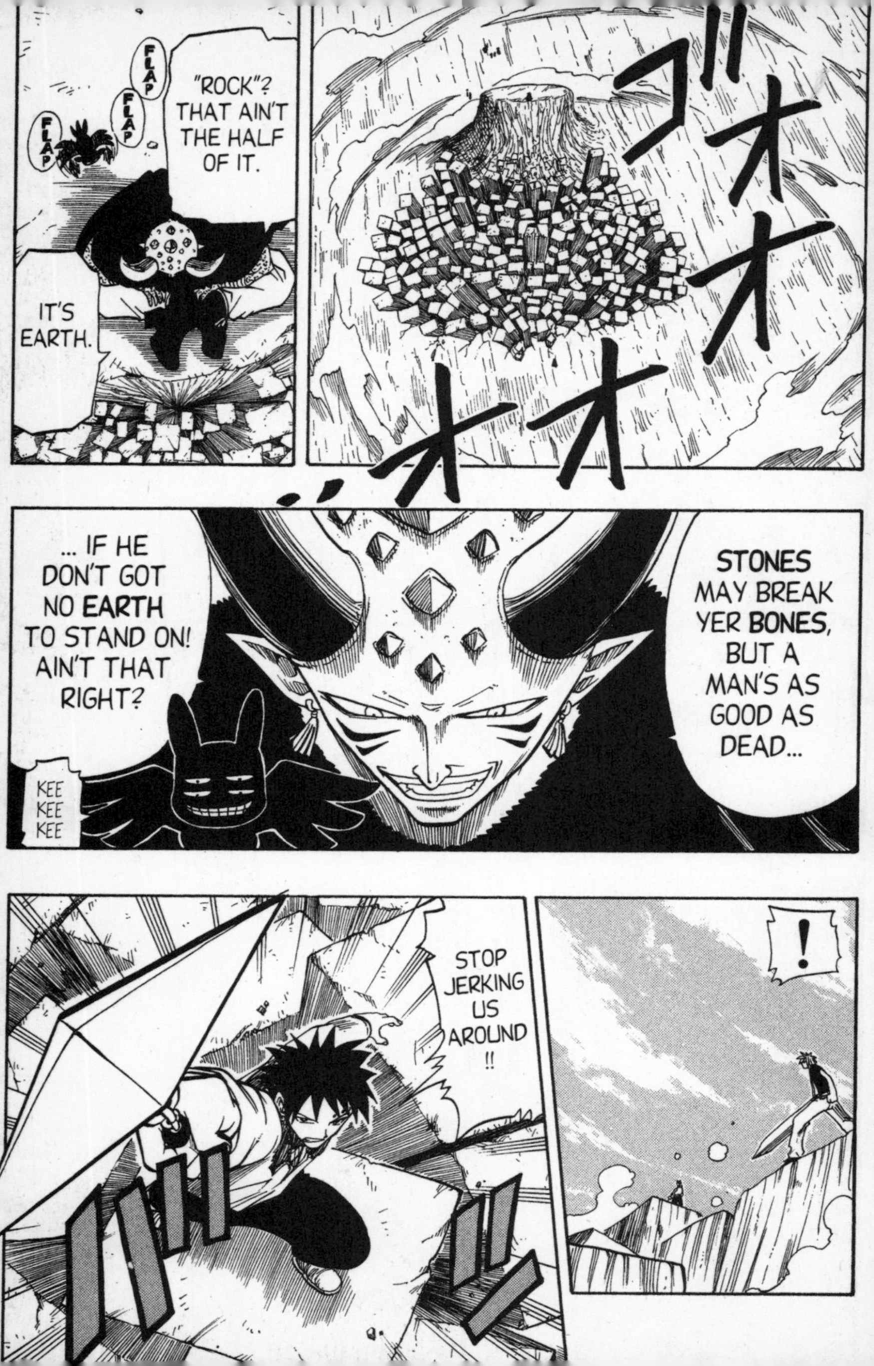
ゴオオオオ…
FLAP FLAP FLAP
"ROCK"? THAT AIN'T THE HALF OF IT.
IT'S EARTH.
STONES MAY BREAK YER BONES, BUT A MAN'S AS GOOD AS DEAD...
... IF HE DON'T GOT NO EARTH TO STAND ON! AIN'T THAT RIGHT?
KEE KEE KEE
!
STOP JERKING US AROUND !!

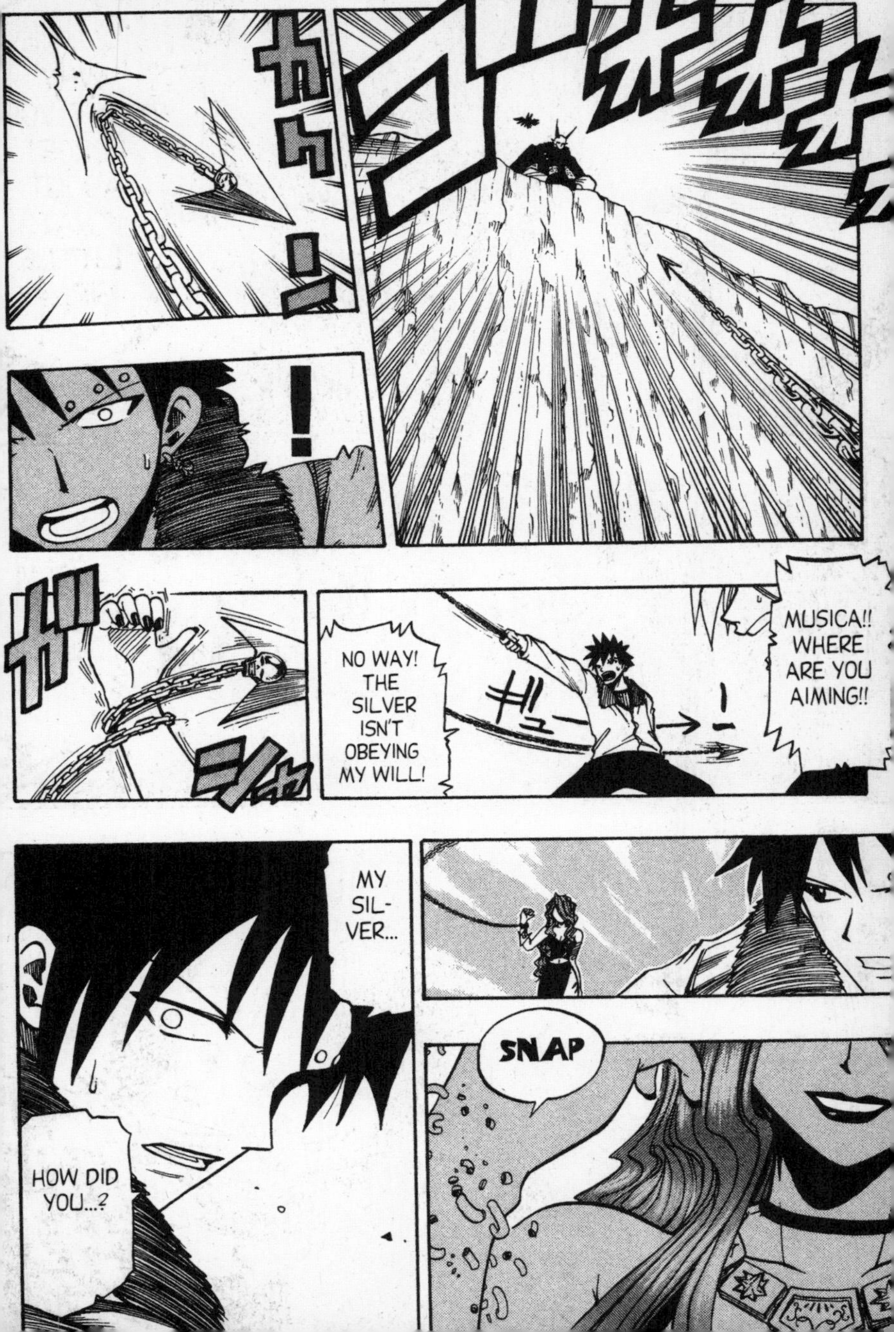

!
MUSICA!! WHERE ARE YOU AIMING!!
NO WAY! THE SILVER ISN'T OBEYING MY WILL!
ギュー
SNAP
MY SIL-VER...
HOW DID YOU...?

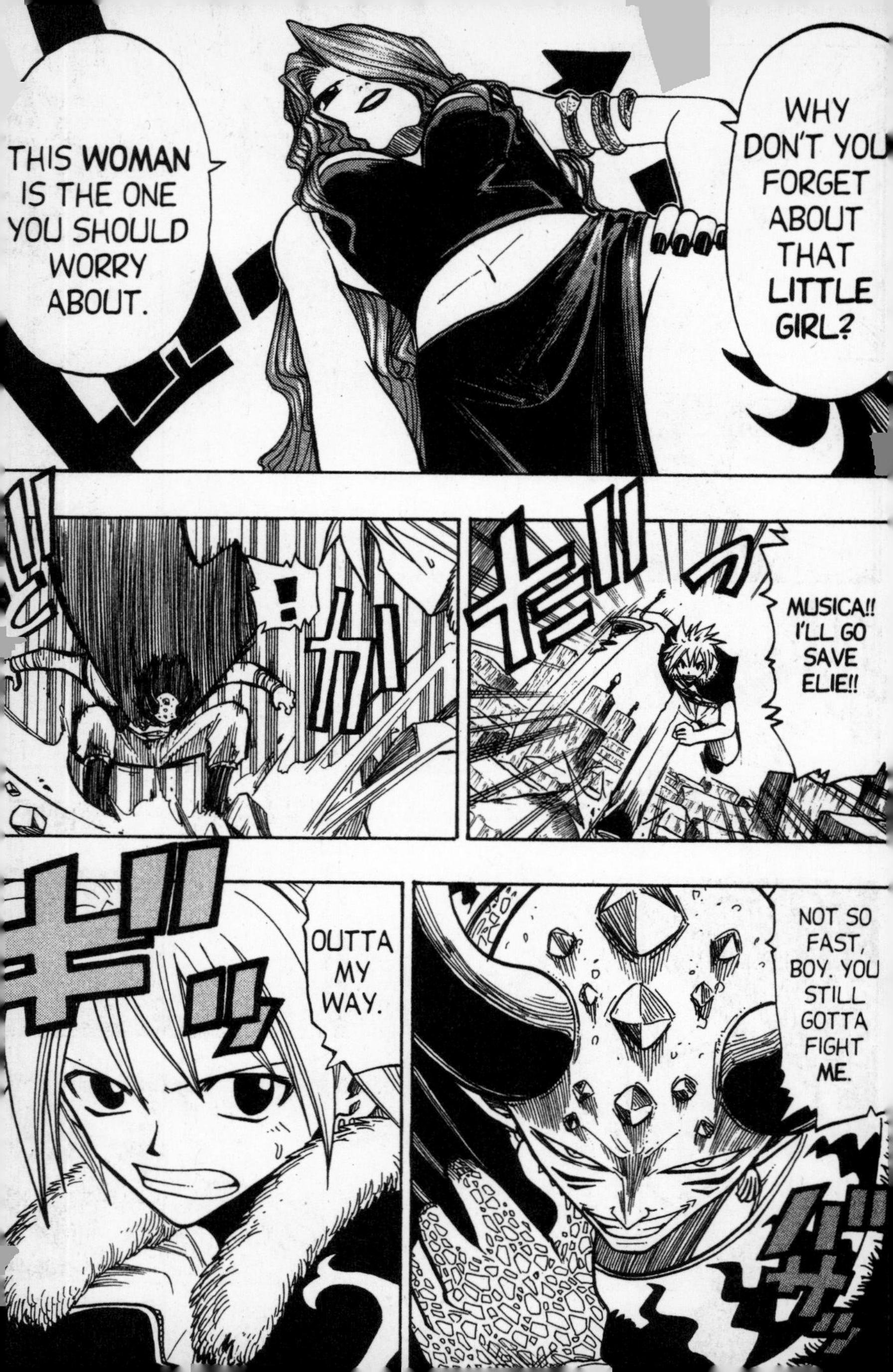
WHY DON'T YOU FORGET ABOUT THAT LITTLE GIRL?
THIS WOMAN IS THE ONE YOU SHOULD WORRY ABOUT.
MUSICA!! I'LL GO SAVE ELIE!!
!
NOT SO FAST, BOY. YOU STILL GOTTA FIGHT ME.
OUTTA MY WAY.

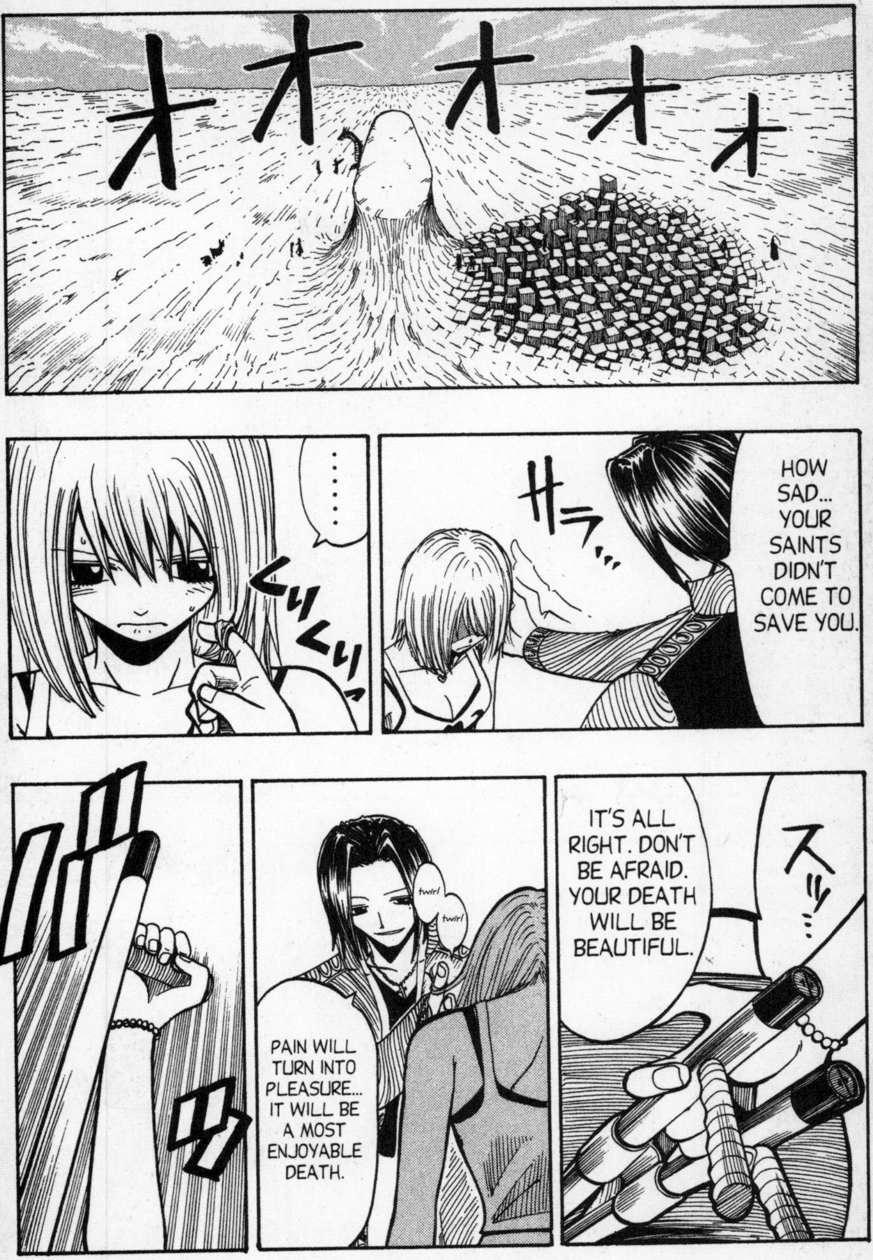

オオオオォ
サラ…
HOW SAD... YOUR SAINTS DIDN'T COME TO SAVE YOU.
......
くりくりっ
IT'S ALL RIGHT. DON'T BE AFRAID. YOUR DEATH WILL BE BEAUTIFUL.
スッ…
twirl
twirl
PAIN WILL TURN INTO PLEASURE... IT WILL BE A MOST ENJOYABLE DEATH.
バッ

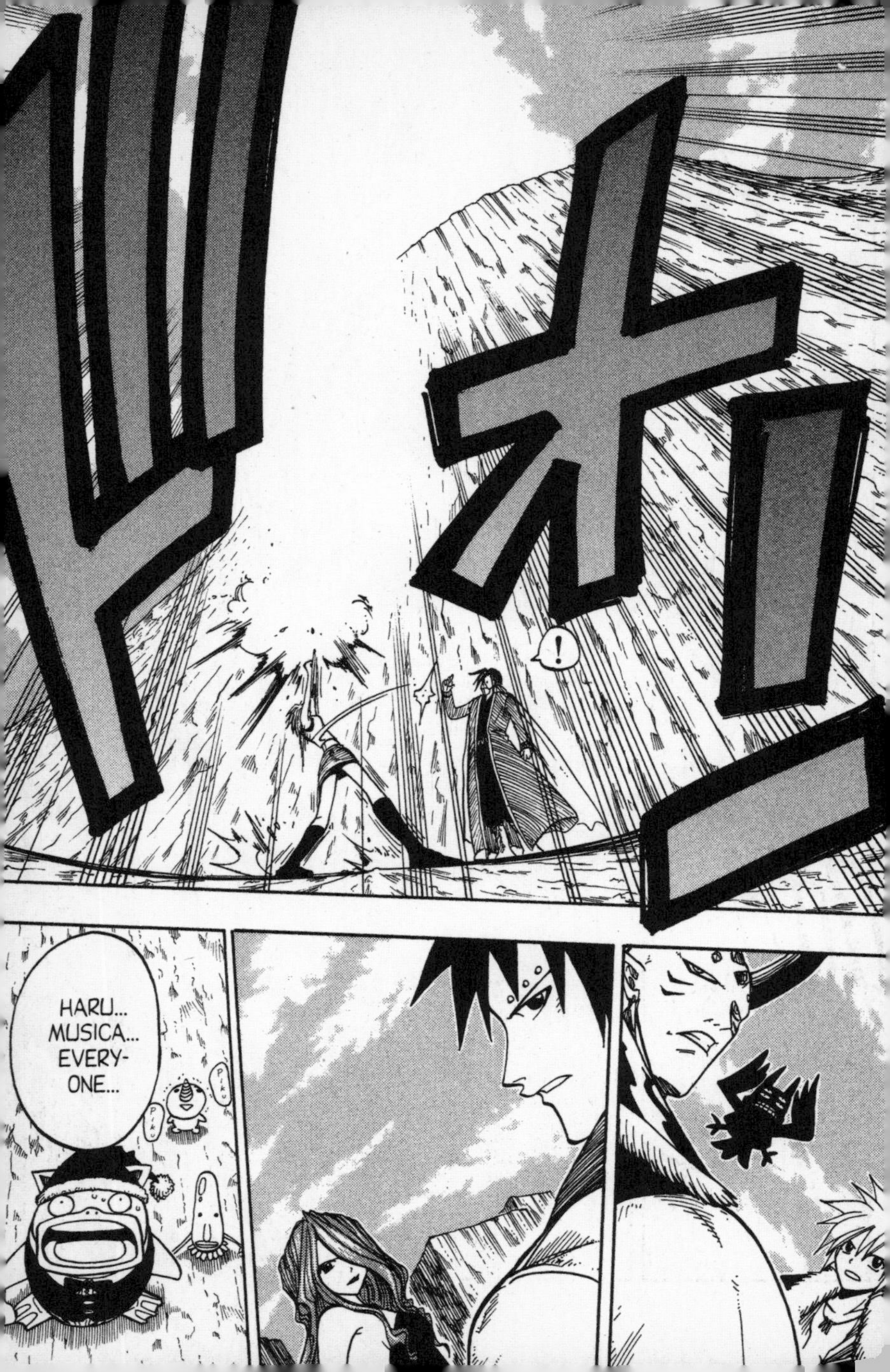
!
HARU... MUSICA... EVERY-ONE...
Piku
Piku

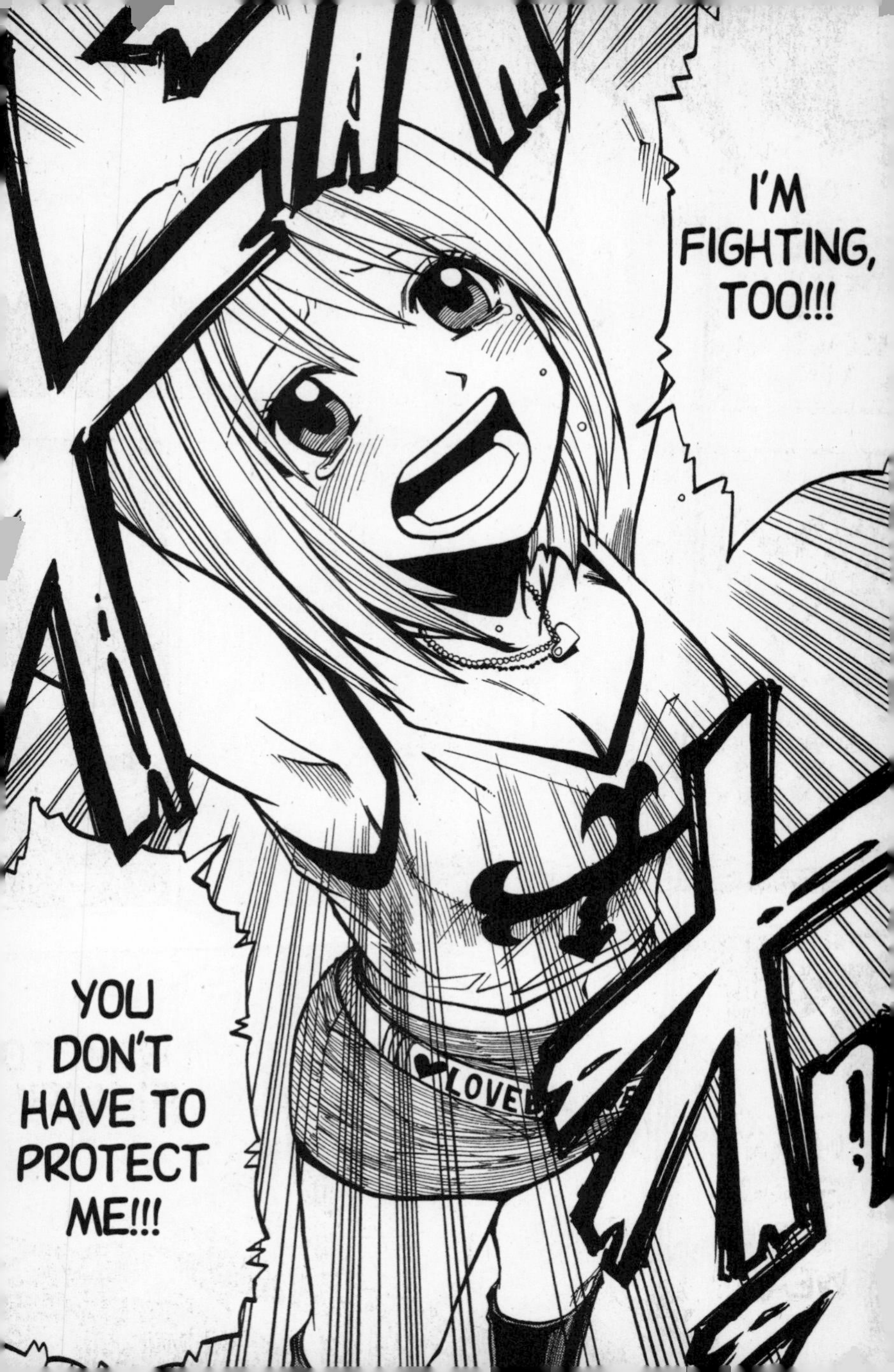
I'M FIGHTING, TOO!!!
YOU DON'T HAVE TO PROTECT ME!!!
LOVE

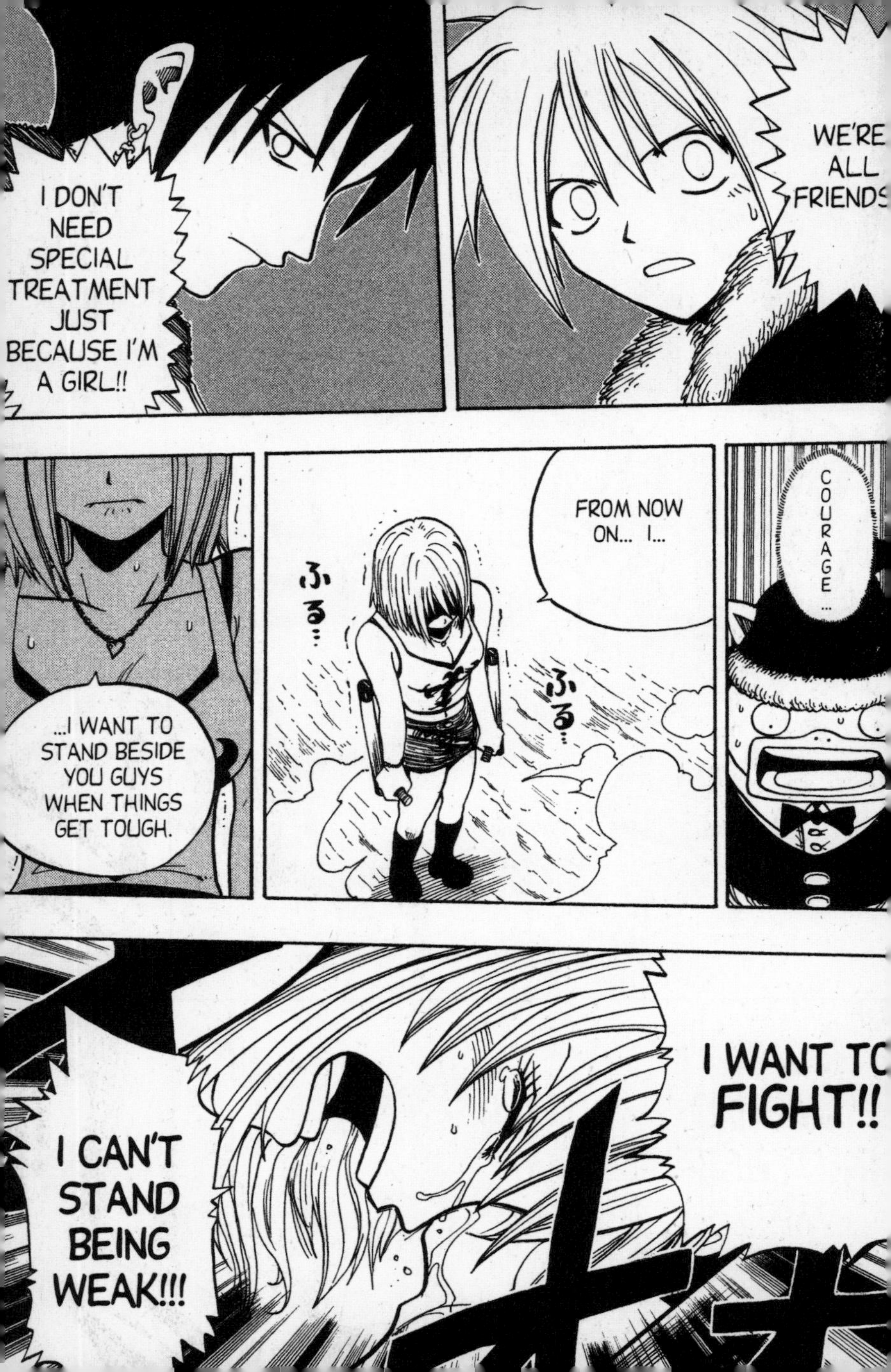
WE'RE ALL FRIENDS
I DON'T NEED SPECIAL TREATMENT JUST BECAUSE I'M A GIRL!!
COURAGE...
FROM NOW ON... I...
ふる…
ふる…
...I WANT TO STAND BESIDE YOU GUYS WHEN THINGS GET TOUGH.
I WANT TO FIGHT!!
I CAN'T STAND BEING WEAK!!!

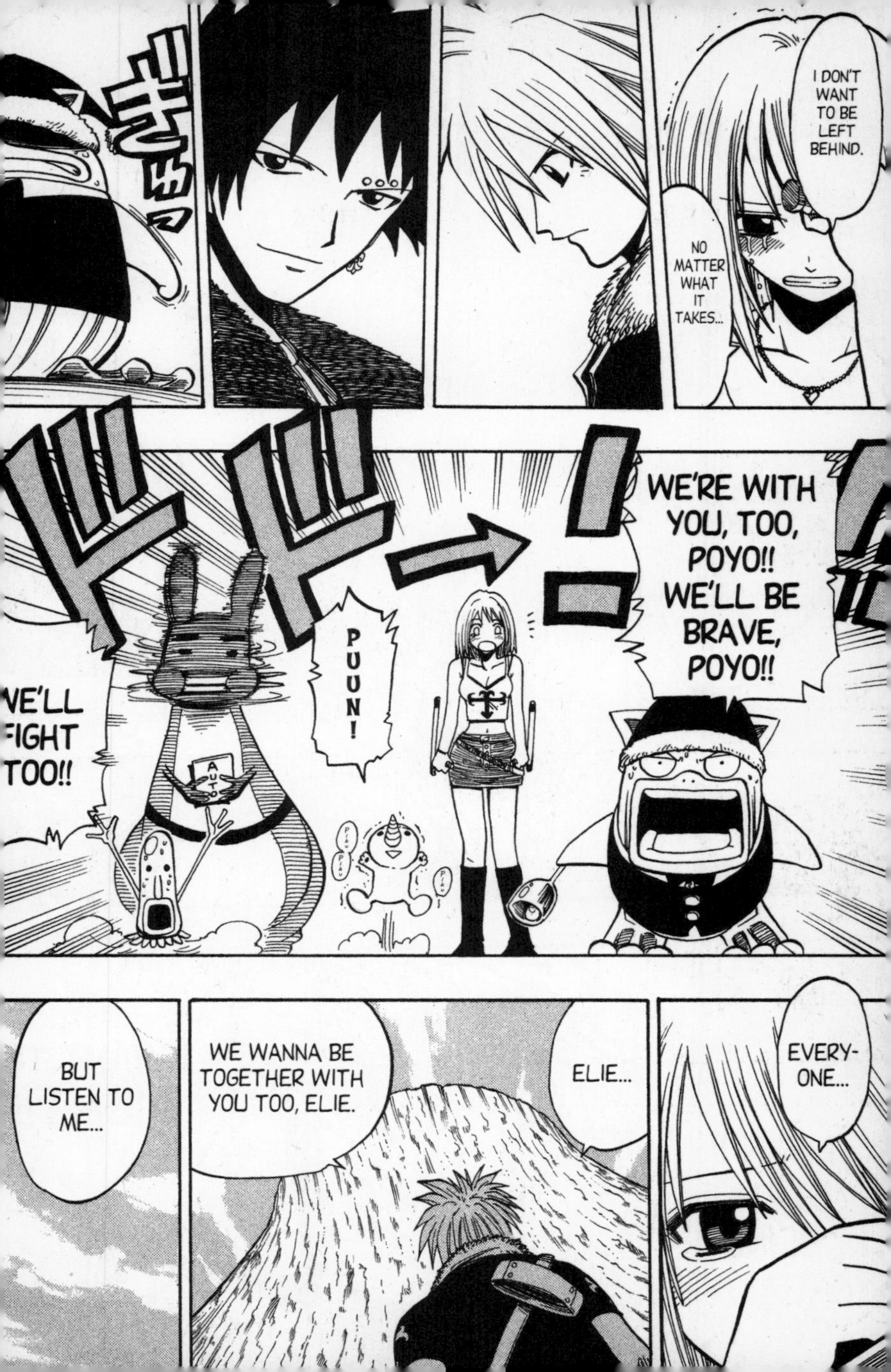
I DON'T WANT TO BE LEFT BEHIND.
NO MATTER WHAT IT TAKES...
ぎゅっ
WE'RE WITH YOU, TOO, POYO!! WE'LL BE BRAVE, POYO!!
PUUN!
WE'LL FIGHT TOO!!
EVERY-ONE...
ELIE...
WE WANNA BE TOGETHER WITH YOU TOO, ELIE.
BUT LISTEN TO ME...

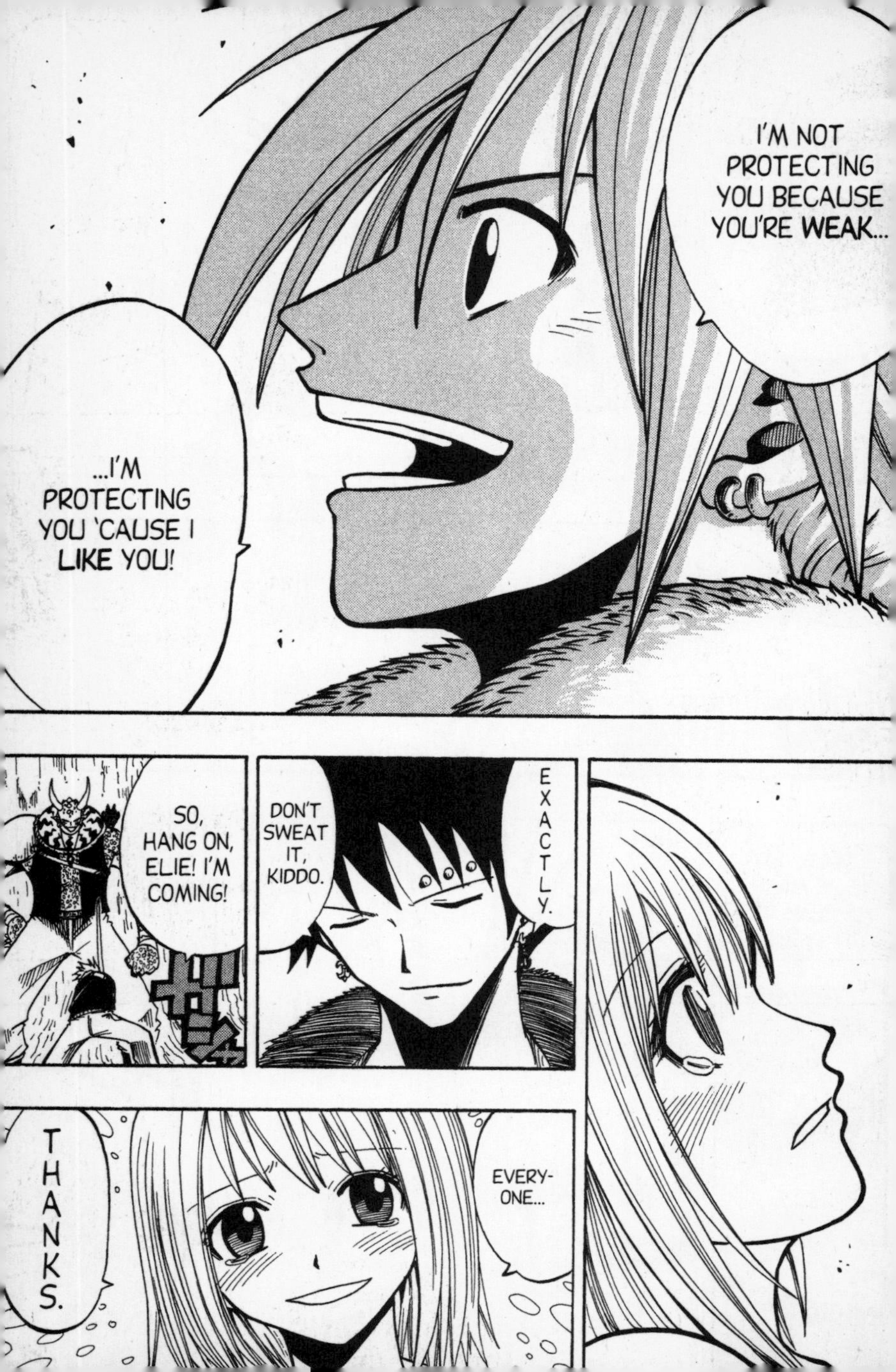
I'M NOT PROTECTING YOU BECAUSE YOU'RE **WEAK**...
...I'M PROTECTING YOU 'CAUSE I **LIKE** YOU!
EXACTLY.
DON'T SWEAT IT, KIDDO.
SO, HANG ON, ELIE! I'M COMING!
EVERY-ONE...
THANKS.

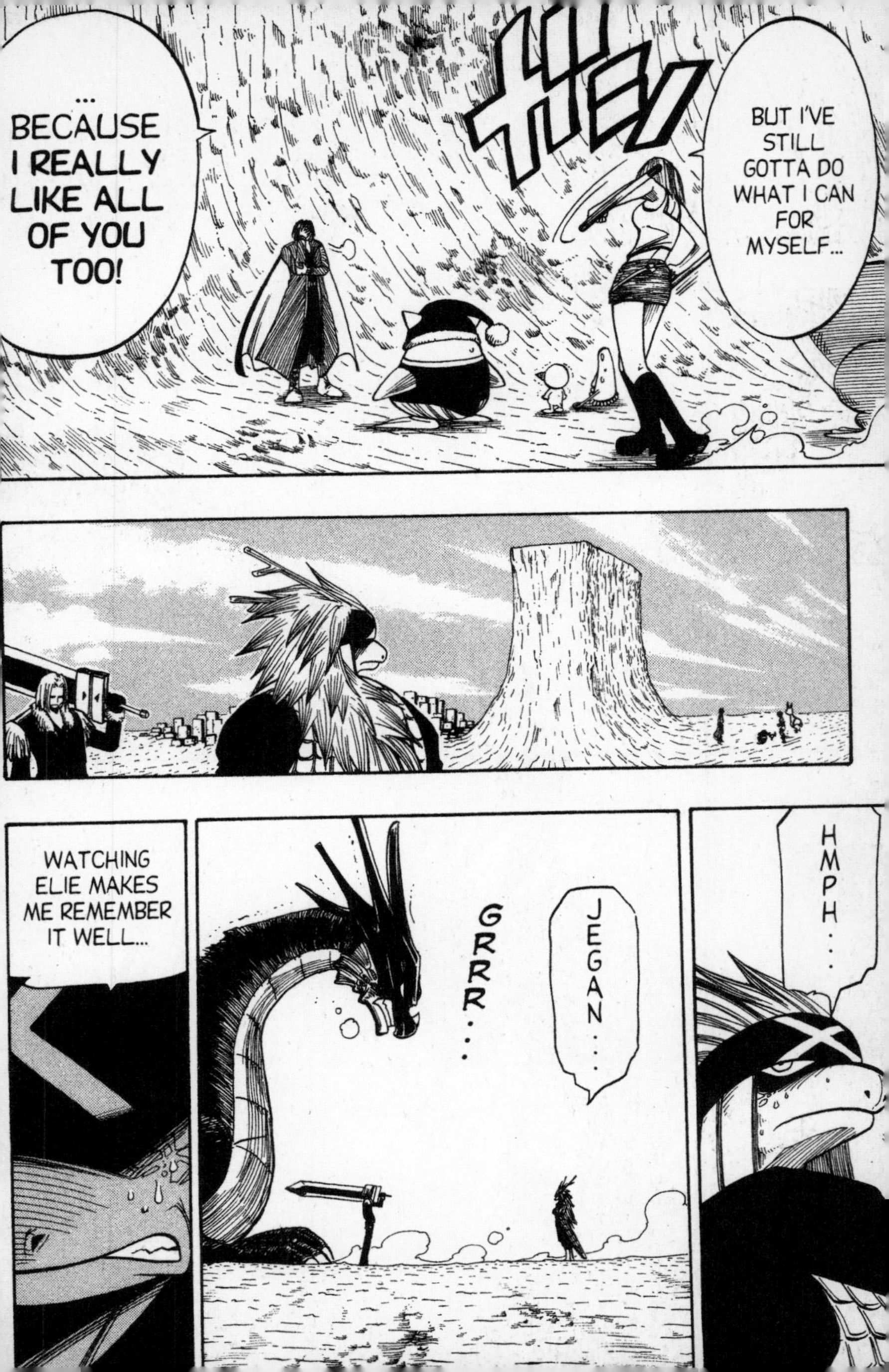
BUT I'VE STILL GOTTA DO WHAT I CAN FOR MYSELF...
... BECAUSE I REALLY LIKE ALL OF YOU TOO!
HMPH...
JEGAN...
GRRR...
WATCHING ELIE MAKES ME REMEMBER IT WELL...

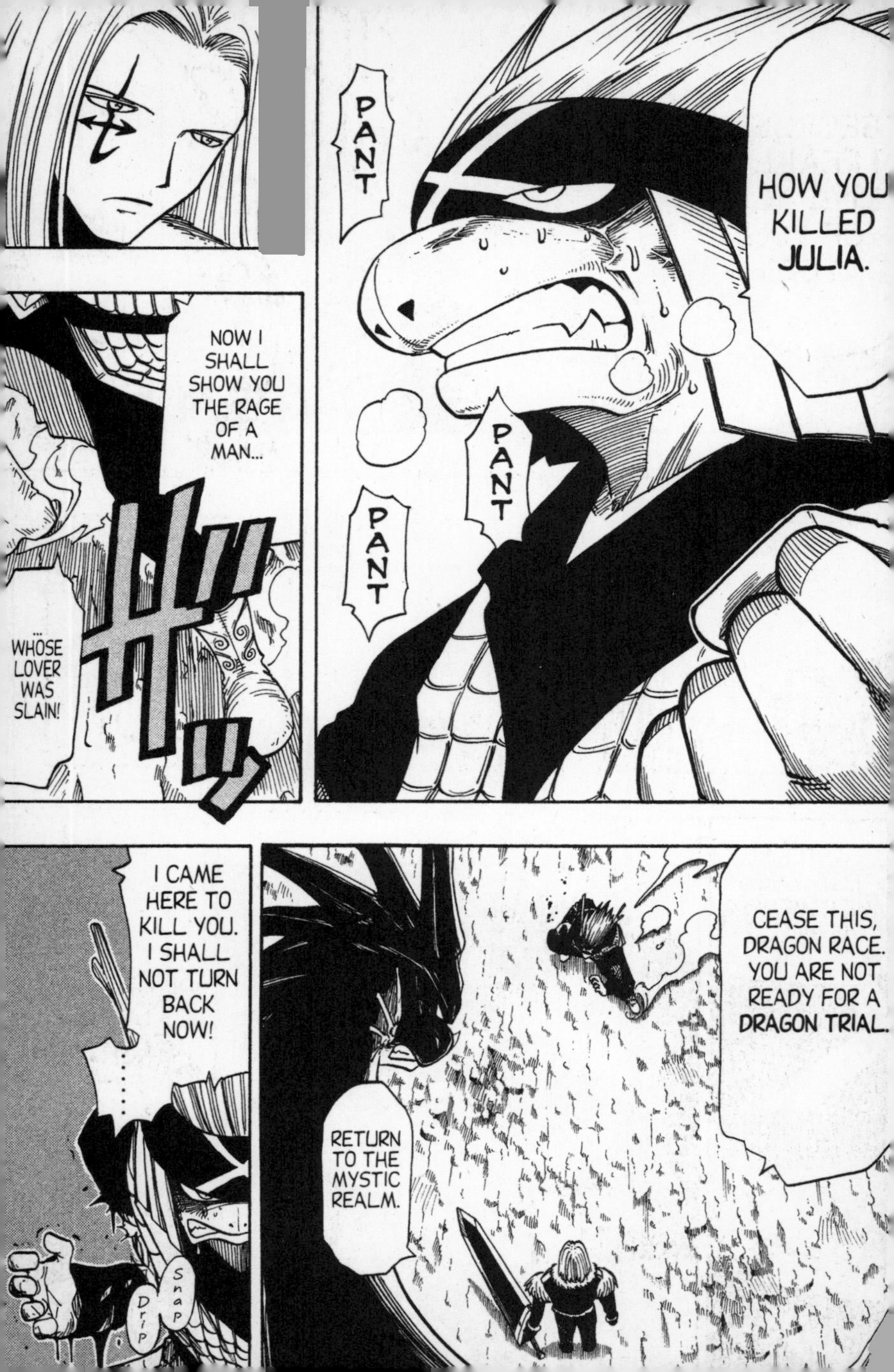
HOW YOU KILLED JULIA.
PANT
PANT
PANT
NOW I SHALL SHOW YOU THE RAGE OF A MAN...
...WHOSE LOVER WAS SLAIN!
CEASE THIS, DRAGON RACE. YOU ARE NOT READY FOR A DRAGON TRIAL.
RETURN TO THE MYSTIC REALM.
I CAME HERE TO KILL YOU. I SHALL NOT TURN BACK NOW!
......
Snap
Drip

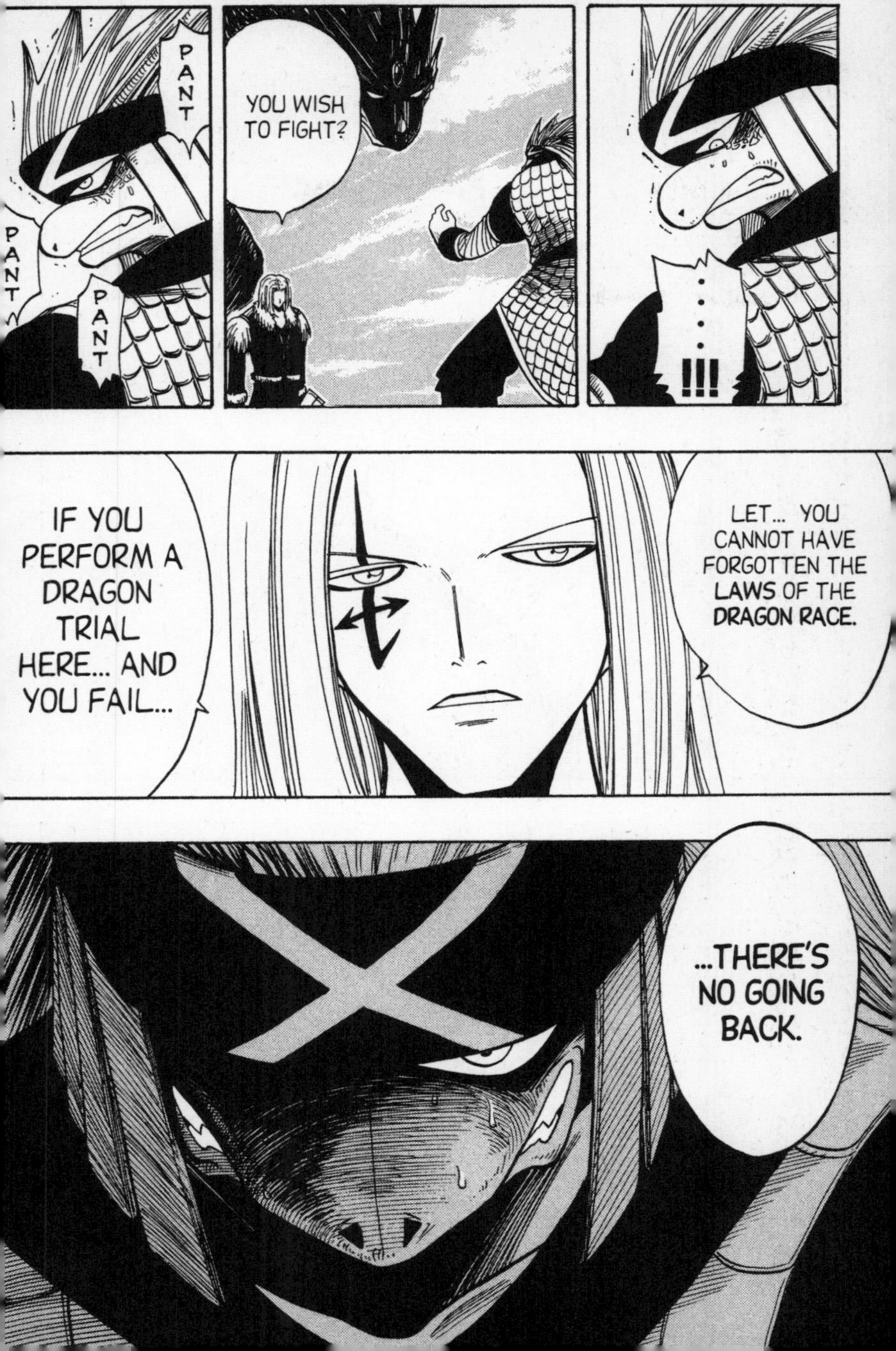

.....
!!!
YOU WISH TO FIGHT?
PANT
PANT
PANT
LET... YOU CANNOT HAVE FORGOTTEN THE LAWS OF THE DRAGON RACE.
IF YOU PERFORM A DRAGON TRIAL HERE... AND YOU FAIL...
...THERE'S NO GOING BACK.

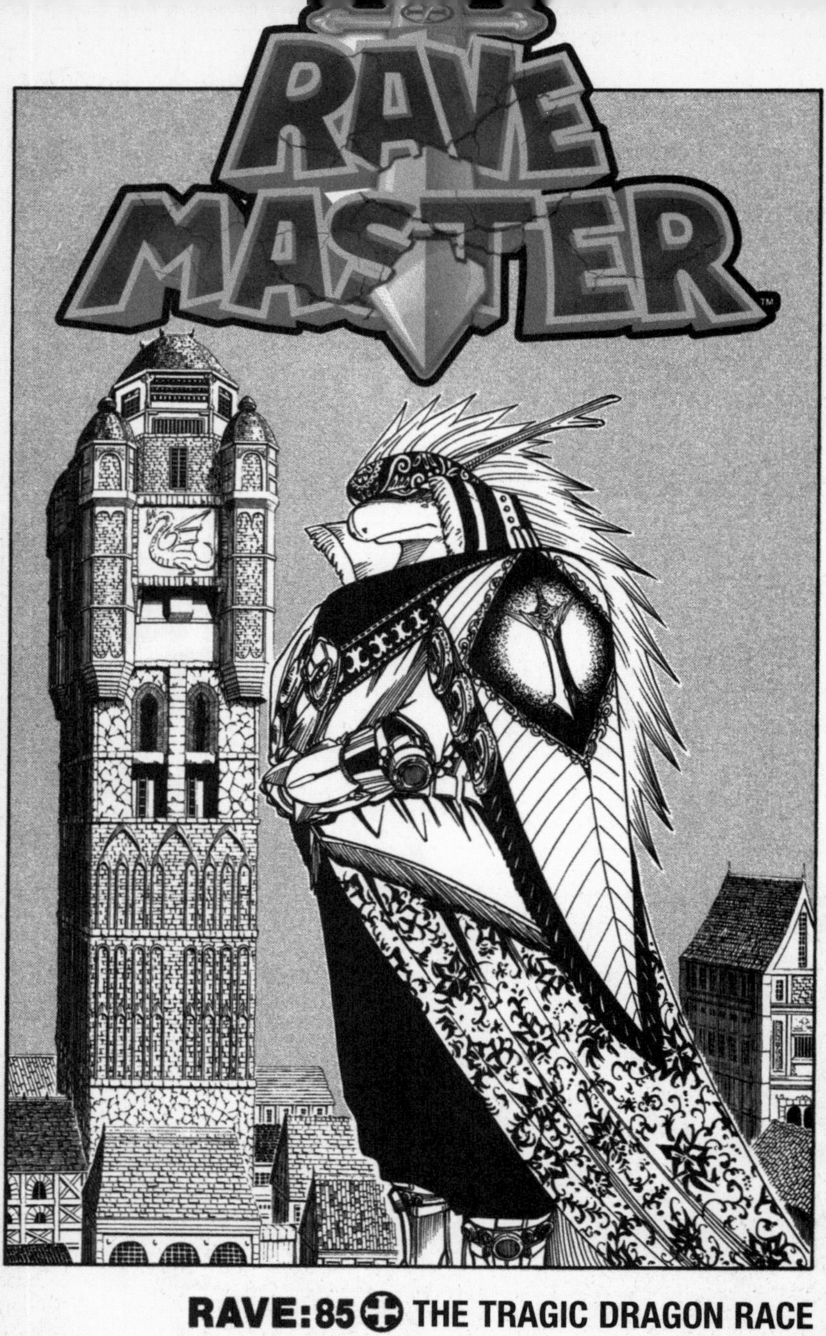
RAVE MASTER

RAVE:85 ✠ THE TRAGIC DRAGON RACE

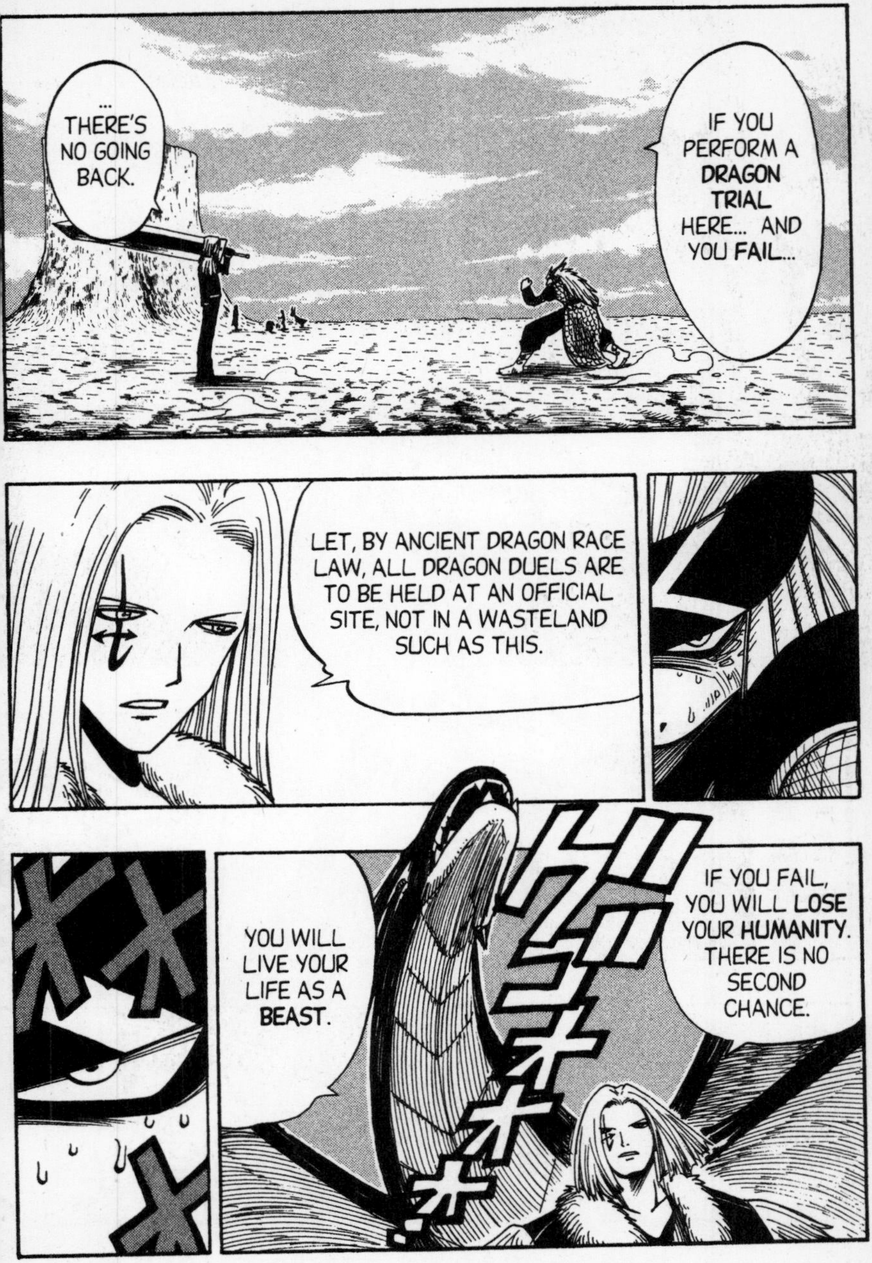
IF YOU PERFORM A DRAGON TRIAL HERE... AND YOU FAIL...
... THERE'S NO GOING BACK.
LET, BY ANCIENT DRAGON RACE LAW, ALL DRAGON DUELS ARE TO BE HELD AT AN OFFICIAL SITE, NOT IN A WASTELAND SUCH AS THIS.
IF YOU FAIL, YOU WILL LOSE YOUR HUMANITY. THERE IS NO SECOND CHANCE.
YOU WILL LIVE YOUR LIFE AS A BEAST.

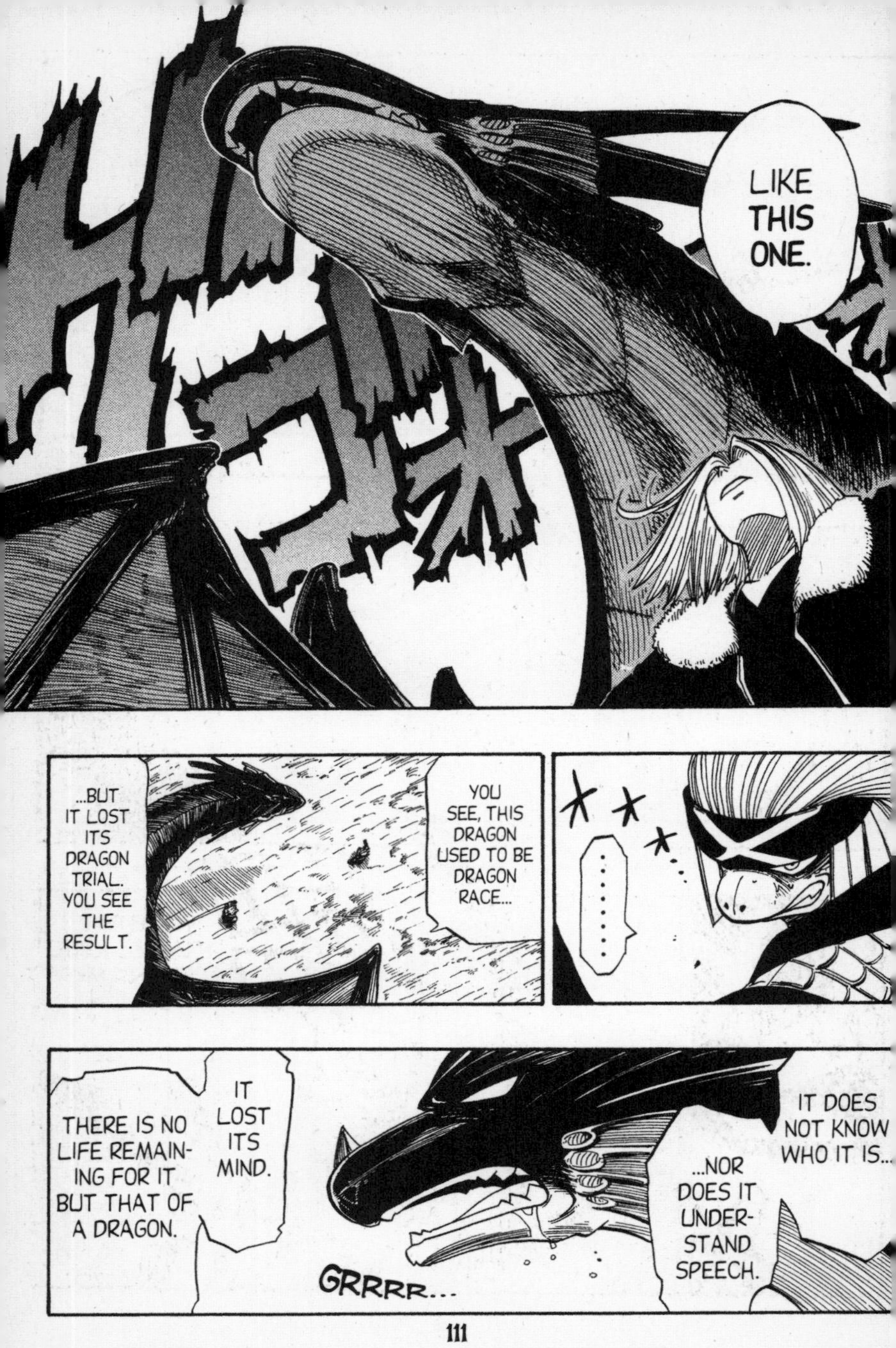
LIKE THIS ONE.
......
YOU SEE, THIS DRAGON USED TO BE DRAGON RACE...
...BUT IT LOST ITS DRAGON TRIAL. YOU SEE THE RESULT.
IT DOES NOT KNOW WHO IT IS...
...NOR DOES IT UNDERSTAND SPEECH.
GRRRR...
IT LOST ITS MIND.
THERE IS NO LIFE REMAINING FOR IT BUT THAT OF A DRAGON.

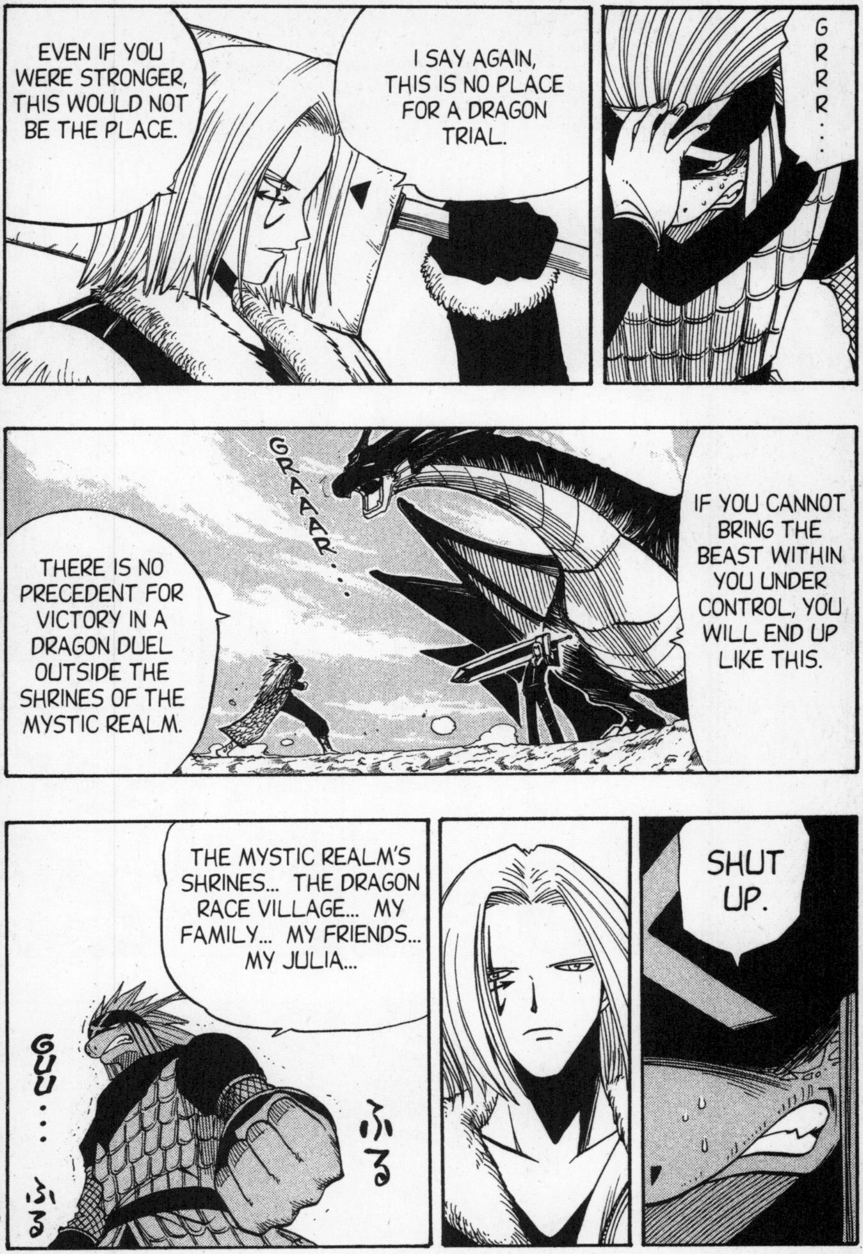
GRRR...
I SAY AGAIN, THIS IS NO PLACE FOR A DRAGON TRIAL.
EVEN IF YOU WERE STRONGER, THIS WOULD NOT BE THE PLACE.
IF YOU CANNOT BRING THE BEAST WITHIN YOU UNDER CONTROL, YOU WILL END UP LIKE THIS.
GRAAAAR...
THERE IS NO PRECEDENT FOR VICTORY IN A DRAGON DUEL OUTSIDE THE SHRINES OF THE MYSTIC REALM.
SHUT UP.
THE MYSTIC REALM'S SHRINES... THE DRAGON RACE VILLAGE... MY FAMILY... MY FRIENDS... MY JULIA...
ふる
GUU...
ふる

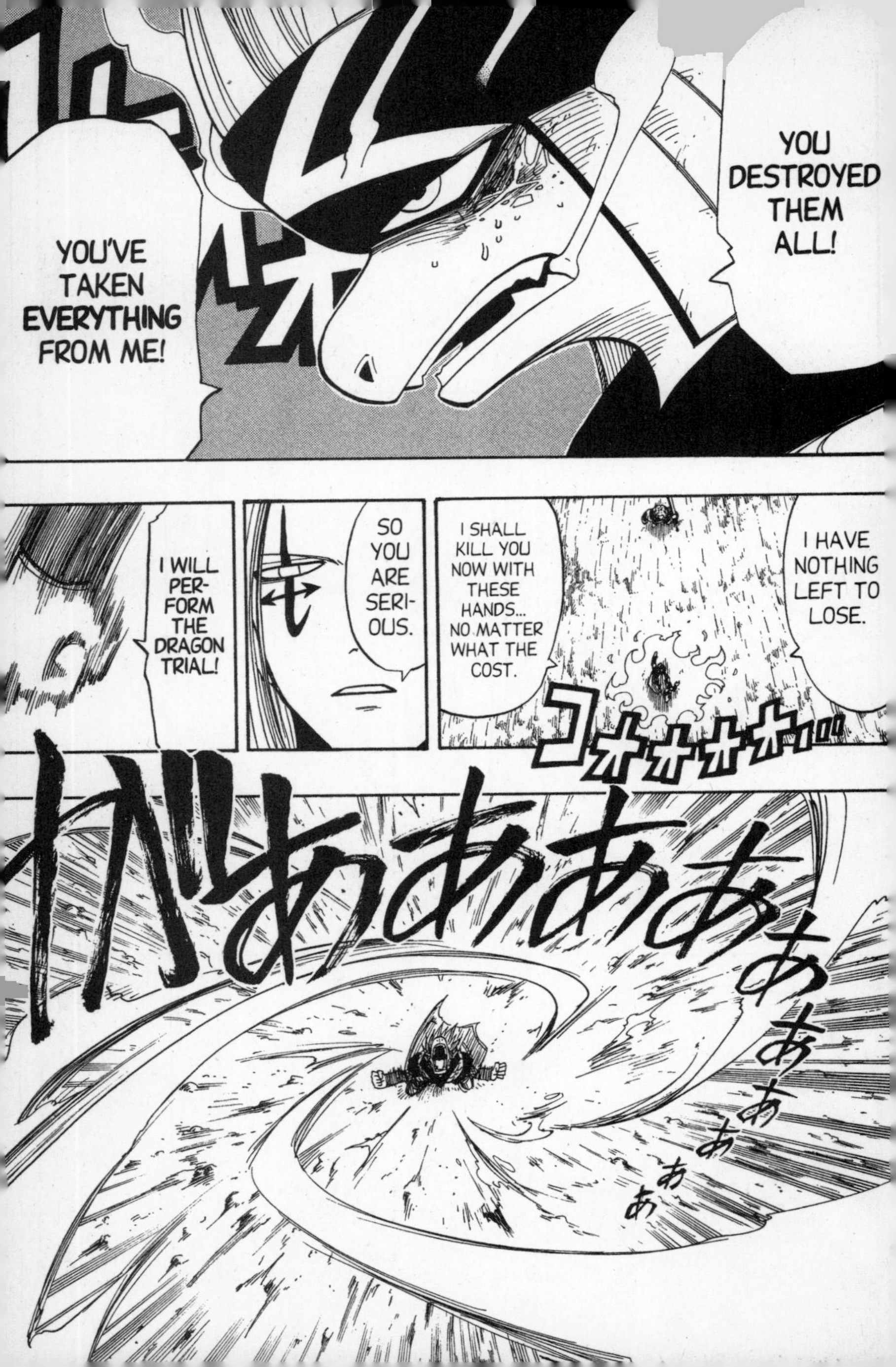
YOU DESTROYED THEM ALL!
YOU'VE TAKEN EVERYTHING FROM ME!
I HAVE NOTHING LEFT TO LOSE.
I SHALL KILL YOU NOW WITH THESE HANDS... NO MATTER WHAT THE COST.
コオオオオ
SO YOU ARE SERI-OUS.
I WILL PER-FORM THE DRAGON TRIAL!

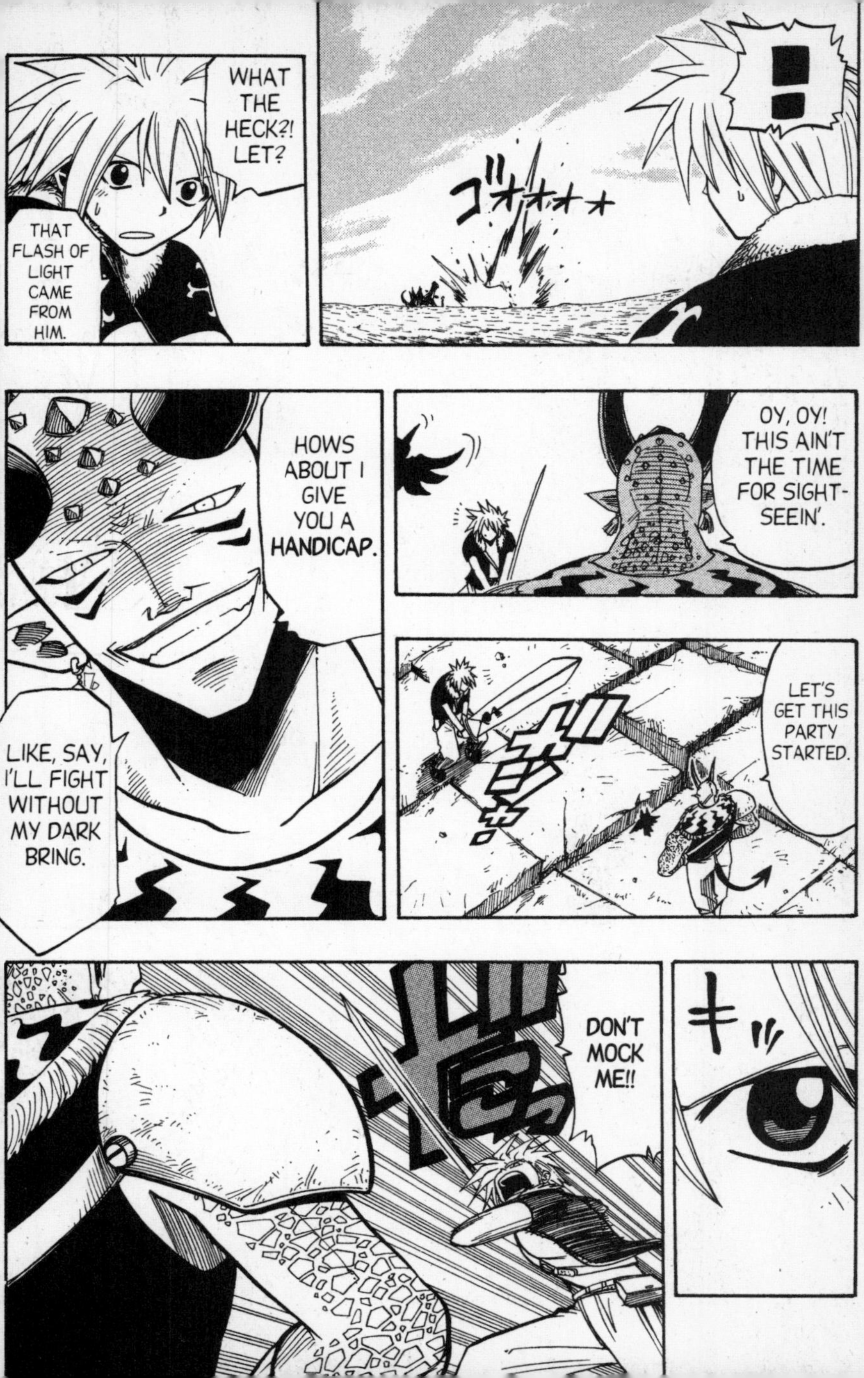
!
WHAT THE HECK?! LET?
THAT FLASH OF LIGHT CAME FROM HIM.
OY, OY! THIS AIN'T THE TIME FOR SIGHT-SEEIN'.
LET'S GET THIS PARTY STARTED.
HOWS ABOUT I GIVE YOU A **HANDICAP**.
LIKE, SAY, I'LL FIGHT WITHOUT MY DARK BRING.
キッ
DON'T MOCK ME!!

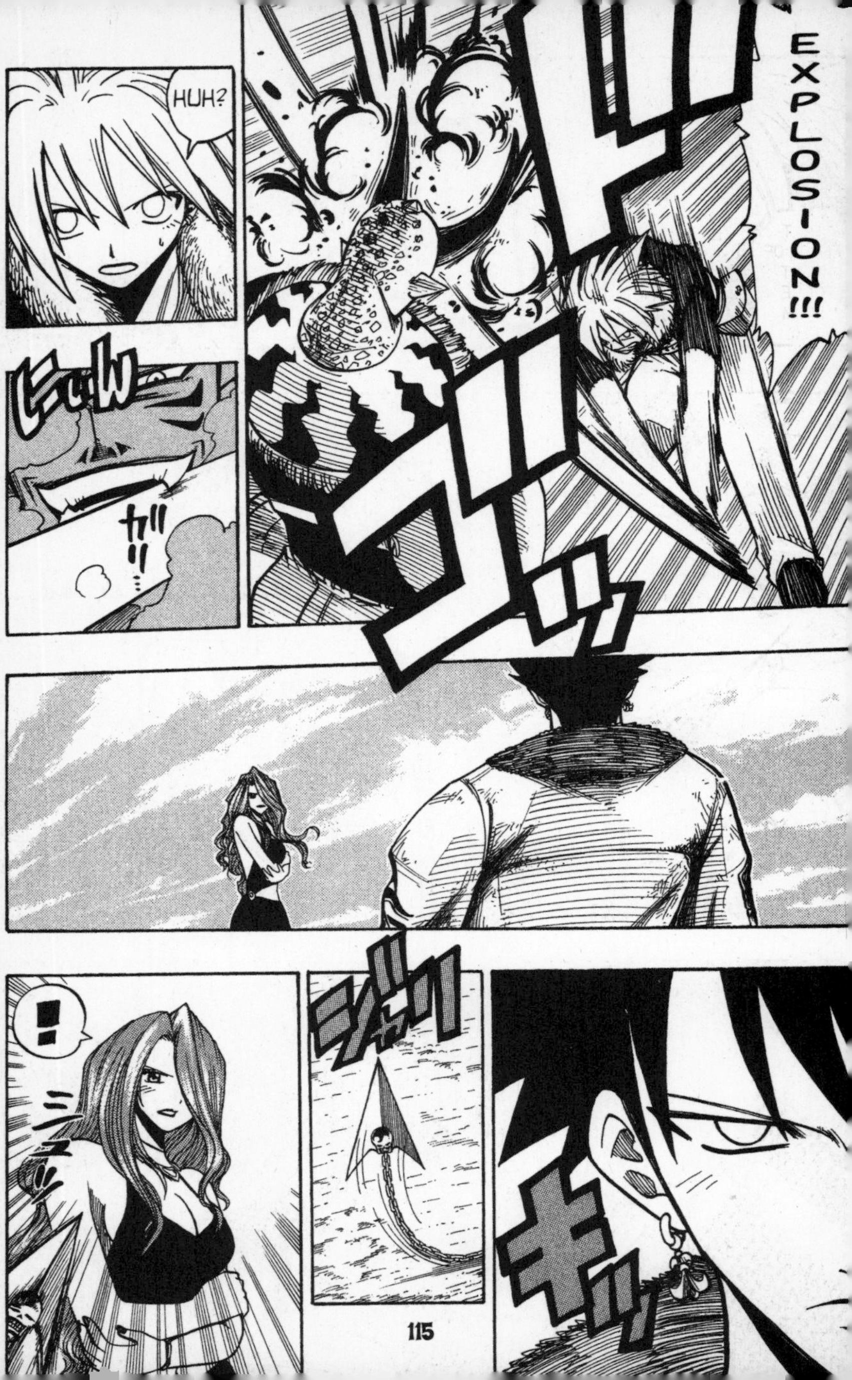
EXPLOSION!!!
HUH?
!!

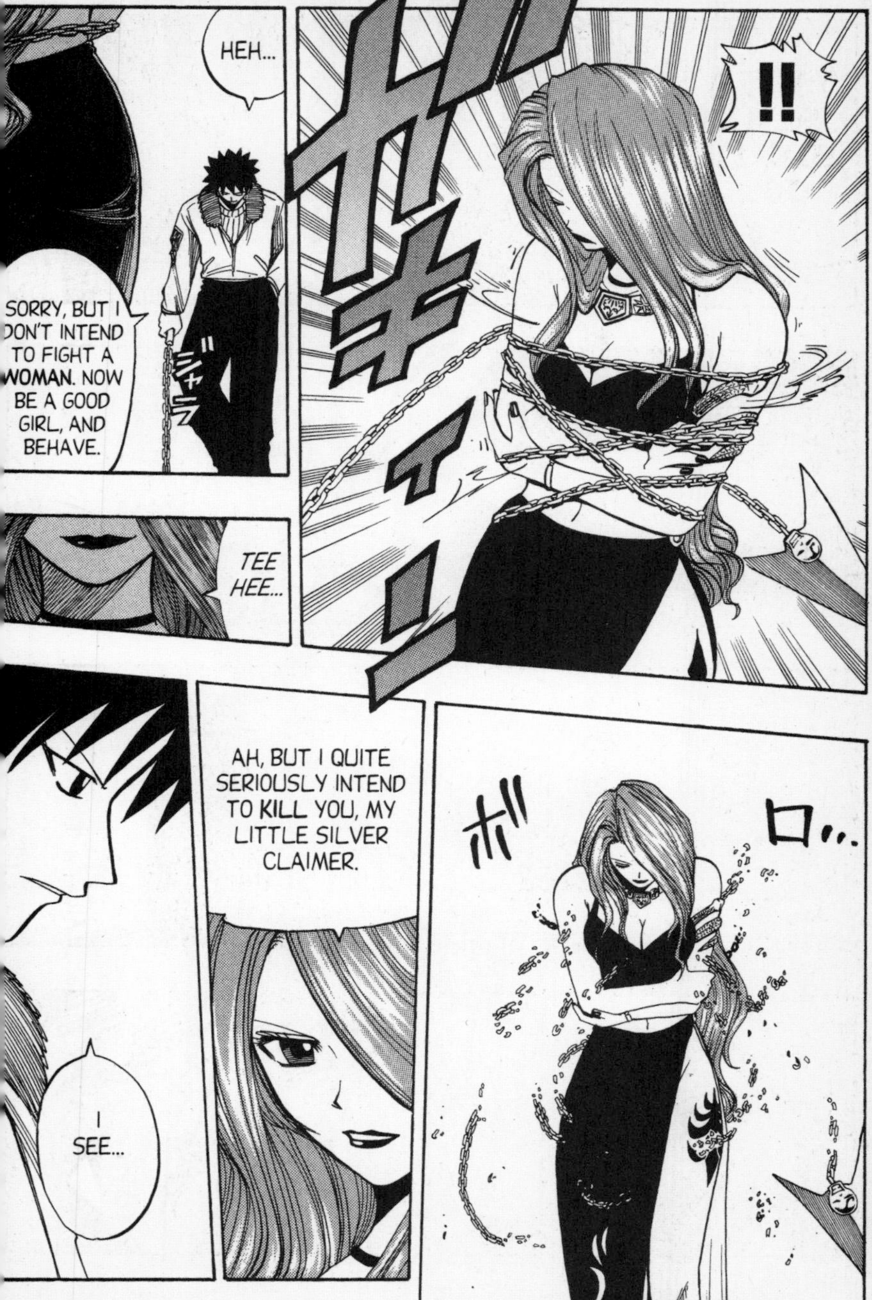
ガキィーン
!!
HEH...
SORRY, BUT I DON'T INTEND TO FIGHT A **WOMAN**. NOW BE A GOOD GIRL, AND BEHAVE.
ジャラ
TEE HEE...
ボロ...
AH, BUT I QUITE SERIOUSLY INTEND TO **KILL** YOU, MY LITTLE SILVER CLAIMER.
I SEE...

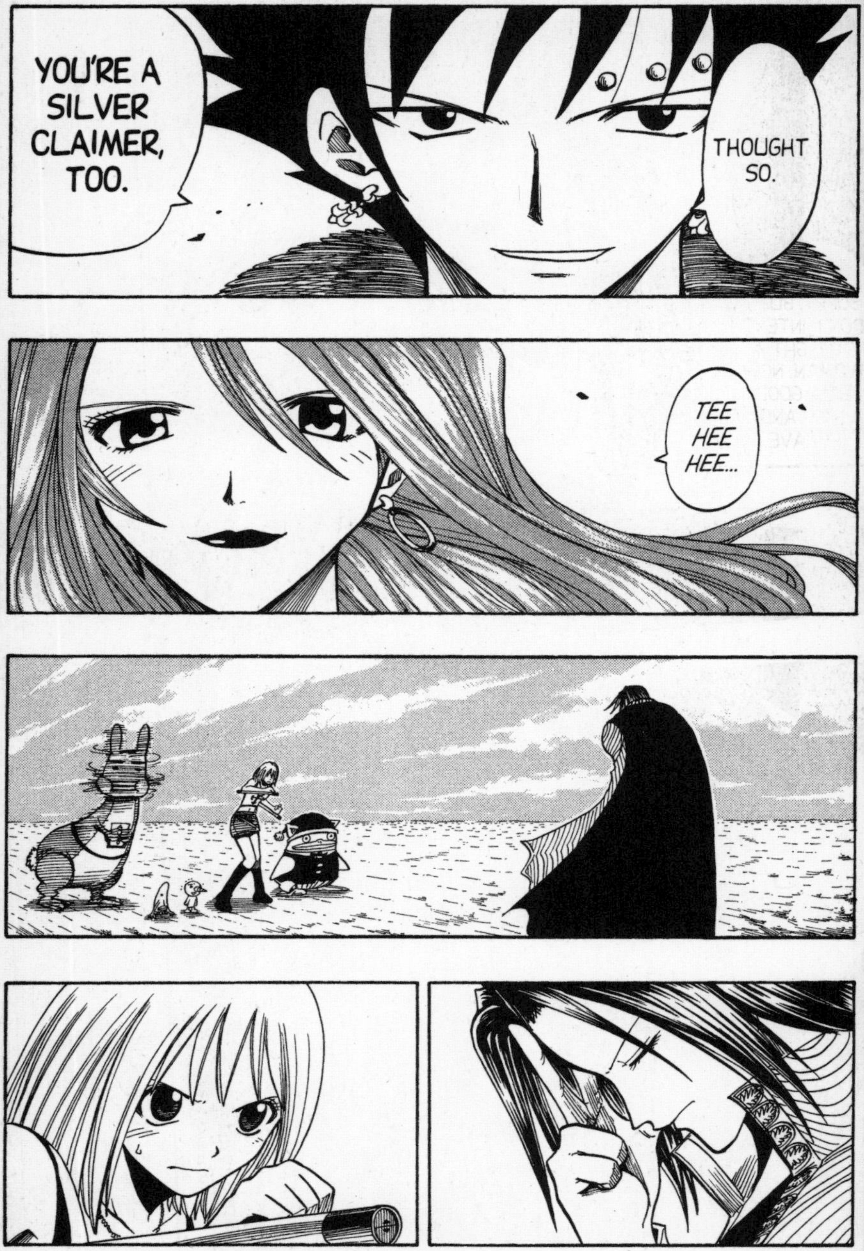
THOUGHT SO.
YOU'RE A SILVER CLAIMER, TOO.
TEE HEE HEE...

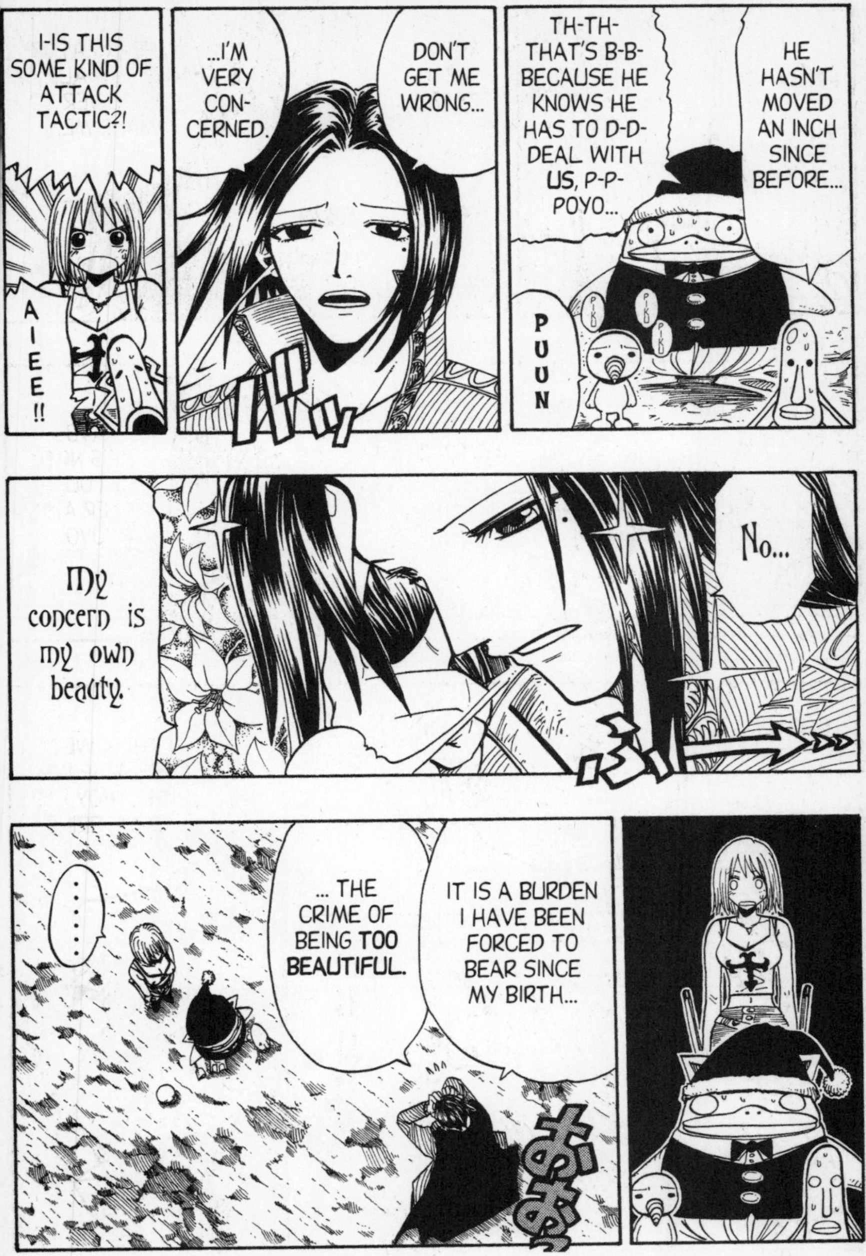
HE HASN'T MOVED AN INCH SINCE BEFORE...
TH-TH-THAT'S B-B-BECAUSE HE KNOWS HE HAS TO D-D-DEAL WITH US, P-P-POYO...
PIKU
PIKU
PIKU
PUUN
DON'T GET ME WRONG...
...I'M VERY CON-CERNED.
I-IS THIS SOME KIND OF ATTACK TACTIC?!
AIEE!!
No...
My concern is my own beauty.
IT IS A BURDEN I HAVE BEEN FORCED TO BEAR SINCE MY BIRTH...
... THE CRIME OF BEING TOO BEAUTIFUL.
......

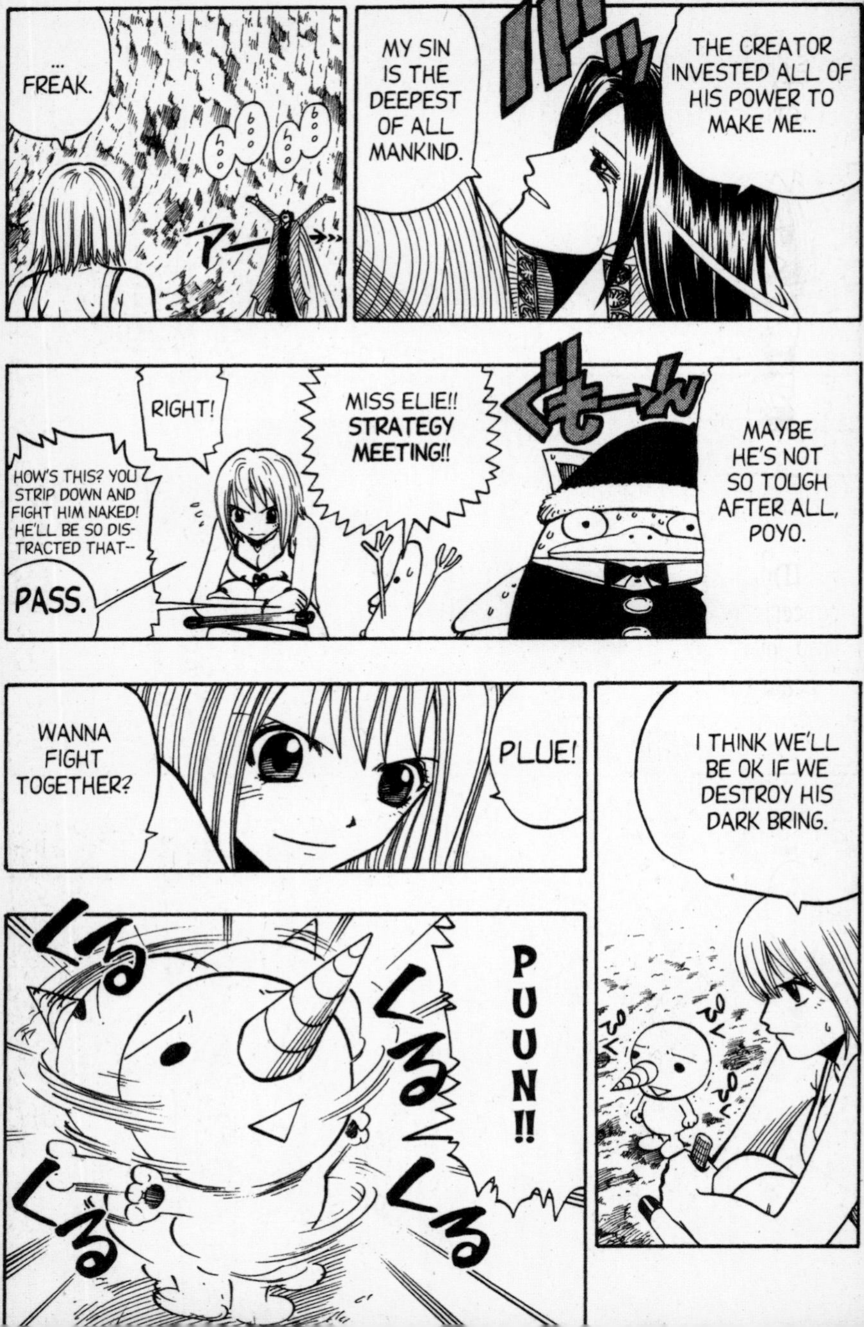

THE CREATOR INVESTED ALL OF HIS POWER TO MAKE ME...
MY SIN IS THE DEEPEST OF ALL MANKIND.
... FREAK.
MAYBE HE'S NOT SO TOUGH AFTER ALL, POYO.
MISS ELIE!! STRATEGY MEETING!!
RIGHT!
HOW'S THIS? YOU STRIP DOWN AND FIGHT HIM NAKED! HE'LL BE SO DIS-TRACTED THAT--
PASS.
I THINK WE'LL BE OK IF WE DESTROY HIS DARK BRING.
PLUE!
WANNA FIGHT TOGETHER?
PUUN!!

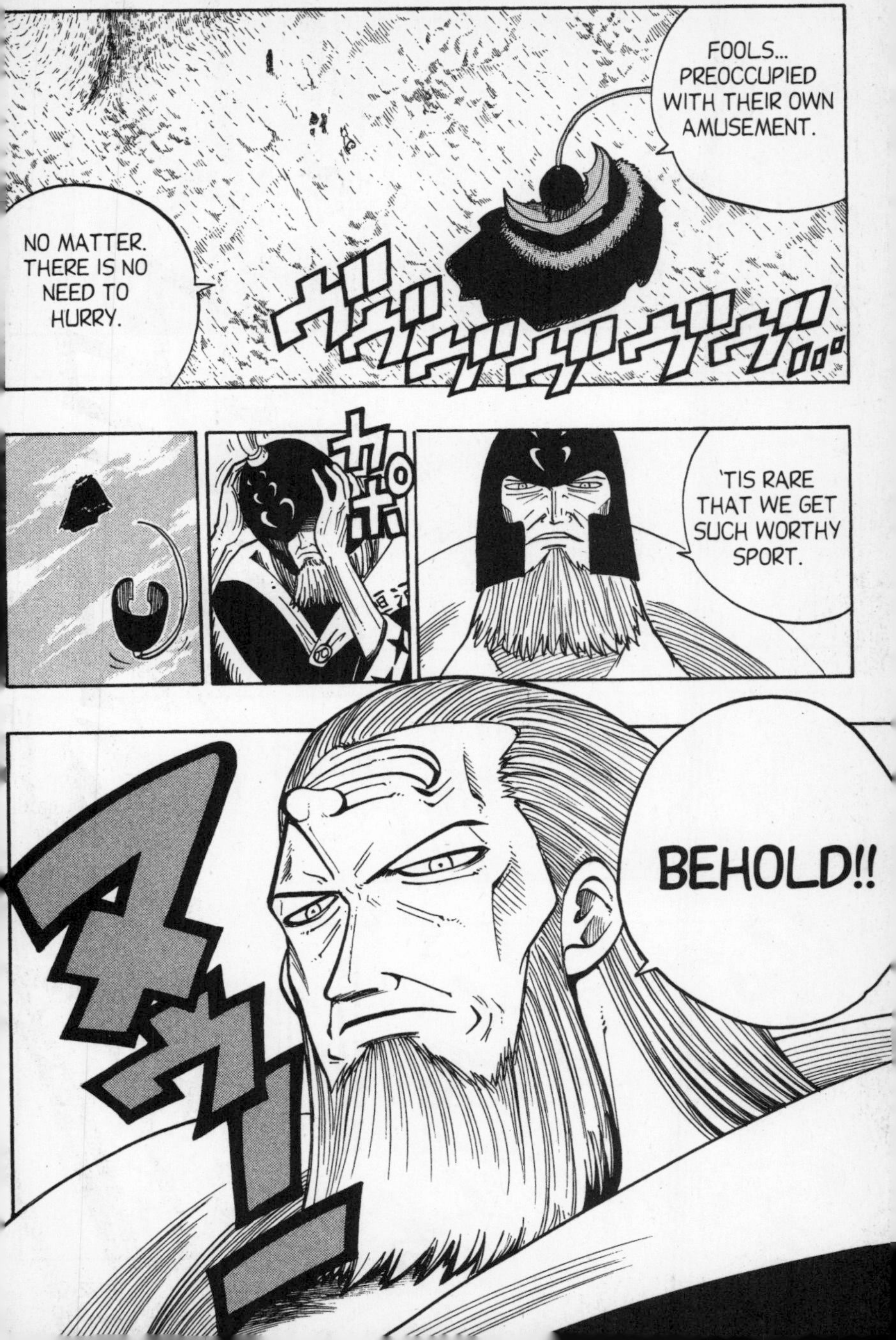
FOOLS... PREOCCUPIED WITH THEIR OWN AMUSEMENT.
NO MATTER. THERE IS NO NEED TO HURRY.
'TIS RARE THAT WE GET SUCH WORTHY SPORT.
BEHOLD!!

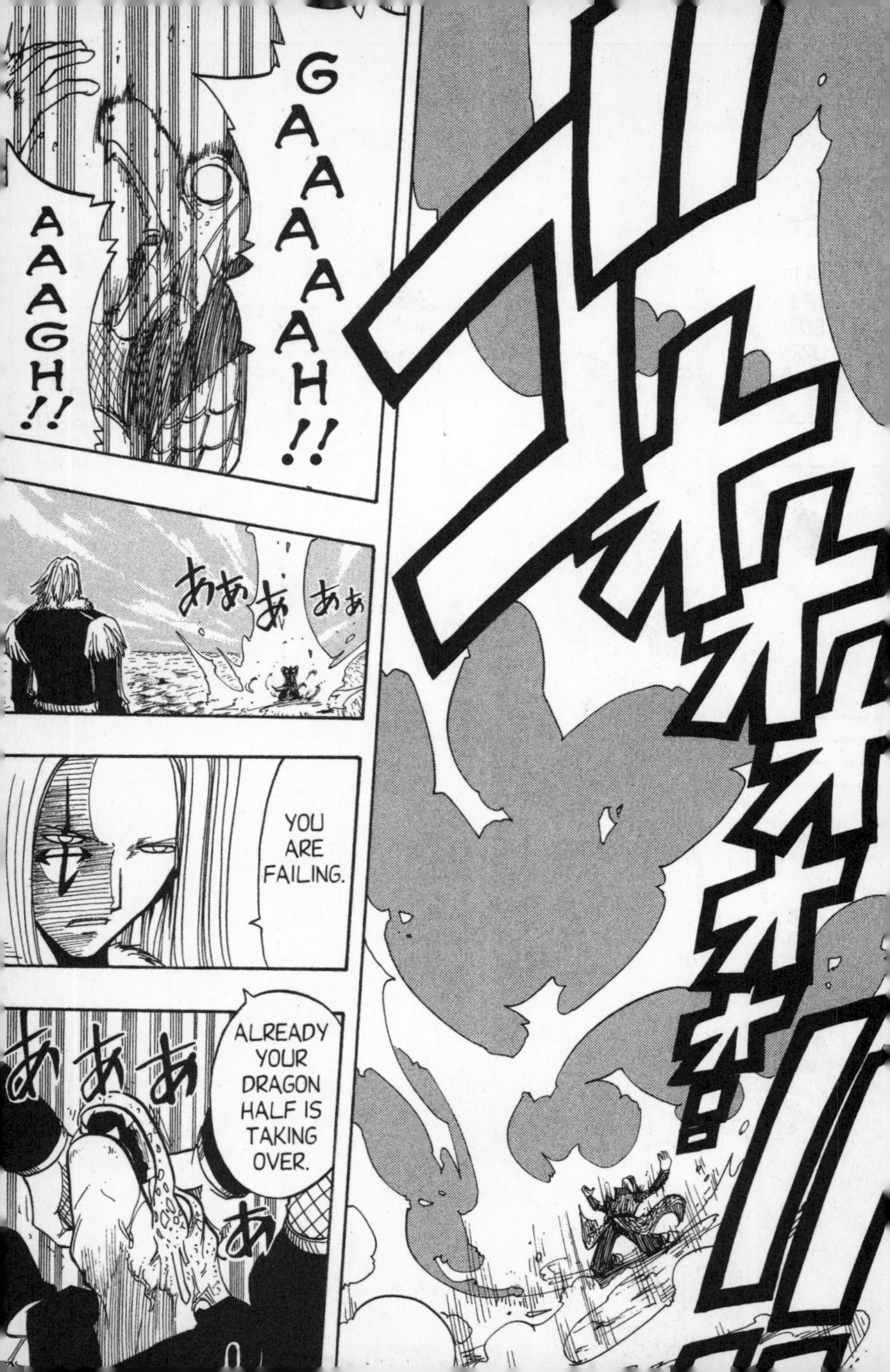
GAAAAAH!!
AAAAGH!!
ああぁ
あ
あぁ
YOU ARE FAILING.
ALREADY YOUR DRAGON HALF IS TAKING OVER.
あああ
あ

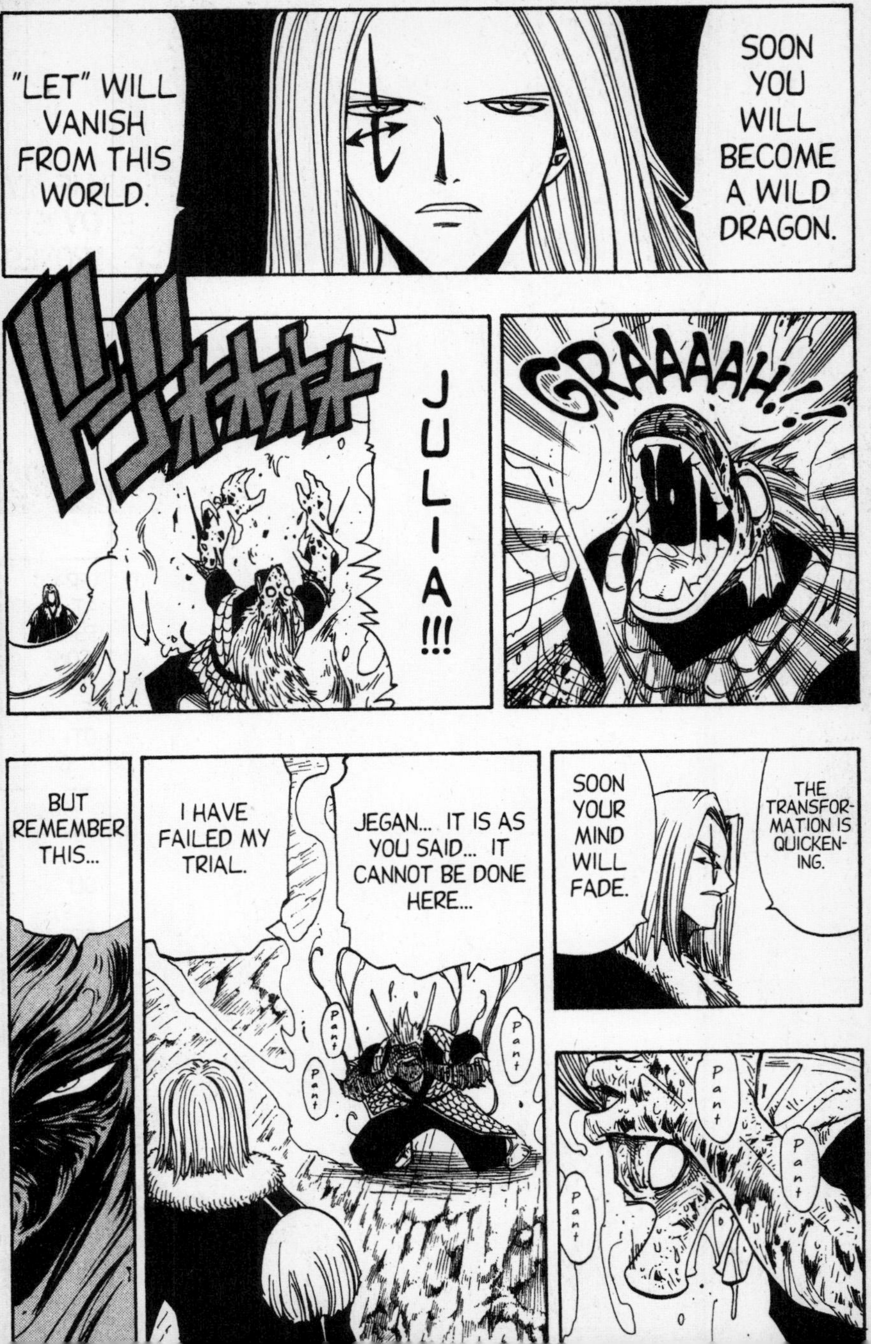
SOON YOU WILL BECOME A WILD DRAGON.
"LET" WILL VANISH FROM THIS WORLD.
GRAAAAH!!
JULIA!!!
ドゴオオオオ
THE TRANSFORMATION IS QUICKENING.
SOON YOUR MIND WILL FADE.
Pant
Pant
Pant
JEGAN... IT IS AS YOU SAID... IT CANNOT BE DONE HERE...
I HAVE FAILED MY TRIAL.
Pant
Pant
Pant
BUT REMEMBER THIS...

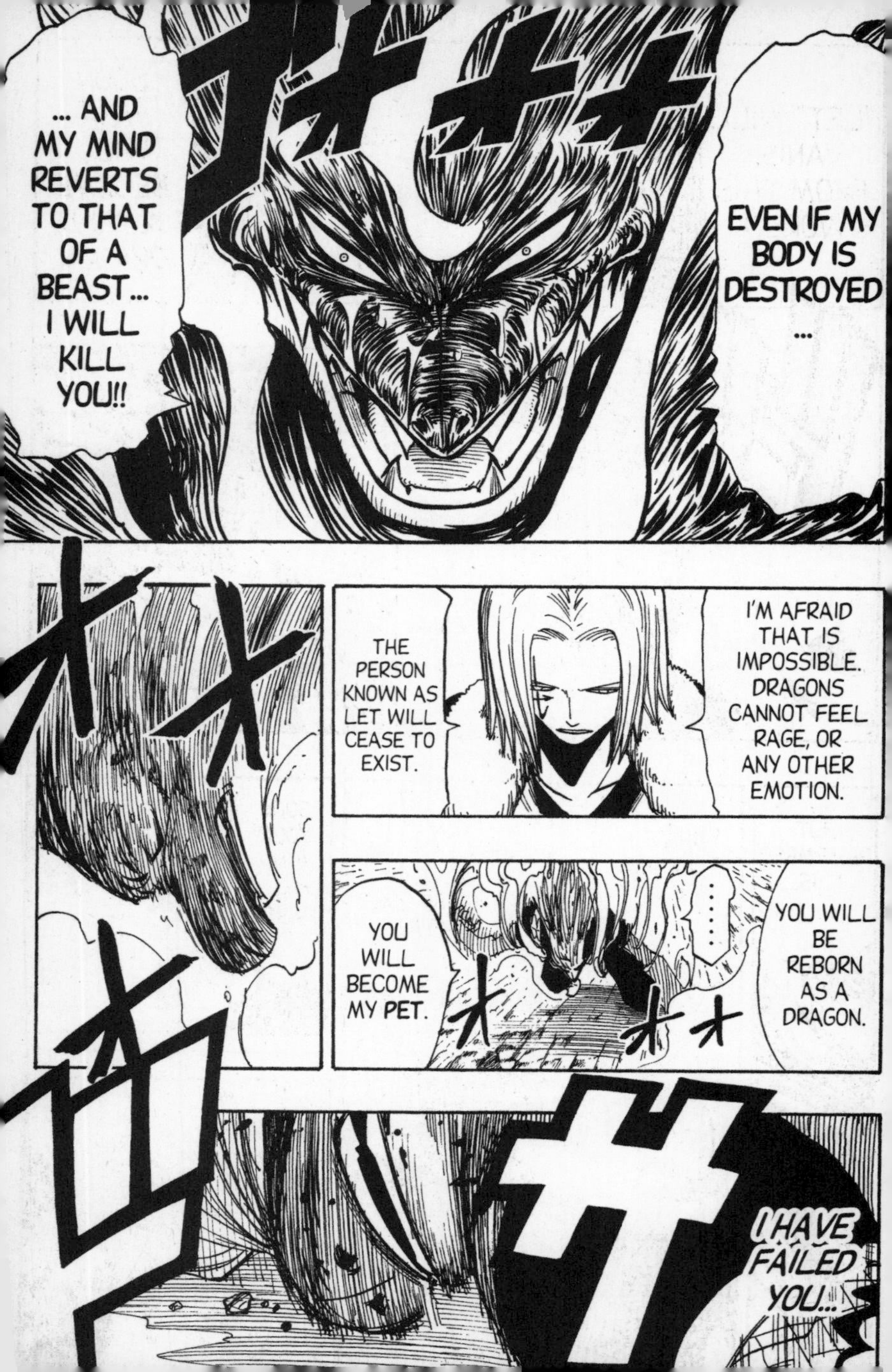
EVEN IF MY BODY IS DESTROYED ...
... AND MY MIND REVERTS TO THAT OF A BEAST... I WILL KILL YOU!!
I'M AFRAID THAT IS IMPOSSIBLE. DRAGONS CANNOT FEEL RAGE, OR ANY OTHER EMOTION.
THE PERSON KNOWN AS LET WILL CEASE TO EXIST.
YOU WILL BE REBORN AS A DRAGON.
......
YOU WILL BECOME MY PET.
I HAVE FAILED YOU...

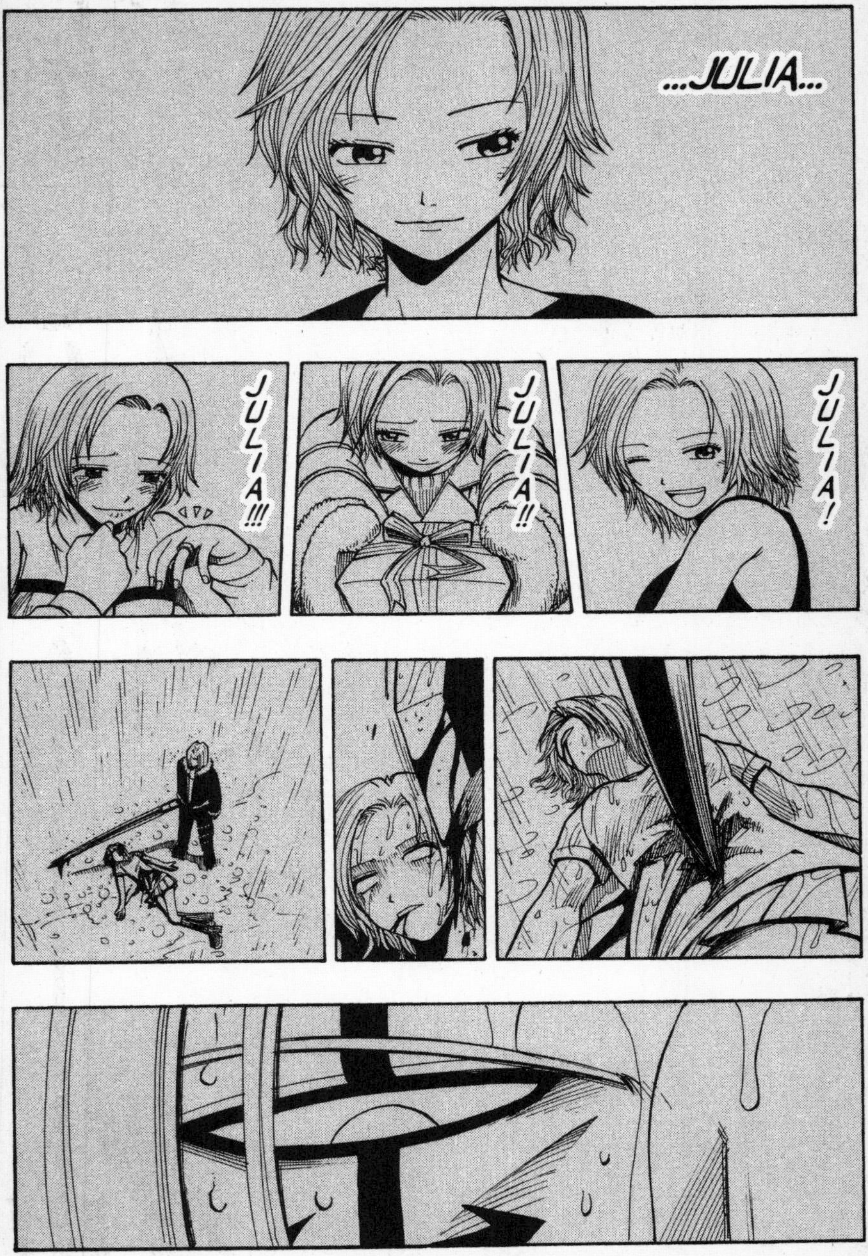
...JULIA...
JULIA!
JULIA!!
JULIA!!!

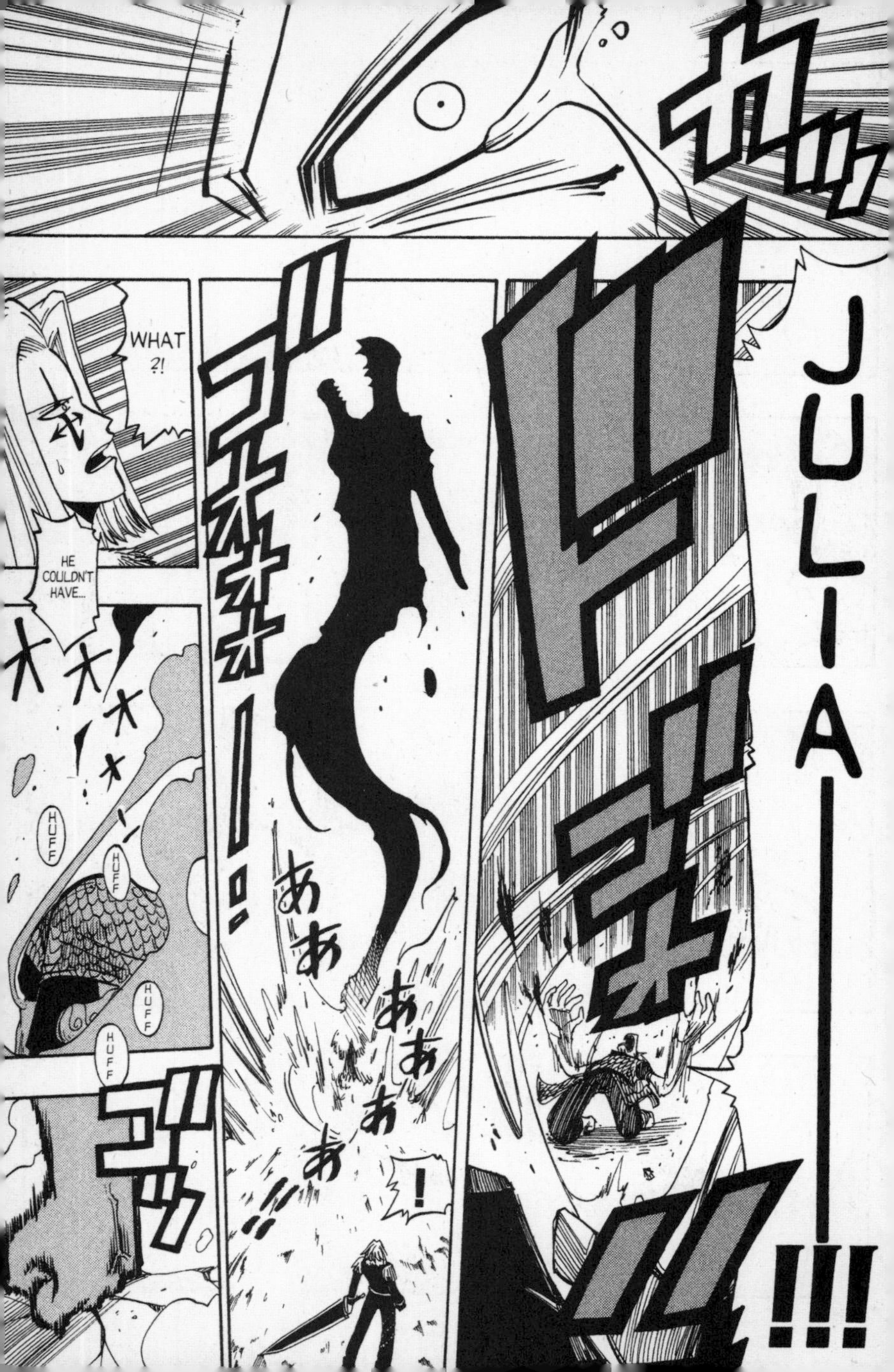
JULIA—!!!
ああああ!!
!
WHAT?!
HE COULDN'T HAVE...
HUFF
HUFF
HUFF
HUFF

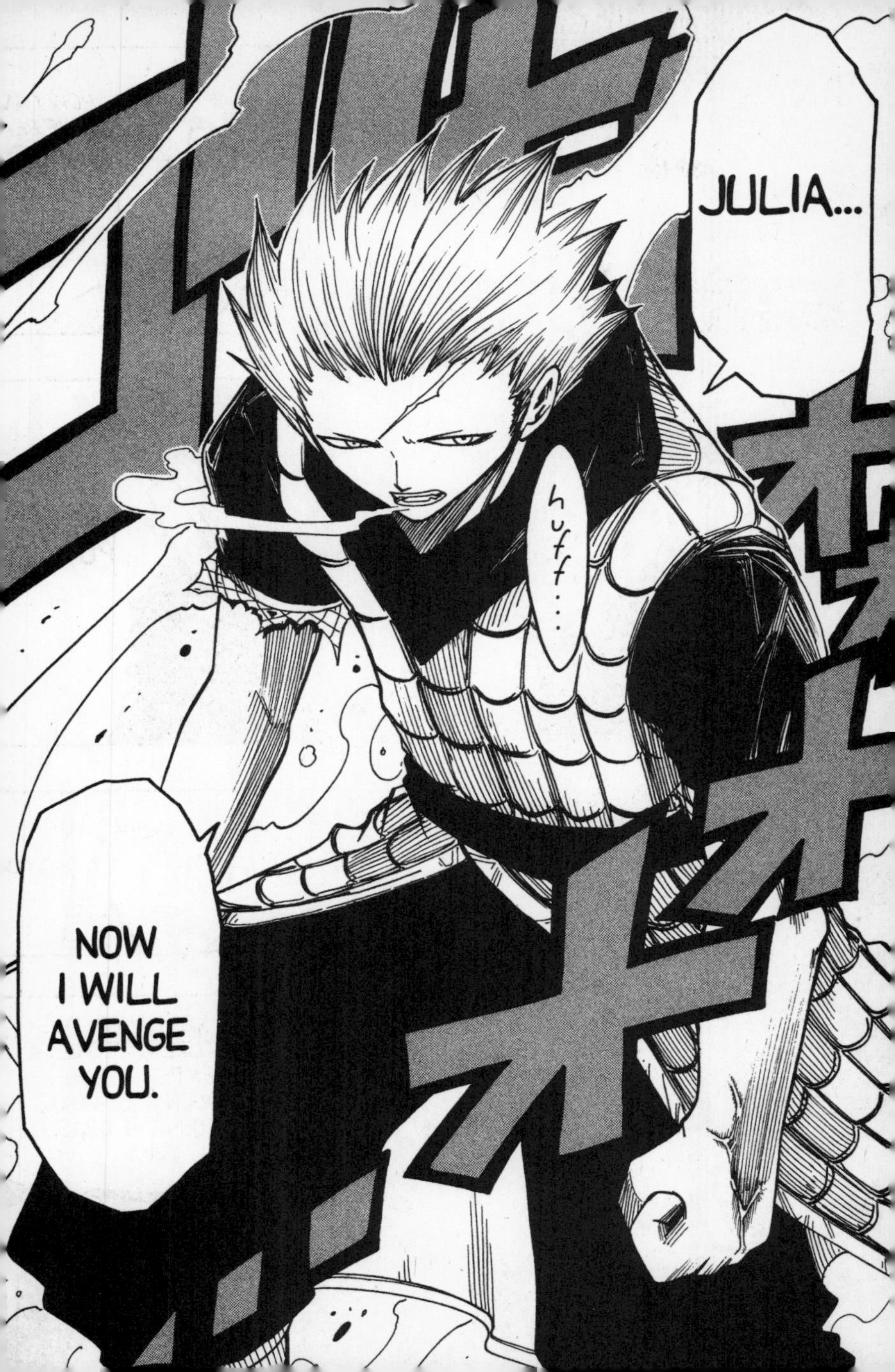
JULIA...
huff...
NOW I WILL AVENGE YOU.

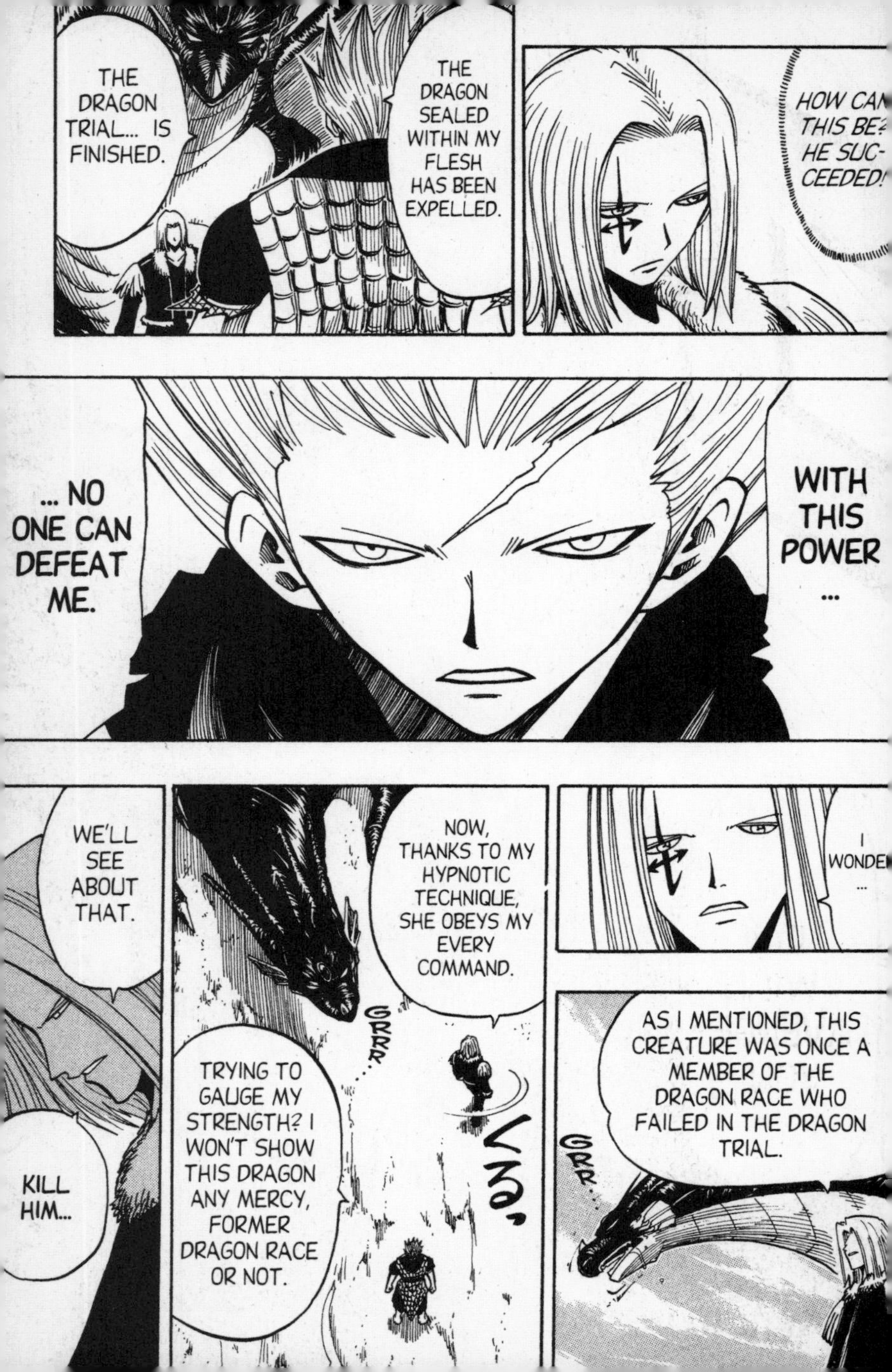
HOW CAN THIS BE?! HE SUC-CEEDED!
THE DRAGON SEALED WITHIN MY FLESH HAS BEEN EXPELLED.
THE DRAGON TRIAL... IS FINISHED.
WITH THIS POWER ...
... NO ONE CAN DEFEAT ME.
I WONDE ...
AS I MENTIONED, THIS CREATURE WAS ONCE A MEMBER OF THE DRAGON RACE WHO FAILED IN THE DRAGON TRIAL.
GRRR...
NOW, THANKS TO MY HYPNOTIC TECHNIQUE, SHE OBEYS MY EVERY COMMAND.
GRRR...
TRYING TO GAUGE MY STRENGTH? I WON'T SHOW THIS DRAGON ANY MERCY, FORMER DRAGON RACE OR NOT.
くる
WE'LL SEE ABOUT THAT.
KILL HIM...

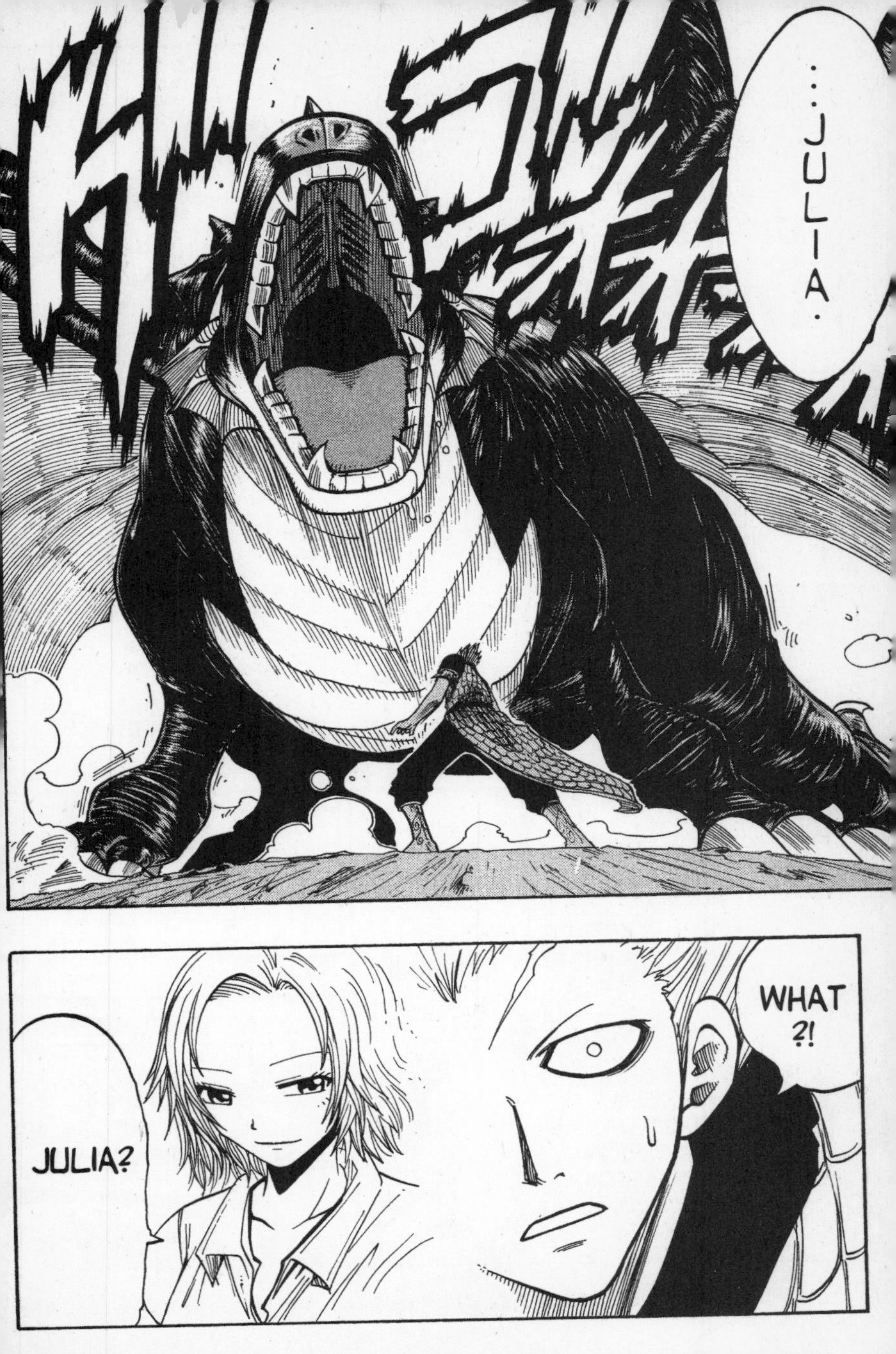
...JULIA.
WHAT ?!
JULIA?

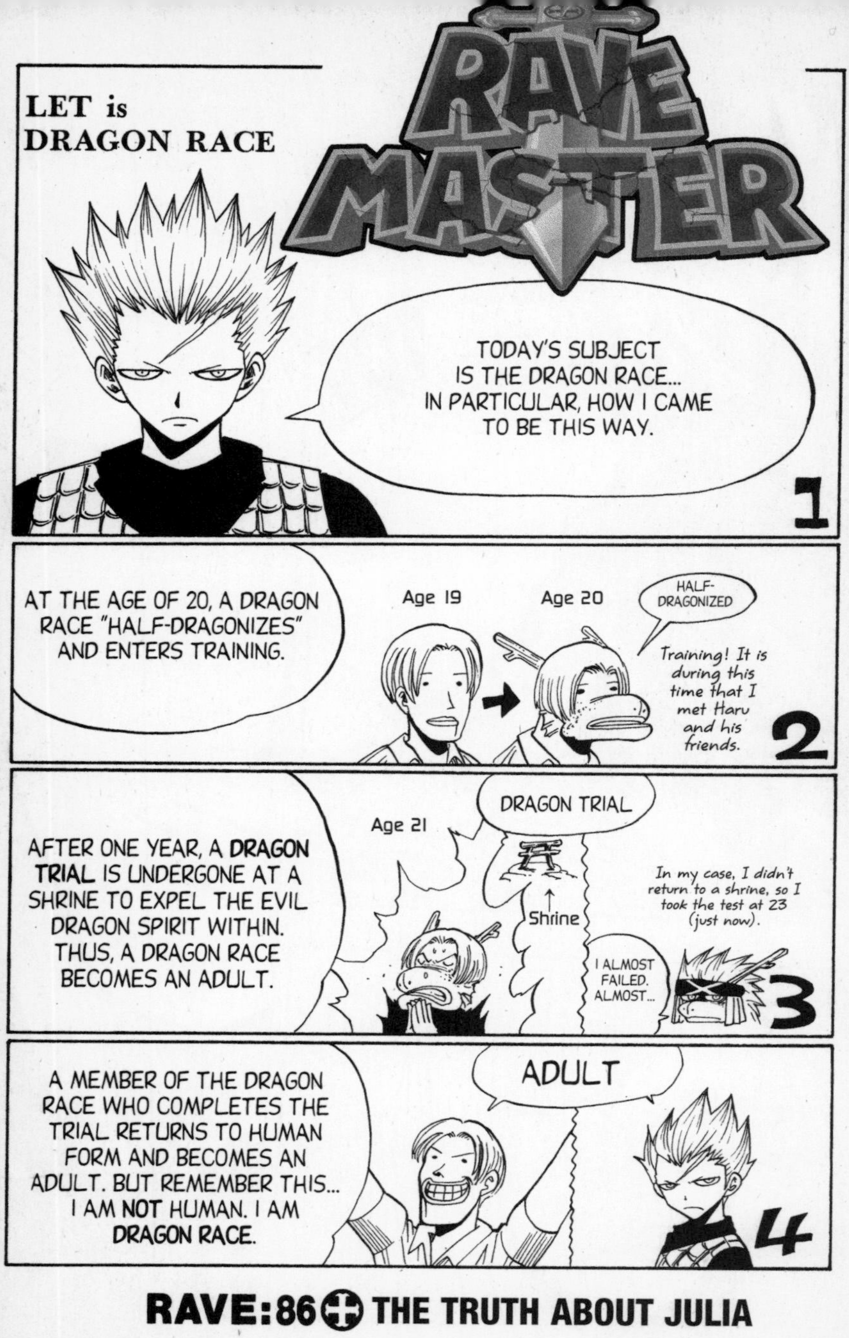
LET is DRAGON RACE
RAVE MASTER
TODAY'S SUBJECT IS THE DRAGON RACE... IN PARTICULAR, HOW I CAME TO BE THIS WAY.
1
HALF-DRAGONIZED
Training! It is during this time that I met Haru and his friends.
Age 20
Age 19
AT THE AGE OF 20, A DRAGON RACE "HALF-DRAGONIZES" AND ENTERS TRAINING.
2
DRAGON TRIAL
Age 21
In my case, I didn't return to a shrine, so I took the test at 23 (just now).
Shrine
I ALMOST FAILED. ALMOST...
AFTER ONE YEAR, A DRAGON TRIAL IS UNDERGONE AT A SHRINE TO EXPEL THE EVIL DRAGON SPIRIT WITHIN. THUS, A DRAGON RACE BECOMES AN ADULT.
3
ADULT
A MEMBER OF THE DRAGON RACE WHO COMPLETES THE TRIAL RETURNS TO HUMAN FORM AND BECOMES AN ADULT. BUT REMEMBER THIS... I AM NOT HUMAN. I AM DRAGON RACE.
4

RAVE:86 ✠ THE TRUTH ABOUT JULIA

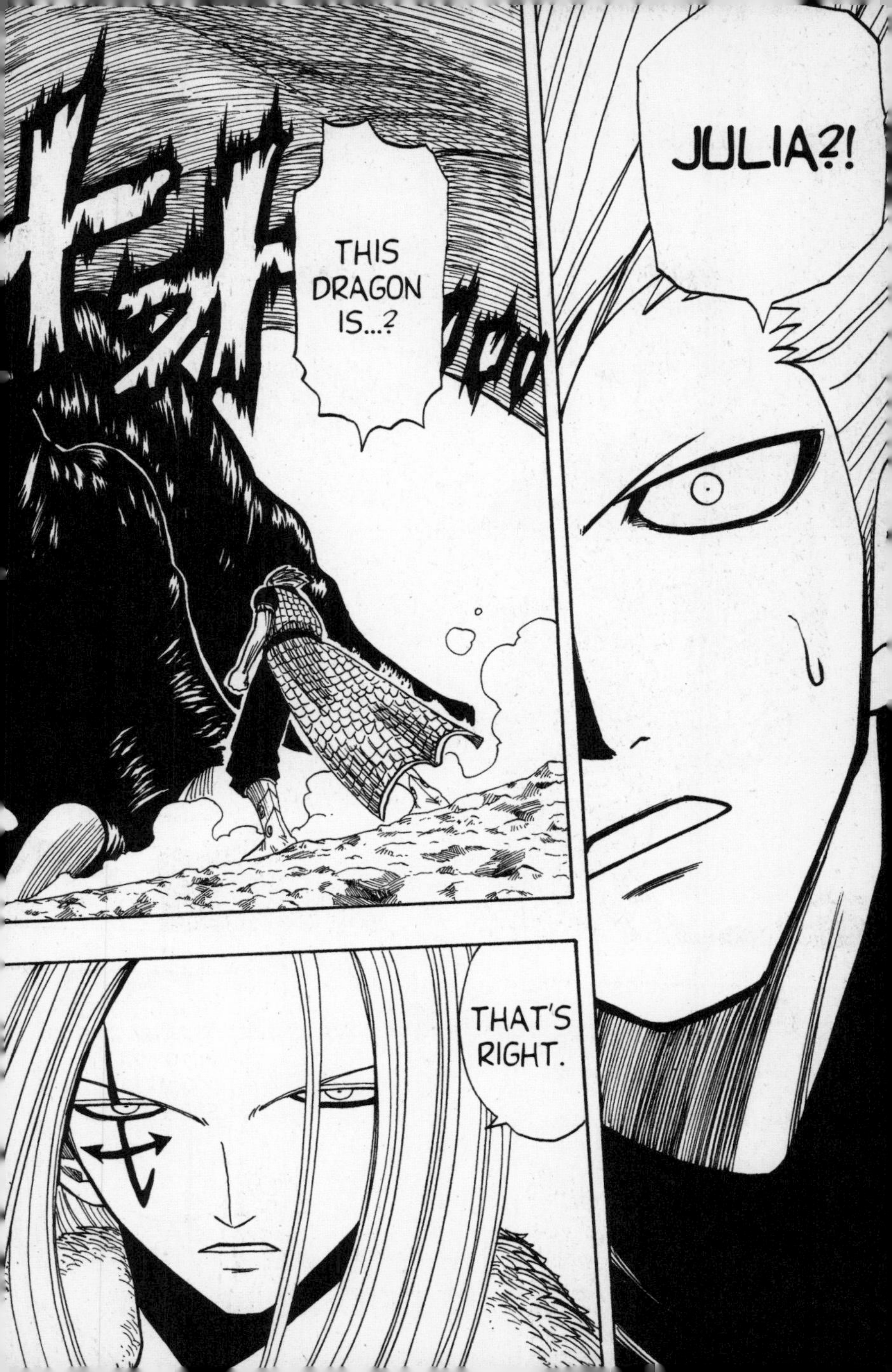
JULIA?!
THIS DRAGON IS...?
THAT'S RIGHT.

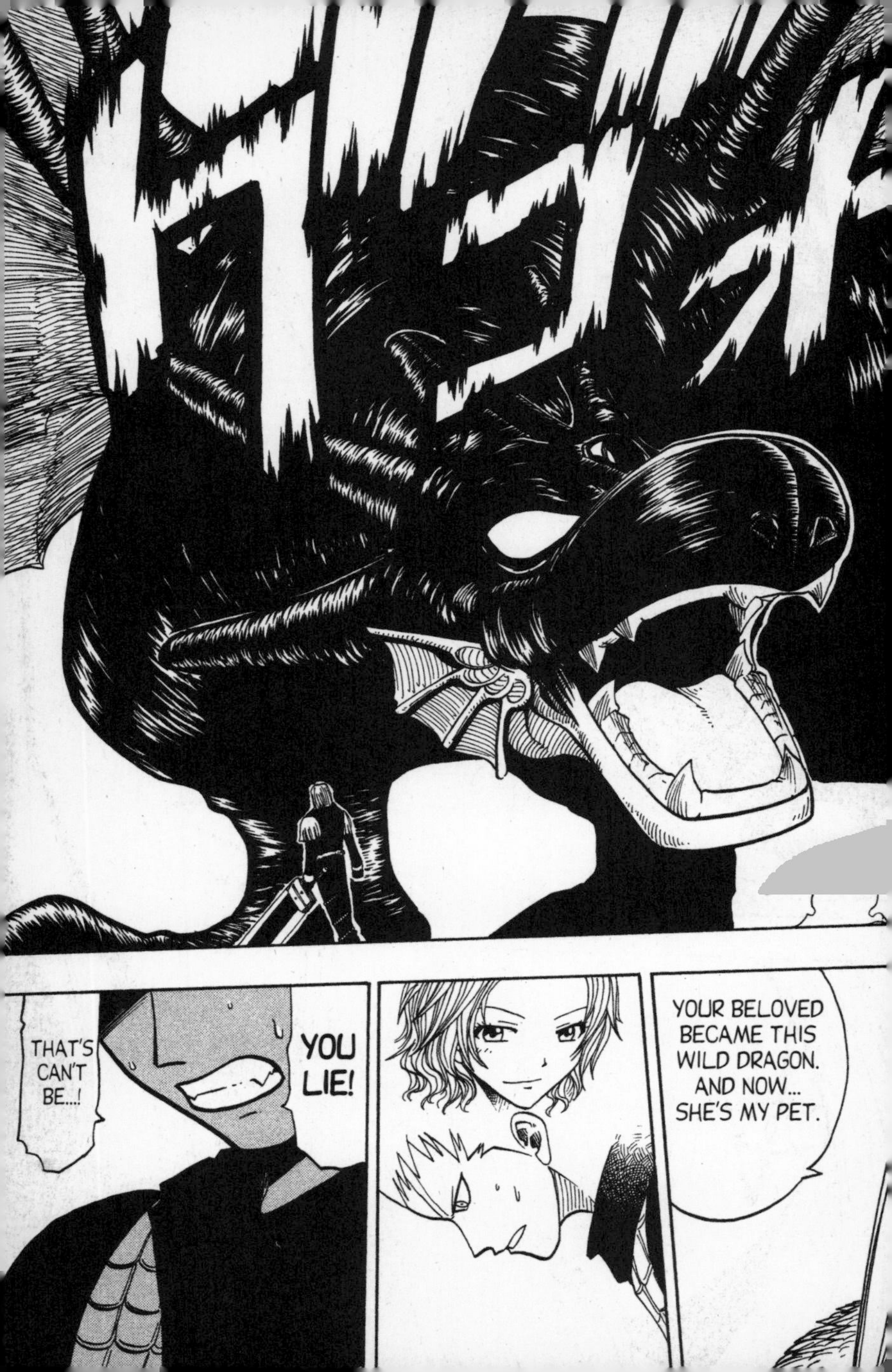
YOUR BELOVED BECAME THIS WILD DRAGON. AND NOW... SHE'S MY PET.
YOU LIE!
THAT'S CAN'T BE...!

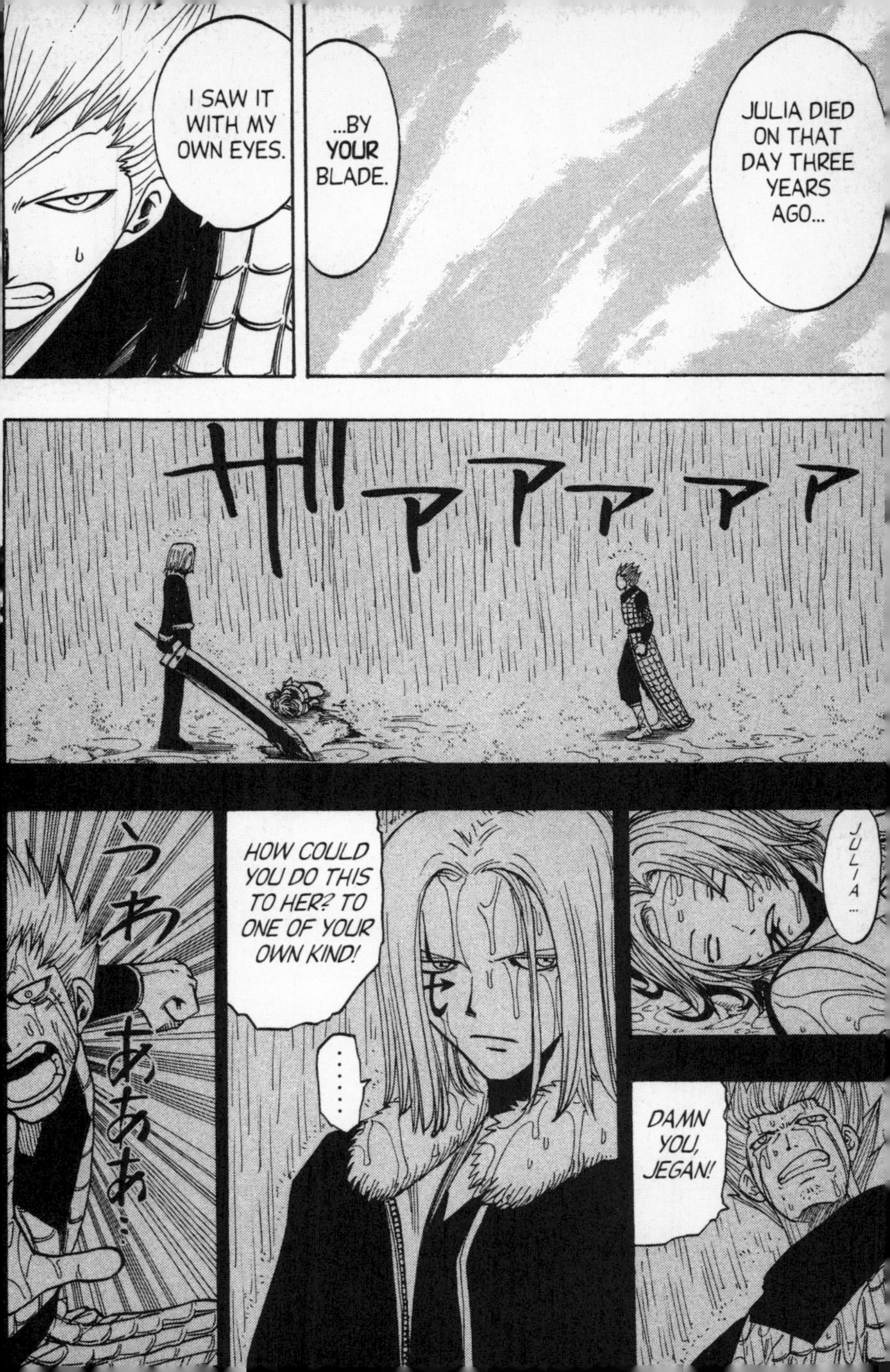
JULIA DIED ON THAT DAY THREE YEARS AGO...
...BY **YOUR** BLADE.
I SAW IT WITH MY OWN EYES.
ザアアアアア
JULIA...
DAMN YOU, JEGAN!
HOW COULD YOU DO THIS TO HER? TO ONE OF YOUR OWN KIND!
......
うああああ...

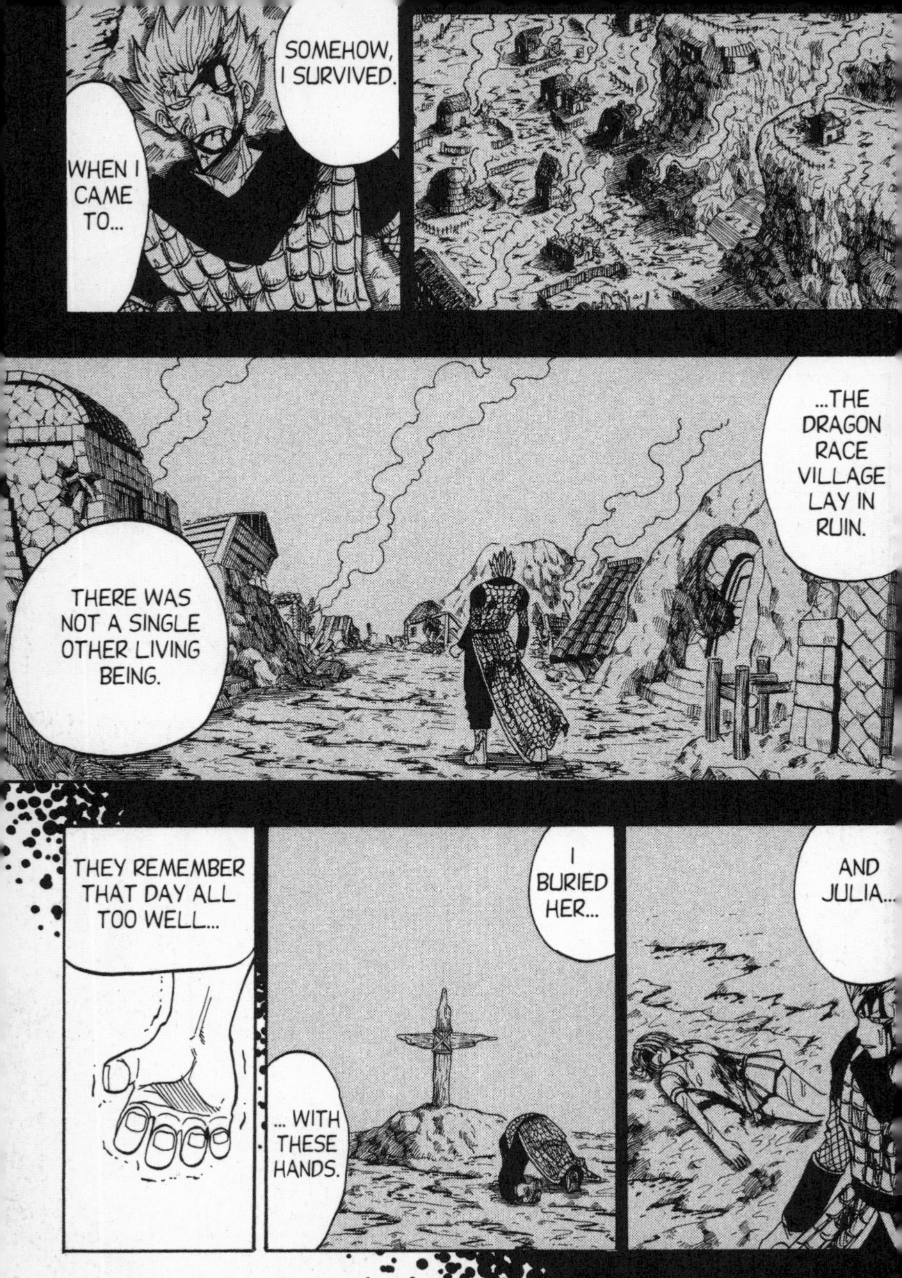
SOMEHOW, I SURVIVED.
WHEN I CAME TO...
...THE DRAGON RACE VILLAGE LAY IN RUIN.
THERE WAS NOT A SINGLE OTHER LIVING BEING.
AND JULIA...
I BURIED HER...
... WITH THESE HANDS.
THEY REMEMBER THAT DAY ALL TOO WELL...

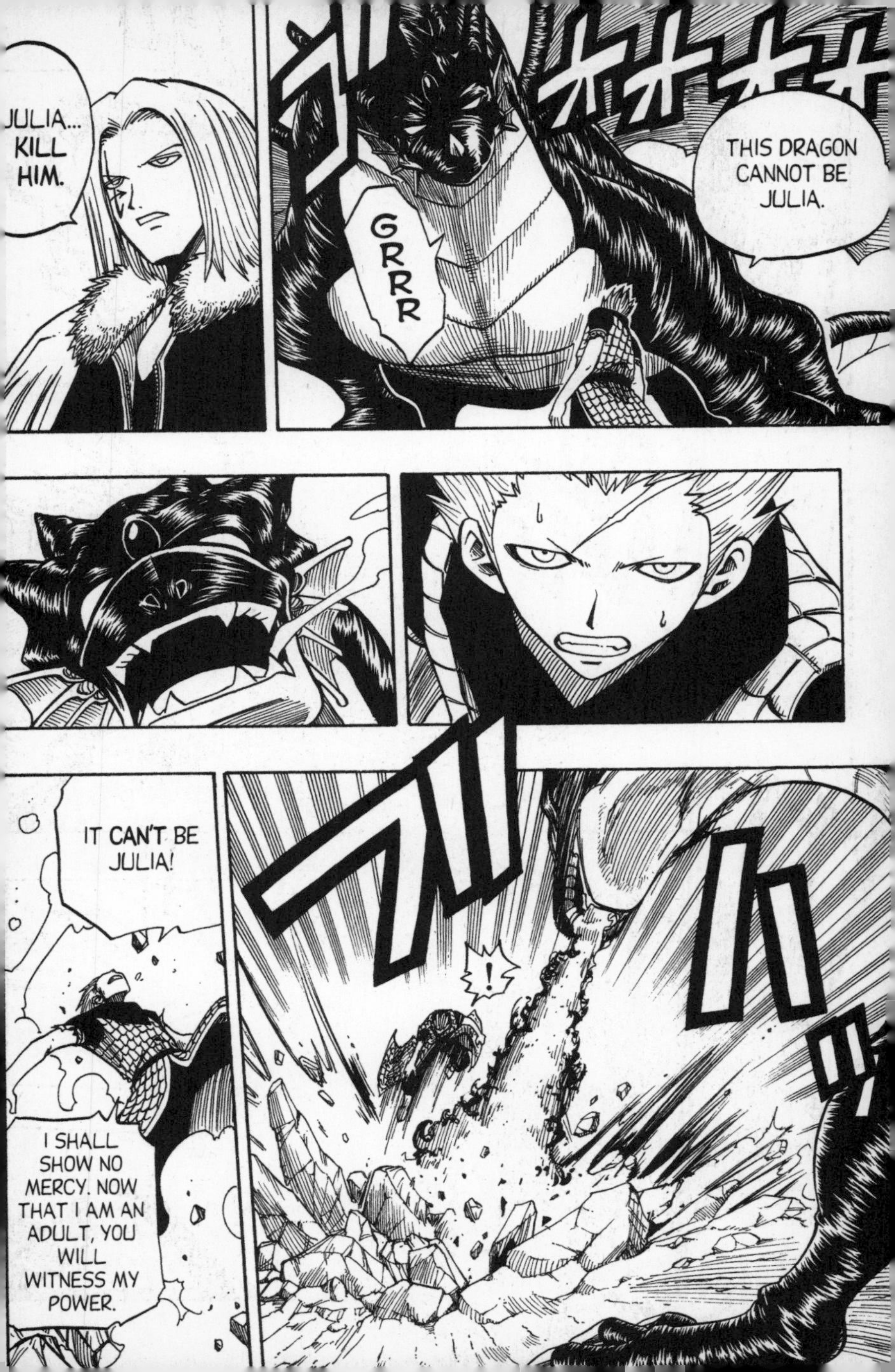
THIS DRAGON CANNOT BE JULIA.
GRRR
JULIA... KILL HIM.
!
IT CAN'T BE JULIA!
I SHALL SHOW NO MERCY. NOW THAT I AM AN ADULT, YOU WILL WITNESS MY POWER.

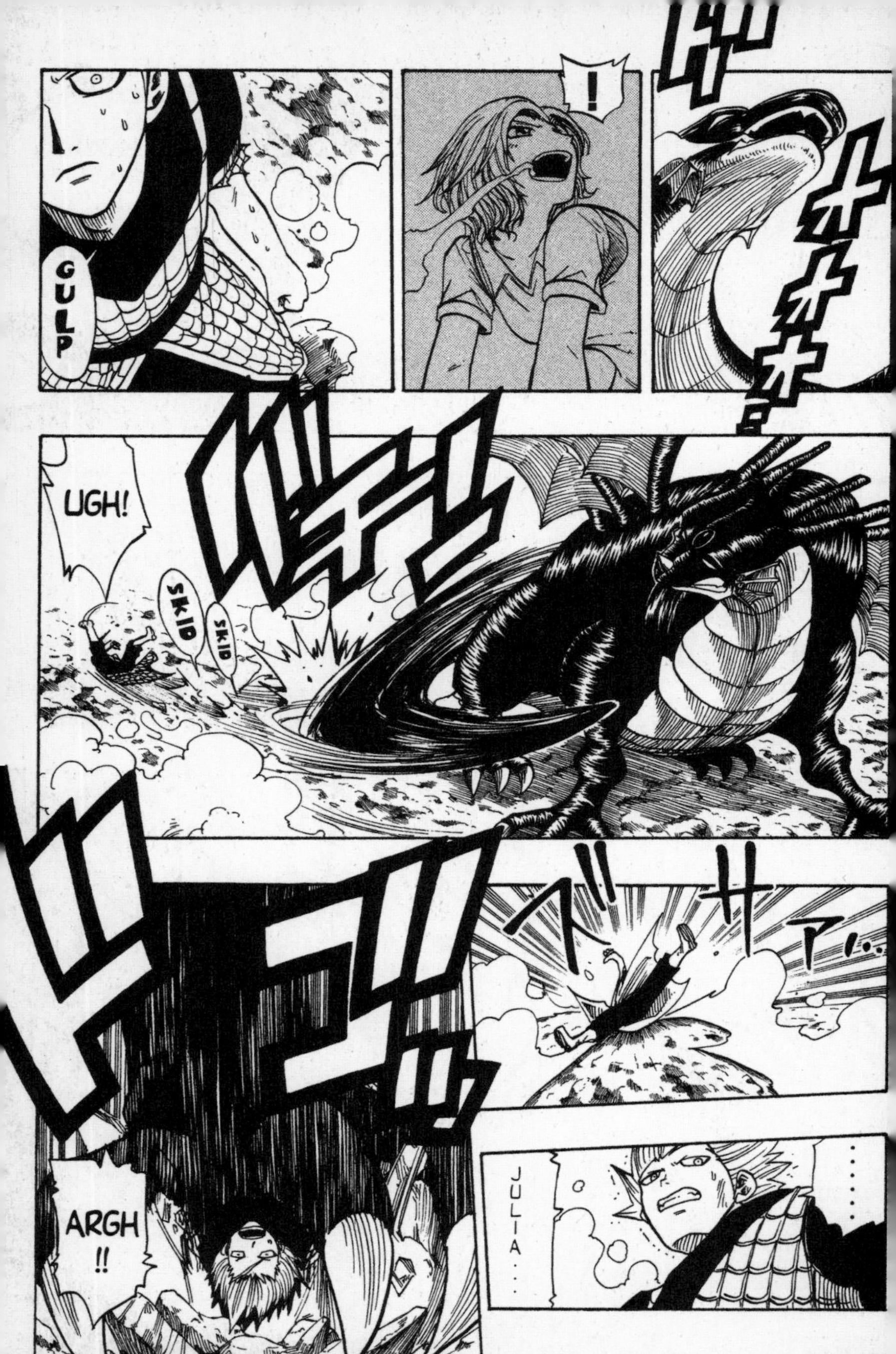
!
GULP
UGH!
SKID
SKID
......
JULIA...
ARGH !!

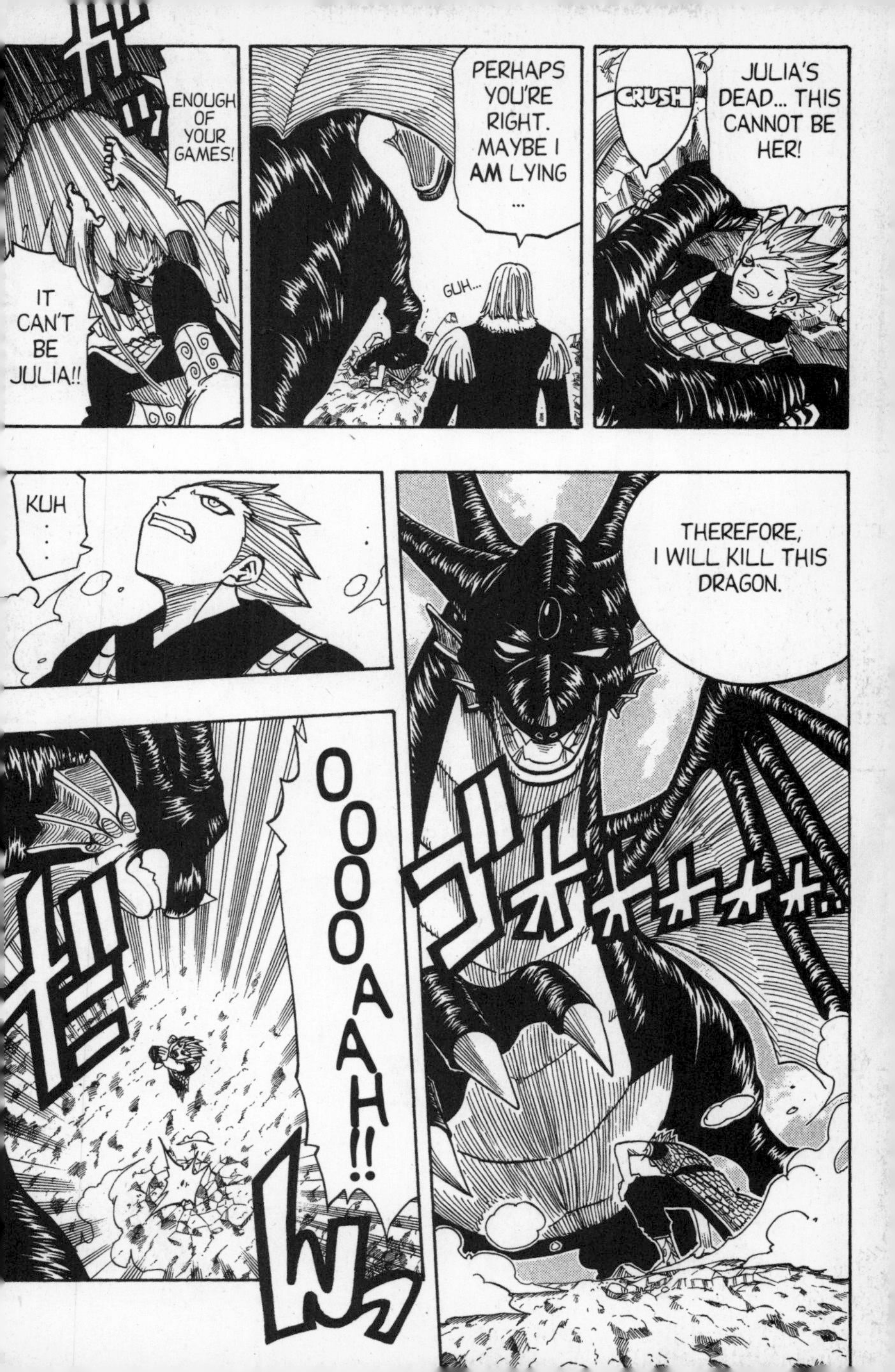
CRUSH
JULIA'S DEAD... THIS CANNOT BE HER!
PERHAPS YOU'RE RIGHT. MAYBE I AM LYING ...
GUH...
ENOUGH OF YOUR GAMES!
IT CAN'T BE JULIA!!
THEREFORE, I WILL KILL THIS DRAGON.
KUH . . .
OOOOAAAH!!

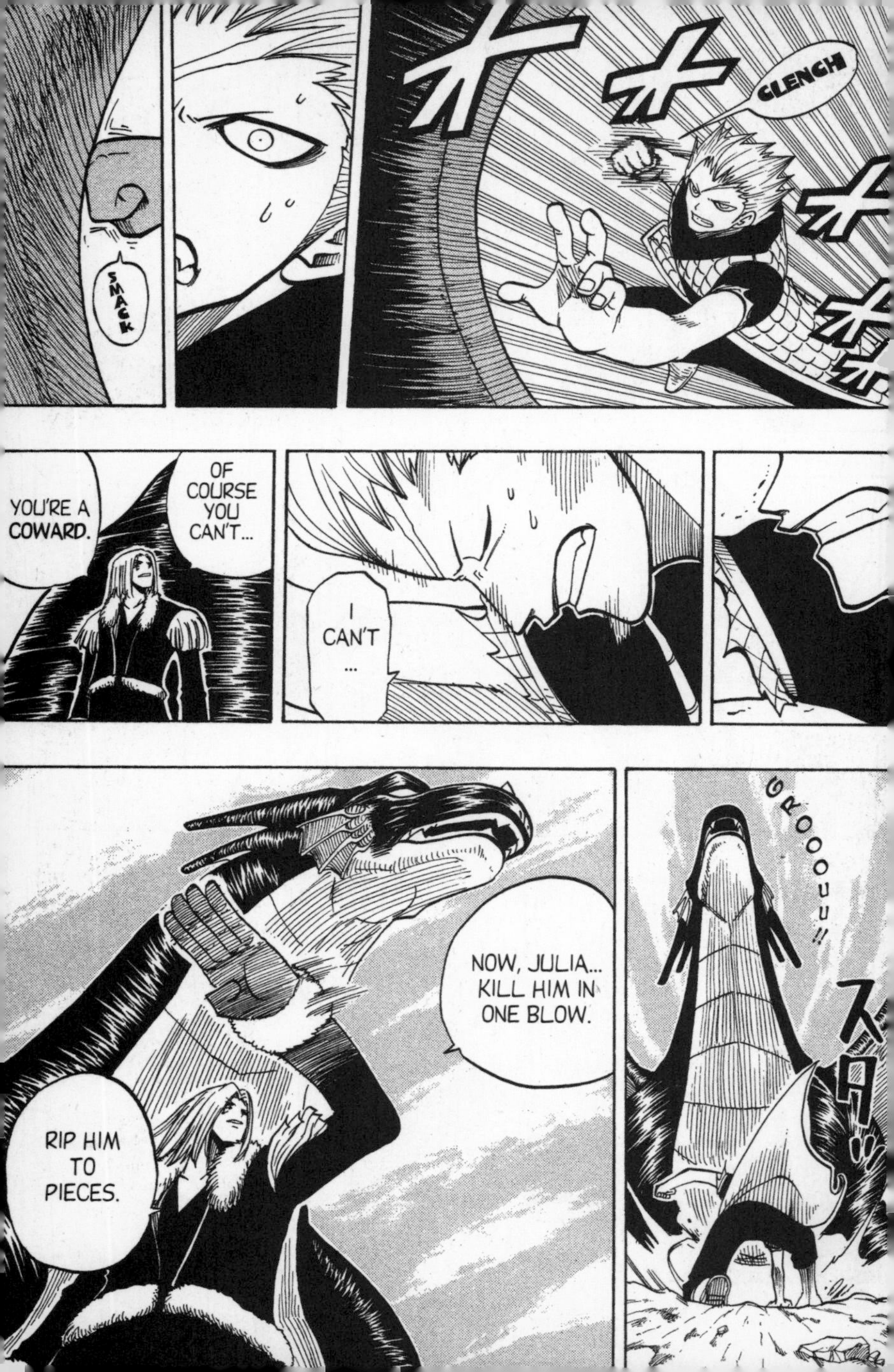
CLENCH
SMACK
I CAN'T ...
OF COURSE YOU CAN'T...
YOU'RE A COWARD.
GROOOUUU!!
NOW, JULIA... KILL HIM IN ONE BLOW.
RIP HIM TO PIECES.

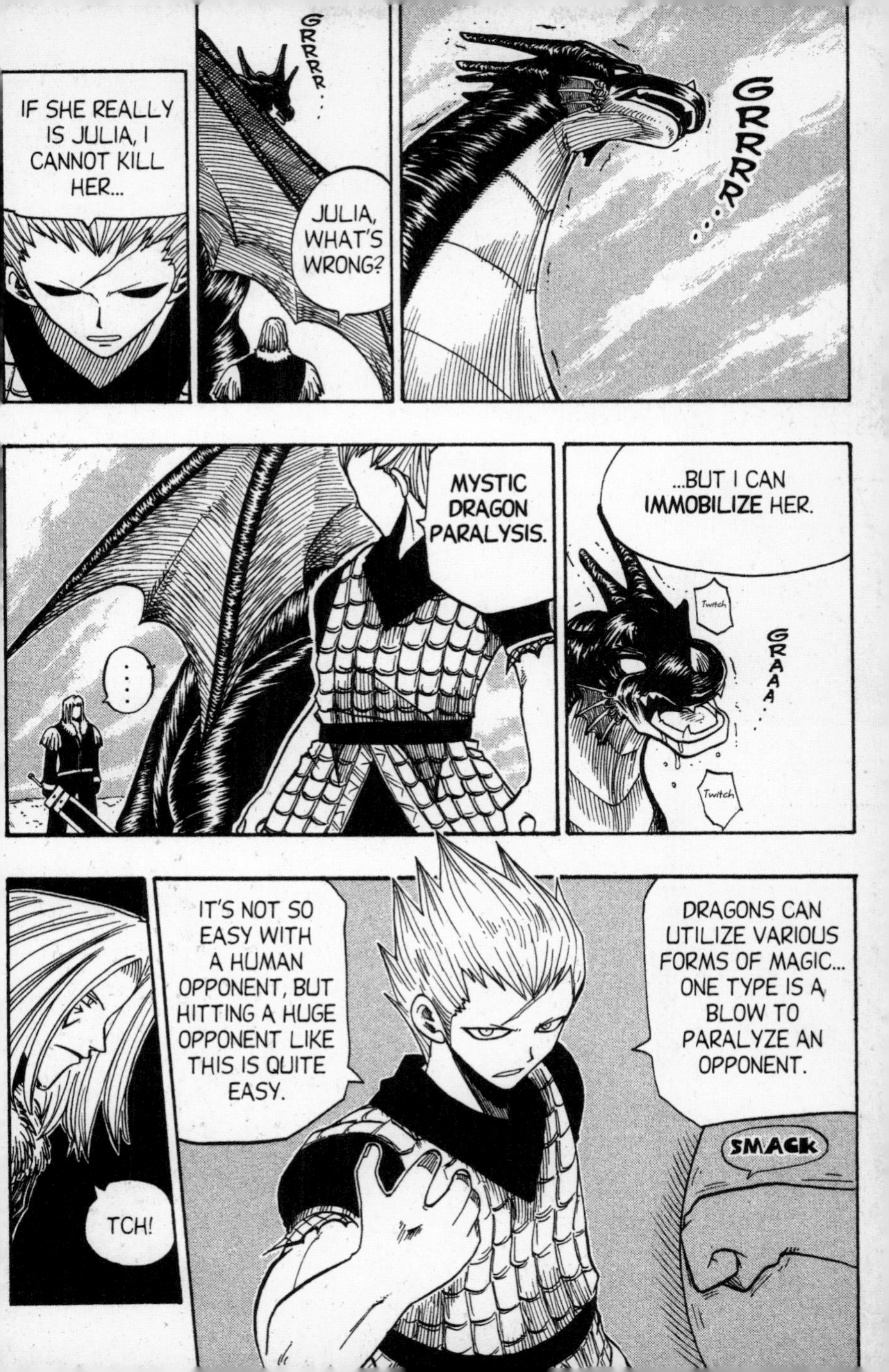
GRRRR...
GRRRR...
JULIA, WHAT'S WRONG?
IF SHE REALLY IS JULIA, I CANNOT KILL HER...
...BUT I CAN IMMOBILIZE HER.
Twitch
GRAAA...
Twitch
MYSTIC DRAGON PARALYSIS.
...
DRAGONS CAN UTILIZE VARIOUS FORMS OF MAGIC... ONE TYPE IS A BLOW TO PARALYZE AN OPPONENT.
SMACK
IT'S NOT SO EASY WITH A HUMAN OPPONENT, BUT HITTING A HUGE OPPONENT LIKE THIS IS QUITE EASY.
TCH!

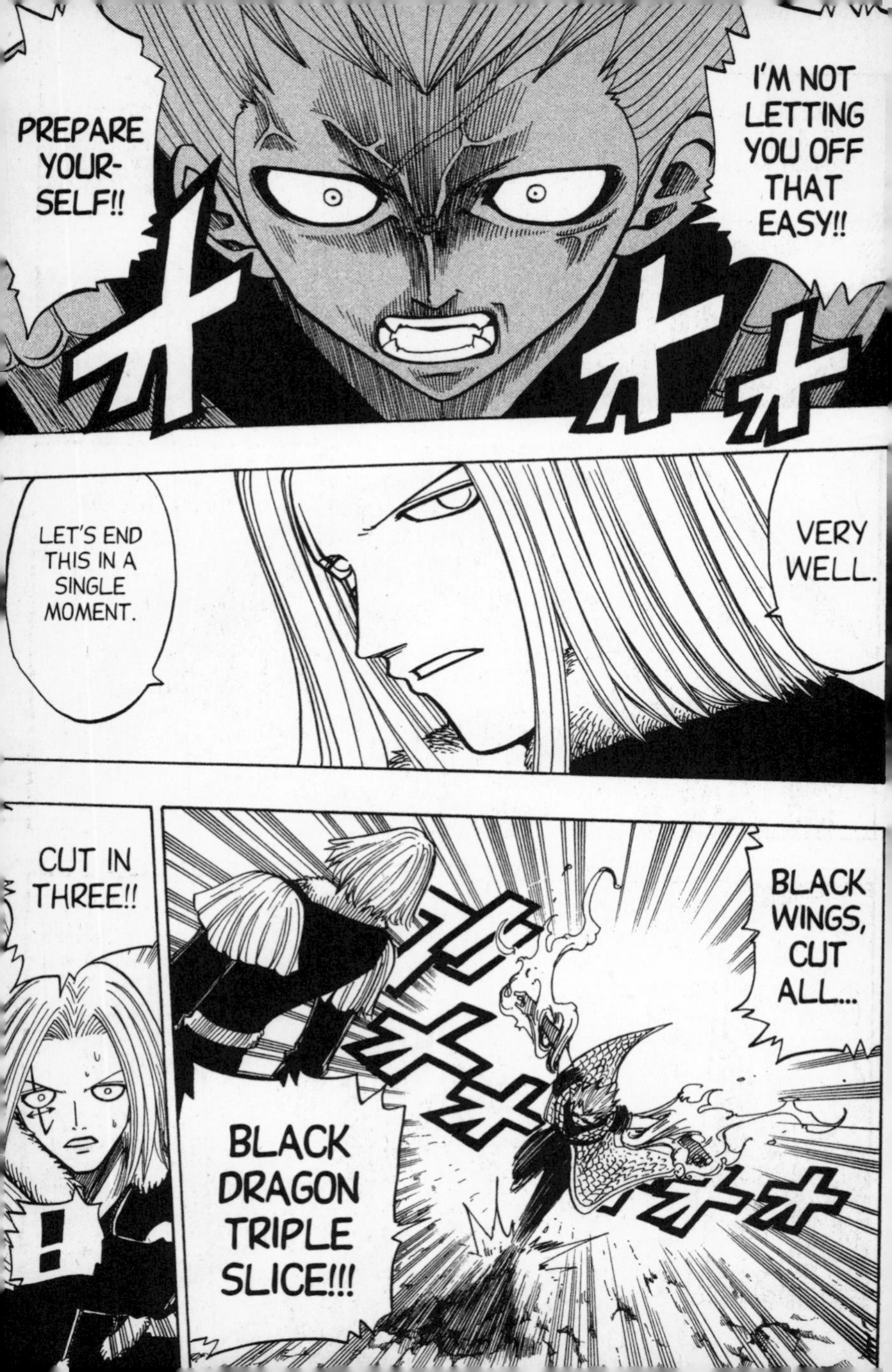
I'M NOT LETTING YOU OFF THAT EASY!!
PREPARE YOUR-SELF!!
VERY WELL.
LET'S END THIS IN A SINGLE MOMENT.
BLACK WINGS, CUT ALL...
BLACK DRAGON TRIPLE SLICE!!!
CUT IN THREE!!
!

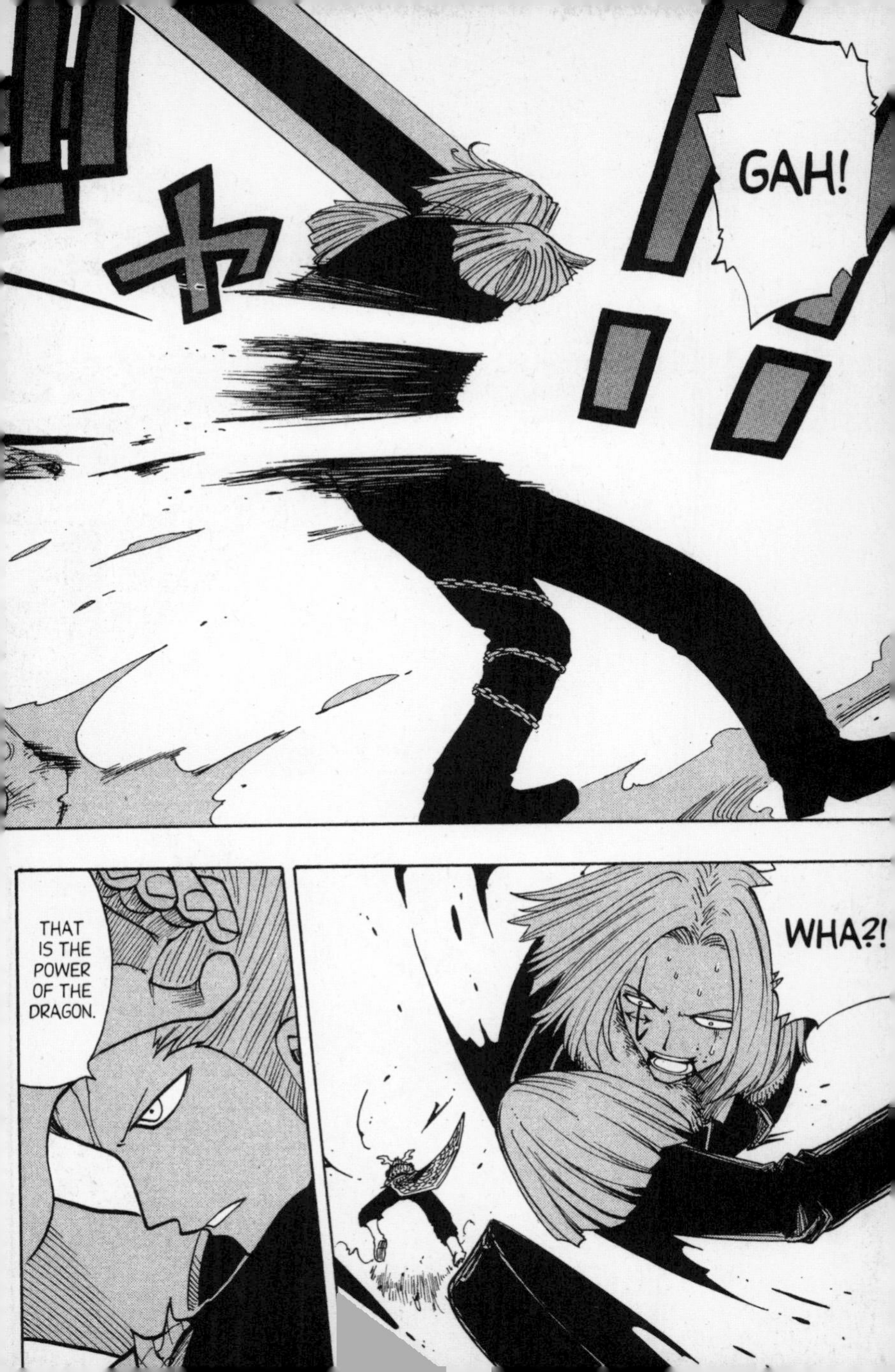
GAH!
WHA?!
THAT IS THE POWER OF THE DRAGON.

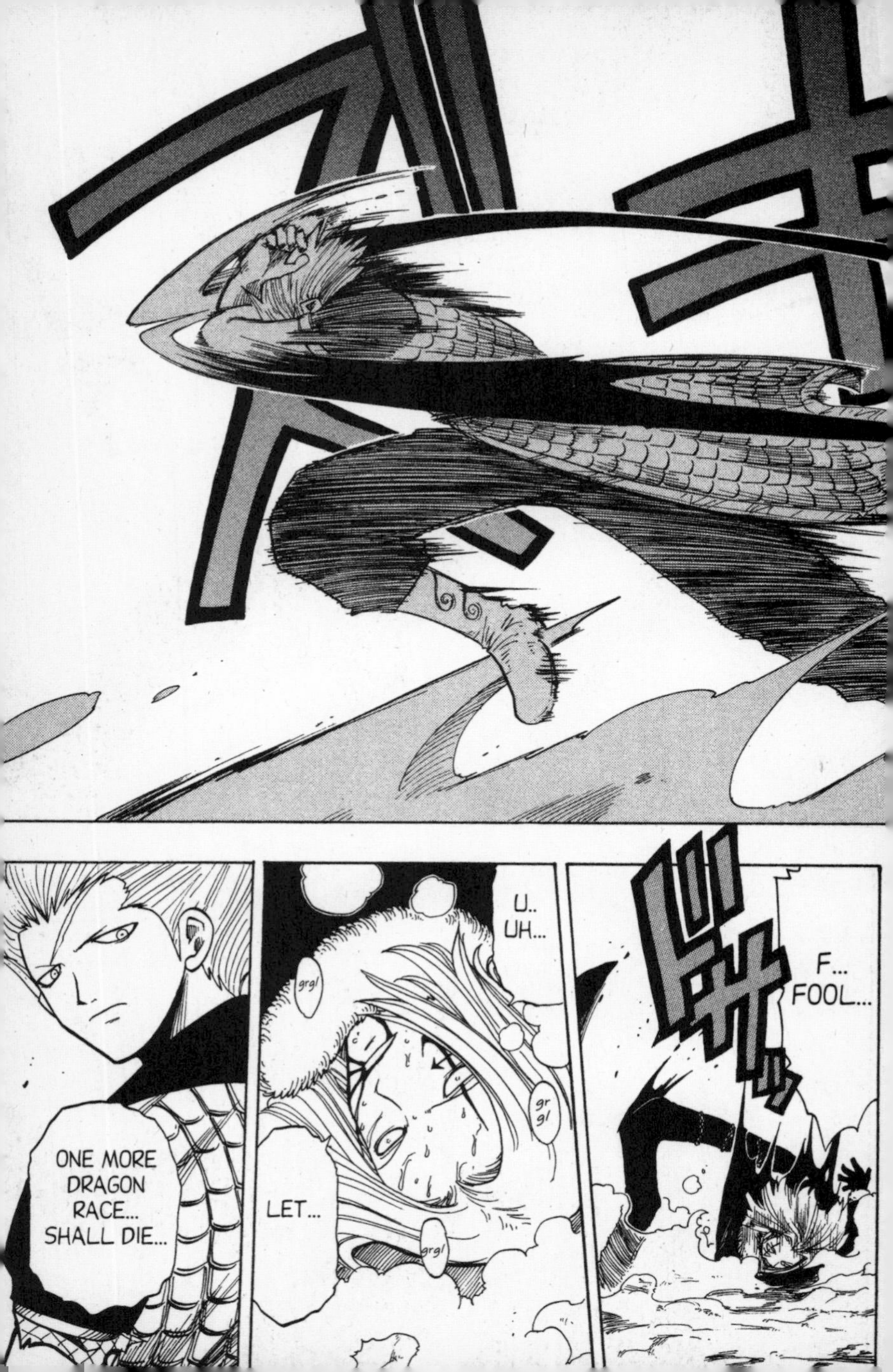
F... FOOL...
U.. UH...
grgl
gr gl
grgl
LET...
grgl
ONE MORE DRAGON RACE... SHALL DIE...

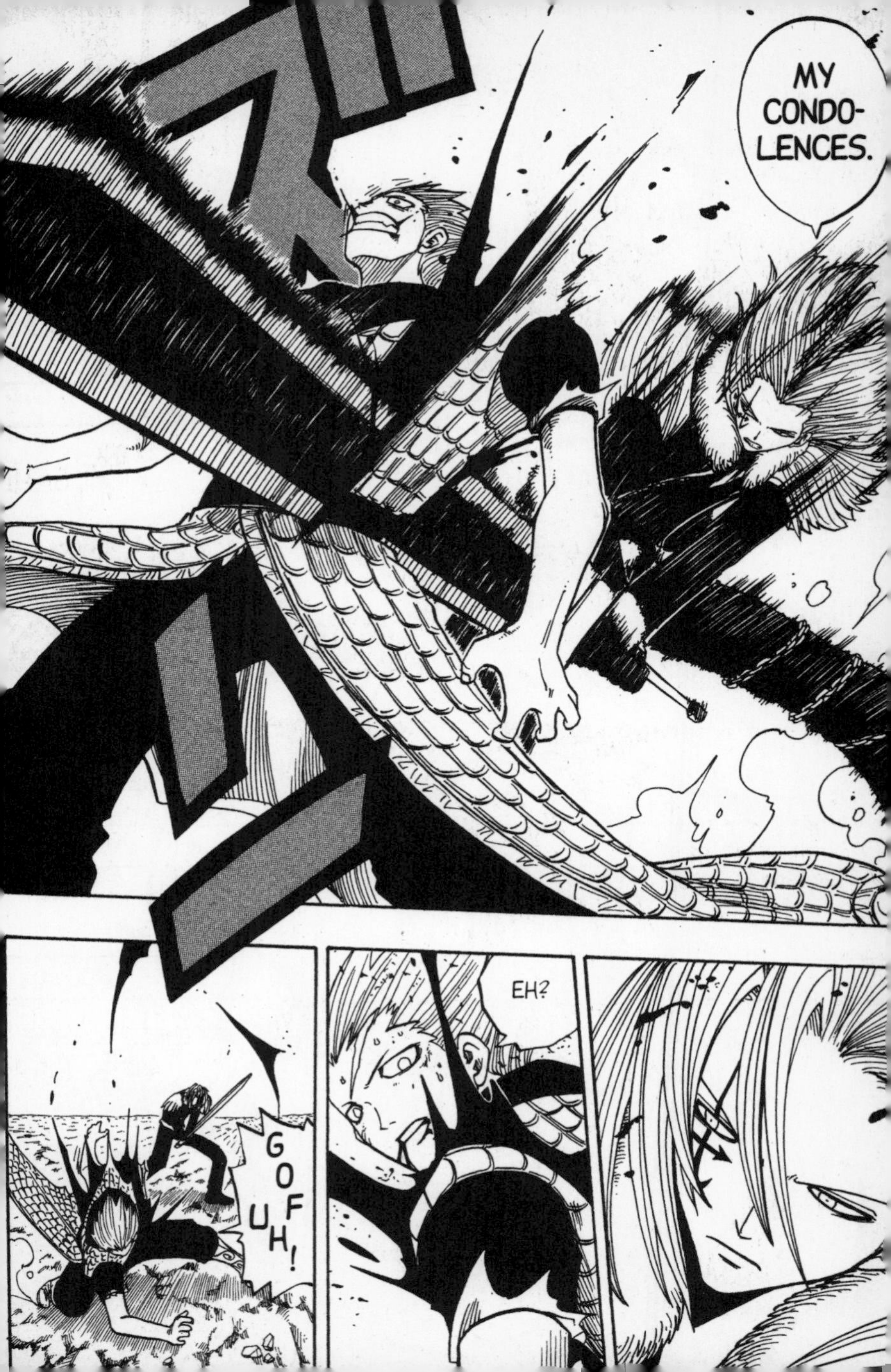
MY CONDO-LENCES.
EH?
GOFUH!

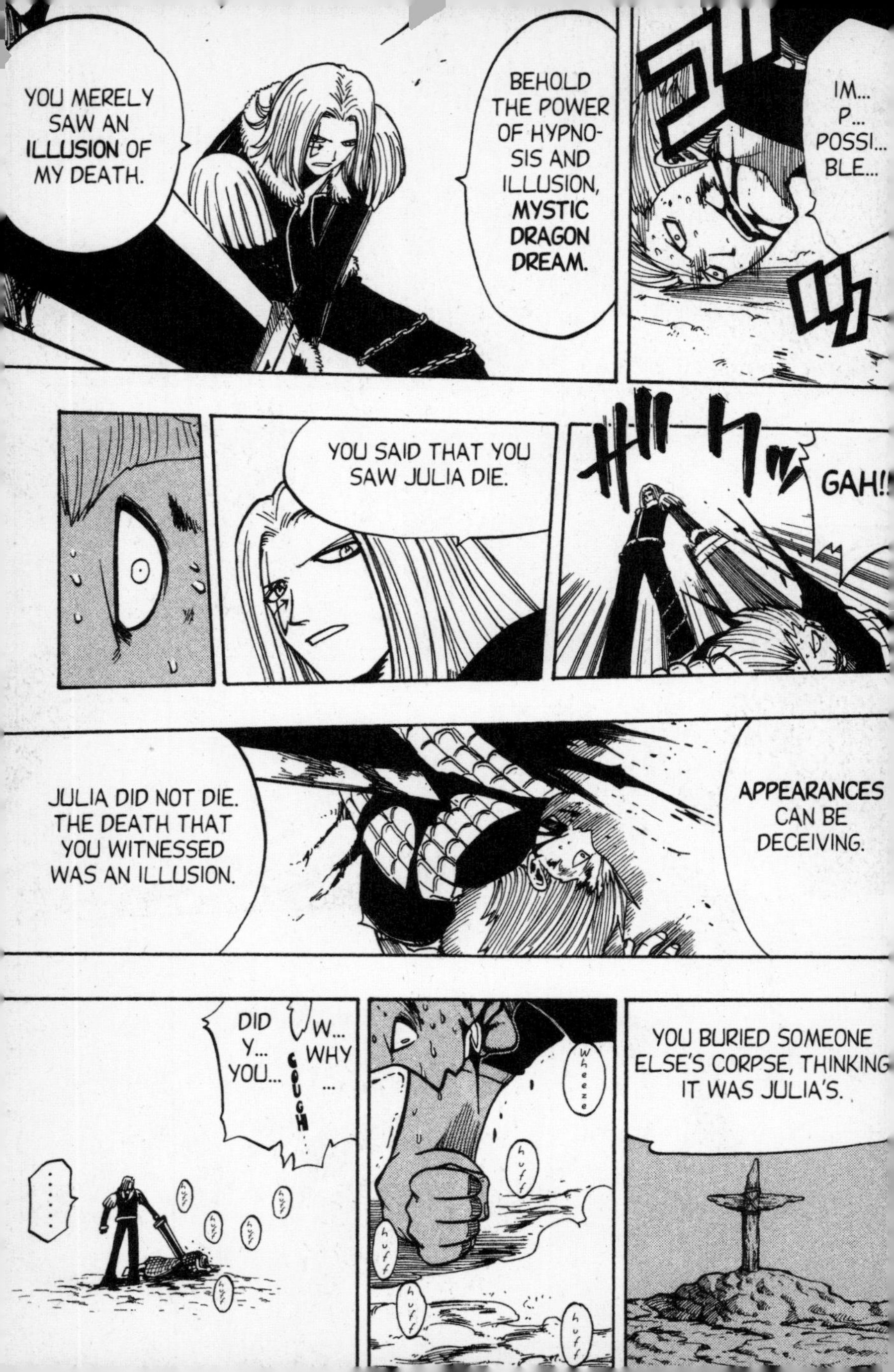

IM... P... POSSI... BLE...
BEHOLD THE POWER OF HYPNO- SIS AND ILLUSION, MYSTIC DRAGON DREAM.
YOU MERELY SAW AN ILLUSION OF MY DEATH.
GAH!!
YOU SAID THAT YOU SAW JULIA DIE.
APPEARANCES CAN BE DECEIVING.
JULIA DID NOT DIE. THE DEATH THAT YOU WITNESSED WAS AN ILLUSION.
YOU BURIED SOMEONE ELSE'S CORPSE, THINKING IT WAS JULIA'S.
Wheeze
huff
huff
huff
huff
W... WHY ...
COUGH
DID Y... YOU...
......
huff
huff
huff
huff
huff

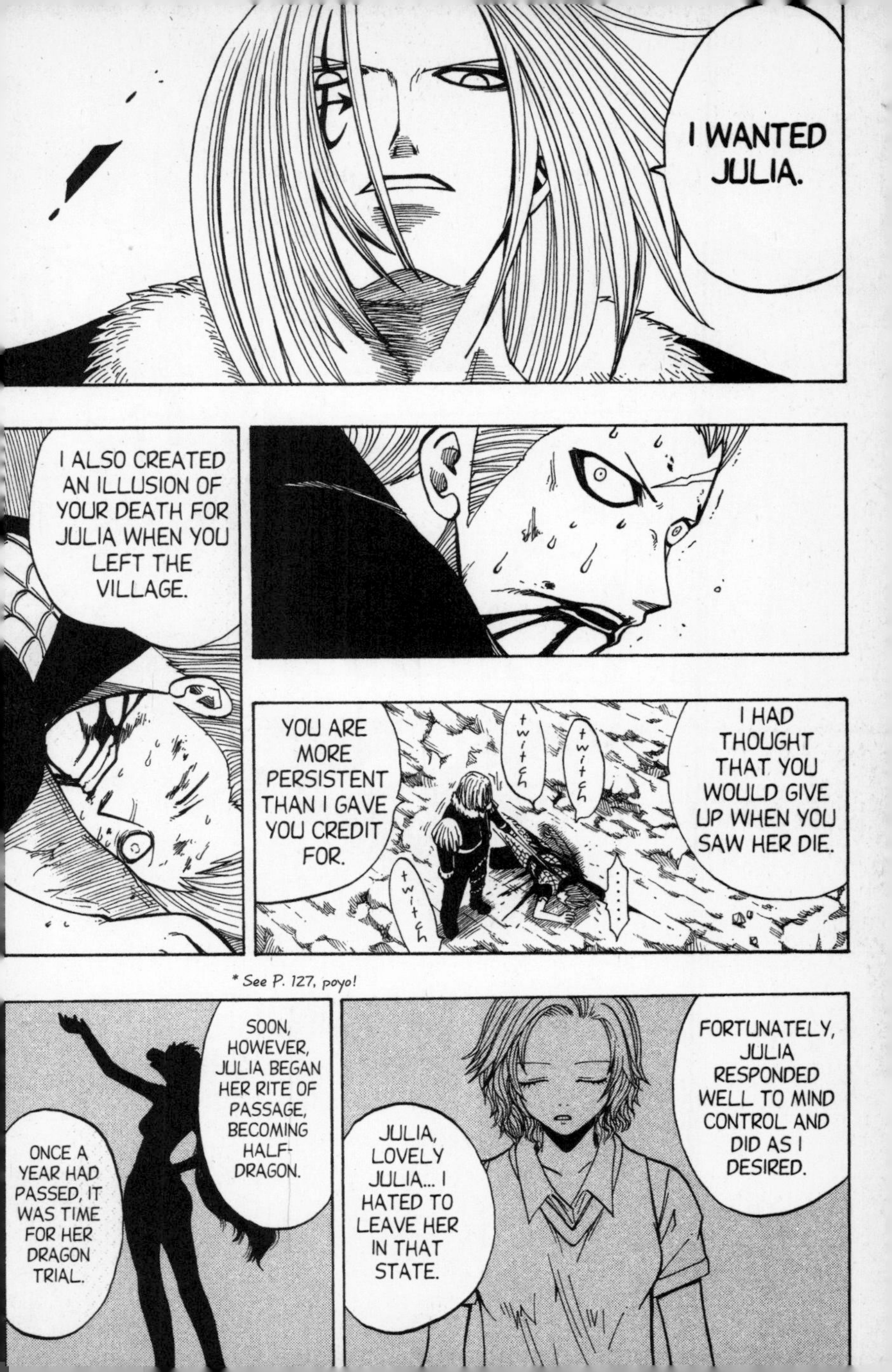
I WANTED JULIA.
I HAD THOUGHT THAT YOU WOULD GIVE UP WHEN YOU SAW HER DIE.
twitch
twitch
......
twitch
YOU ARE MORE PERSISTENT THAN I GAVE YOU CREDIT FOR.
I ALSO CREATED AN ILLUSION OF YOUR DEATH FOR JULIA WHEN YOU LEFT THE VILLAGE.
FORTUNATELY, JULIA RESPONDED WELL TO MIND CONTROL AND DID AS I DESIRED.
JULIA, LOVELY JULIA... I HATED TO LEAVE HER IN THAT STATE.
SOON, HOWEVER, JULIA BEGAN HER RITE OF PASSAGE, BECOMING HALF-DRAGON.
ONCE A YEAR HAD PASSED, IT WAS TIME FOR HER DRAGON TRIAL.

* See P. 127, poyo!

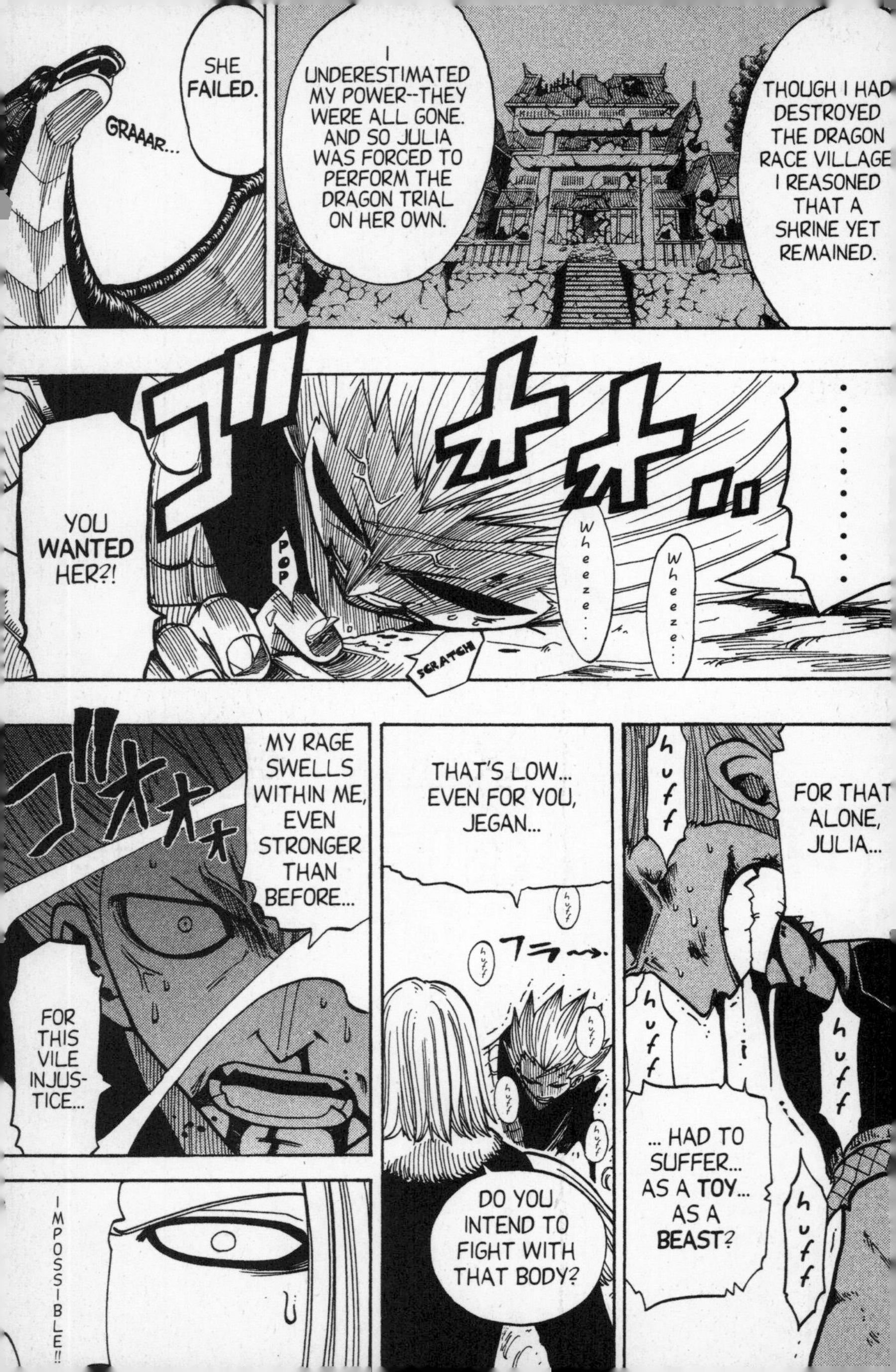
THOUGH I HAD DESTROYED THE DRAGON RACE VILLAGE I REASONED THAT A SHRINE YET REMAINED.
I UNDERESTIMATED MY POWER--THEY WERE ALL GONE. AND SO JULIA WAS FORCED TO PERFORM THE DRAGON TRIAL ON HER OWN.
SHE FAILED.
GRAAAR...
....
Wheeze...
Wheeze...
SCRATCH
POP
YOU WANTED HER?!
FOR THAT ALONE, JULIA...
huff
huff
huff
... HAD TO SUFFER... AS A TOY... AS A BEAST?
huff
THAT'S LOW... EVEN FOR YOU, JEGAN...
DO YOU INTEND TO FIGHT WITH THAT BODY?
MY RAGE SWELLS WITHIN ME, EVEN STRONGER THAN BEFORE...
FOR THIS VILE INJUSTICE...
IMPOSSIBLE!!

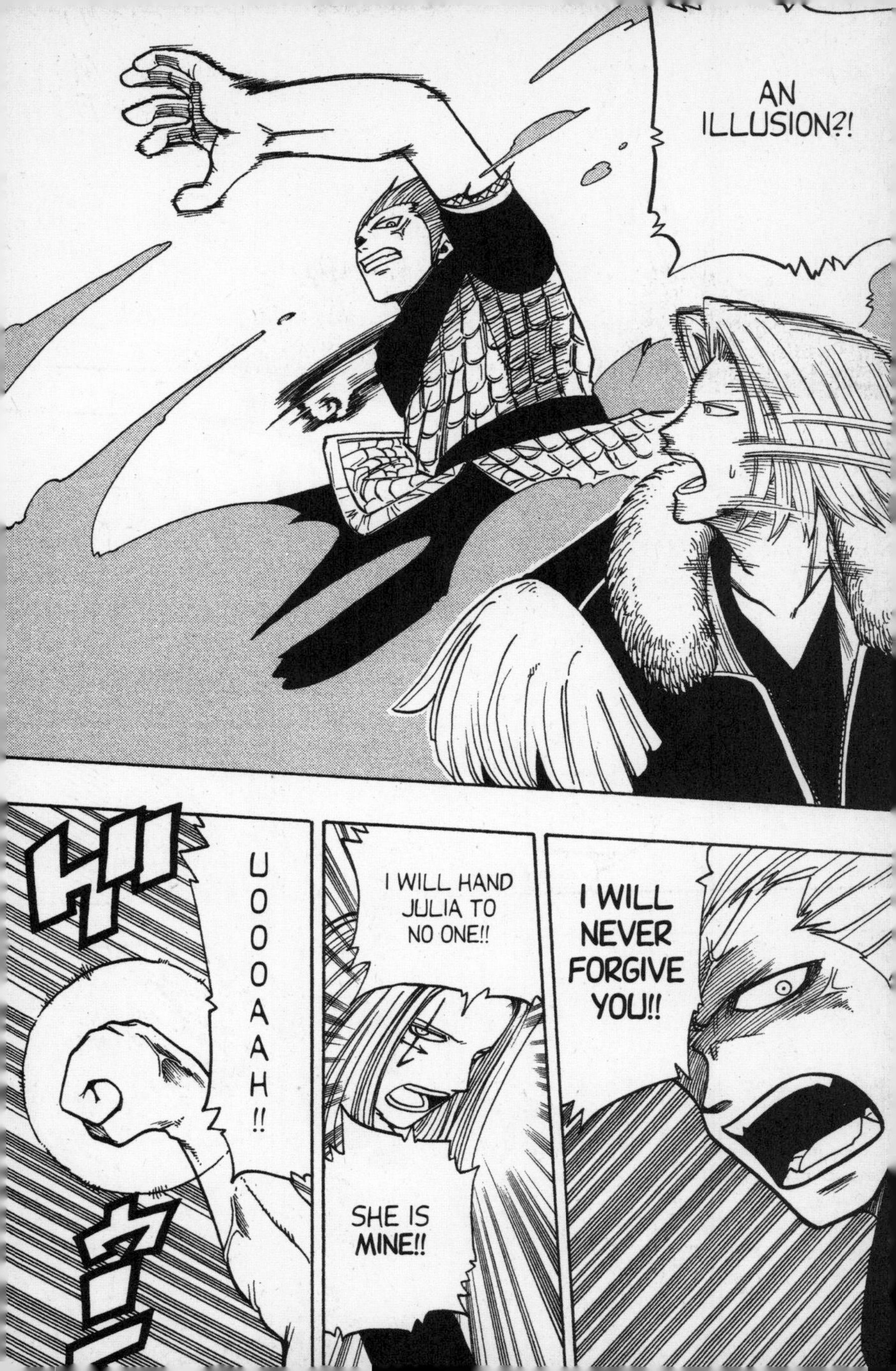
AN ILLUSION?!
I WILL NEVER FORGIVE YOU!!
I WILL HAND JULIA TO NO ONE!!
SHE IS MINE!!
UOOOAAH!!

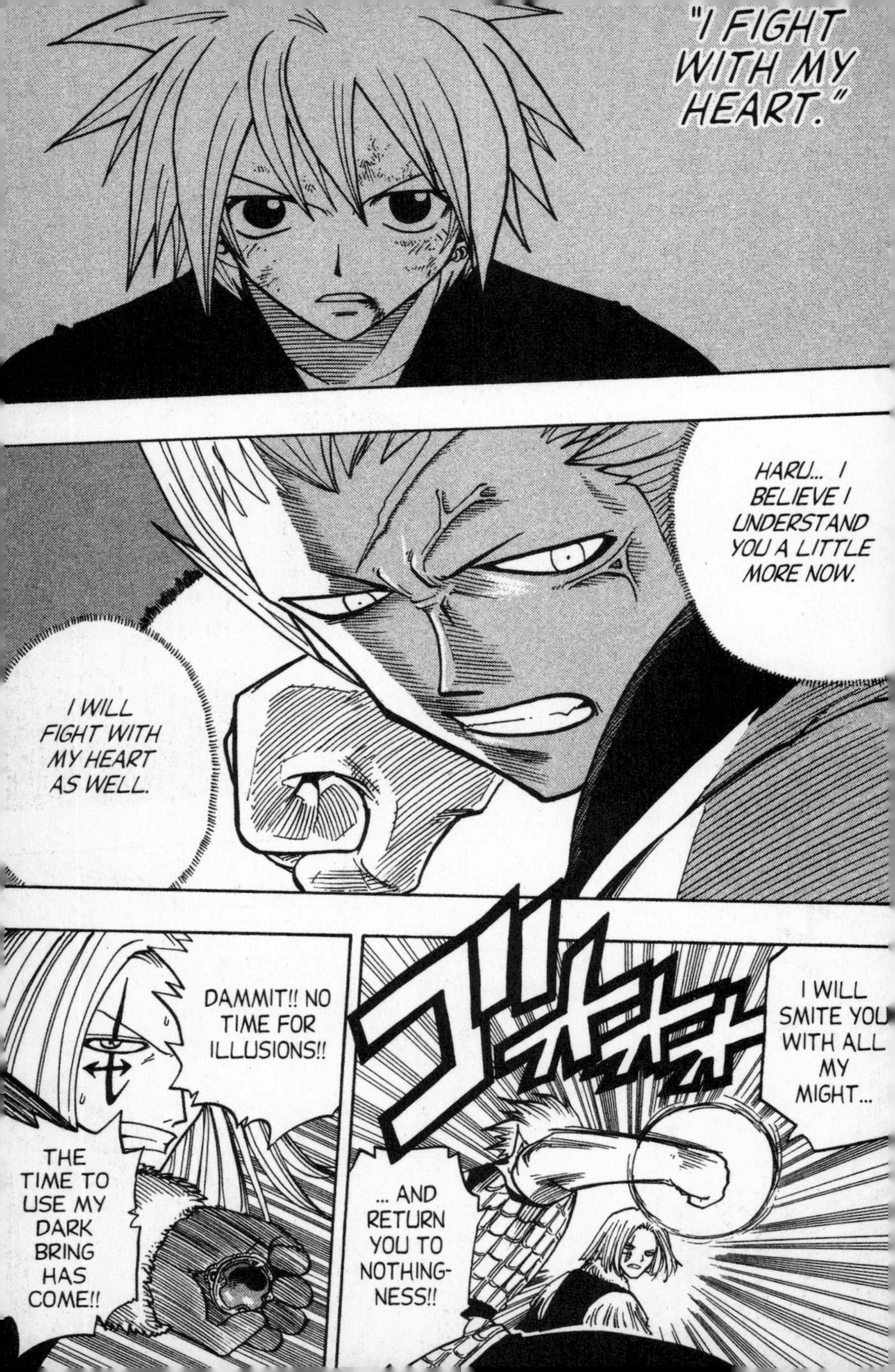
"I FIGHT WITH MY HEART."
HARU... I BELIEVE I UNDERSTAND YOU A LITTLE MORE NOW.
I WILL FIGHT WITH MY HEART AS WELL.
I WILL SMITE YOU WITH ALL MY MIGHT...
... AND RETURN YOU TO NOTHING-NESS!!
DAMMIT!! NO TIME FOR ILLUSIONS!!
THE TIME TO USE MY DARK BRING HAS COME!!

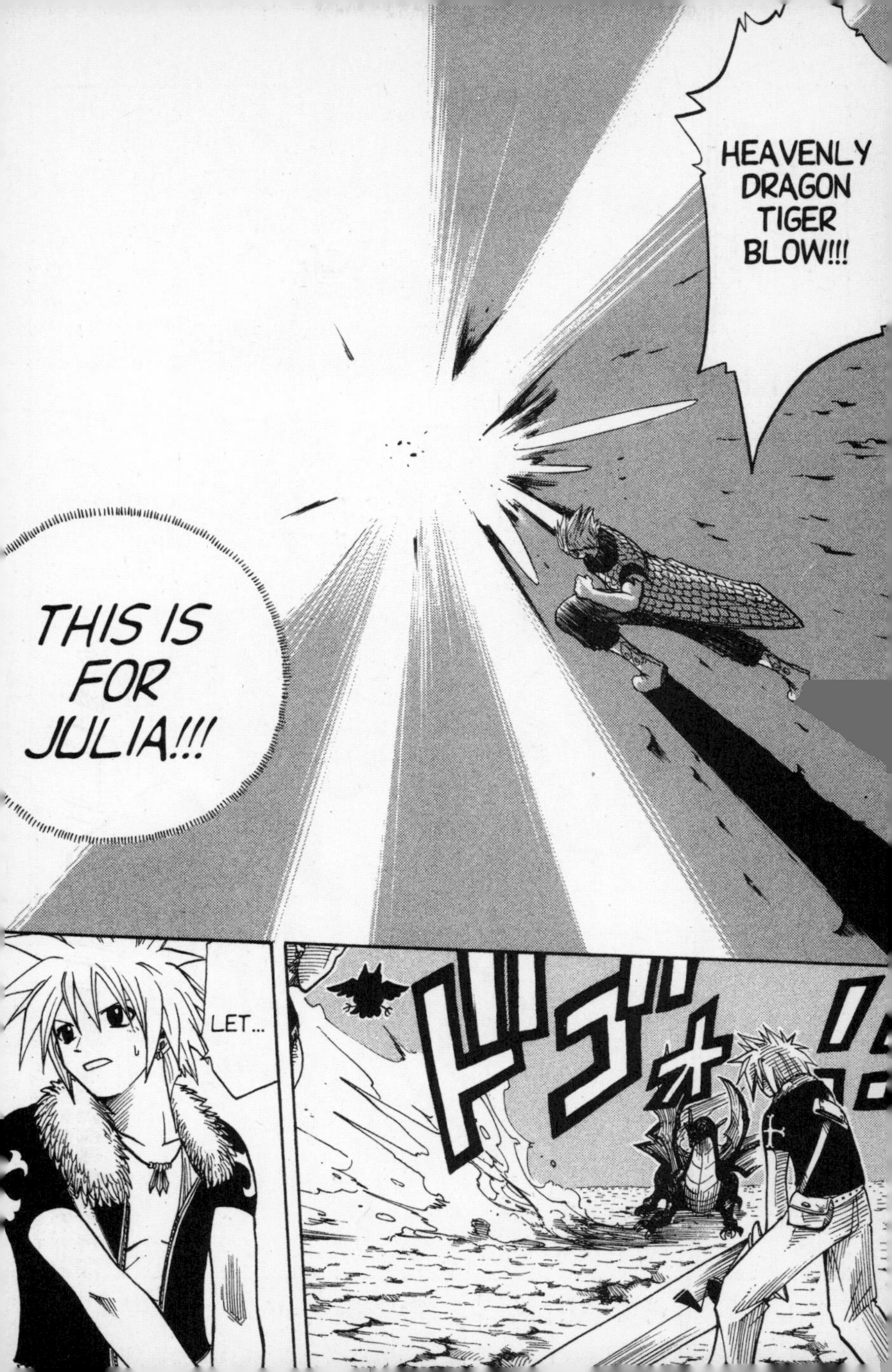
HEAVENLY DRAGON TIGER BLOW!!!
THIS IS FOR JULIA!!!
ドゴォ!!
LET...

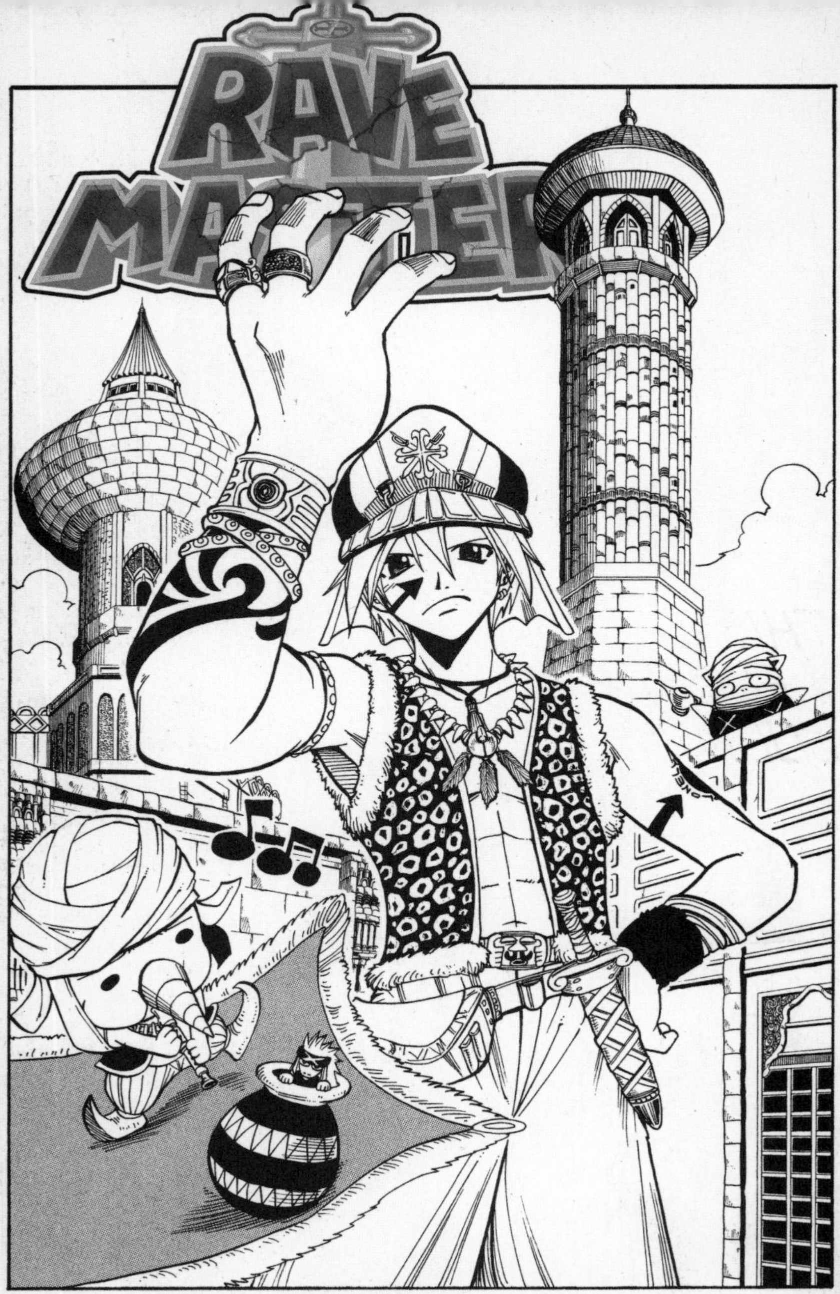

RAVE:87 ✠ SILVER RAY

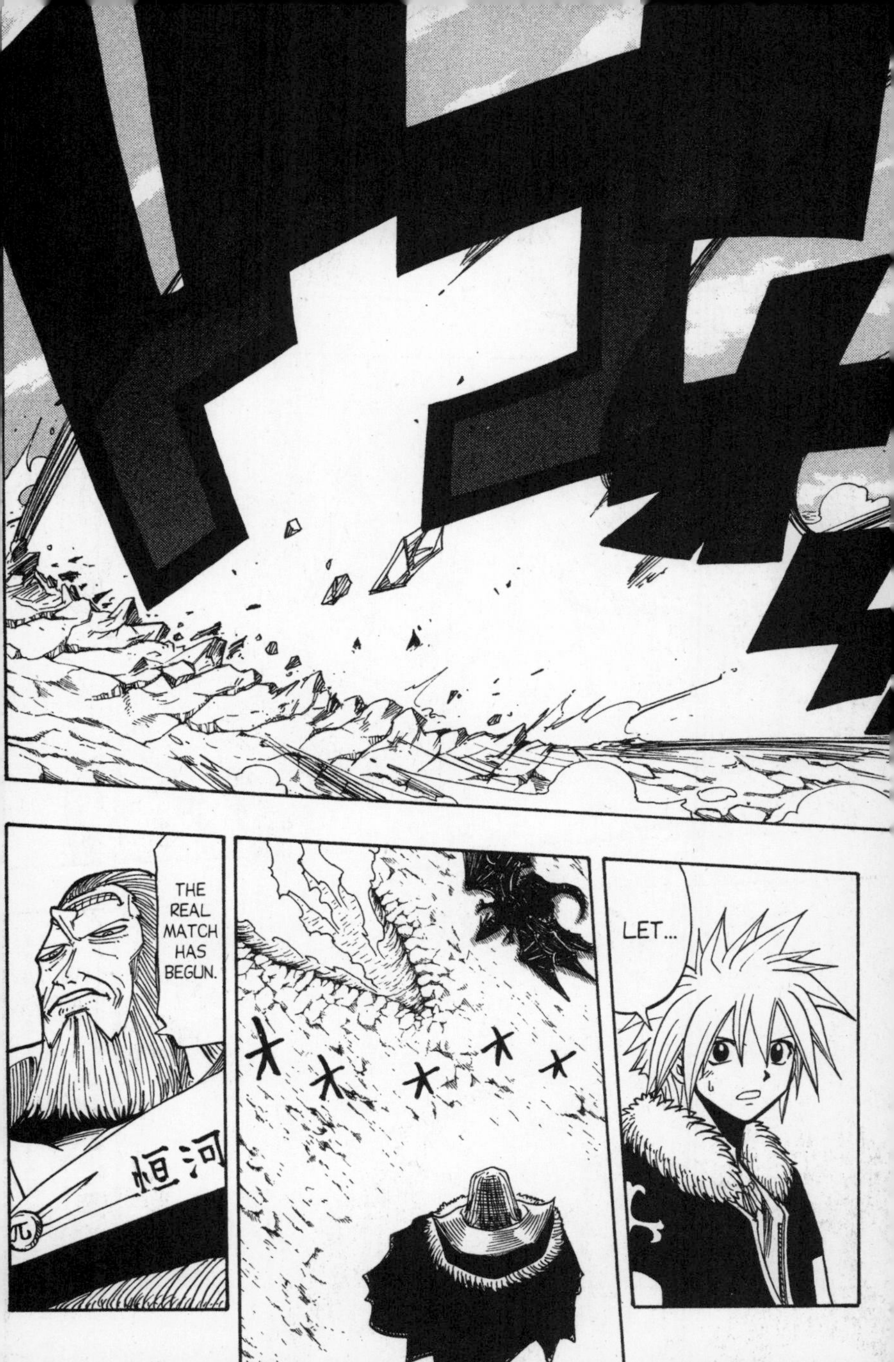
LET...
THE REAL MATCH HAS BEGUN.
恒河

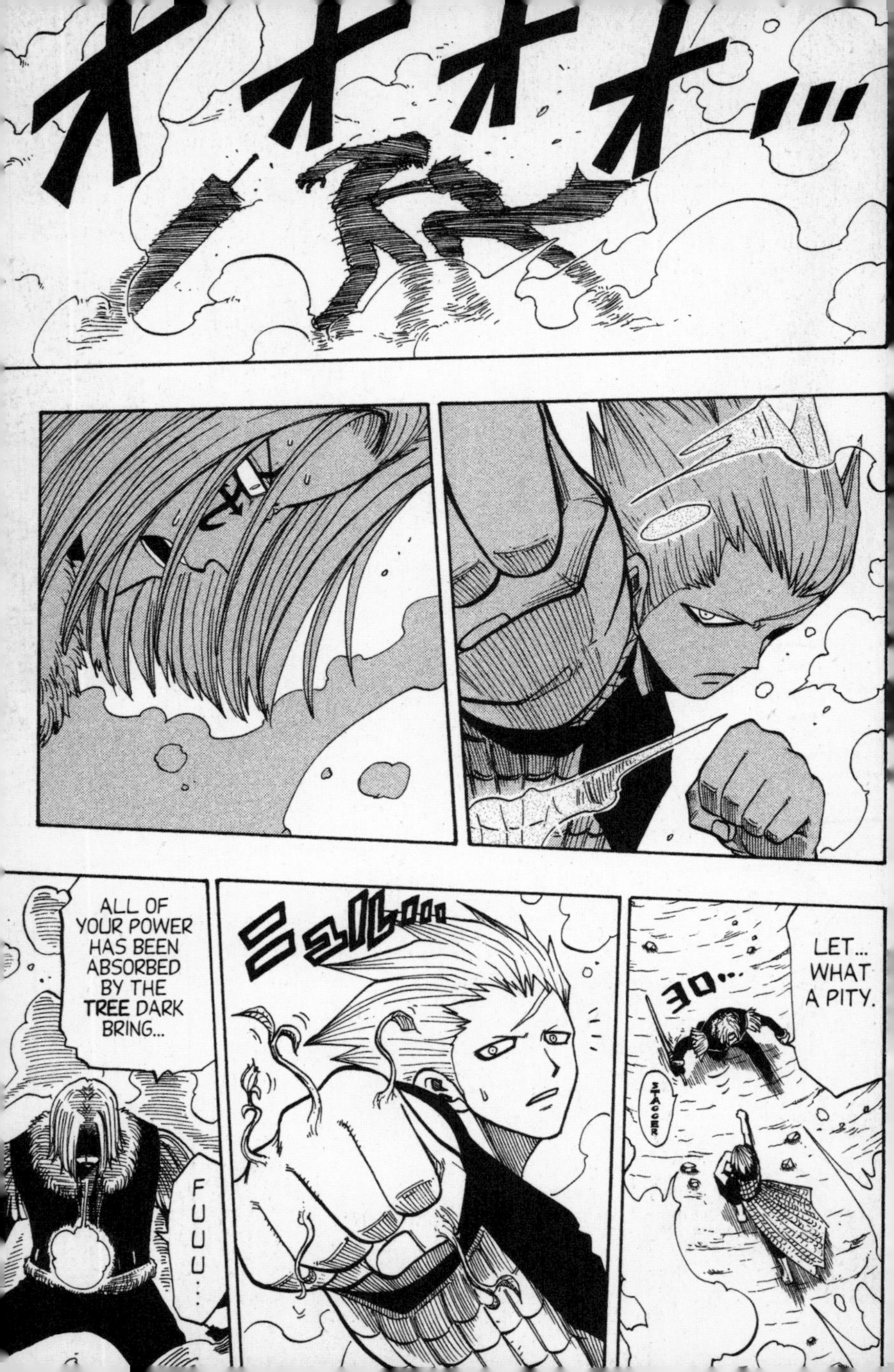

オオオオ…
LET... WHAT A PITY.
ヨロ…
STAGGER
ALL OF YOUR POWER HAS BEEN ABSORBED BY THE **TREE** DARK BRING...
FUUU...

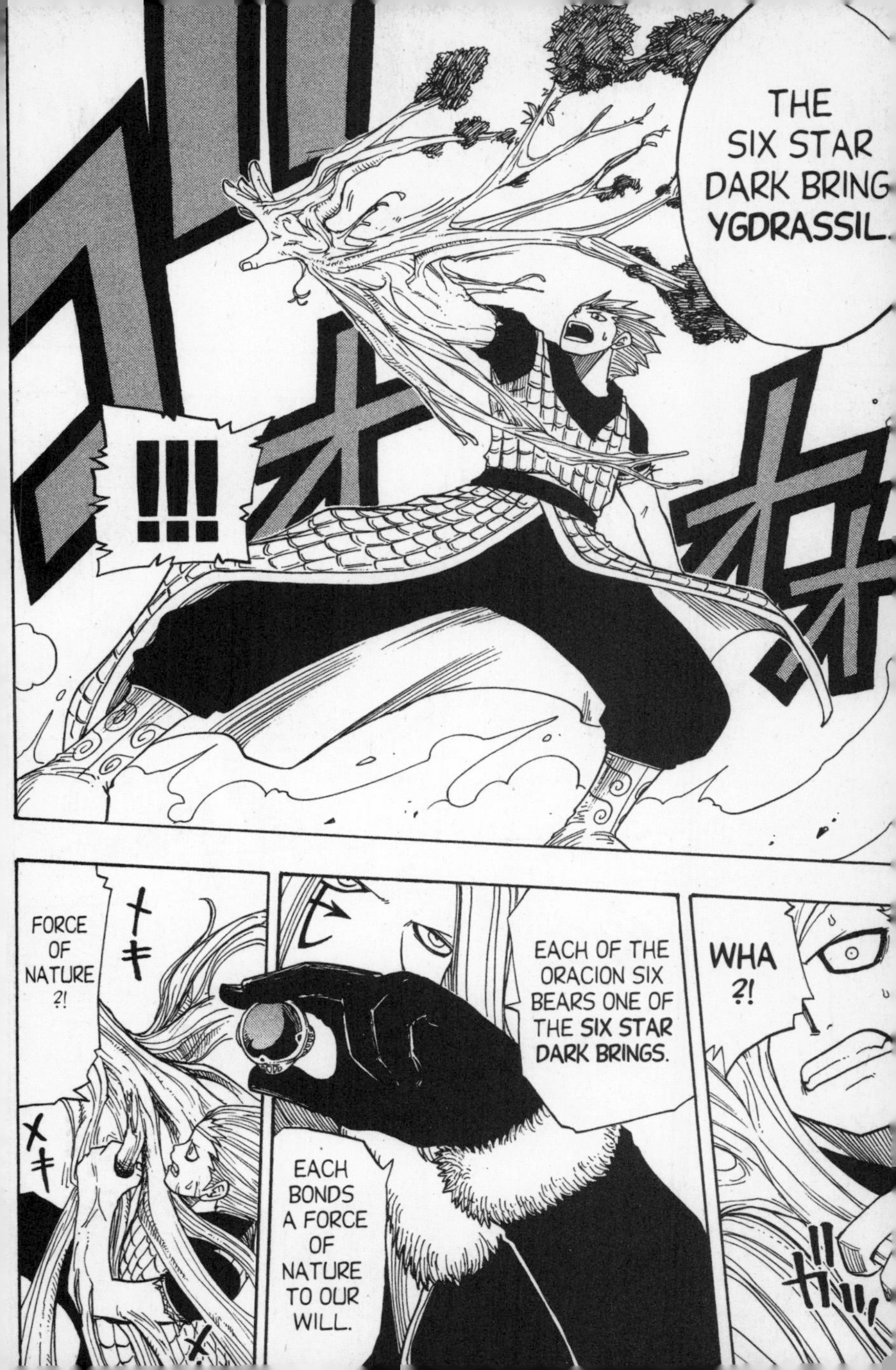
THE SIX STAR DARK BRING YGDRASSIL.
!!!
WHA ?!
EACH OF THE ORACION SIX BEARS ONE OF THE SIX STAR DARK BRINGS.
EACH BONDS A FORCE OF NATURE TO OUR WILL.
FORCE OF NATURE ?!

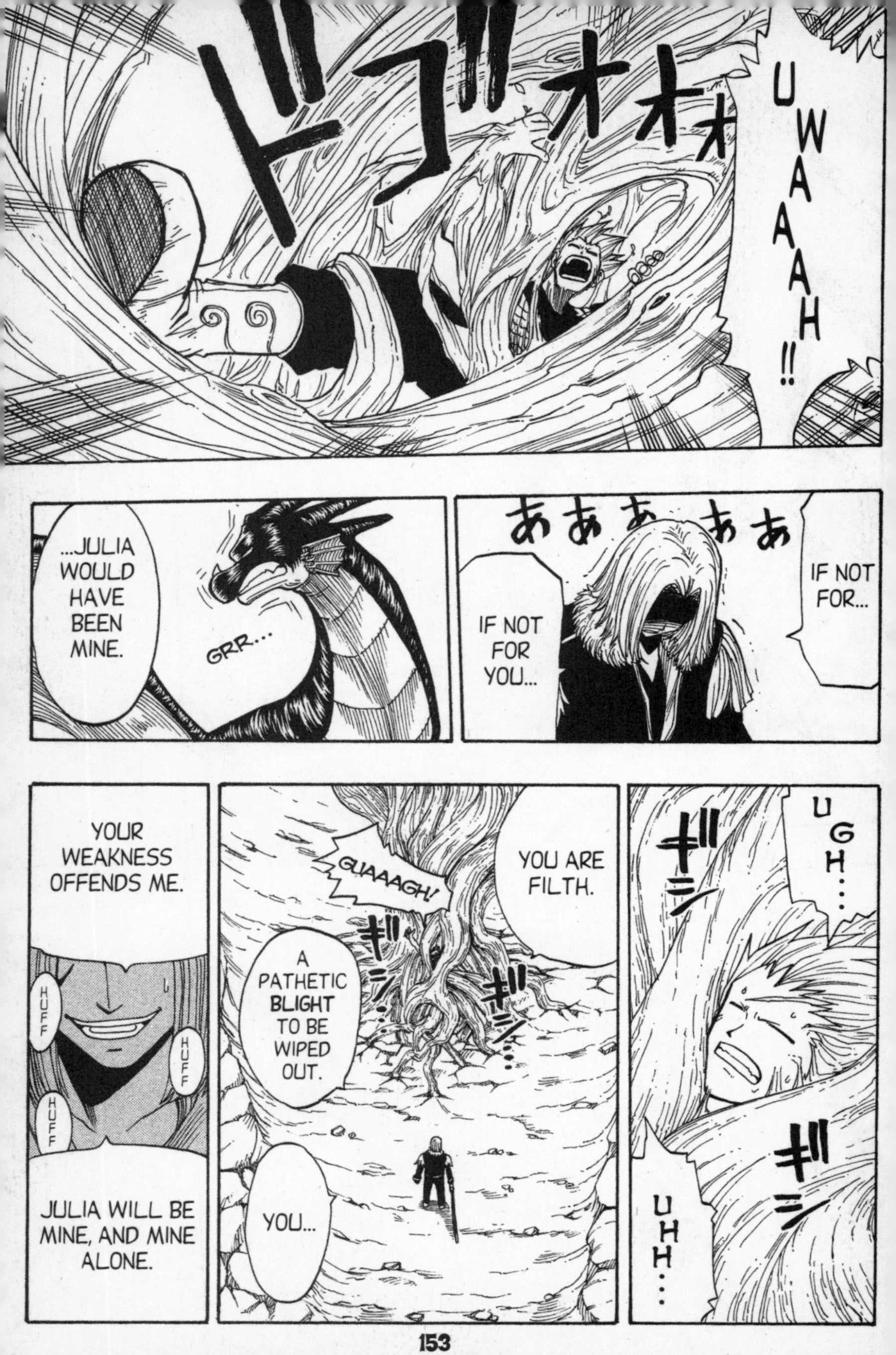
ドゴオオ
UWAAAAH!!
IF NOT FOR...
IF NOT FOR YOU...
あああぁぁ
...JULIA WOULD HAVE BEEN MINE.
GRR...
UGH...
ギシ
ギシ
UHH...
YOU ARE FILTH.
GUAAAAGH!
ギシ
ギシ
A PATHETIC BLIGHT TO BE WIPED OUT.
YOU...
YOUR WEAKNESS OFFENDS ME.
HUFF
HUFF
HUFF
JULIA WILL BE MINE, AND MINE ALONE.

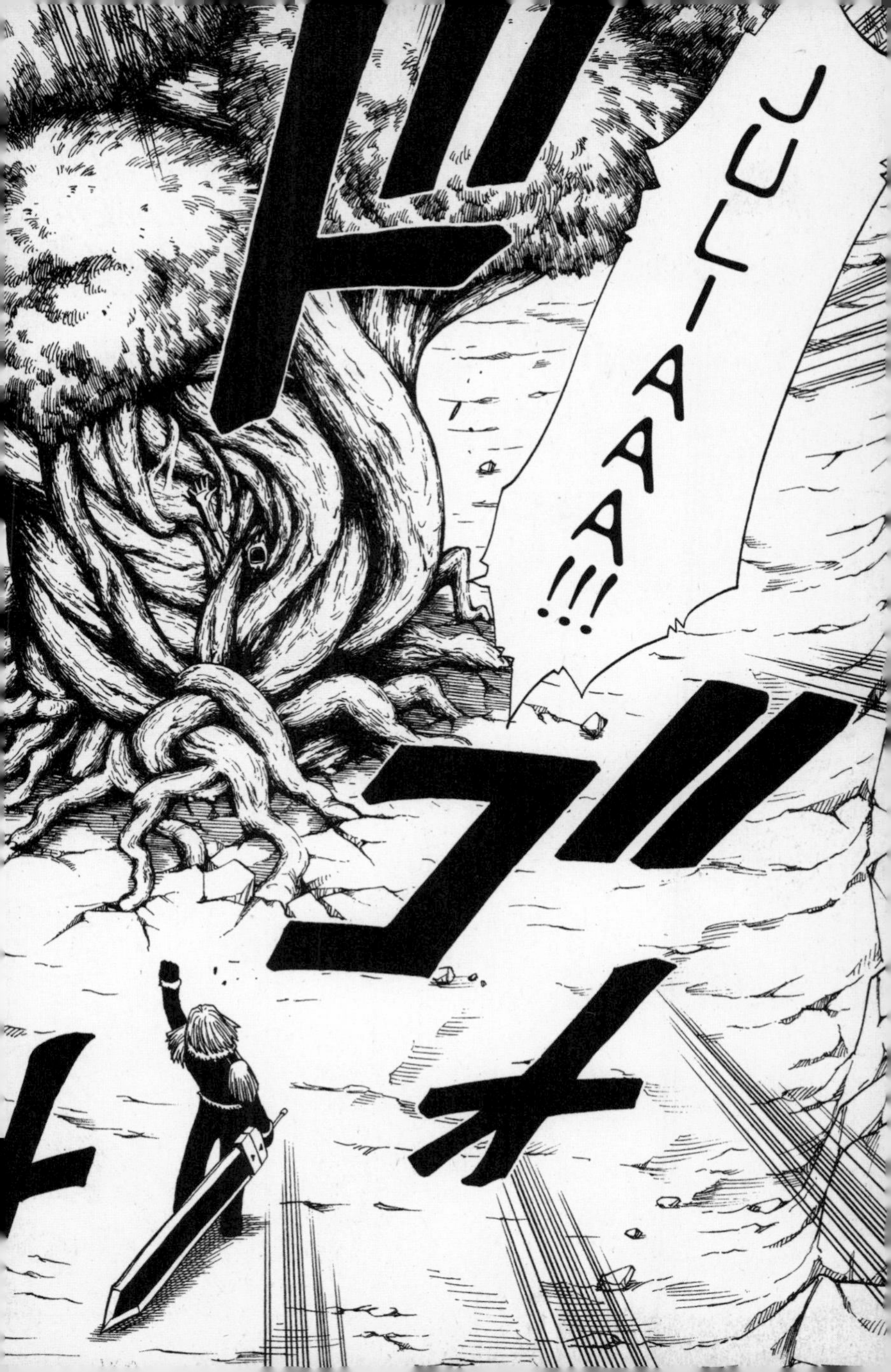
JULIAAA!!!

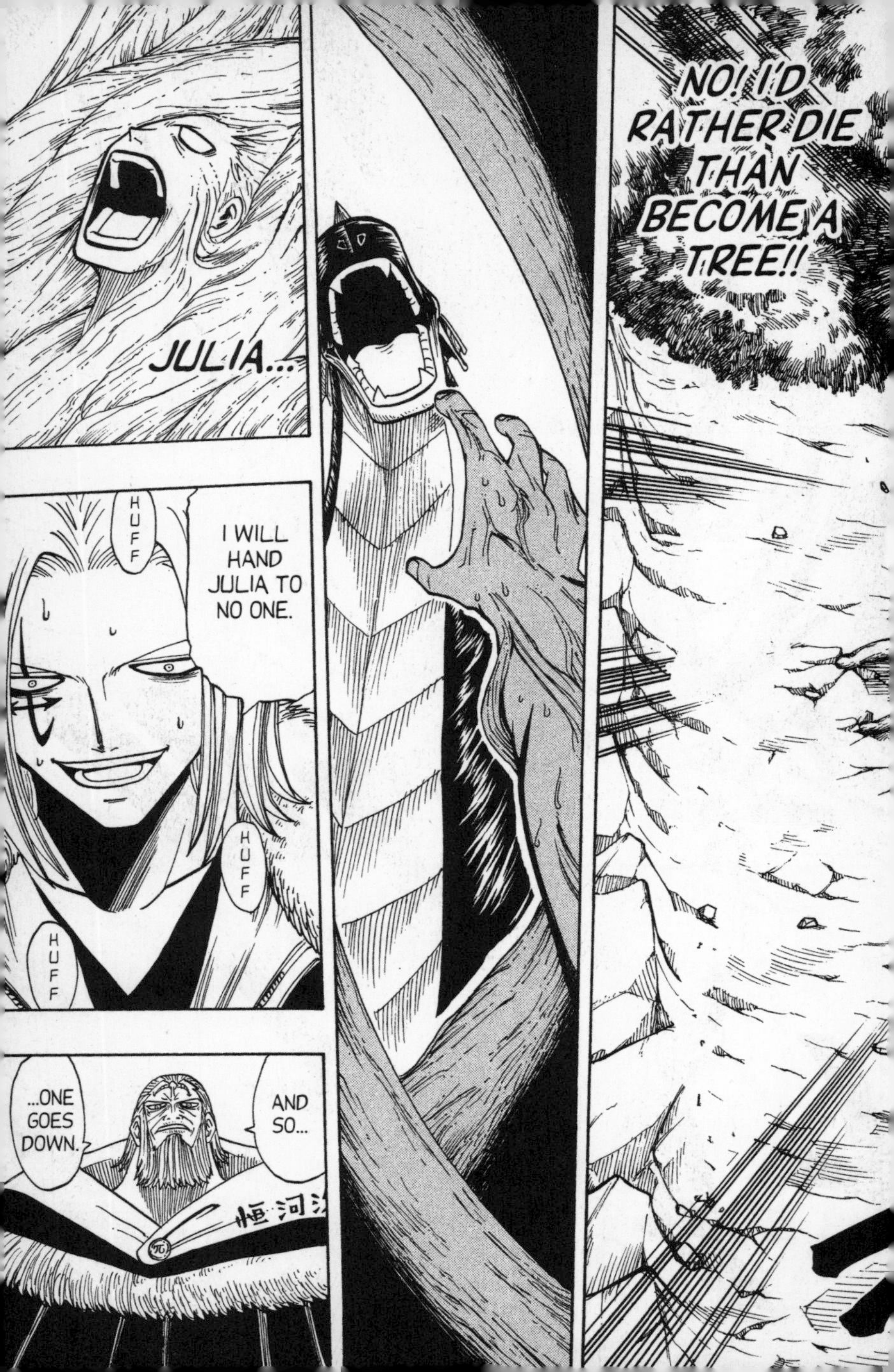
NO! I'D RATHER DIE THAN BECOME A TREE!!
JULIA...
I WILL HAND JULIA TO NO ONE.
HUFF
HUFF
HUFF
AND SO...
...ONE GOES DOWN.

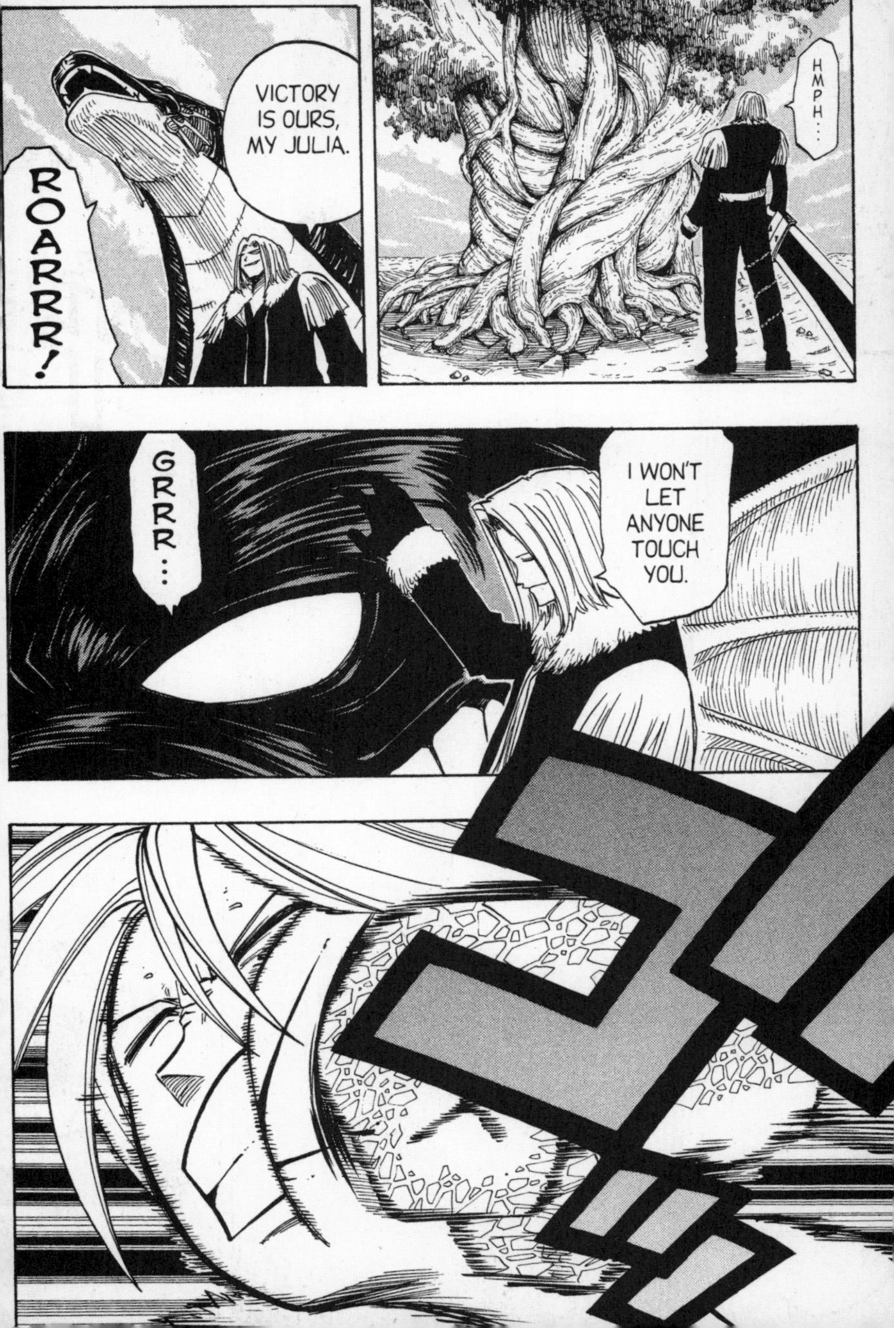
HMPH...
VICTORY IS OURS, MY JULIA.
ROARRR!
I WON'T LET ANYONE TOUCH YOU.
GRRR...

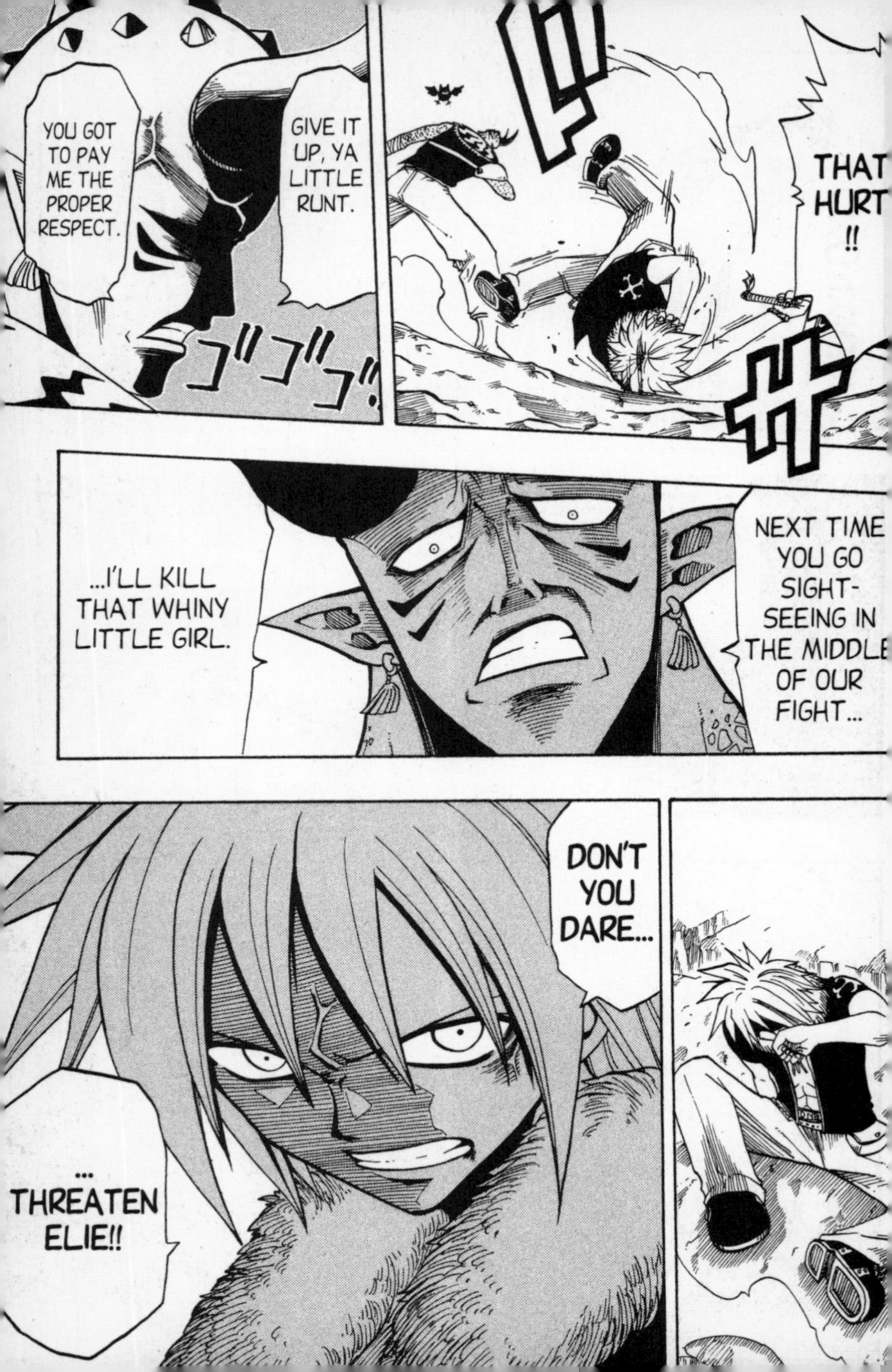
THAT HURT!!
GIVE IT UP, YA LITTLE RUNT.
YOU GOT TO PAY ME THE PROPER RESPECT.
ゴゴゴ
NEXT TIME YOU GO SIGHT-SEEING IN THE MIDDLE OF OUR FIGHT...
...I'LL KILL THAT WHINY LITTLE GIRL.
DON'T YOU DARE...
...THREATEN ELIE!!

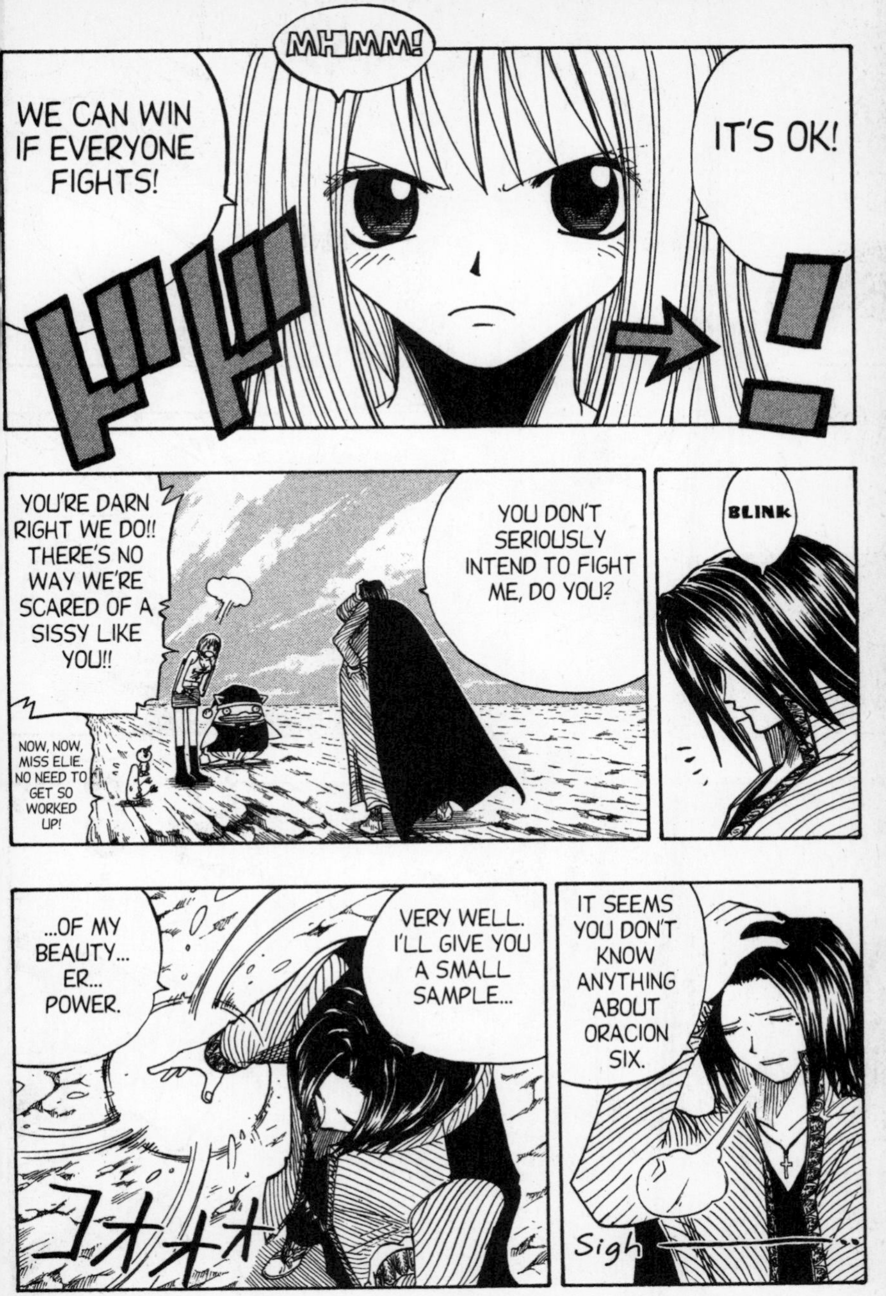
IT'S OK!
MHMM!
WE CAN WIN IF EVERYONE FIGHTS!
BLINK
YOU DON'T SERIOUSLY INTEND TO FIGHT ME, DO YOU?
YOU'RE DARN RIGHT WE DO!! THERE'S NO WAY WE'RE SCARED OF A SISSY LIKE YOU!!
NOW, NOW, MISS ELIE. NO NEED TO GET SO WORKED UP!
IT SEEMS YOU DON'T KNOW ANYTHING ABOUT ORACION SIX.
Sigh
VERY WELL. I'LL GIVE YOU A SMALL SAMPLE...
...OF MY BEAUTY... ER... POWER.
コオオオ

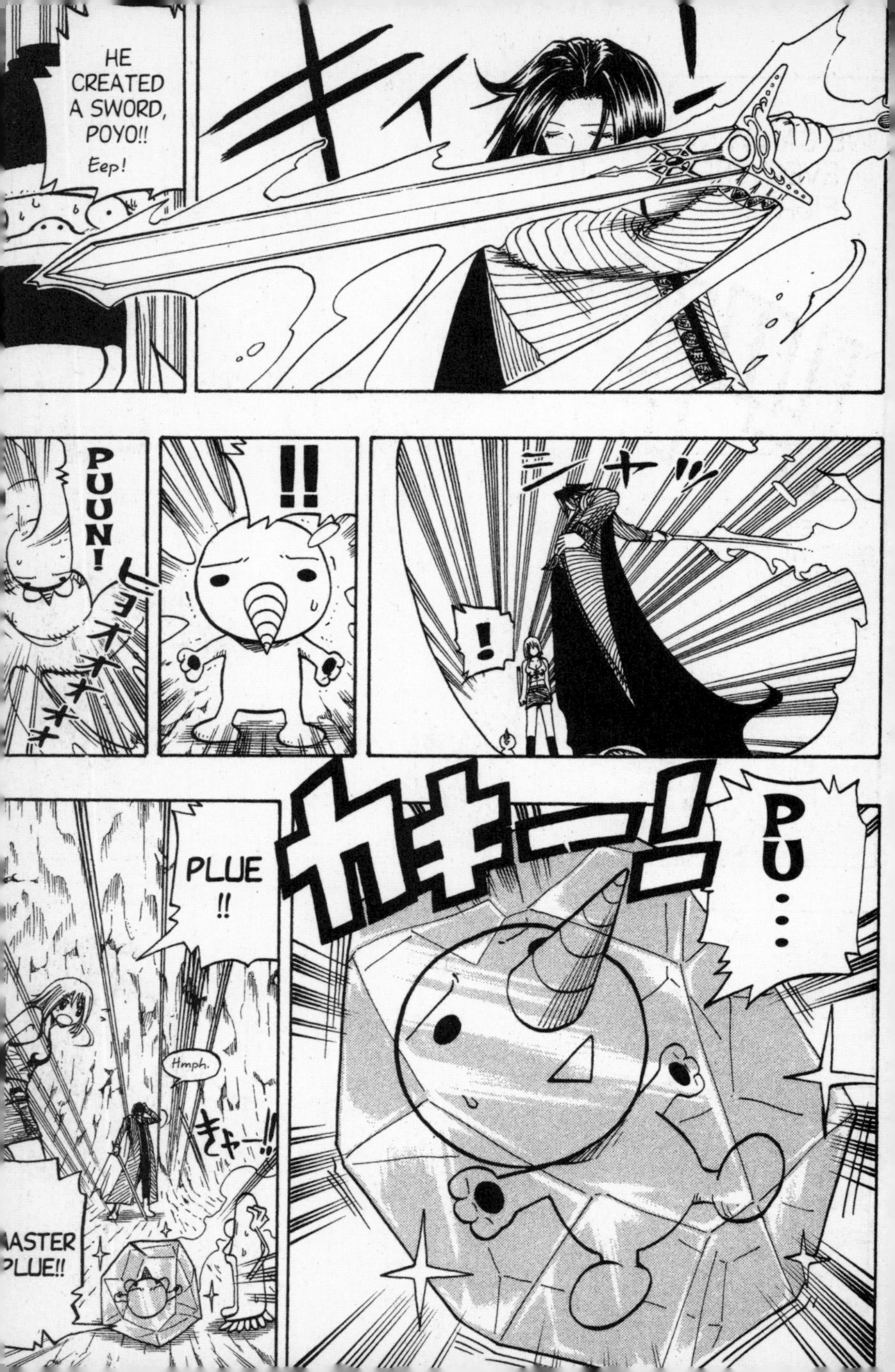
キィー
HE CREATED A SWORD, POYO!!
Eep!
!
!!
PUUN!
カキーン!
PU...
PLUE !!
Hmph.
きゃー!!
MASTER PLUE!!

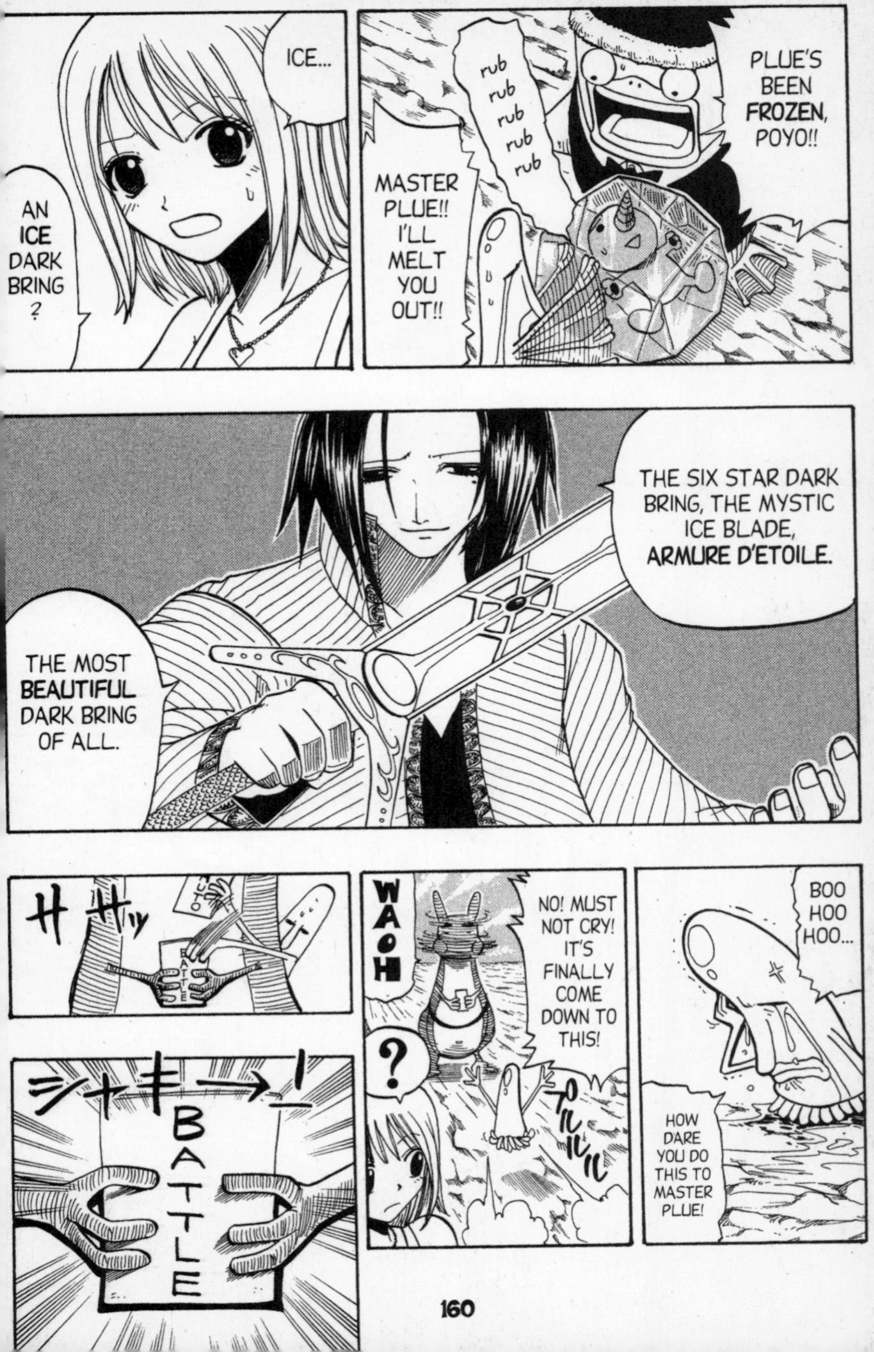

PLUE'S BEEN FROZEN, POYO!!
rub rub rub rub rub
MASTER PLUE!! I'LL MELT YOU OUT!!
ICE...
AN ICE DARK BRING?
THE SIX STAR DARK BRING, THE MYSTIC ICE BLADE, ARMURE D'ETOILE.
THE MOST BEAUTIFUL DARK BRING OF ALL.
BOO HOO HOO...
HOW DARE YOU DO THIS TO MASTER PLUE!
NO! MUST NOT CRY! IT'S FINALLY COME DOWN TO THIS!
WAOH
?
プルルル
サ サッ
AUTO
BATTLE
シャキーン!
BATTLE

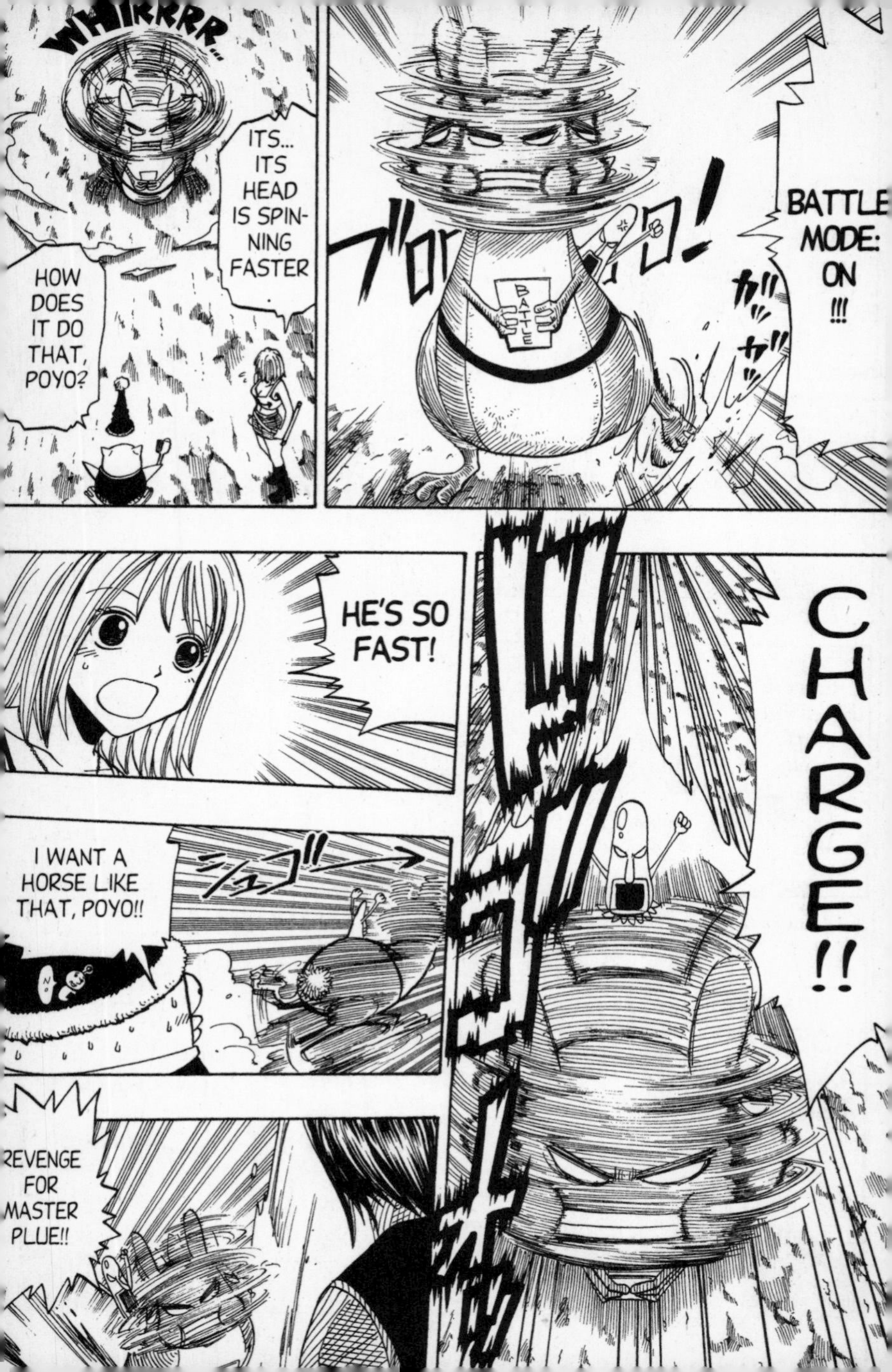
BATTLE
BATTLE MODE: ON!!!
WHIRRRR...
ITS... ITS HEAD IS SPIN-NING FASTER
HOW DOES IT DO THAT, POYO?
CHARGE!!
HE'S SO FAST!
I WANT A HORSE LIKE THAT, POYO!!
REVENGE FOR MASTER PLUE!!

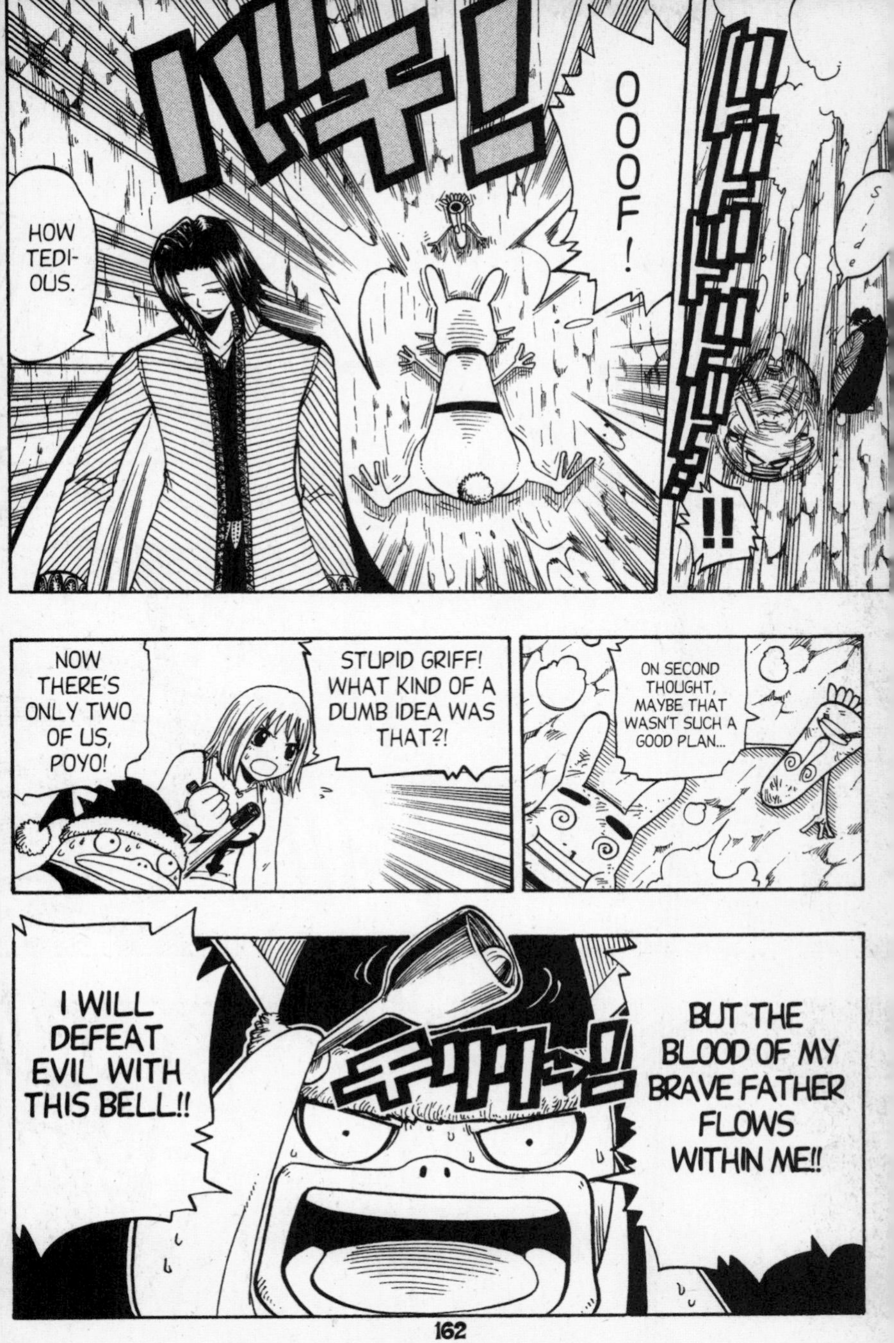
Slide
OOOF!
HOW TEDIOUS.
ON SECOND THOUGHT, MAYBE THAT WASN'T SUCH A GOOD PLAN...
STUPID GRIFF! WHAT KIND OF A DUMB IDEA WAS THAT?!
NOW THERE'S ONLY TWO OF US, POYO!
BUT THE BLOOD OF MY BRAVE FATHER FLOWS WITHIN ME!!
I WILL DEFEAT EVIL WITH THIS BELL!!

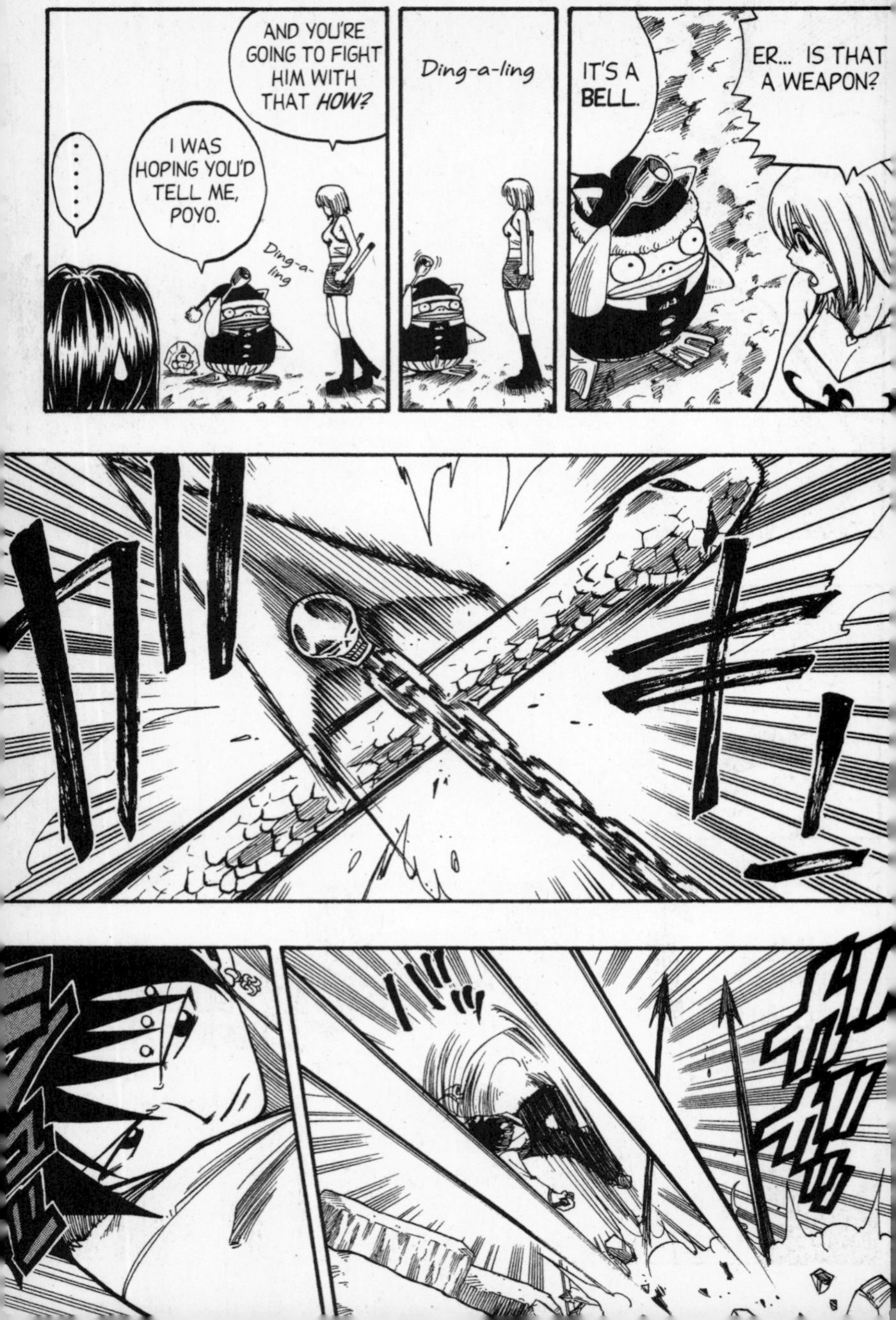
ER... IS THAT A WEAPON?
IT'S A BELL.
Ding-a-ling
AND YOU'RE GOING TO FIGHT HIM WITH THAT *HOW?*
I WAS HOPING YOU'D TELL ME, POYO.
Ding-a-ling
......

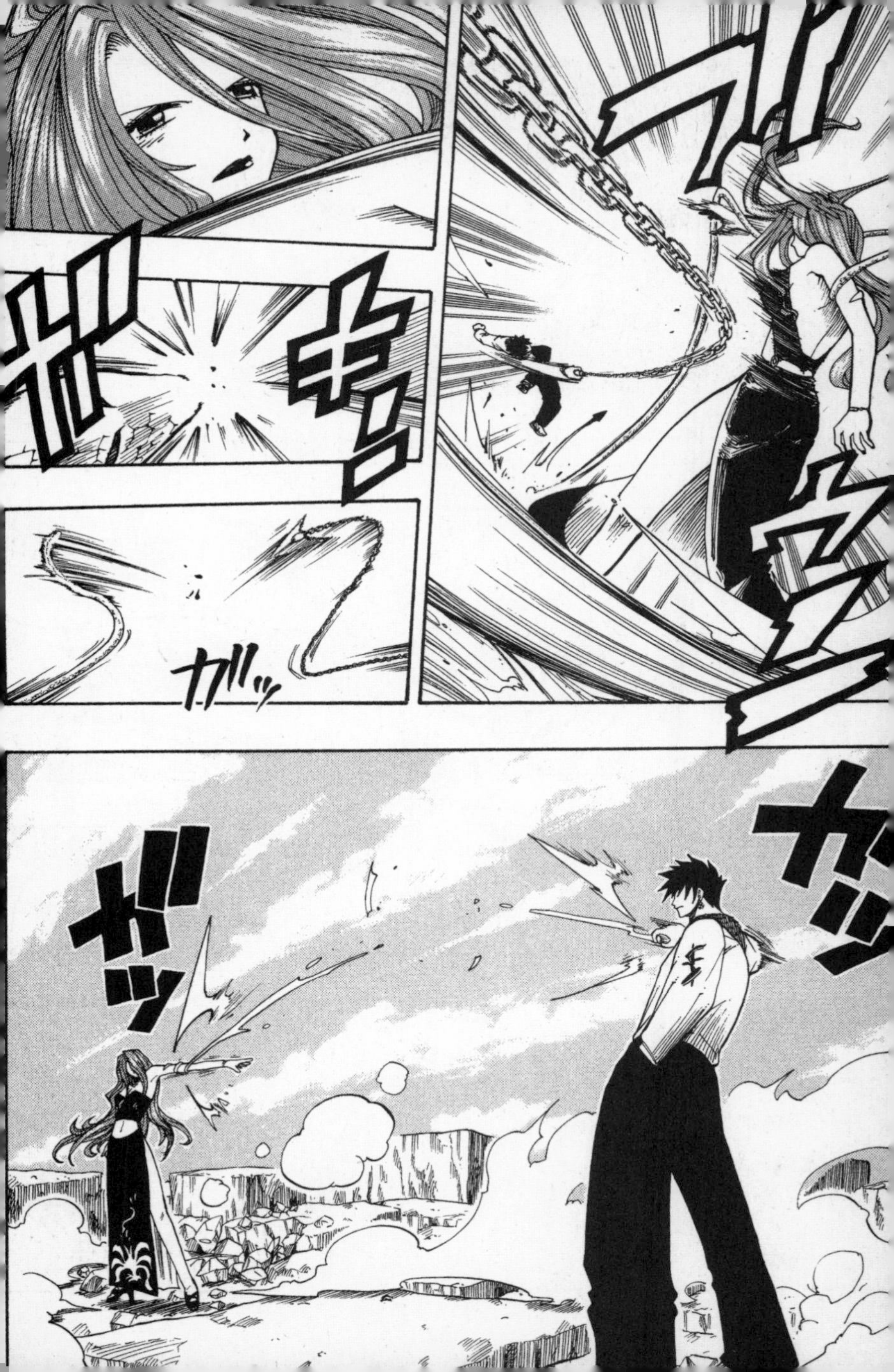
カッ
ガッ

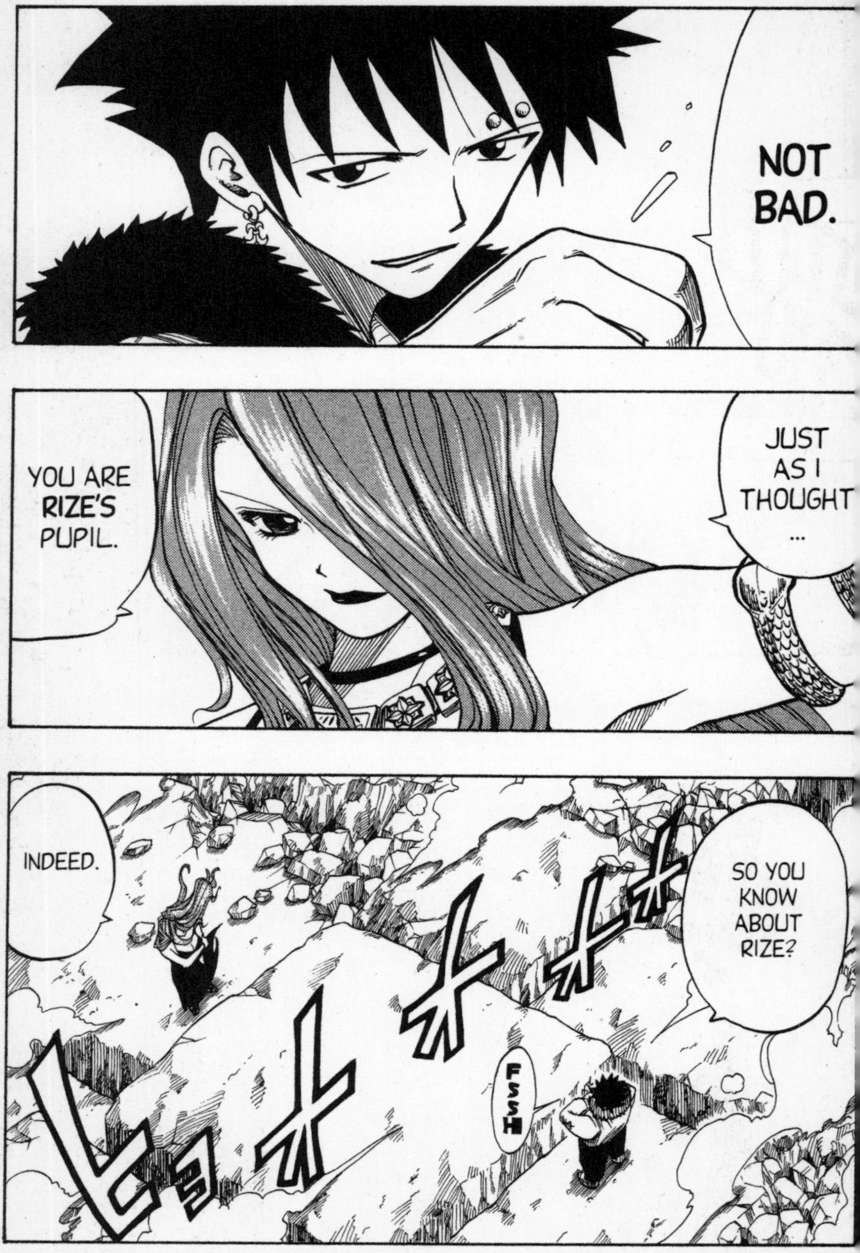
NOT BAD.
JUST AS I THOUGHT ...
YOU ARE RIZE'S PUPIL.
SO YOU KNOW ABOUT RIZE?
FSSH
INDEED.

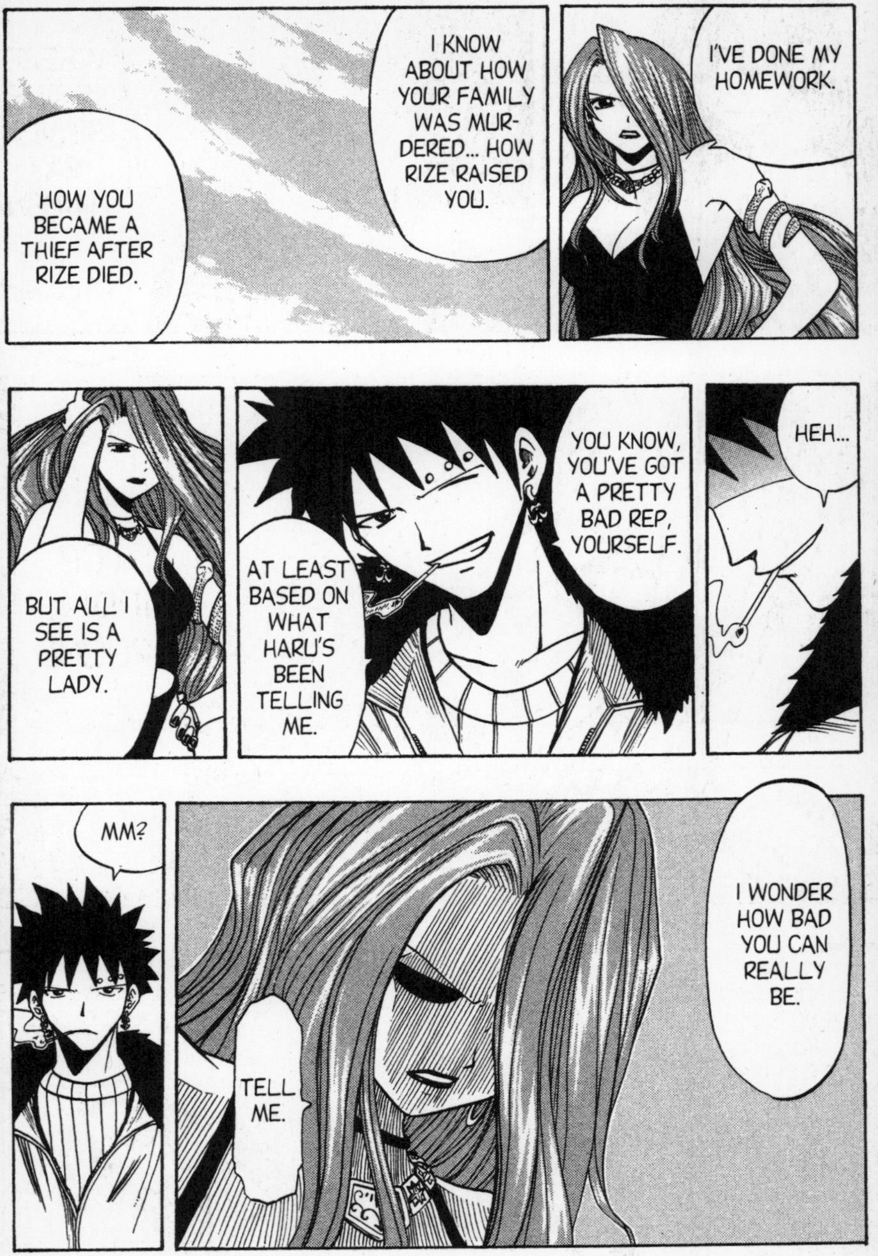
I'VE DONE MY HOMEWORK.
I KNOW ABOUT HOW YOUR FAMILY WAS MUR-DERED... HOW RIZE RAISED YOU.
HOW YOU BECAME A THIEF AFTER RIZE DIED.
HEH...
YOU KNOW, YOU'VE GOT A PRETTY BAD REP, YOURSELF.
AT LEAST BASED ON WHAT HARU'S BEEN TELLING ME.
BUT ALL I SEE IS A PRETTY LADY.
I WONDER HOW BAD YOU CAN REALLY BE.
TELL ME.
MM?

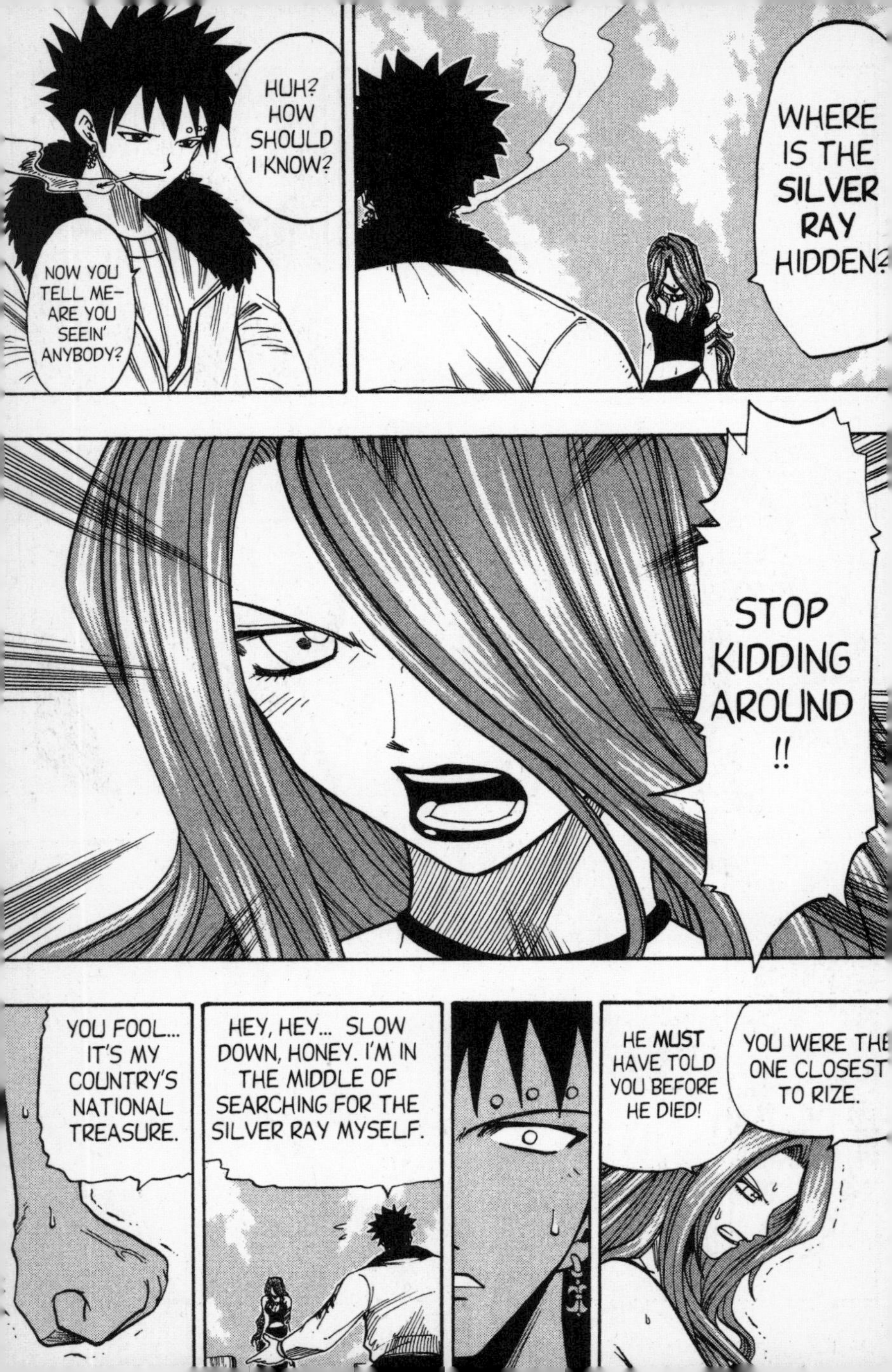
WHERE IS THE SILVER RAY HIDDEN?
HUH? HOW SHOULD I KNOW?
NOW YOU TELL ME— ARE YOU SEEIN' ANYBODY?
STOP KIDDING AROUND !!
YOU WERE THE ONE CLOSEST TO RIZE.
HE **MUST** HAVE TOLD YOU BEFORE HE DIED!
HEY, HEY... SLOW DOWN, HONEY. I'M IN THE MIDDLE OF SEARCHING FOR THE SILVER RAY MYSELF.
YOU FOOL... IT'S MY COUNTRY'S NATIONAL TREASURE.

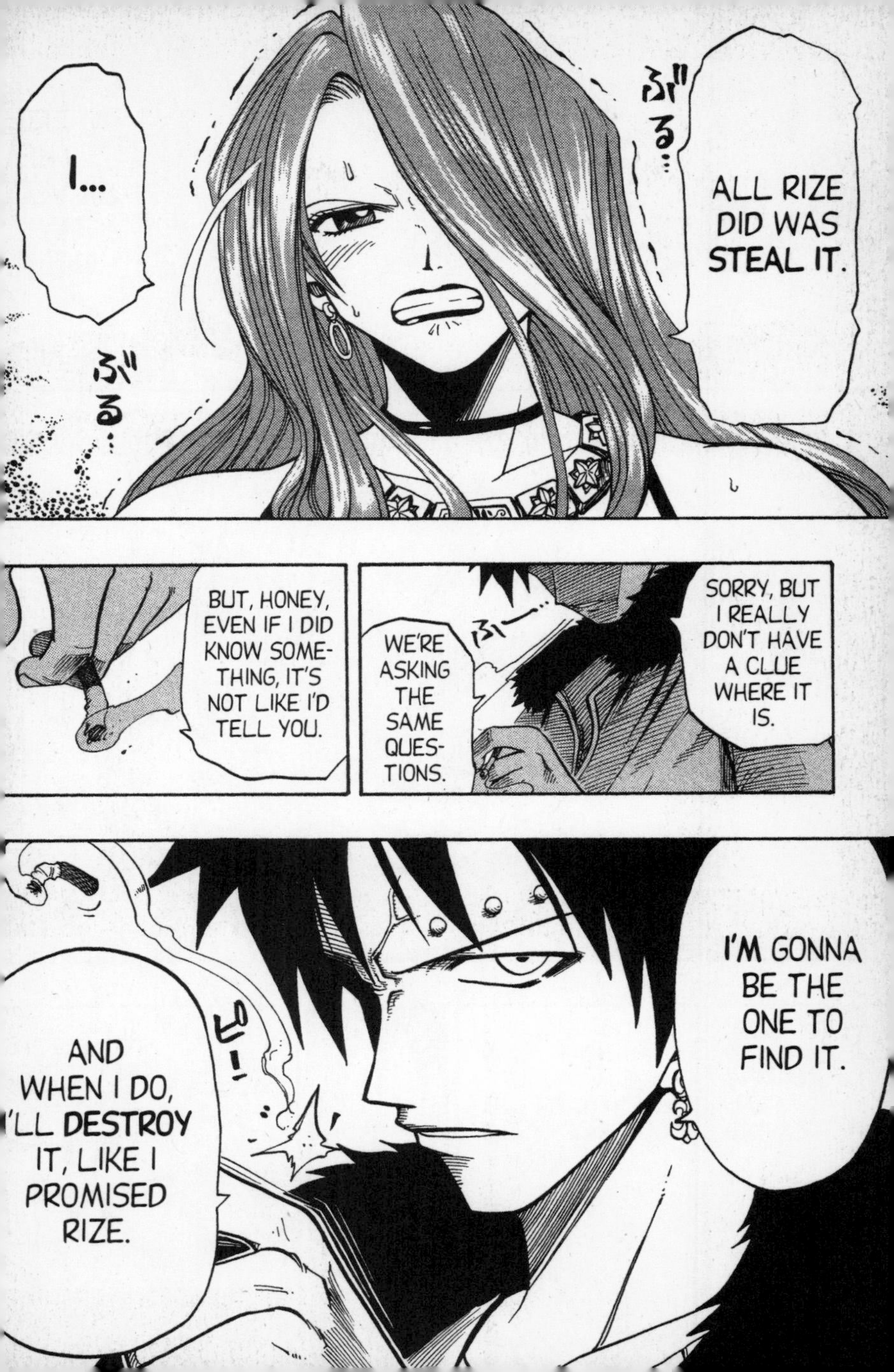
ALL RIZE DID WAS STEAL IT.
ぶる…
I...
ぶる…
SORRY, BUT I REALLY DON'T HAVE A CLUE WHERE IT IS.
ふー…
WE'RE ASKING THE SAME QUESTIONS.
BUT, HONEY, EVEN IF I DID KNOW SOMETHING, IT'S NOT LIKE I'D TELL YOU.
I'M GONNA BE THE ONE TO FIND IT.
ピ!
AND WHEN I DO, I'LL DESTROY IT, LIKE I PROMISED RIZE.

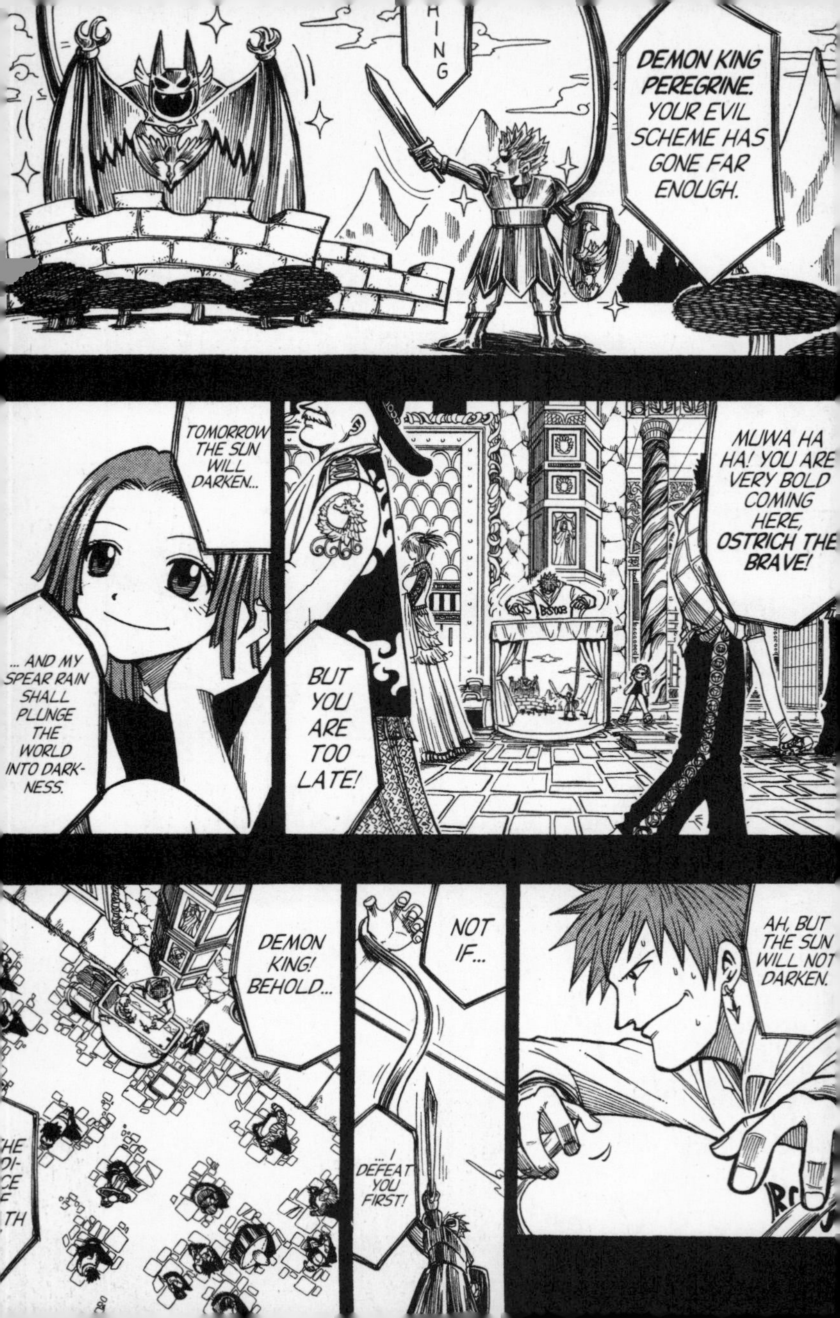
HING
DEMON KING PEREGRINE. YOUR EVIL SCHEME HAS GONE FAR ENOUGH.
MUWA HA HA! YOU ARE VERY BOLD COMING HERE, OSTRICH THE BRAVE!
BUT YOU ARE TOO LATE!
TOMORROW THE SUN WILL DARKEN...
... AND MY SPEAR RAIN SHALL PLUNGE THE WORLD INTO DARK-NESS.
AH, BUT THE SUN WILL NOT DARKEN.
NOT IF...
... I DEFEAT YOU FIRST!
DEMON KING! BEHOLD...

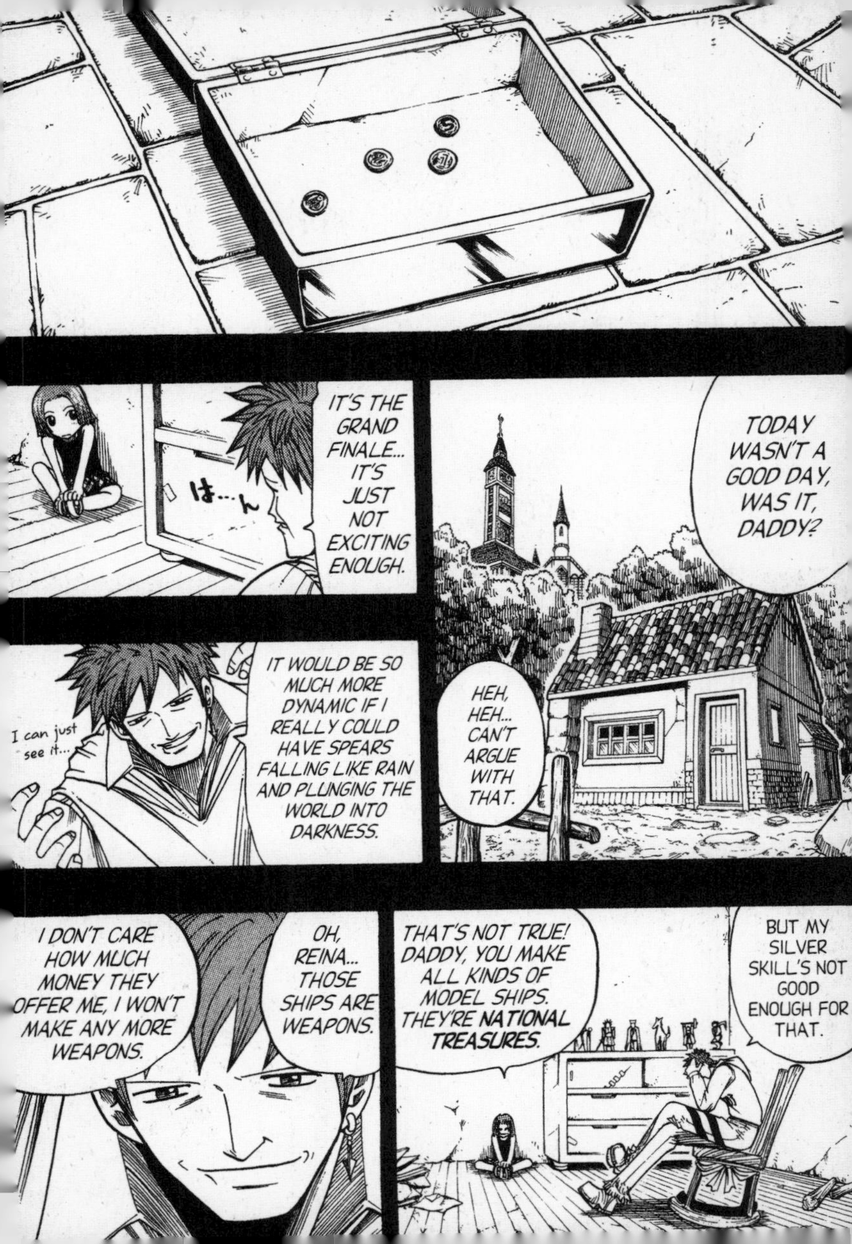
TODAY WASN'T A GOOD DAY, WAS IT, DADDY?
HEH, HEH... CAN'T ARGUE WITH THAT.
IT'S THE GRAND FINALE... IT'S JUST NOT EXCITING ENOUGH.
は…ん
IT WOULD BE SO MUCH MORE DYNAMIC IF I REALLY COULD HAVE SPEARS FALLING LIKE RAIN AND PLUNGING THE WORLD INTO DARKNESS.
I can just see it...
BUT MY SILVER SKILL'S NOT GOOD ENOUGH FOR THAT.
THAT'S NOT TRUE! DADDY, YOU MAKE ALL KINDS OF MODEL SHIPS. THEY'RE **NATIONAL TREASURES**.
OH, REINA... THOSE SHIPS ARE WEAPONS.
I DON'T CARE HOW MUCH MONEY THEY OFFER ME, I WON'T MAKE ANY MORE WEAPONS.

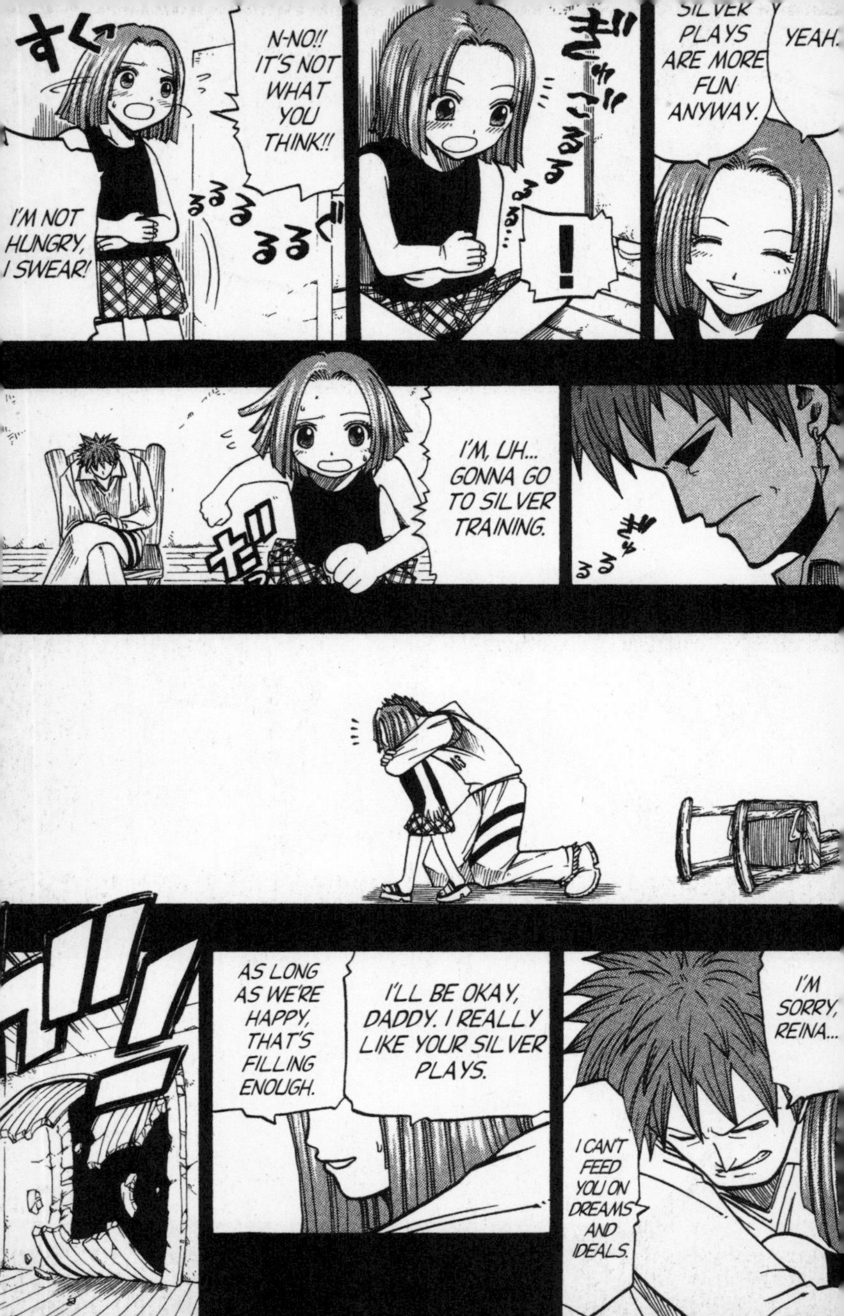
YEAH.
SILVER PLAYS ARE MORE FUN ANYWAY.
ぎゅるるる
るる…
!
すくっ
N-NO!! IT'S NOT WHAT YOU THINK!!
るるる
でっ
るる
I'M NOT HUNGRY, I SWEAR!
ぎゅるる
I'M, UH... GONNA GO TO SILVER TRAINING.
だっ
I'M SORRY, REINA...
I CAN'T FEED YOU ON DREAMS AND IDEALS.
I'LL BE OKAY, DADDY. I REALLY LIKE YOUR SILVER PLAYS.
AS LONG AS WE'RE HAPPY, THAT'S FILLING ENOUGH.
!!

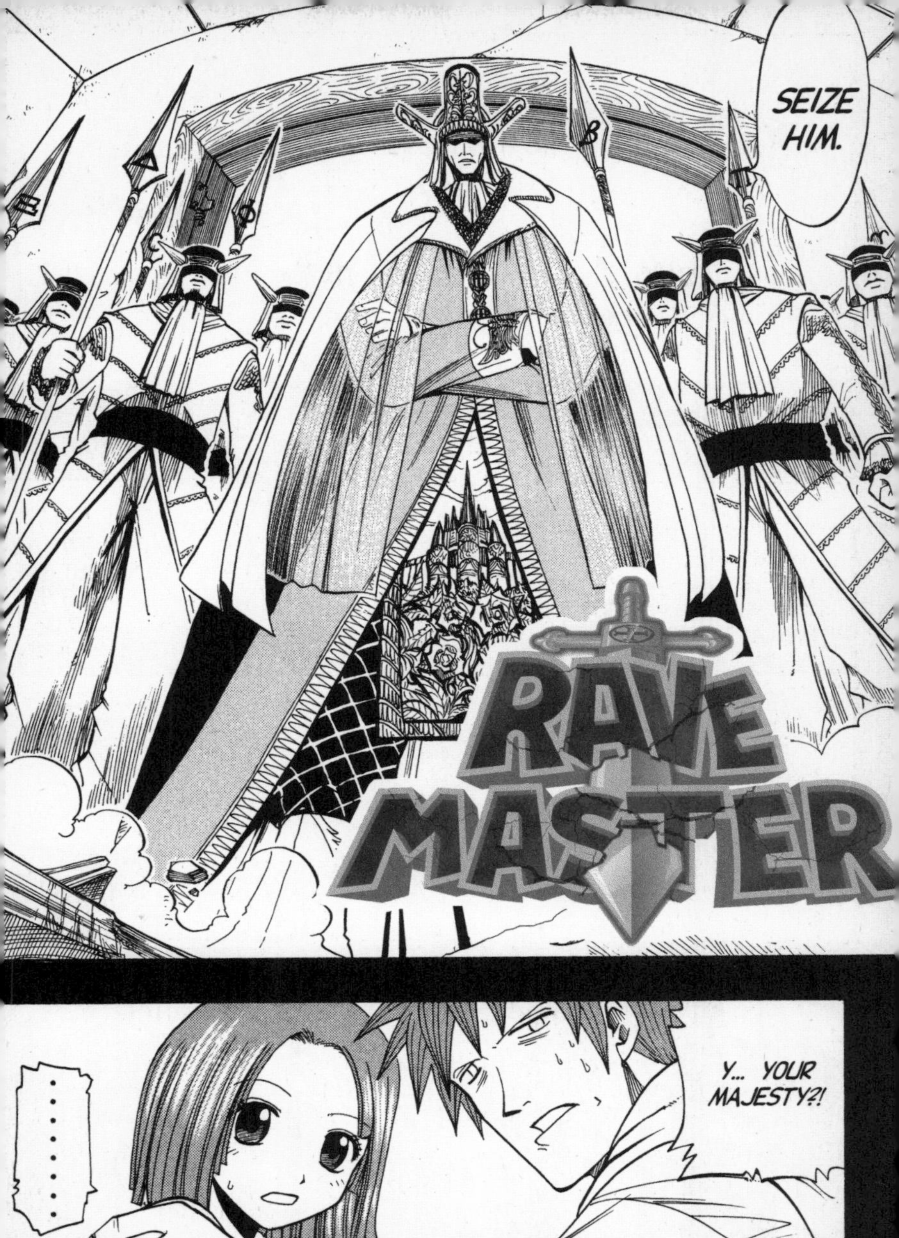
SEIZE HIM.
RAVE MASTER
Y... YOUR MAJESTY?!
......

RAVE:88 SILVER CLAIMER REMINISCENCE

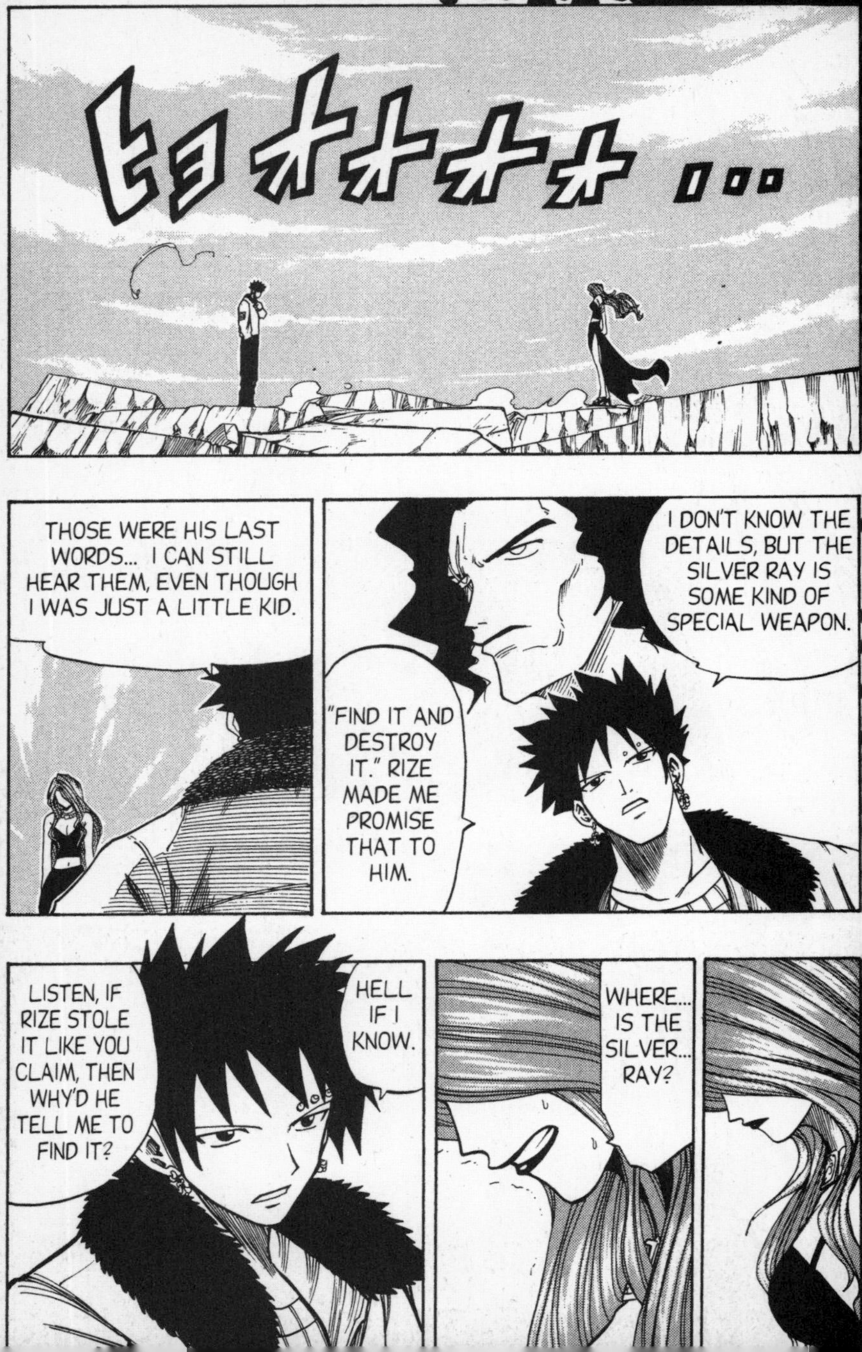

ヒョオオオオオ...
I DON'T KNOW THE DETAILS, BUT THE SILVER RAY IS SOME KIND OF SPECIAL WEAPON.
"FIND IT AND DESTROY IT." RIZE MADE ME PROMISE THAT TO HIM.
THOSE WERE HIS LAST WORDS... I CAN STILL HEAR THEM, EVEN THOUGH I WAS JUST A LITTLE KID.
WHERE... IS THE SILVER... RAY?
HELL IF I KNOW.
LISTEN, IF RIZE STOLE IT LIKE YOU CLAIM, THEN WHY'D HE TELL ME TO FIND IT?

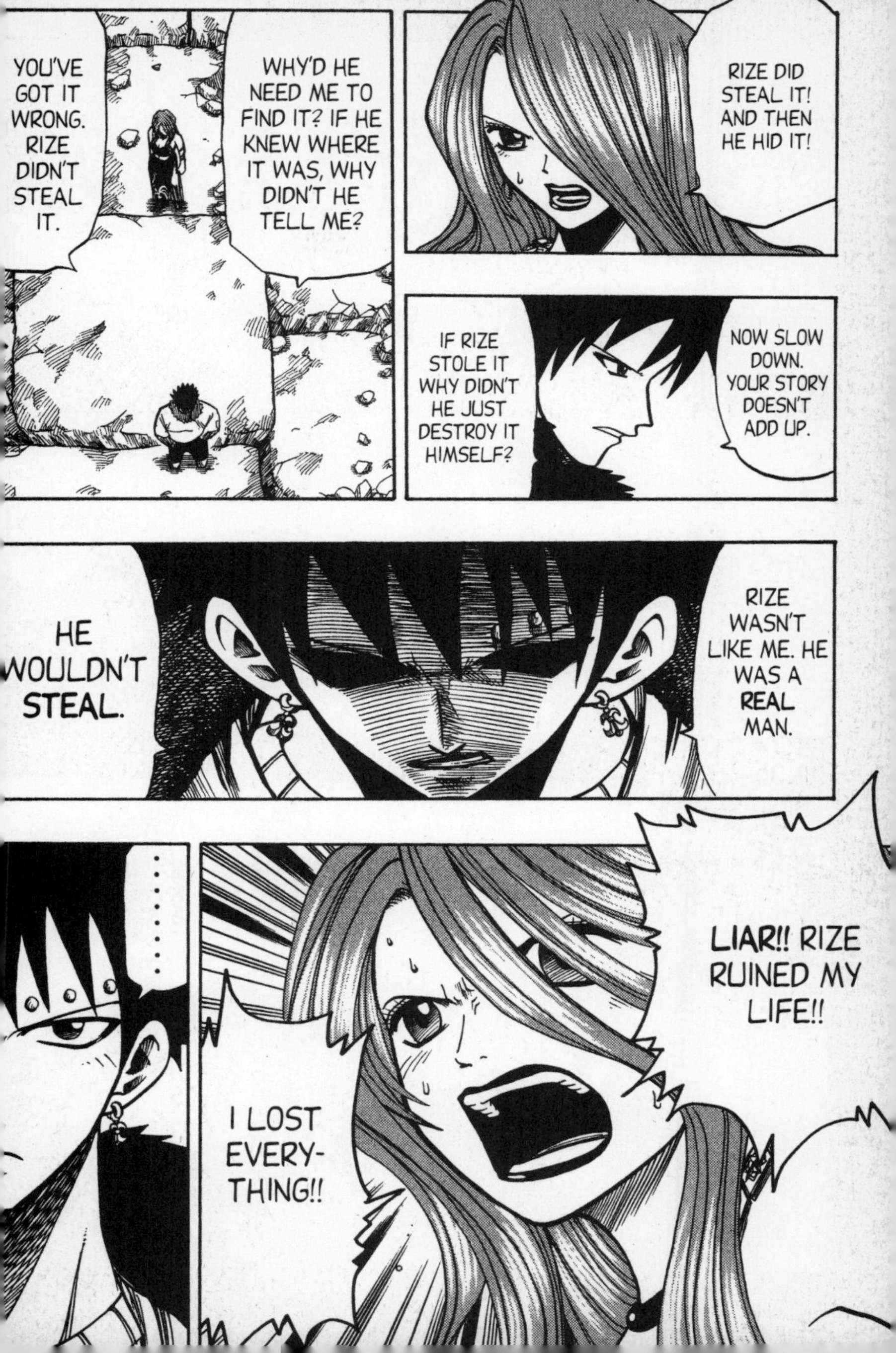
RIZE DID STEAL IT! AND THEN HE HID IT!
NOW SLOW DOWN. YOUR STORY DOESN'T ADD UP.
IF RIZE STOLE IT WHY DIDN'T HE JUST DESTROY IT HIMSELF?
WHY'D HE NEED ME TO FIND IT? IF HE KNEW WHERE IT WAS, WHY DIDN'T HE TELL ME?
YOU'VE GOT IT WRONG. RIZE DIDN'T STEAL IT.
RIZE WASN'T LIKE ME. HE WAS A **REAL** MAN.
HE WOULDN'T **STEAL.**
LIAR!! RIZE RUINED MY LIFE!!
I LOST EVERY-THING!!
......

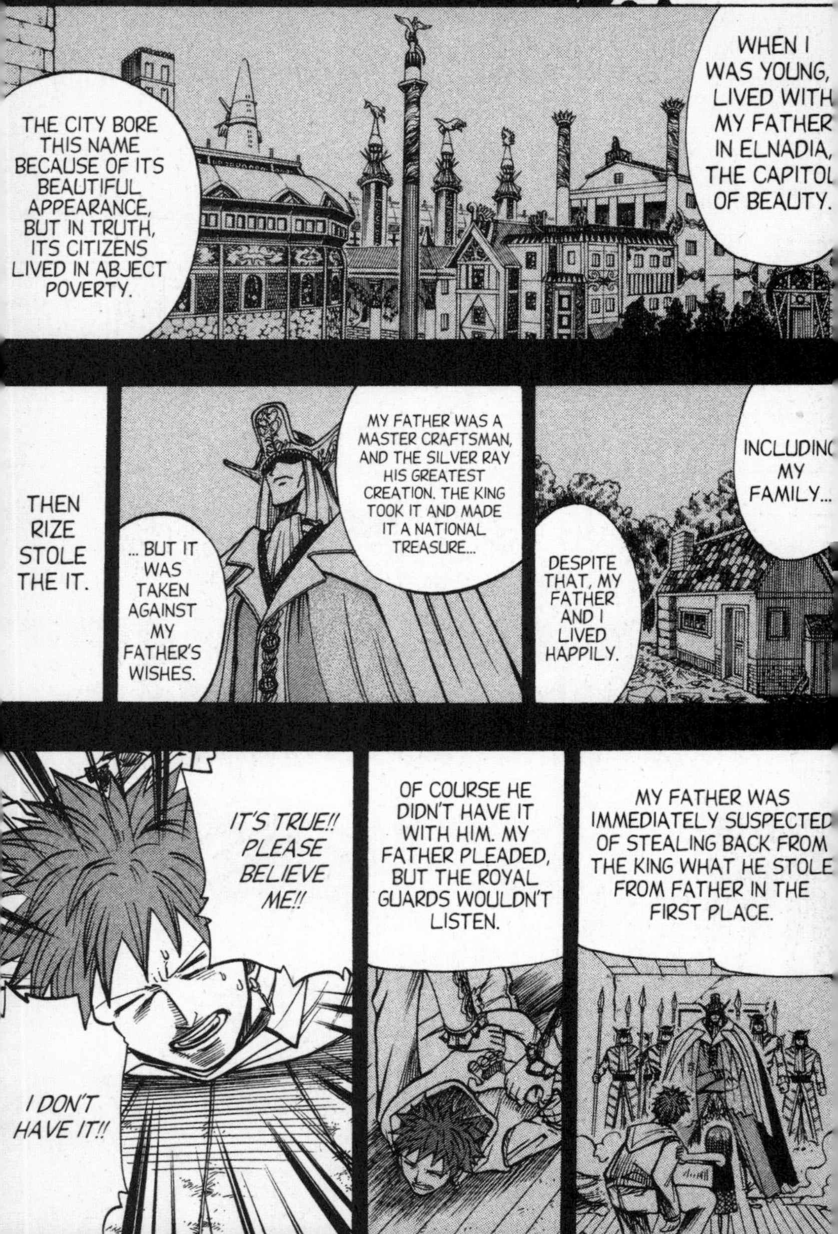
WHEN I WAS YOUNG, LIVED WITH MY FATHER IN ELNADIA, THE CAPITOL OF BEAUTY.
THE CITY BORE THIS NAME BECAUSE OF ITS BEAUTIFUL APPEARANCE, BUT IN TRUTH, ITS CITIZENS LIVED IN ABJECT POVERTY.
INCLUDING MY FAMILY...
DESPITE THAT, MY FATHER AND I LIVED HAPPILY.
MY FATHER WAS A MASTER CRAFTSMAN, AND THE SILVER RAY HIS GREATEST CREATION. THE KING TOOK IT AND MADE IT A NATIONAL TREASURE...
... BUT IT WAS TAKEN AGAINST MY FATHER'S WISHES.
THEN RIZE STOLE THE IT.
MY FATHER WAS IMMEDIATELY SUSPECTED OF STEALING BACK FROM THE KING WHAT HE STOLE FROM FATHER IN THE FIRST PLACE.
OF COURSE HE DIDN'T HAVE IT WITH HIM. MY FATHER PLEADED, BUT THE ROYAL GUARDS WOULDN'T LISTEN.
IT'S TRUE!! PLEASE BELIEVE ME!!
I DON'T HAVE IT!!

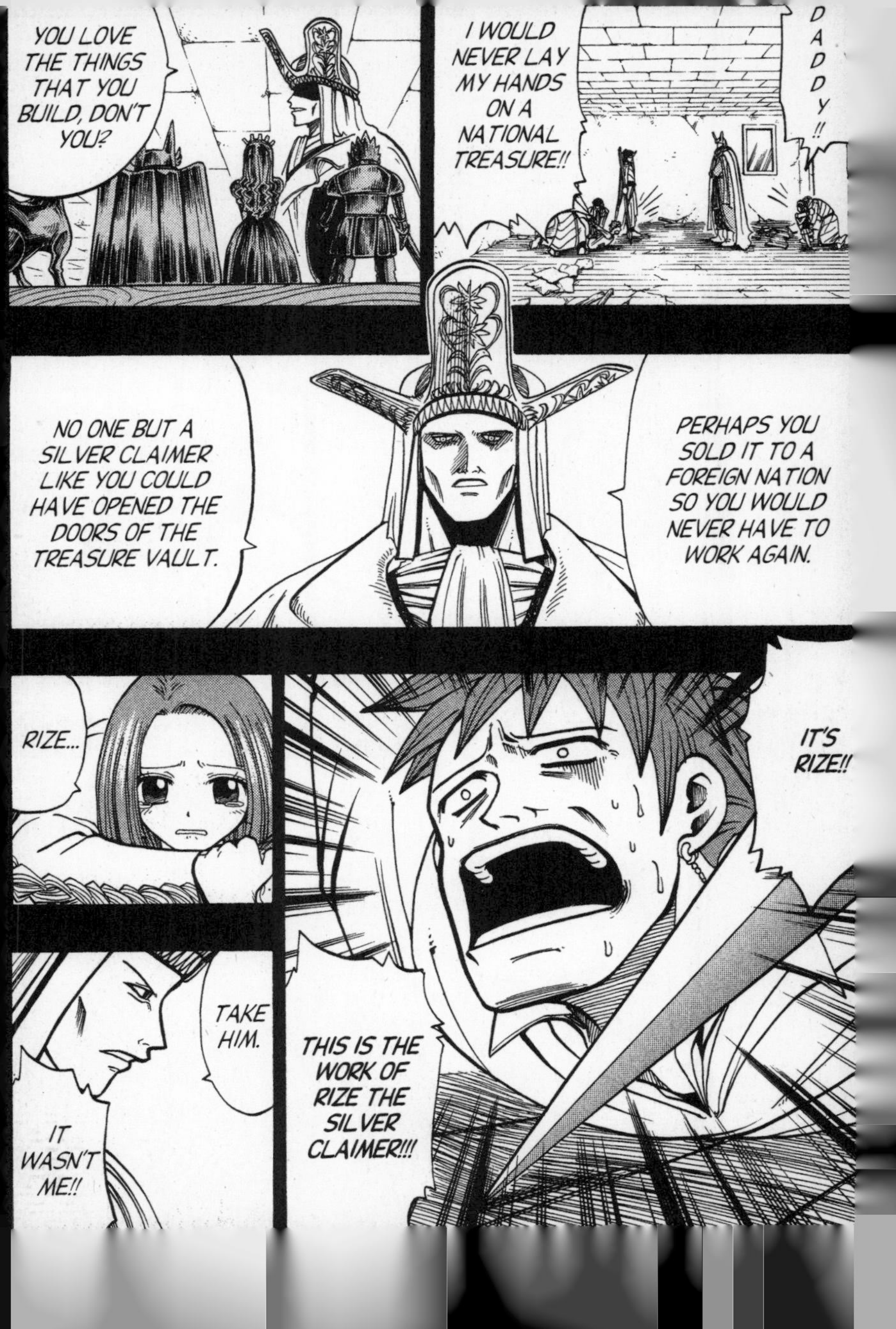
DADDY!!
I WOULD NEVER LAY MY HANDS ON A NATIONAL TREASURE!!
YOU LOVE THE THINGS THAT YOU BUILD, DON'T YOU?
PERHAPS YOU SOLD IT TO A FOREIGN NATION SO YOU WOULD NEVER HAVE TO WORK AGAIN.
NO ONE BUT A SILVER CLAIMER LIKE YOU COULD HAVE OPENED THE DOORS OF THE TREASURE VAULT.
IT'S RIZE!!
THIS IS THE WORK OF RIZE THE SILVER CLAIMER!!!
RIZE...
TAKE HIM.
IT WASN'T ME!!

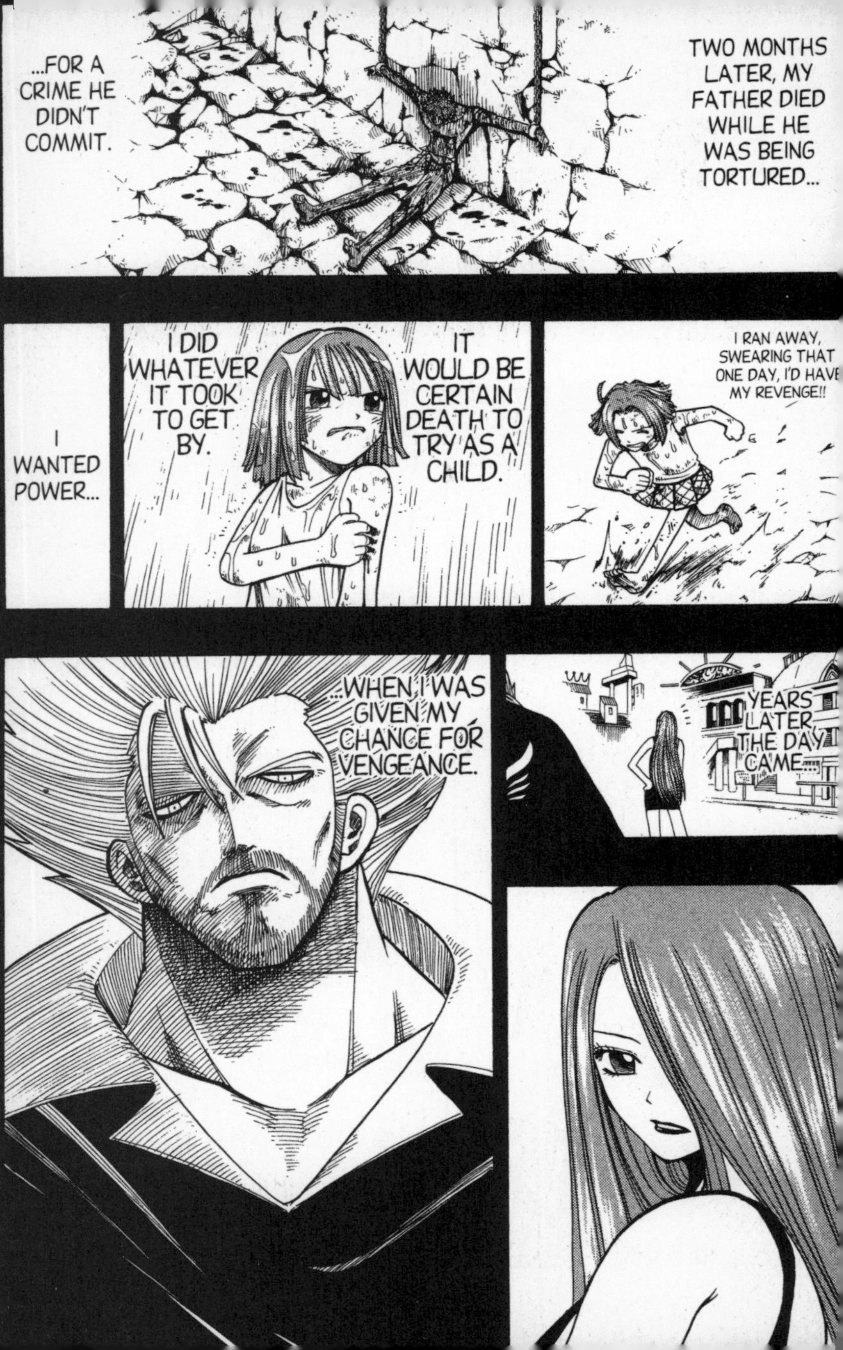
TWO MONTHS LATER, MY FATHER DIED WHILE HE WAS BEING TORTURED...
...FOR A CRIME HE DIDN'T COMMIT.
I RAN AWAY, SWEARING THAT ONE DAY, I'D HAVE MY REVENGE!!
IT WOULD BE CERTAIN DEATH TO TRY AS A CHILD.
I DID WHATEVER IT TOOK TO GET BY.
I WANTED POWER...
YEARS LATER, THE DAY CAME...
...WHEN I WAS GIVEN MY CHANCE FOR VENGEANCE.

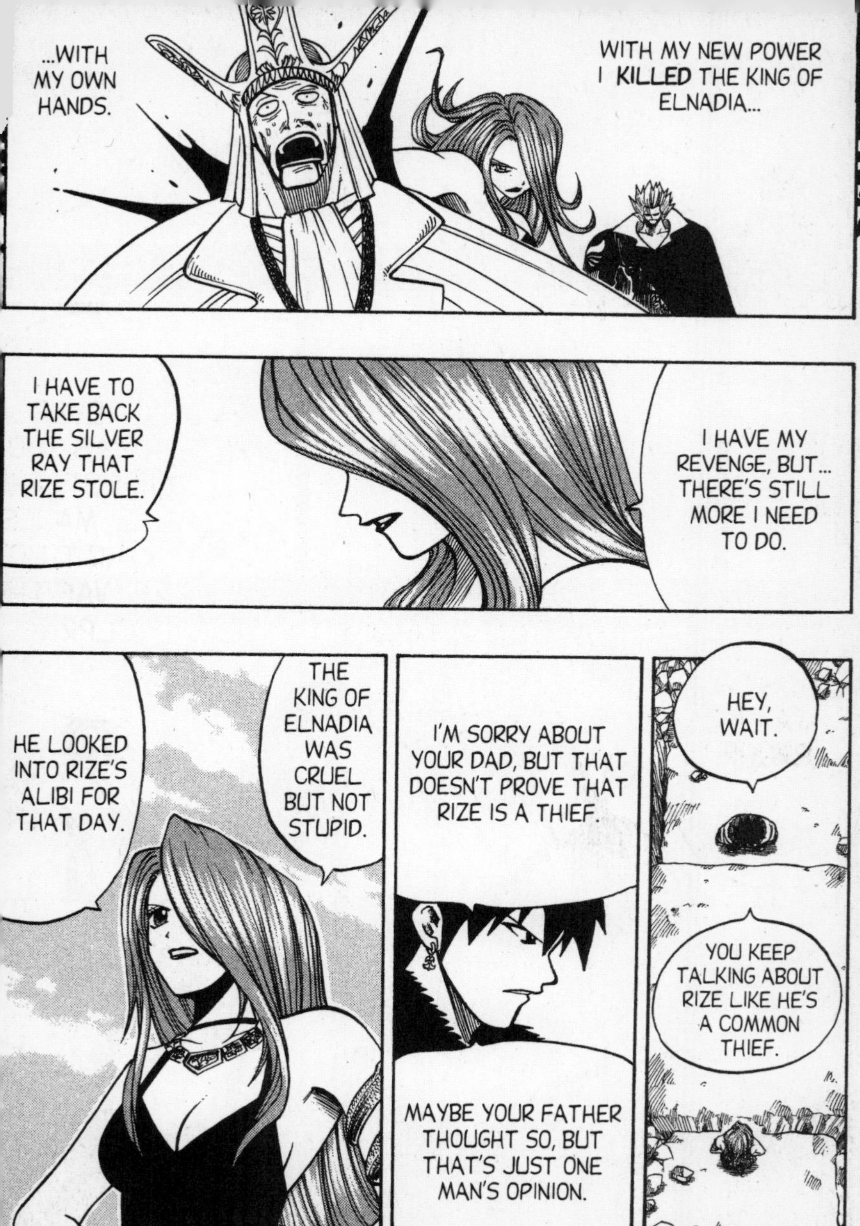
WITH MY NEW POWER I **KILLED** THE KING OF ELNADIA...
...WITH MY OWN HANDS.
I HAVE MY REVENGE, BUT... THERE'S STILL MORE I NEED TO DO.
I HAVE TO TAKE BACK THE SILVER RAY THAT RIZE STOLE.
HEY, WAIT.
YOU KEEP TALKING ABOUT RIZE LIKE HE'S A COMMON THIEF.
I'M SORRY ABOUT YOUR DAD, BUT THAT DOESN'T PROVE THAT RIZE IS A THIEF.
MAYBE YOUR FATHER THOUGHT SO, BUT THAT'S JUST ONE MAN'S OPINION.
THE KING OF ELNADIA WAS CRUEL BUT NOT STUPID.
HE LOOKED INTO RIZE'S ALIBI FOR THAT DAY.

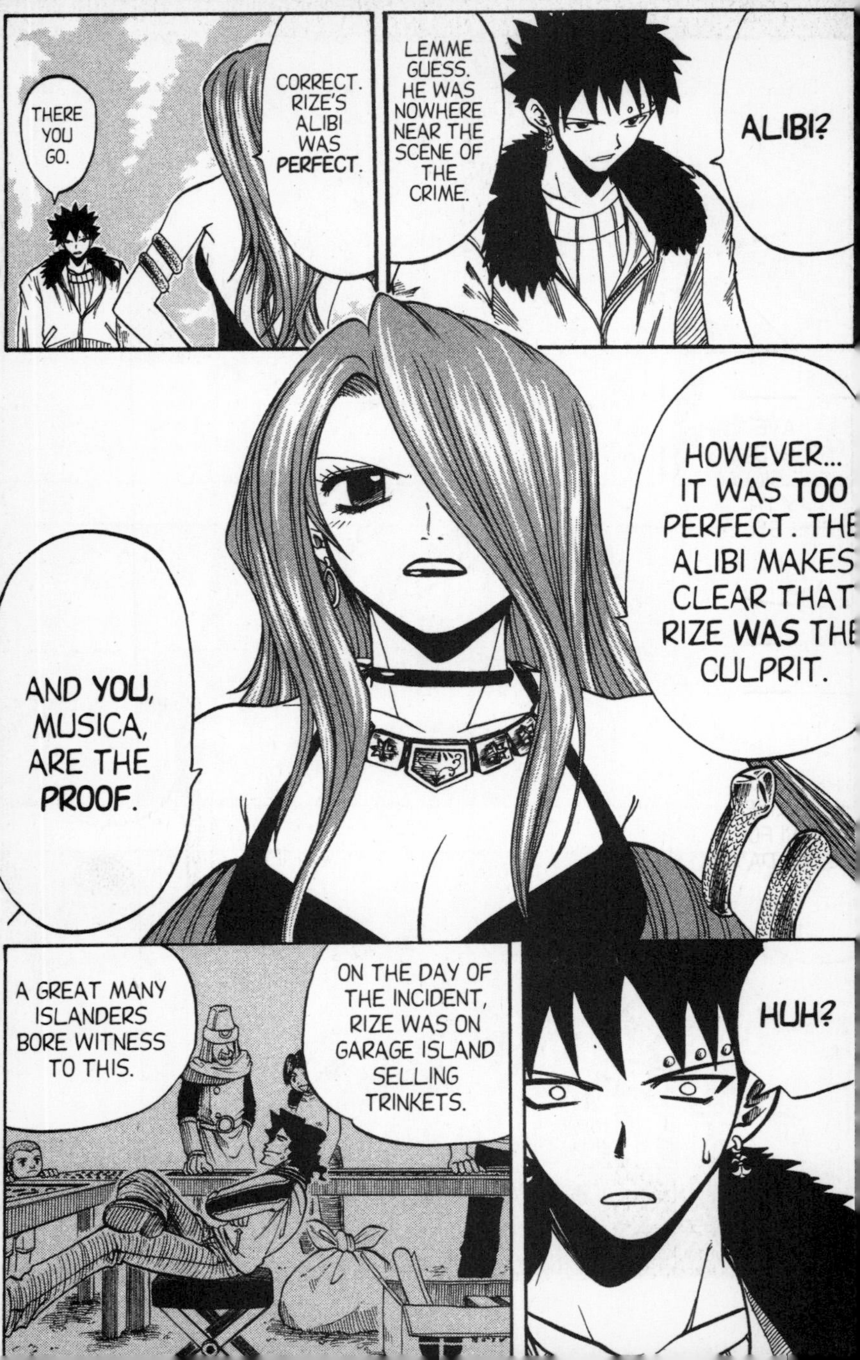
ALIBI?
LEMME GUESS. HE WAS NOWHERE NEAR THE SCENE OF THE CRIME.
CORRECT. RIZE'S ALIBI WAS PERFECT.
THERE YOU GO.
HOWEVER... IT WAS TOO PERFECT. THE ALIBI MAKES CLEAR THAT RIZE WAS THE CULPRIT.
AND YOU, MUSICA, ARE THE PROOF.
HUH?
ON THE DAY OF THE INCIDENT, RIZE WAS ON GARAGE ISLAND SELLING TRINKETS.
A GREAT MANY ISLANDERS BORE WITNESS TO THIS.

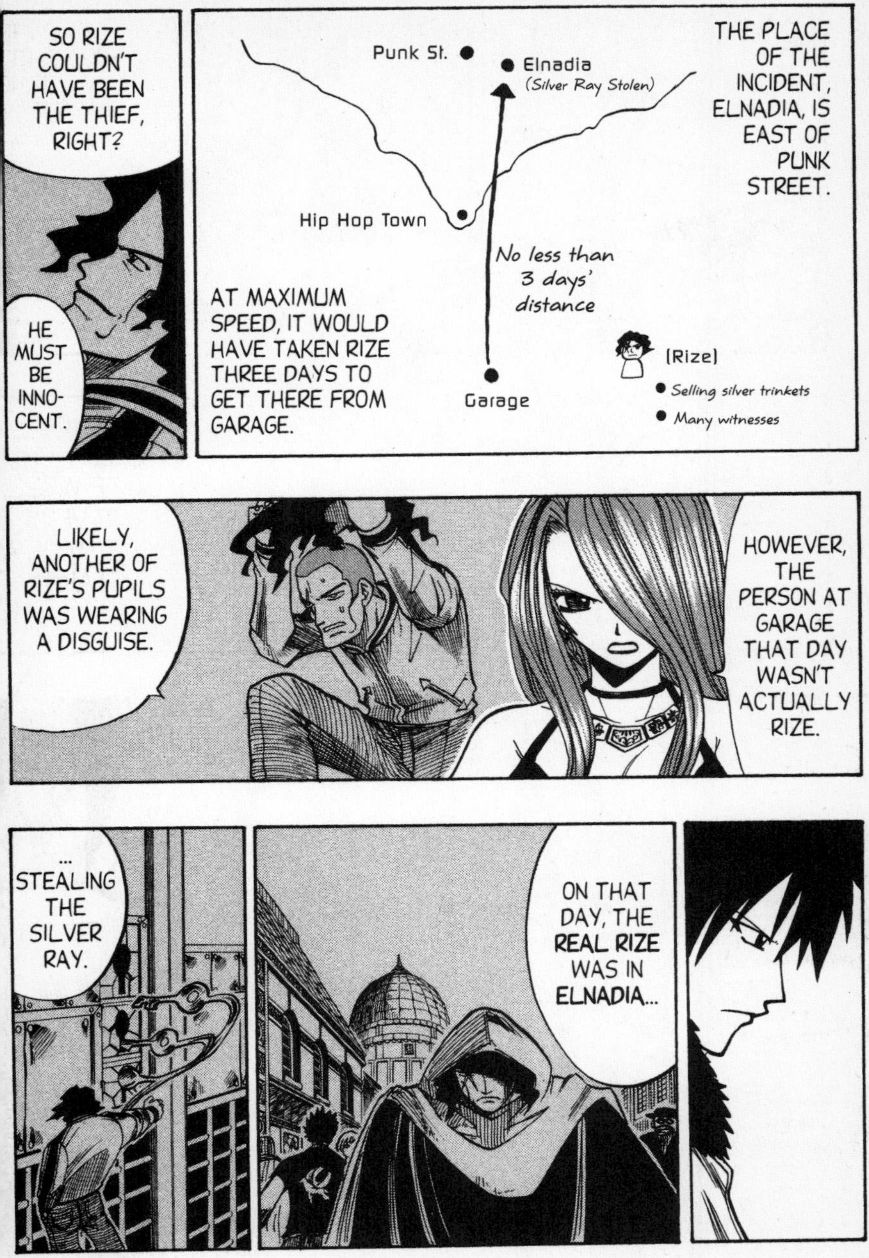
THE PLACE OF THE INCIDENT, ELNADIA, IS EAST OF PUNK STREET.
Punk St.
Elnadia
(Silver Ray Stolen)
Hip Hop Town
No less than 3 days' distance
Garage
[Rize]
Selling silver trinkets
Many witnesses
AT MAXIMUM SPEED, IT WOULD HAVE TAKEN RIZE THREE DAYS TO GET THERE FROM GARAGE.
SO RIZE COULDN'T HAVE BEEN THE THIEF, RIGHT?
HE MUST BE INNO-CENT.
HOWEVER, THE PERSON AT GARAGE THAT DAY WASN'T ACTUALLY RIZE.
LIKELY, ANOTHER OF RIZE'S PUPILS WAS WEARING A DISGUISE.
ON THAT DAY, THE **REAL RIZE** WAS IN **ELNADIA**...
...STEALING THE SILVER RAY.

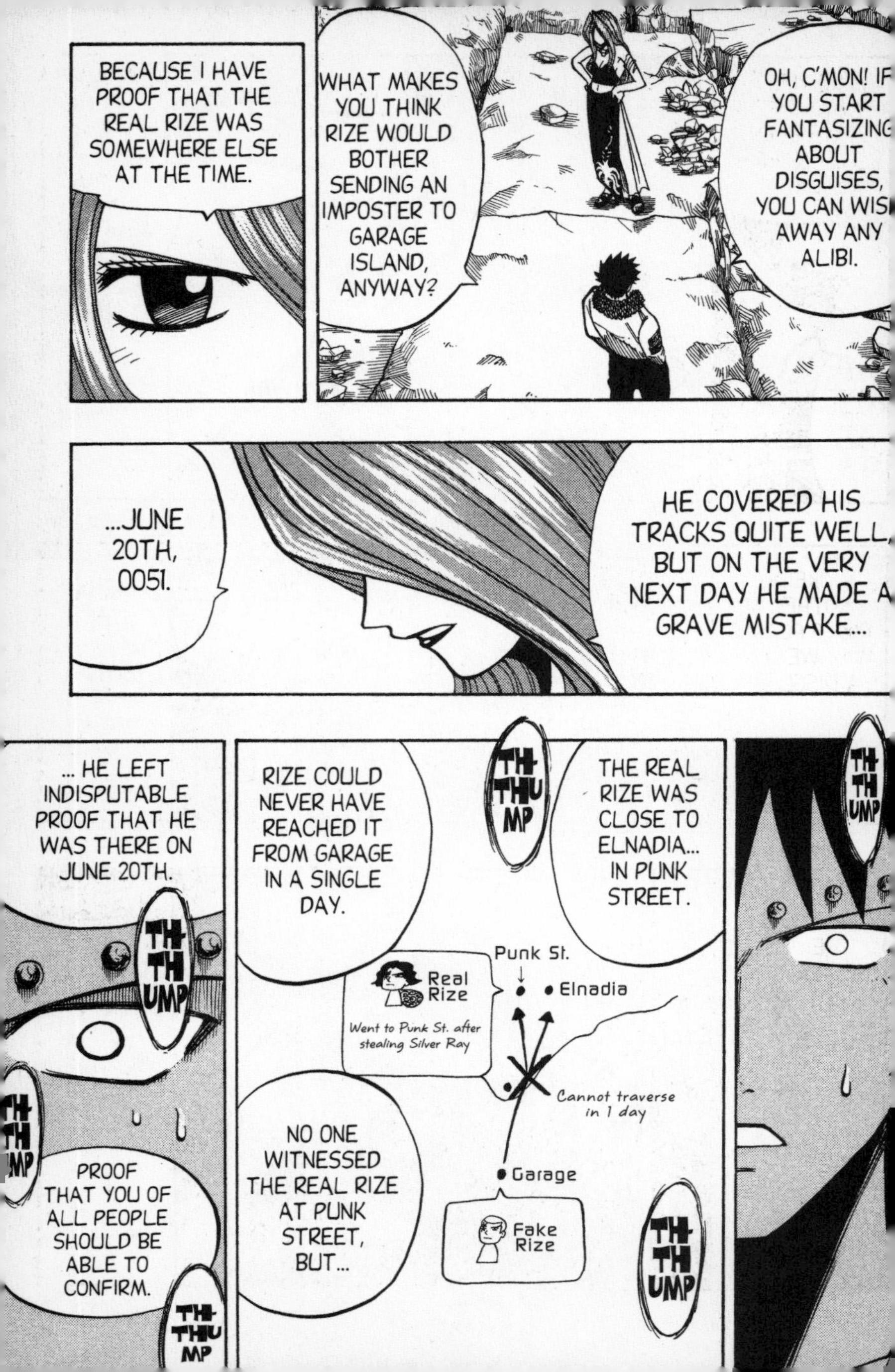
OH, C'MON! IF YOU START FANTASIZING ABOUT DISGUISES, YOU CAN WISH AWAY ANY ALIBI.
WHAT MAKES YOU THINK RIZE WOULD BOTHER SENDING AN IMPOSTER TO GARAGE ISLAND, ANYWAY?
BECAUSE I HAVE PROOF THAT THE REAL RIZE WAS SOMEWHERE ELSE AT THE TIME.
HE COVERED HIS TRACKS QUITE WELL, BUT ON THE VERY NEXT DAY HE MADE A GRAVE MISTAKE...
...JUNE 20TH, 0051.
TH-TH-UMP
TH-THU-MP
THE REAL RIZE WAS CLOSE TO ELNADIA... IN PUNK STREET.
RIZE COULD NEVER HAVE REACHED IT FROM GARAGE IN A SINGLE DAY.
Punk St.
Elnadia
Real Rize
Went to Punk St. after stealing Silver Ray
Cannot traverse in 1 day
Garage
Fake Rize
NO ONE WITNESSED THE REAL RIZE AT PUNK STREET, BUT...
TH-TH-UMP
... HE LEFT INDISPUTABLE PROOF THAT HE WAS THERE ON JUNE 20TH.
TH-TH-UMP
PROOF THAT YOU OF ALL PEOPLE SHOULD BE ABLE TO CONFIRM.
TH-THU-MP

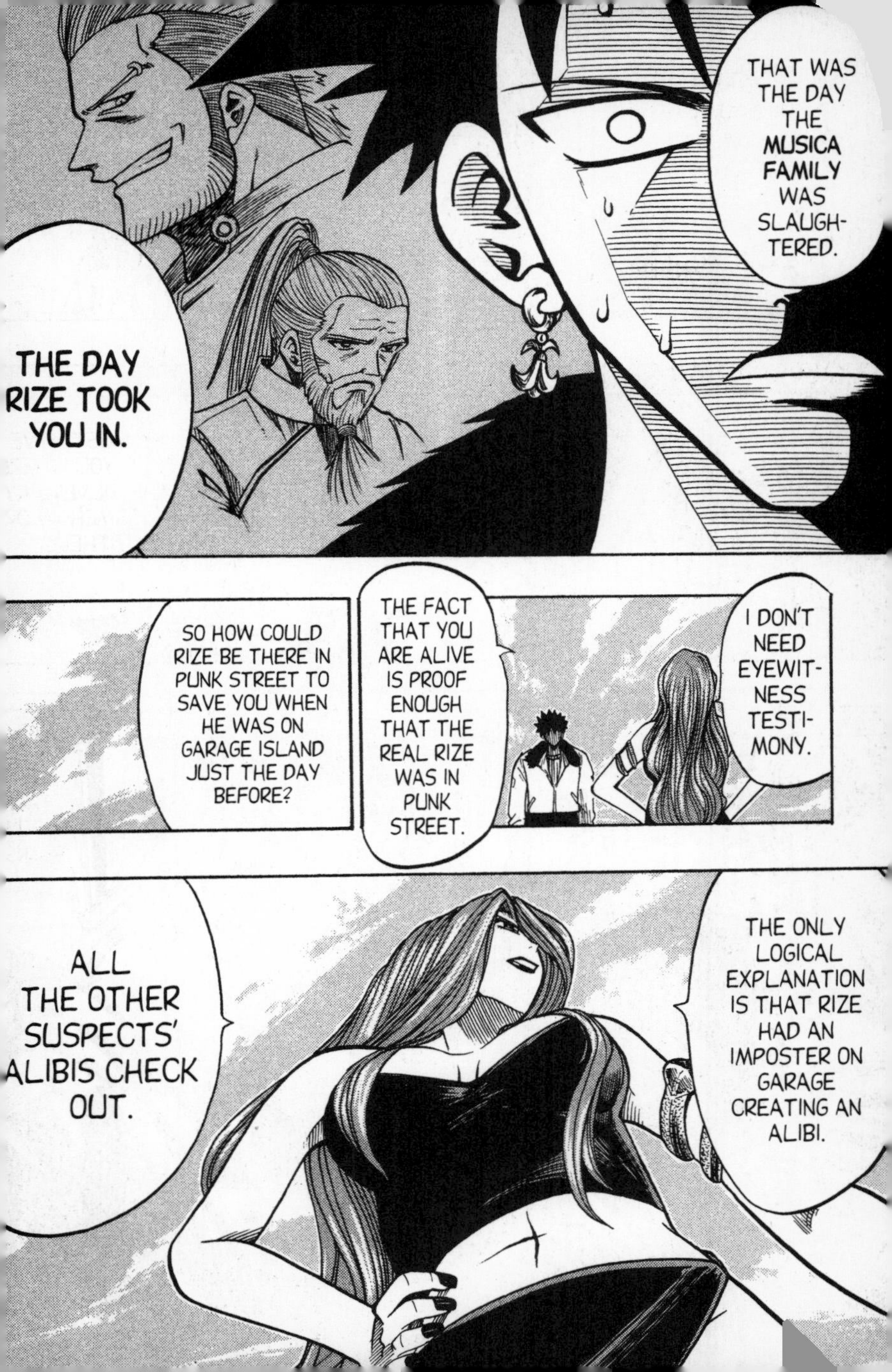
THAT WAS THE DAY THE MUSICA FAMILY WAS SLAUGHTERED.
THE DAY RIZE TOOK YOU IN.
I DON'T NEED EYEWITNESS TESTIMONY.
THE FACT THAT YOU ARE ALIVE IS PROOF ENOUGH THAT THE REAL RIZE WAS IN PUNK STREET.
SO HOW COULD RIZE BE THERE IN PUNK STREET TO SAVE YOU WHEN HE WAS ON GARAGE ISLAND JUST THE DAY BEFORE?
THE ONLY LOGICAL EXPLANATION IS THAT RIZE HAD AN IMPOSTER ON GARAGE CREATING AN ALIBI.
ALL THE OTHER SUSPECTS' ALIBIS CHECK OUT.

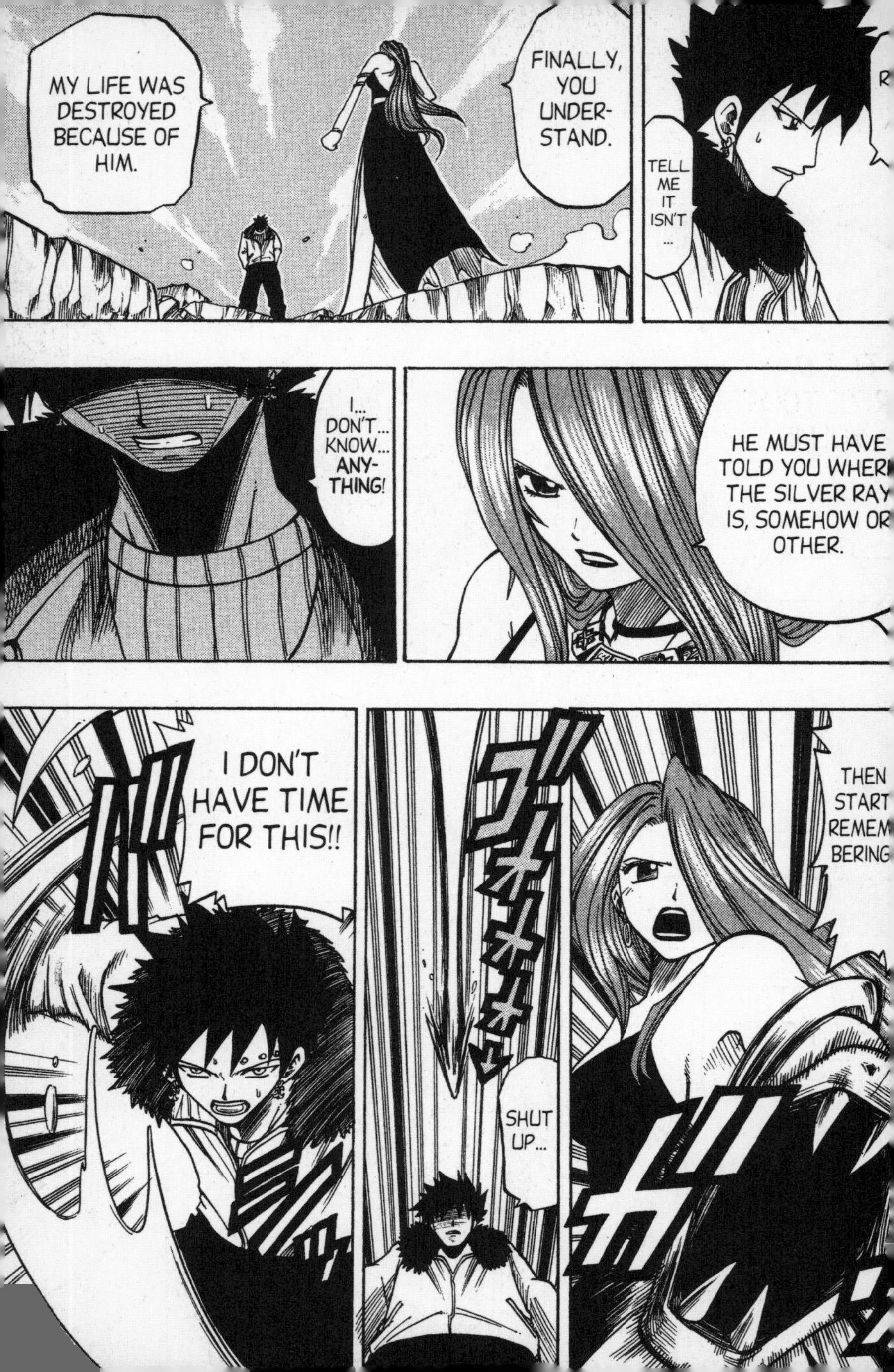
TELL ME IT ISN'T ...
FINALLY, YOU UNDER-STAND.
MY LIFE WAS DESTROYED BECAUSE OF HIM.
HE MUST HAVE TOLD YOU WHER THE SILVER RAY IS, SOMEHOW OR OTHER.
I... DON'T... KNOW... ANY-THING!
THEN START REMEM BERING
SHUT UP...
I DON'T HAVE TIME FOR THIS!!

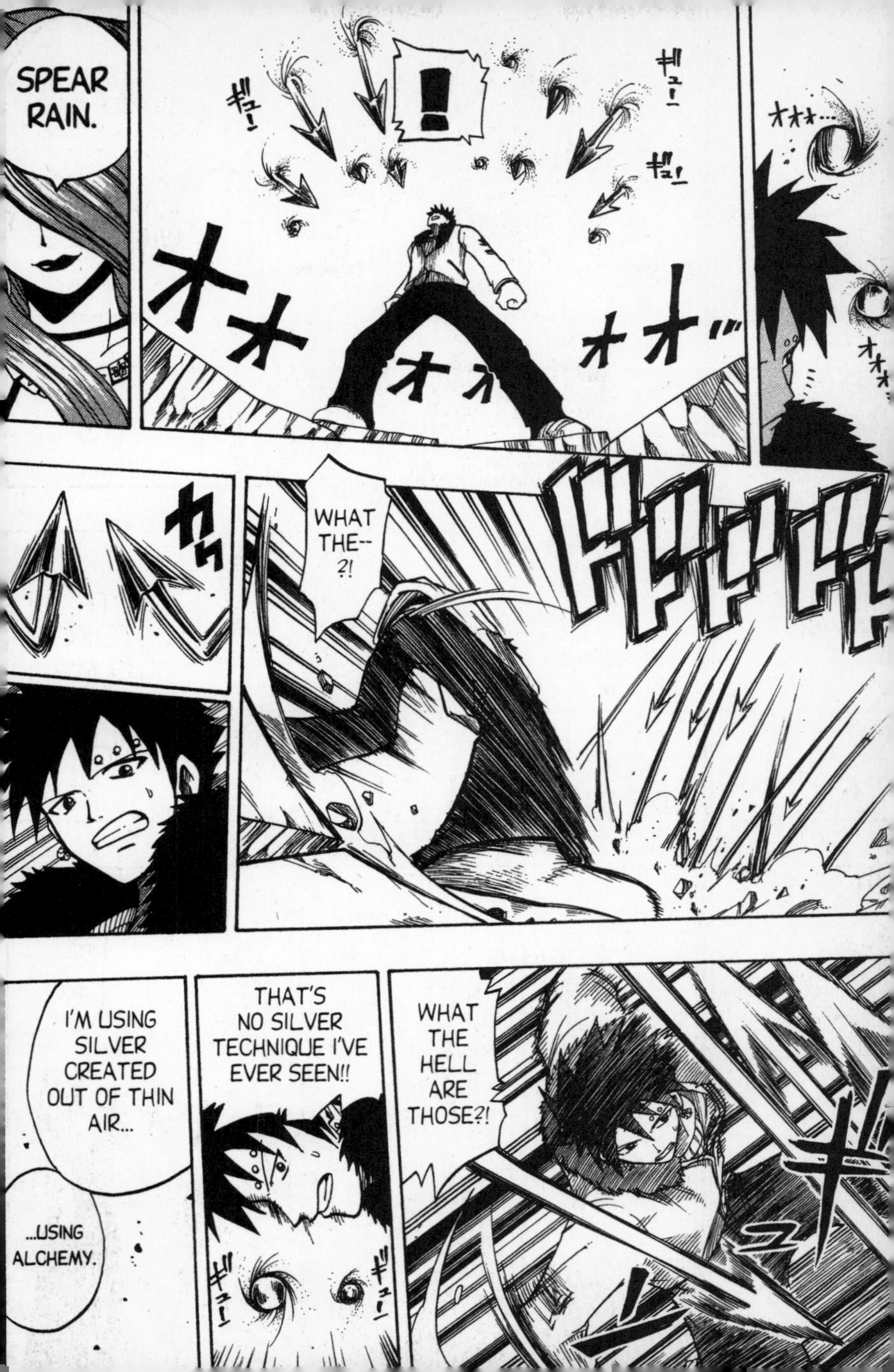
!
SPEAR RAIN.
WHAT THE--?!
WHAT THE HELL ARE THOSE?!
THAT'S NO SILVER TECHNIQUE I'VE EVER SEEN!!
I'M USING SILVER CREATED OUT OF THIN AIR...
...USING ALCHEMY.

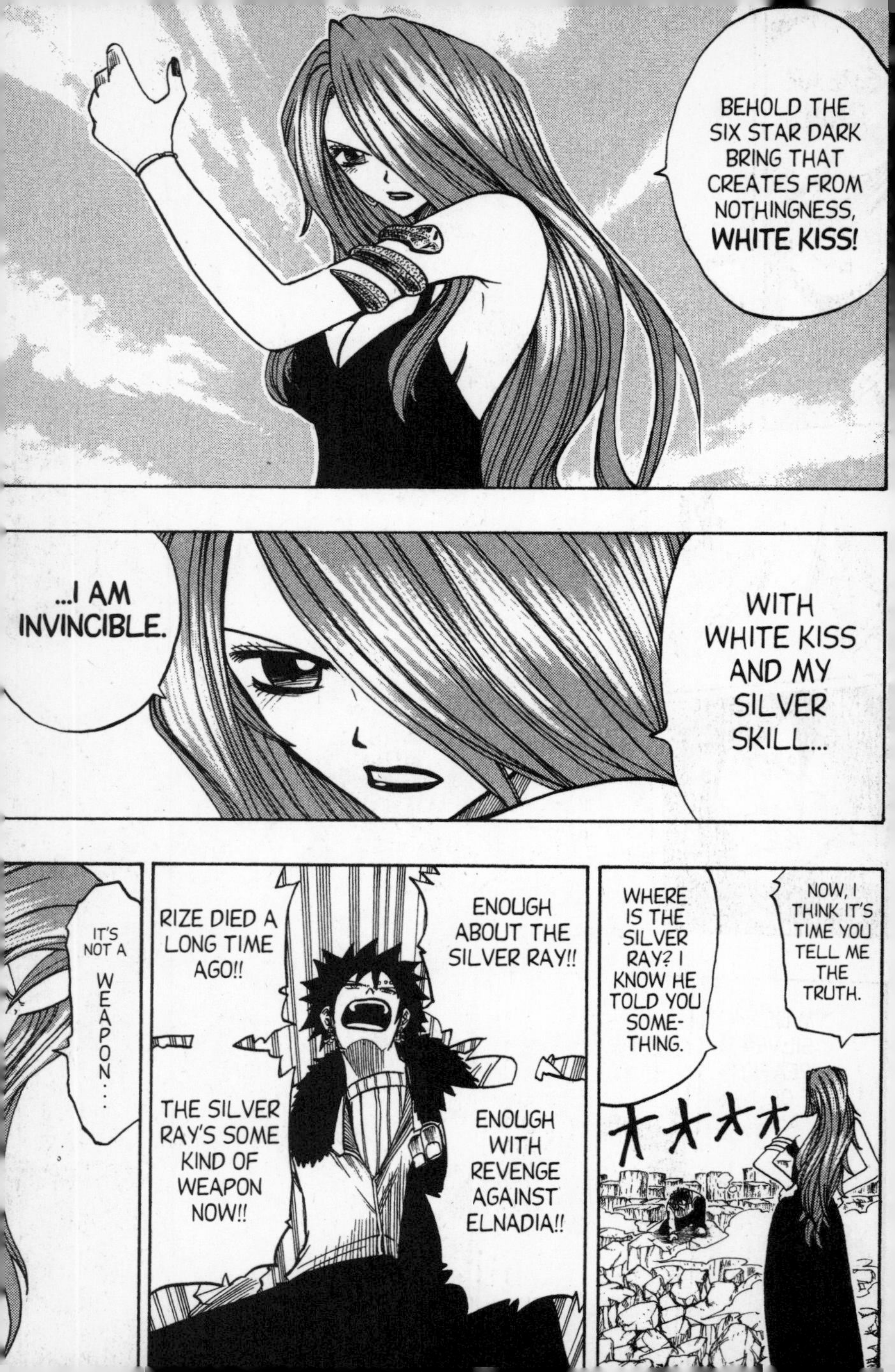
BEHOLD THE SIX STAR DARK BRING THAT CREATES FROM NOTHINGNESS, WHITE KISS!
WITH WHITE KISS AND MY SILVER SKILL...
...I AM INVINCIBLE.
NOW, I THINK IT'S TIME YOU TELL ME THE TRUTH.
WHERE IS THE SILVER RAY? I KNOW HE TOLD YOU SOMETHING.
ENOUGH ABOUT THE SILVER RAY!!
RIZE DIED A LONG TIME AGO!!
ENOUGH WITH REVENGE AGAINST ELNADIA!!
THE SILVER RAY'S SOME KIND OF WEAPON NOW!!
IT'S NOT A WEAPON...

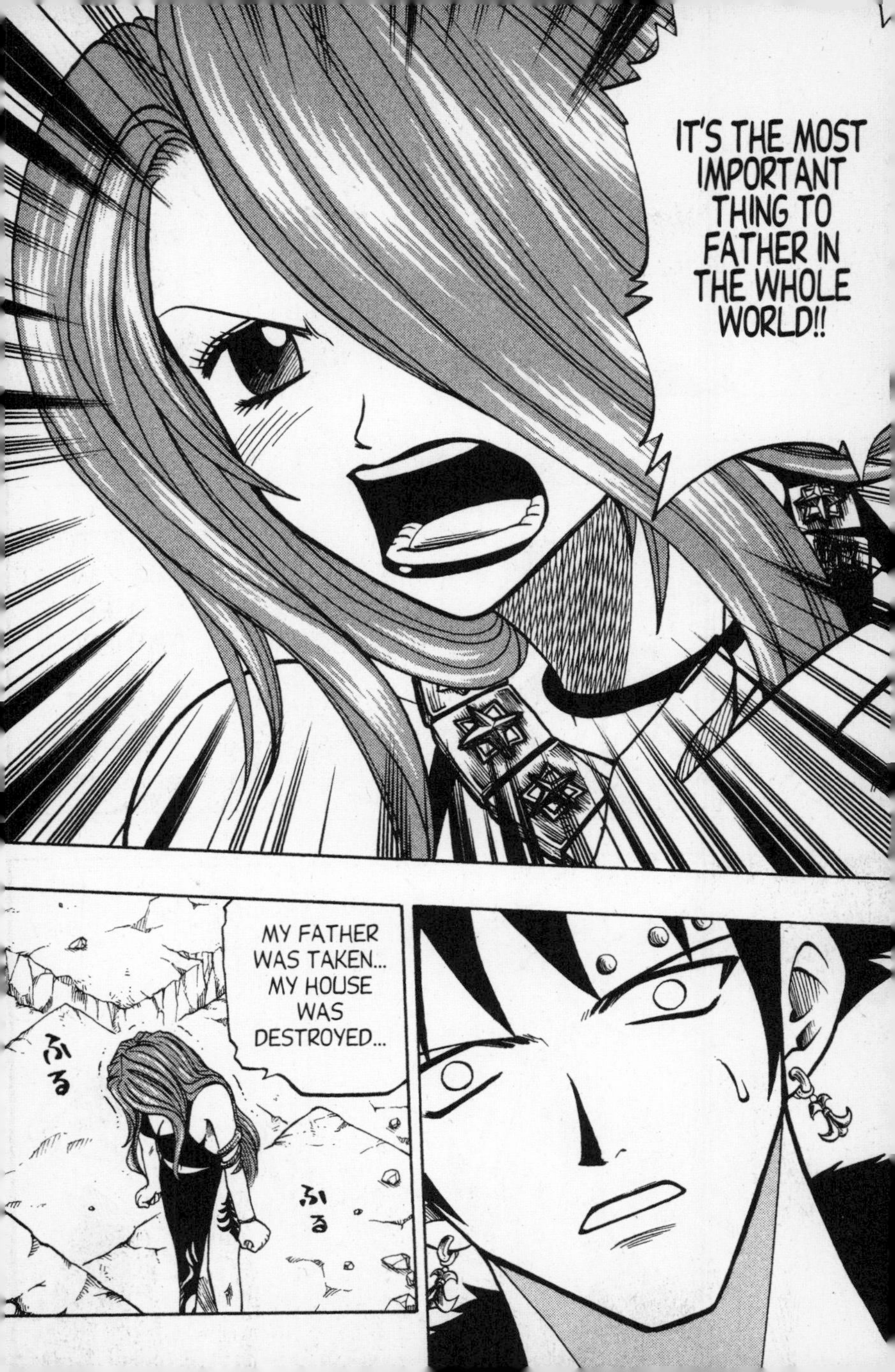
IT'S THE MOST IMPORTANT THING TO FATHER IN THE WHOLE WORLD!!
MY FATHER WAS TAKEN... MY HOUSE WAS DESTROYED...
ふる
ふる

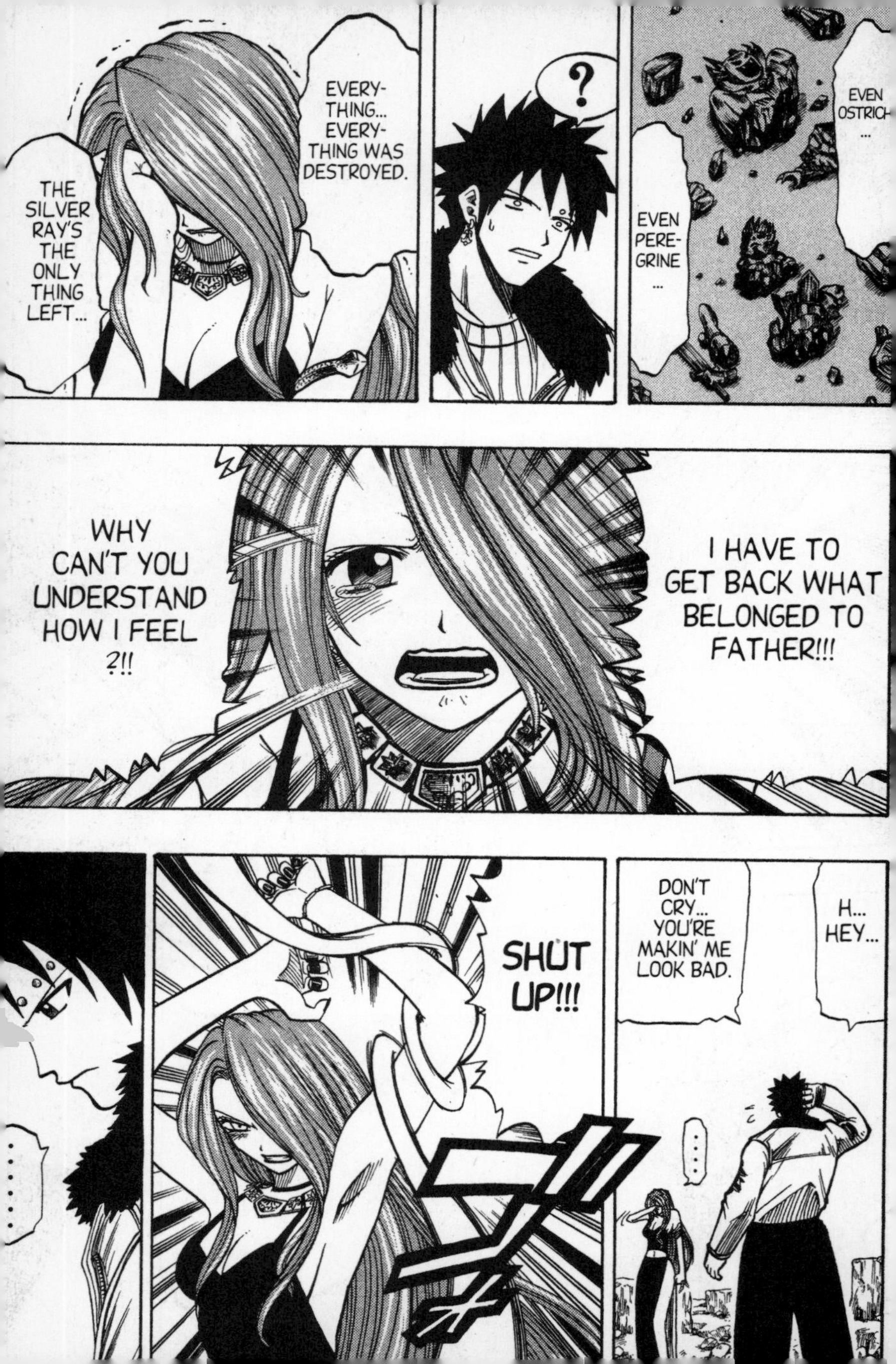
EVEN OSTRICH...
EVEN PEREGRINE...
?
EVERY-THING... EVERY-THING WAS DESTROYED.
THE SILVER RAY'S THE ONLY THING LEFT...
I HAVE TO GET BACK WHAT BELONGED TO FATHER!!!
WHY CAN'T YOU UNDERSTAND HOW I FEEL?!!
H... HEY...
DON'T CRY... YOU'RE MAKIN' ME LOOK BAD.
.....
SHUT UP!!!
......

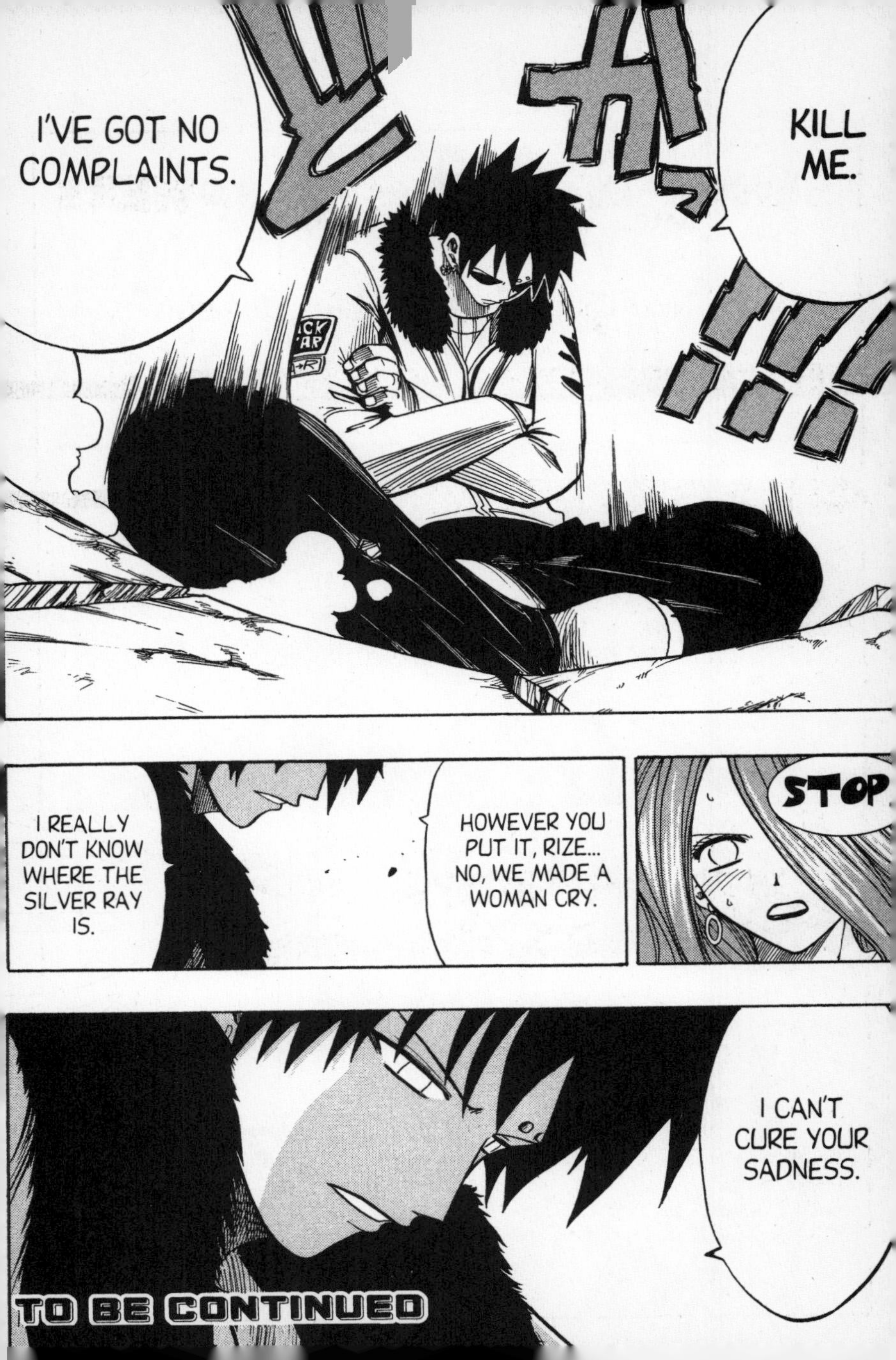
KILL ME.
I'VE GOT NO COMPLAINTS.
STOP
HOWEVER YOU PUT IT, RIZE... NO, WE MADE A WOMAN CRY.
I REALLY DON'T KNOW WHERE THE SILVER RAY IS.
I CAN'T CURE YOUR SADNESS.
TO BE CONTINUED

SWORD OF TEN: TEN POWERS

5. The Twin Dragon Sword: Blue Crimson

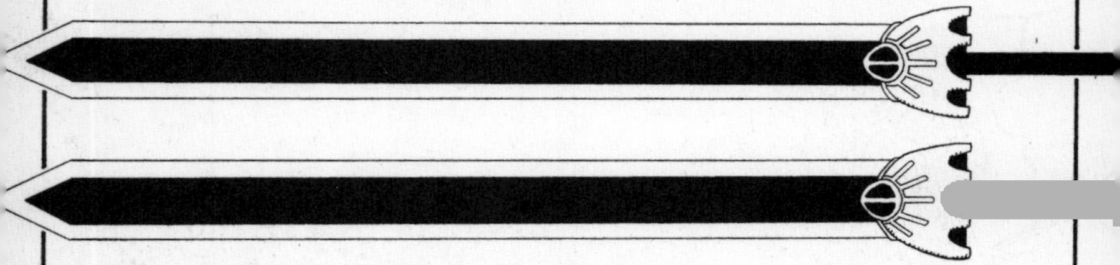

TWIN ENCHANTED BLADES OF FIRE AND ICE. CAPABLE OF VARIOUS ATTACK TECHNIQUES IN THE HAND OF A MASTER... WHICH HARU IS NOT... YET.
BLUE IS, WELL... BLUE, FOR ICE, WHILE CRIMSON IS... CRIMSON, FOR FIRE.

6. The Vacuum Sword: Mel Force

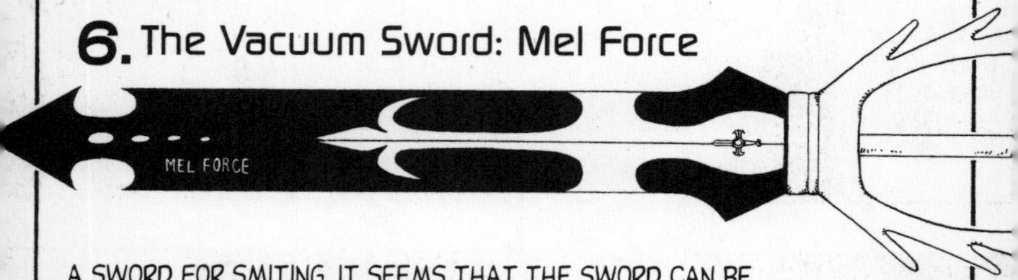
MEL FORCE

A SWORD FOR SMITING. IT SEEMS THAT THE SWORD CAN BE USED TO PARALYZE AN OPPONENT.
IT IS BELIEVED THAT SHIBA NEVER EMPLOYED THE FOUR REMAINING FORMS OF THE TEN POWERS.

OH, ALSO I GET A LOT OF QUESTIONS ASKING IF THE SWORD HARU IS SEEN HOLDING ON THE CHAPTER COVER FOR CHAPTER 73 (BOOK 9) IS THE FINAL SHAPE OF THE TEN POWERS. IT'S NOT, THAT'S NOTHING.

WE HAVE HAD SOME CHANGES IN PERSONNEL

HEYA.

ASSISTANT'S PAGE

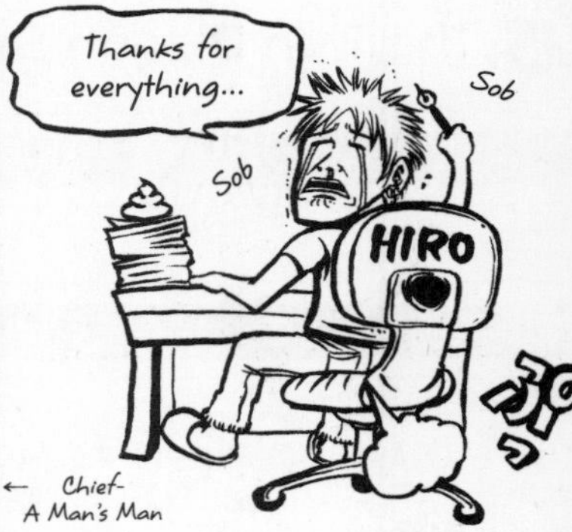

Thanks for everything...
Sob
Sob
HIRO

← Chief-
A Man's Man

Formerly homeless. Dumber than me.

The new guy.
↓Catching on quick!

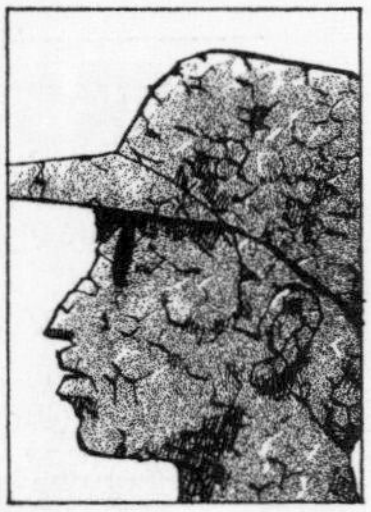

Assistant #1
Kouji Nakamura

Profile Etc.
2nd Volume
Reference
Photo: Post-
Petrification

Known Residences: Mashima-san's workplace (Kodansha) Tokyo's Hinoshi district (as of 2001)

Favorite Activities: Drawing & Shading Backgrounds
Rubbing Nose
Playing Historical Simulation Games

Special Talent: Harassing his subordinates

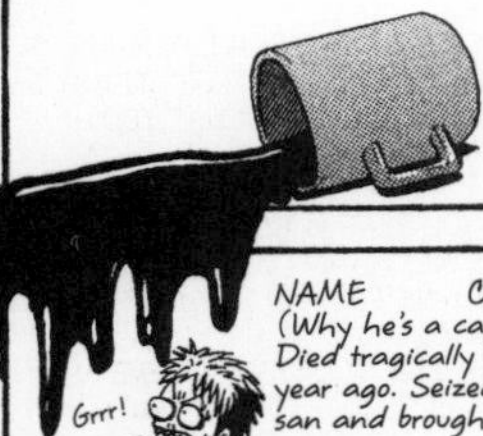

Oops, spilled your cup of coffee, Kaz. Heh heh heh...

Your unhoned skill is in the way of my work!
The New Guy, de Condo.

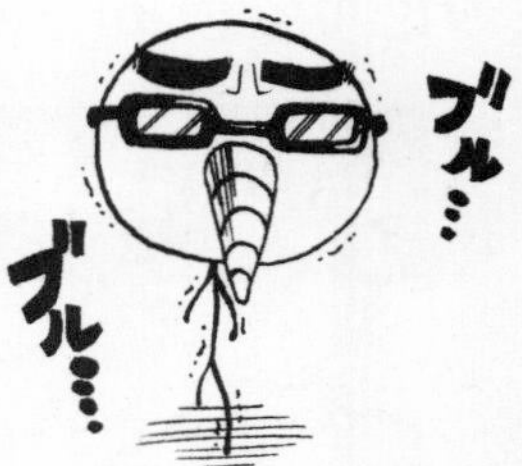

My Job

- Shading (You missed a spot!)
- Erasing (Fold the manuscript!)
- Line Drawing (Put that curtain over there!)
- Toning (Cut the manuscript!)

I am Mashima-san's tool! If there's no RAVE, then I don't eat, so friends, readers, everyone support RAVE!!

NAME Captain Kaz (22)
(Why he's a captain is s-e-c-r-e-t _)
Died tragically in a Kabuki play one year ago. Seized on site by Mashima-san and brought back here.

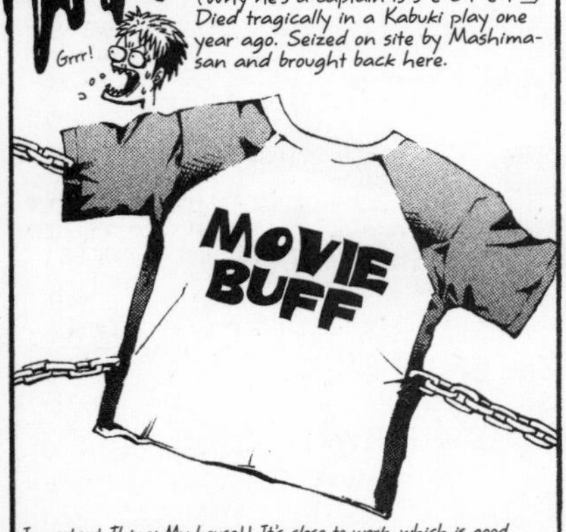

Grrr!
MOVIE BUFF

Important Thing: My house!! It's close to work, which is good
Addiction: Photography! I'm addicting all my friends too.
Frequently Visited: Shinjuku, Shihikita Station
Alma Mater: Nagasaki. I'm a Kyushu Man.
I Like: Stress reduction thru talkin' to friends!!
Special Talent: Massages. Body's important!
Strength: Clapping my fingers together! (Meaning Unknown)
Role: Drawing backgrounds, take-out, errands, photocopy, fax

RAVE MASTER™

Fan Art!

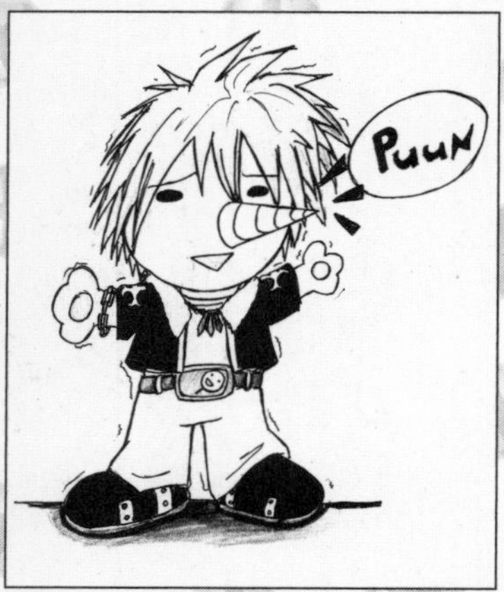

PUUN

RAVE MASTER PLUE! I LIKE THE ALL THE LITTLE DETAILS–LIKE THE LOLLIPOP BELT BUCKLE. COOL IDEA!

ASHLEY G.
MEDICAL LAKE, WA

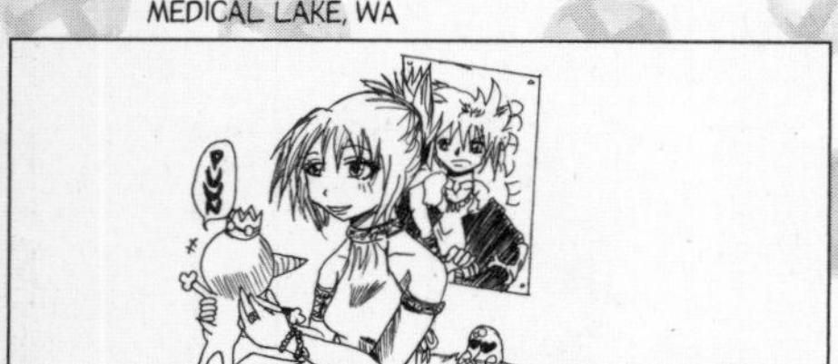

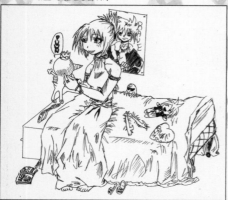

"ELIE'S ROOM." SO PRETTY! I LIKE HOW YOU EVEN GAVE HER "LOVE BELIEVER" BRAND SLIPPERS. NICE GRIFF CAMEO, TOO!

SABRINA D.
AGE 14
NORTH POLE, AK

HEY ASPIRING MANGA ARTISTS! WANT TO SEE YOUR PICTURES IN PRINT? WELL, IF YOU THINK YOU CAN DRAW A COOL-LOOKING HARU, A SEXY ELIE OR A FUNNY PLUE, SEND 'EM THIS WAY! WE'LL PICK ONE LUCKY WINNER FROM EACH ROUND AND SEND THEM A SPECIAL PRIZE! WHAT DO HAVE TO LOSE? NOTHING!

HOW TO SUBMIT:

1) SEND YOUR WORK VIA REGULAR MAIL (NOT E-MAIL) TO:

RAVE MASTER FAN ART
C/O TOKYOPOP
5900 WILSHIRE BLVD.
SUITE 2000
LOS ANGELES, CA 90036

2) ALL WORK SUBMITTED SHOULD BE IN BLACK-AND-WHITE AND NO LARGER THAN 8.5" X 11". (AND TRY NOT TO FOLD IT TOO MANY TIMES!)

3) ANYTHING YOU SEND WILL NOT BE RETURNED. IF YOU WANT TO KEEP YOUR ORIGINAL, IT'S FINE TO SEND US A COPY.

4) PLEASE INCLUDE YOUR FULL NAME, AGE, CITY AND STATE FOR US TO PRINT WITH YOUR WORK. IF YOU'D RATHER US USE A PEN NAME, PLEASE INCLUDE THAT TOO.

5) IMPORTANT: IF YOU'RE UNDER THE AGE OF 18, YOU MUST HAVE YOUR PARENT'S PERMISSION IN ORDER FOR US TO PRINT YOUR WORK. ANY SUBMISSIONS WITHOUT A SIGNED NOTE OF PARENTAL CONSENT CANNOT BE USED.

6) FOR FULL DETAILS, PLEASE CHECK OUT HTTP://WWW.TOKYOPOP.COM/ABOUTUS/FANART.PHP

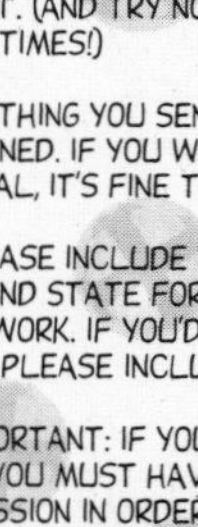

DRAW US! PUUN!

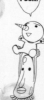

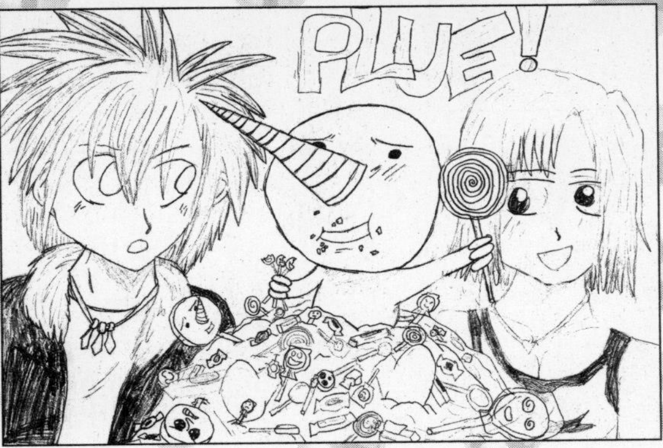
PLUE!

AW, SWEET! LOOK AT ALL THAT CANDY! PLUE MUST BE IN HEAVEN RIGHT NOW. THANKS, TONY!

TONY B.
AGE 11
GLADSTONE, MO

THE ORIGINAL THREESOME. IT'S NICE TO SEE THEM THEM ALL SO HAPPY! THANKS A BUNCH, ALECIA

ALECIA B.
AGE 13
WILDWOOD, MO!

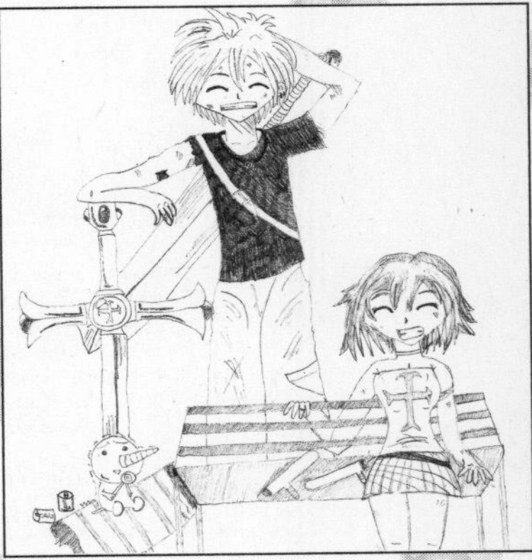

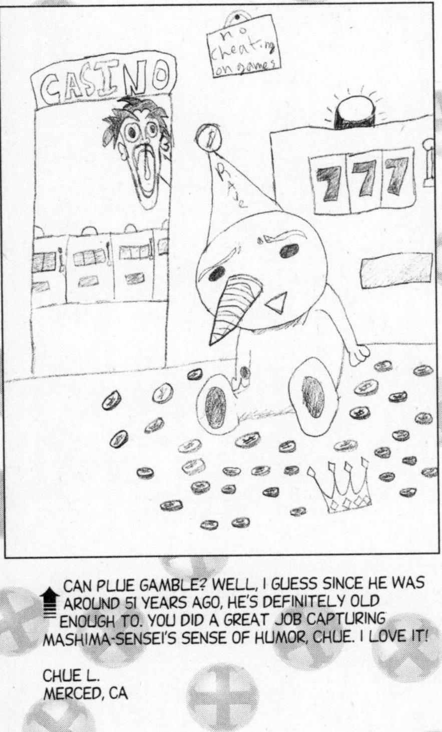
CASINO
no cheating on games
777

CAN PLUE GAMBLE? WELL, I GUESS SINCE HE WAS AROUND 51 YEARS AGO, HE'S DEFINITELY OLD ENOUGH TO. YOU DID A GREAT JOB CAPTURING MASHIMA-SENSEI'S SENSE OF HUMOR, CHUE. I LOVE IT!

CHUE L.
MERCED, CA

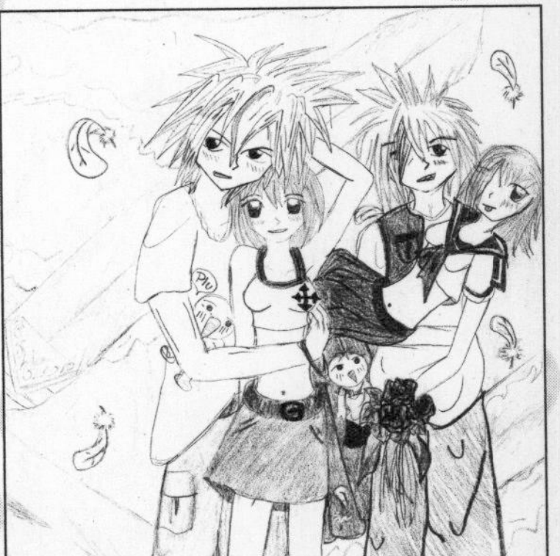

TWO VIEWS OF HARU AND ELIE. AREN'T THEY A CUTE COUPLE? HOPEFULLY THEY CAN GET SOME TIME TO RELAX IN THE NEXT VOLUME. THANKS, CYNTHIA!

CYNTHIA S.
STREAMWOOD, IL

AW, SNAP! I TOTALLY BLEW IT! I RECEIVED THESE AWESOME PIECES OF ART AND LOST THE ARTISTS' NAMES! WHOEVER YOU TWO ARE, YOUR WORK ROCKS.

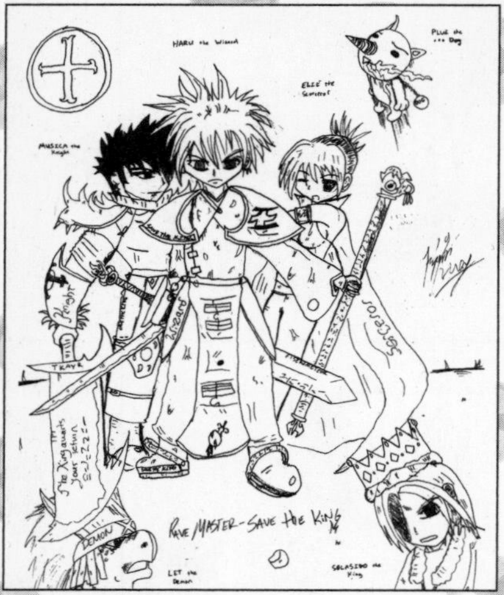
Rave MASTER - SAVE the King

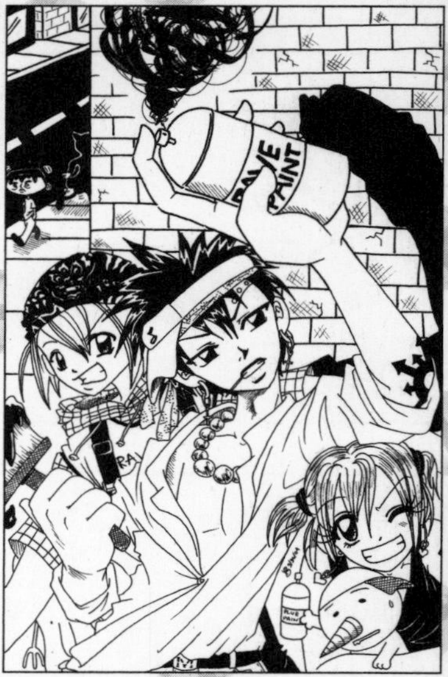
RAVE PAINT

WHAT A GREAT CONCEPT! MASHIMA-SENSEI LOVES SWORDS AND SORCERY, SO REST ASSURED THAT YOU'LL SEE MORE PICTURES OF THE RAVE CREW IN FANTASY GEAR PRETTY SOON! Y'KNOW WHAT'S THE WEIRDEST THING ABOUT THIS DRAWING? PLUE WITH EARS! EARS?! VERY COOL.

BISHI MUSICA LEADS A GRAFFITI ADVENTURE! SUCH A FUN PIC. YOU EVEN WORKED A PUDDING-HEAD AND JIGGLE-BUTT INTO THE BACKGROUND! THIS DRAWING COULD EASILY HAVE BEEN ONE OF MASHIMA-SENSEI'S CHAPTER BREAKS. AWESOME!

HARU AND FUNKY PLUE. YOU ROCK TOO, T-BONE! P'SHAW!

TOMMY "T-BONE" M.
AGE 11
HANOVER, NH

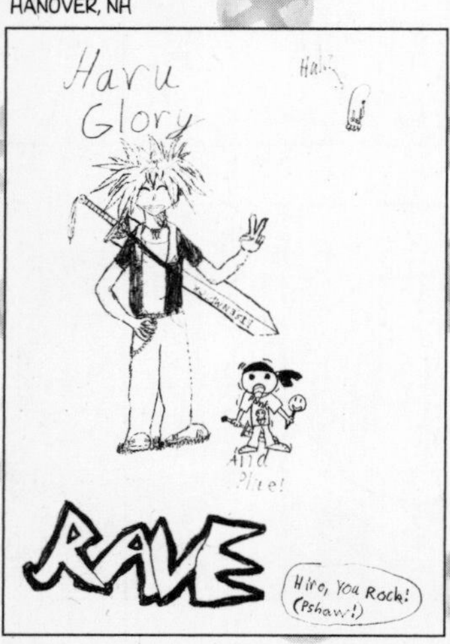
Haru Glory
And Plue!
RAVE
Hiro, You Rock! (Pshaw!)

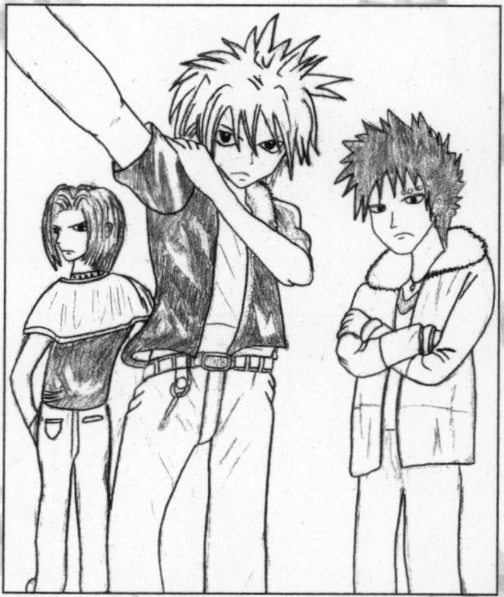

HARU AND THE TOUGH GUYS FROM VOLUME 7. WILL WE EVER SEE SOLASIDO AGAIN?

JORDAN T.
LOS ANGELES, CA

RAVE0077 Levin watches the House
Episode 10 - Image Change

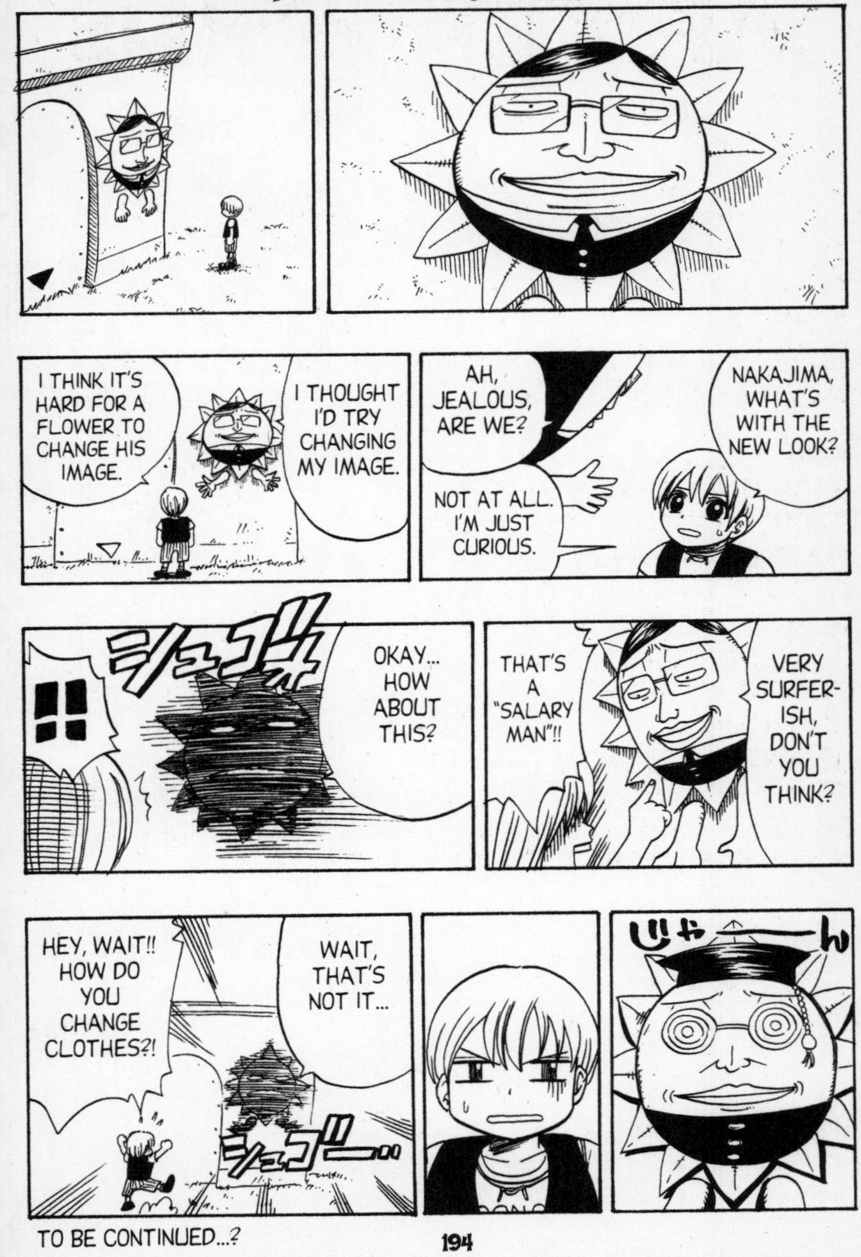
NAKAJIMA, WHAT'S WITH THE NEW LOOK?
AH, JEALOUS, ARE WE?
NOT AT ALL. I'M JUST CURIOUS.
I THOUGHT I'D TRY CHANGING MY IMAGE.
I THINK IT'S HARD FOR A FLOWER TO CHANGE HIS IMAGE.
VERY SURFER-ISH, DON'T YOU THINK?
THAT'S A "SALARY MAN"!!
OKAY... HOW ABOUT THIS?
シュゴォ
!!
じゃーーん
WAIT, THAT'S NOT IT...
HEY, WAIT!! HOW DO YOU CHANGE CLOTHES?!
シュゴー…

TO BE CONTINUED...?

"AFTERWORDS"

DOT COM!! MASHIMA HERE. BEEN PRETTY BUSY LATELY. I LOVE BEING A MANGA ARTIST, BUT IT'S A BUSY LIFE. BUSY DOING WHAT? COLOR ART! FOR THE MAGAZINE, I'M DOING A RAVE CALENDAR, PLUS SOME OTHER ILLUSTRATIONS, SO LOTS OF DRAWING AND PAINTING. YES, IT'S A BUSY LIFE, BUT THOSE GRUMBLES ARE HAPPY GRUMBLES. I'D MUCH RATHER DO THIS THAN ANY OTHER JOB.

NOW, ABOUT VOL. 11. THIS TIME, BESIDES THE MAIN STORY OF THE RAVE MASTER VS. DARK BRING MASTER, THERE'S JEGAN VS. LET AND MUSICA VS. REINA FOR SUBPLOTS. AFTER DEBATING THE PROS AND CONS, I DECIDED THIS WOULD BE WHERE LET REGAINS HIS HUMANOID FORM, RATHER THAN WHERE I'D ORIGINALLY PLANNED IT (BACK IN VOL. 8). I'D ALREADY SUGGESTED THAT REINA IS A SILVER CLAIMER (VOL. 6, P. 129), BUT NOW YOU KNOW IT'S TRUE. OH, HERE'S A LITTLE SECRET... YOU KNOW THAT BIRD ALWAYS AROUND BELIAL? WANNA KNOW HIS NAME? ISN'T IT OBVIOUS? **GRAVE**!! A VERY FITTING NAME FOR BELIAL'S SIDEKICK, IF I DO SAY SO MYSELF.

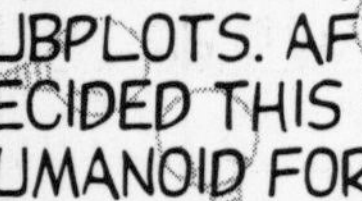
MASHIMA.

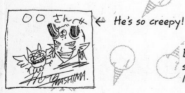

← *He's so creepy!*

By the way, I'll make some RAVE art of King like this soon. →

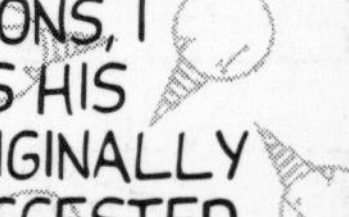
RAVE
MASHIMA.

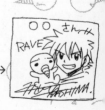

The Great Character Hunt!

WOW, THE CAST OF RAVE MASTER HAS GOTTEN BIG, HASN'T IT? AS A REFRESHER, WE TOOK THE ENTIRE CAST SO FAR AND CRAMMED ALL THEIR NAMES INTO THIS GREAT BIG WAD OF LETTERS. SEE THAT LIST? THEY'RE ALL IN THERE. PLUS, SINCE MASHIMA-SENSEI IS SUCH A LORD OF THE RINGS FAN, WE THREW IN A FOURSOME OF HOBBITS TO BOOT! ALL NAMES ARE LISTED HORIZONTALLY OR VERTICALLY, FORWARDS AND BACKWARDS (SORRY, NO DIAGONALS!). SEE IF YOU CAN FIND THEM ALL!

A	J	A	H	X	R	M	U	D	E	E	P	S	N	O	W	C	F	I	J
N	I	D	L	E	T	F	J	E	G	A	N	W	I	Y	R	P	L	U	E
I	G	A	L	E	R	A	R	E	G	R	O	O	V	E	T	L	E	N	I
E	G	W	N	D	L	F	P	R	M	O	D	M	E	L	O	D	I	A	D
R	L	V	A	F	Y	R	Z	H	A	N	I	U	L	I	U	S	N	K	C
H	E	B	I	L	L	A	B	O	N	G	S	S	F	E	A	V	A	A	L
M	B	O	T	O	N	N	B	U	X	L	A	I	R	E	B	L	P	J	E
E	U	N	A	W	M	K	I	N	G	A	L	C	O	R	I	A	S	I	A
R	T	I	M	H	A	E	S	D	G	C	O	A	D	E	H	S	E	M	M
R	T	P	L	A	D	N	G	D	E	E	S	Z	O	M	S	A	N	A	A
Y	G	P	A	R	U	B	Y	H	N	L	S	A	M	I	N	G	I	R	L
C	A	I	D	U	H	I	R	O	M	A	S	H	I	M	A	N	P	E	T
R	N	P	Z	G	S	L	T	I	A	N	G	L	E	A	Y	A	L	F	E
F	G	C	U	L	I	L	I	T	H	C	A	T	T	L	E	Y	A	P	S
F	L	H	D	O	R	Y	U	N	R	E	S	H	A	T	W	F	U	A	E
I	J	I	H	R	A	C	A	S	O	R	I	O	N	E	T	T	E	W	K
R	Q	N	K	Y	R	O	L	G	E	L	A	G	U	S	K	N	A	L	B
G	E	O	R	C	O	X	O	T	R	A	H	G	I	E	S	M	F	I	H

HARU GLORY
PLUE
ELIE
MUSICA
GRIFF
LET
RUBY
HEBI
NAKAJIMA
CATTLEYA
GENMA
BOTON
LEVIN
GALE GLORY
SHIBA
DALMATIAN
ALPINE SPANIEL
DEERHOUND

CLEA MALTESE
RESHA
MELODIA
LASAGNA
CHINO
SOLASIDO
REMI MALTESE
FUA
PAWL
SEIG HART
KING
GALE RAREGROOVE
SHUDA
REINA
JEGAN
BERIAL
IULIUS
HAJA

GEORCO
LANCE
ROSA
GO
RON GLACE
LTIANGLE
RACAS
RIONETTE
DORYU
FRANKEN BILLY
LILITH
WOLF
DEEP SNOW
WADA
BLANK
JEID
HIRO MASHIMA

The Rave Master has fallen?!
Who can stop the Oracion Six?

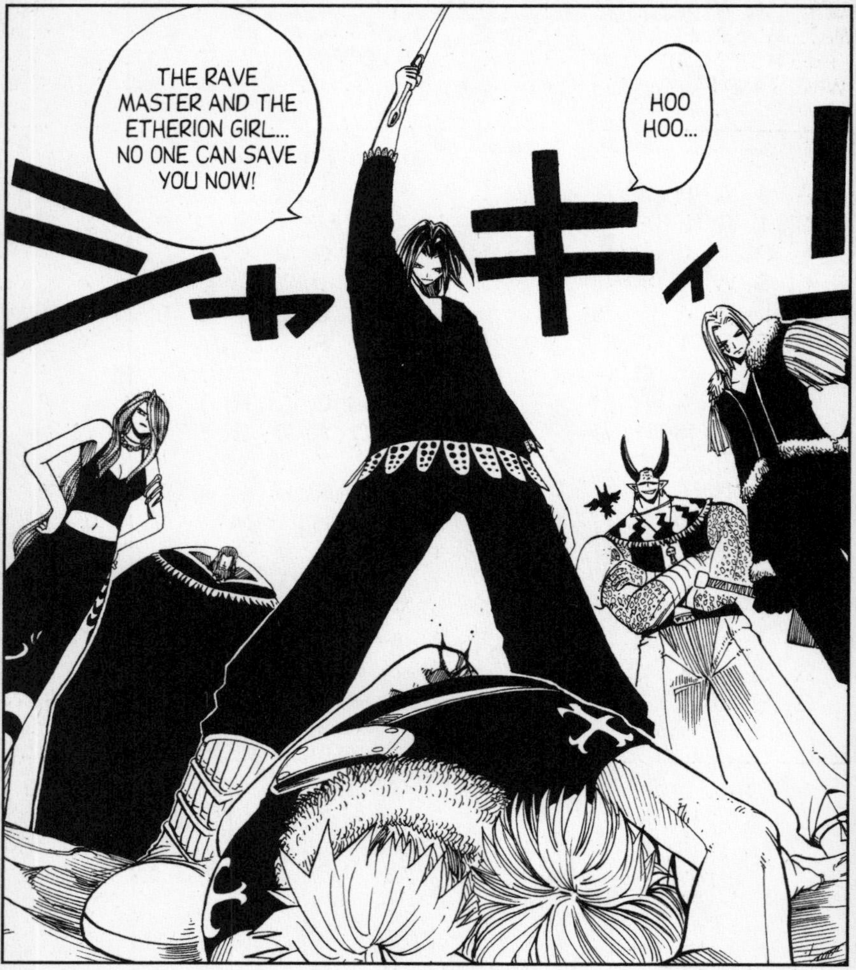
HOO HOO...
THE RAVE MASTER AND THE ETHERION GIRL... NO ONE CAN SAVE YOU NOW!

With the Timestream in jeopardy, an old foe returns.
The battle of titans comes to a shocking conclusion!

Rave Master volume 12
Available December 2004

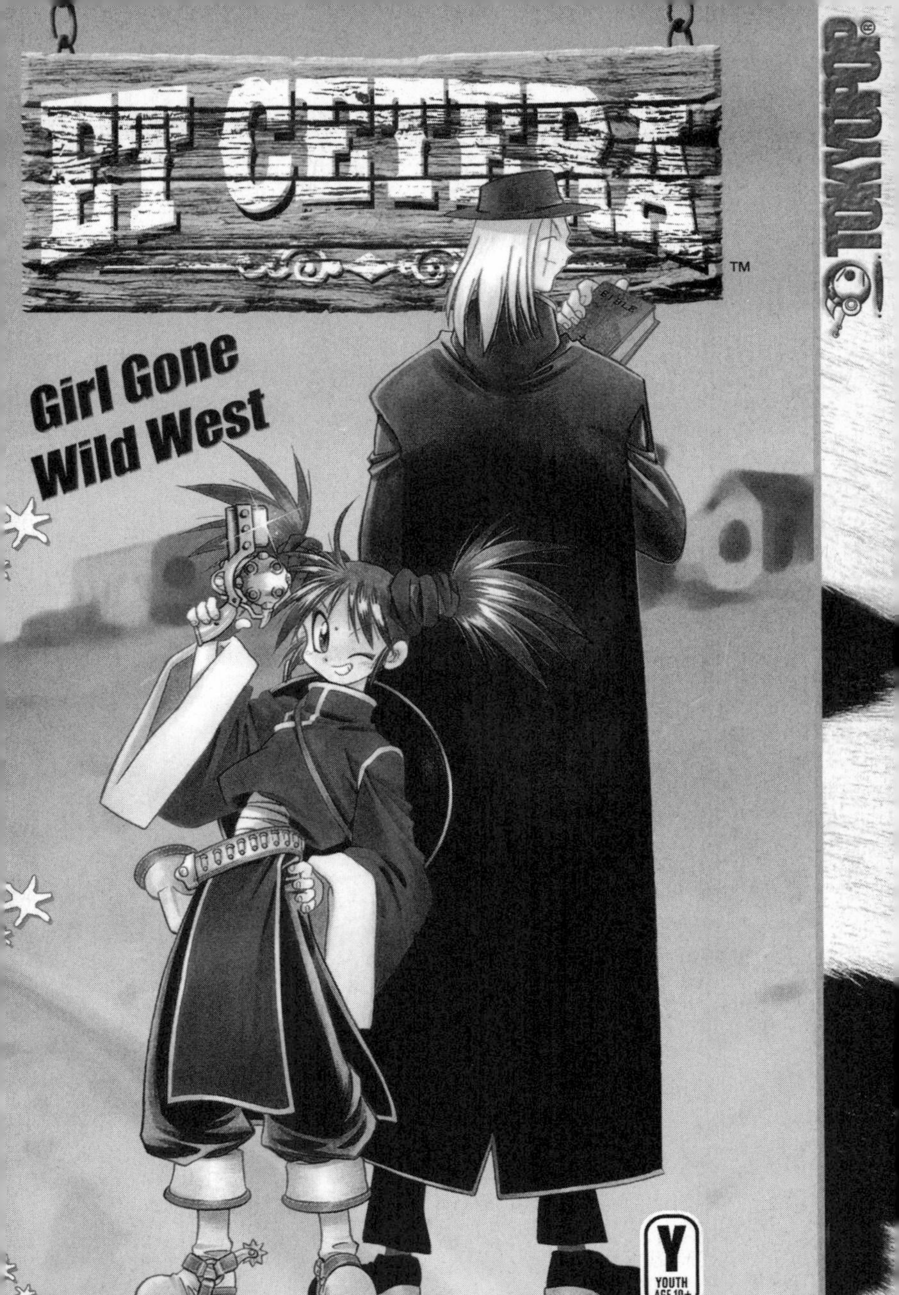
TM
Y
YOUTH
AGE 10+
TOKYOPOP

Girl Gone Wild West

www.TOKYOPOP.com

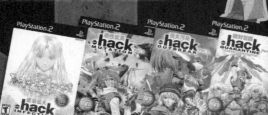

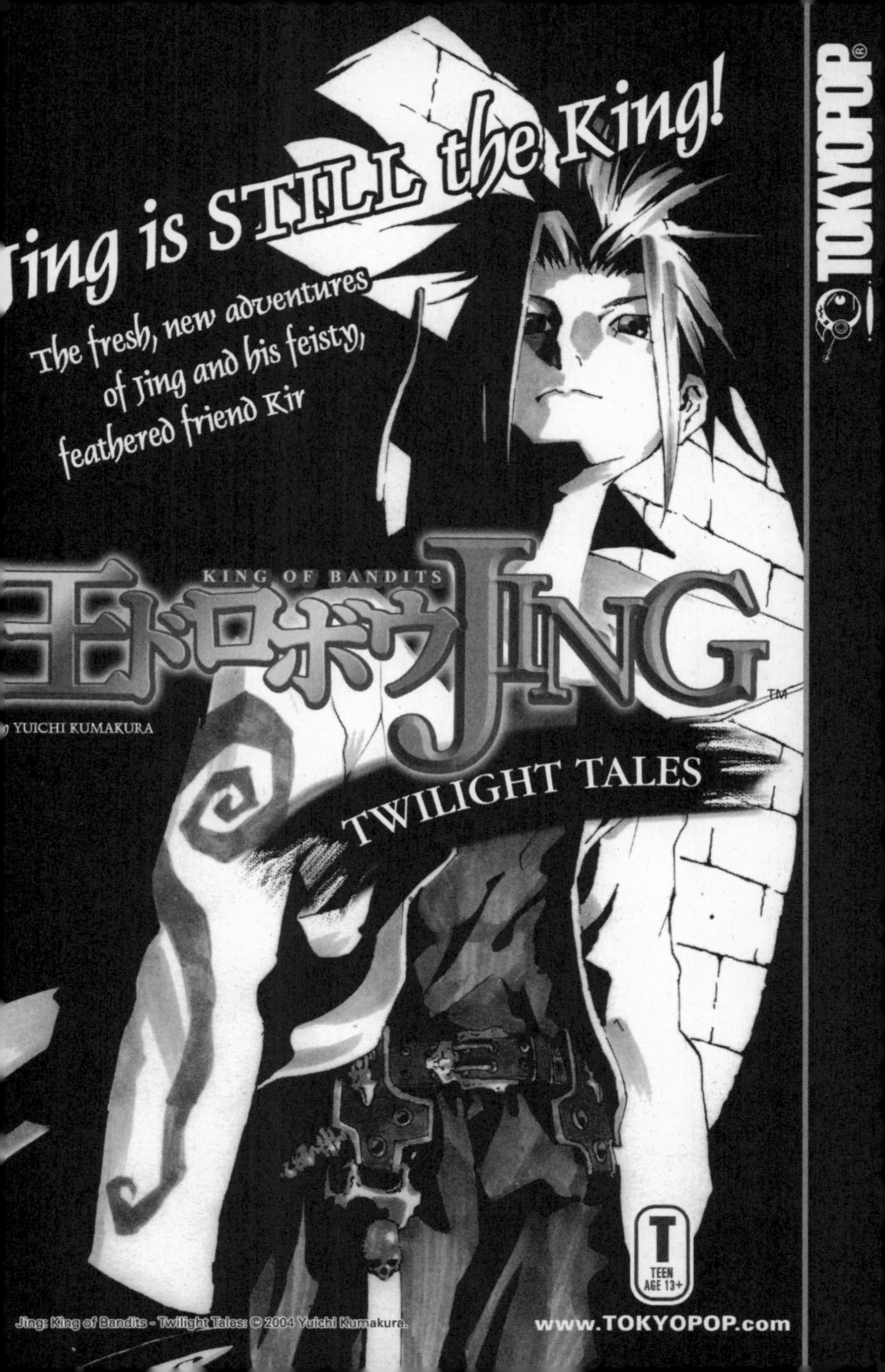
Jing is STILL the King!
The fresh, new adventures of Jing and his feisty, feathered friend Kir
KING OF BANDITS
王ドロボウ JING
YUICHI KUMAKURA
TWILIGHT TALES
T TEEN AGE 13+
Jing: King of Bandits - Twilight Tales: © 2004 Yuichi Kumakura.
www.TOKYOPOP.com
TOKYOPOP

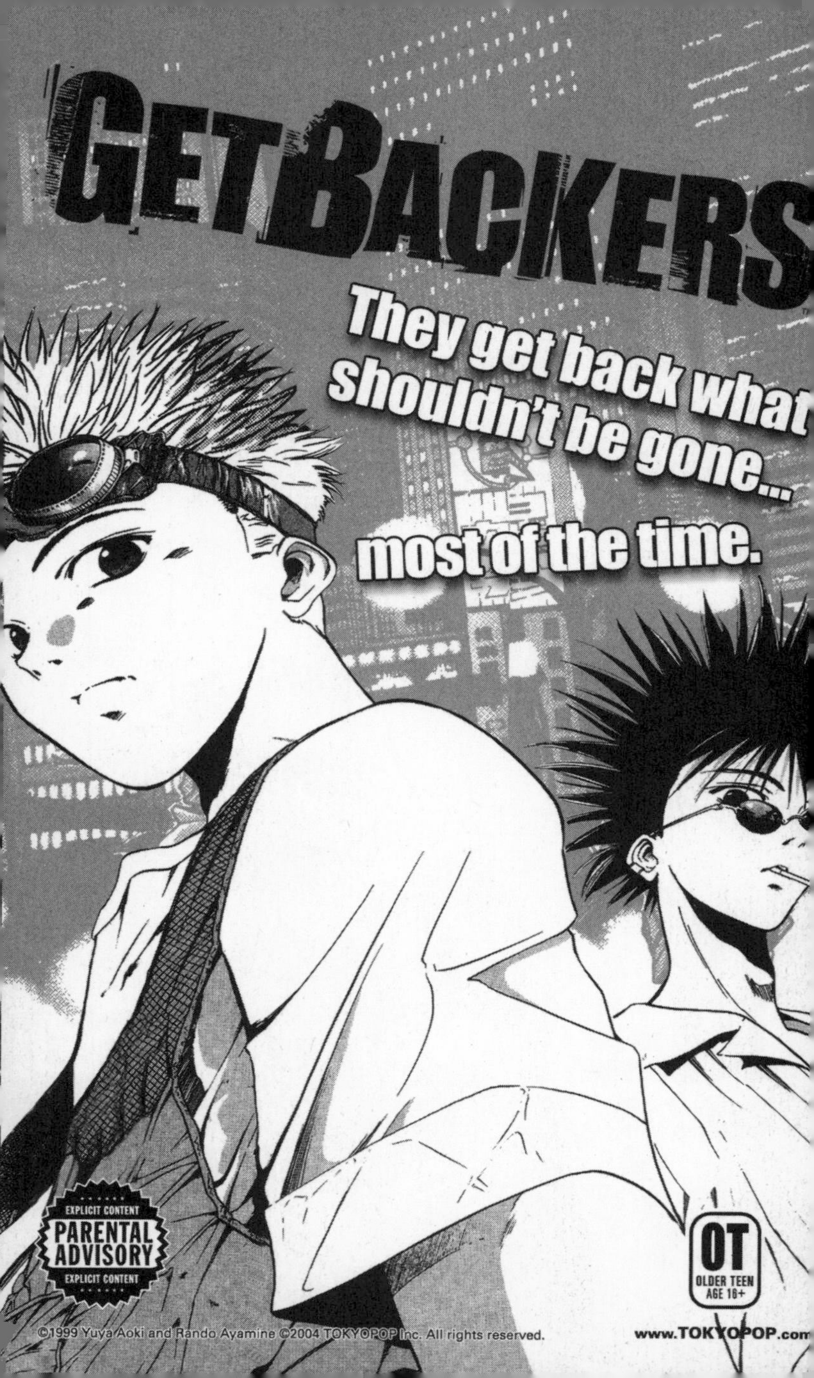
GETBACKERS
They get back what shouldn't be gone...
most of the time.
EXPLICIT CONTENT
PARENTAL ADVISORY
EXPLICIT CONTENT
OT
OLDER TEEN AGE 16+
©1999 Yuya Aoki and Rando Ayamine ©2004 TOKYOPOP Inc. All rights reserved.
www.TOKYOPOP.com

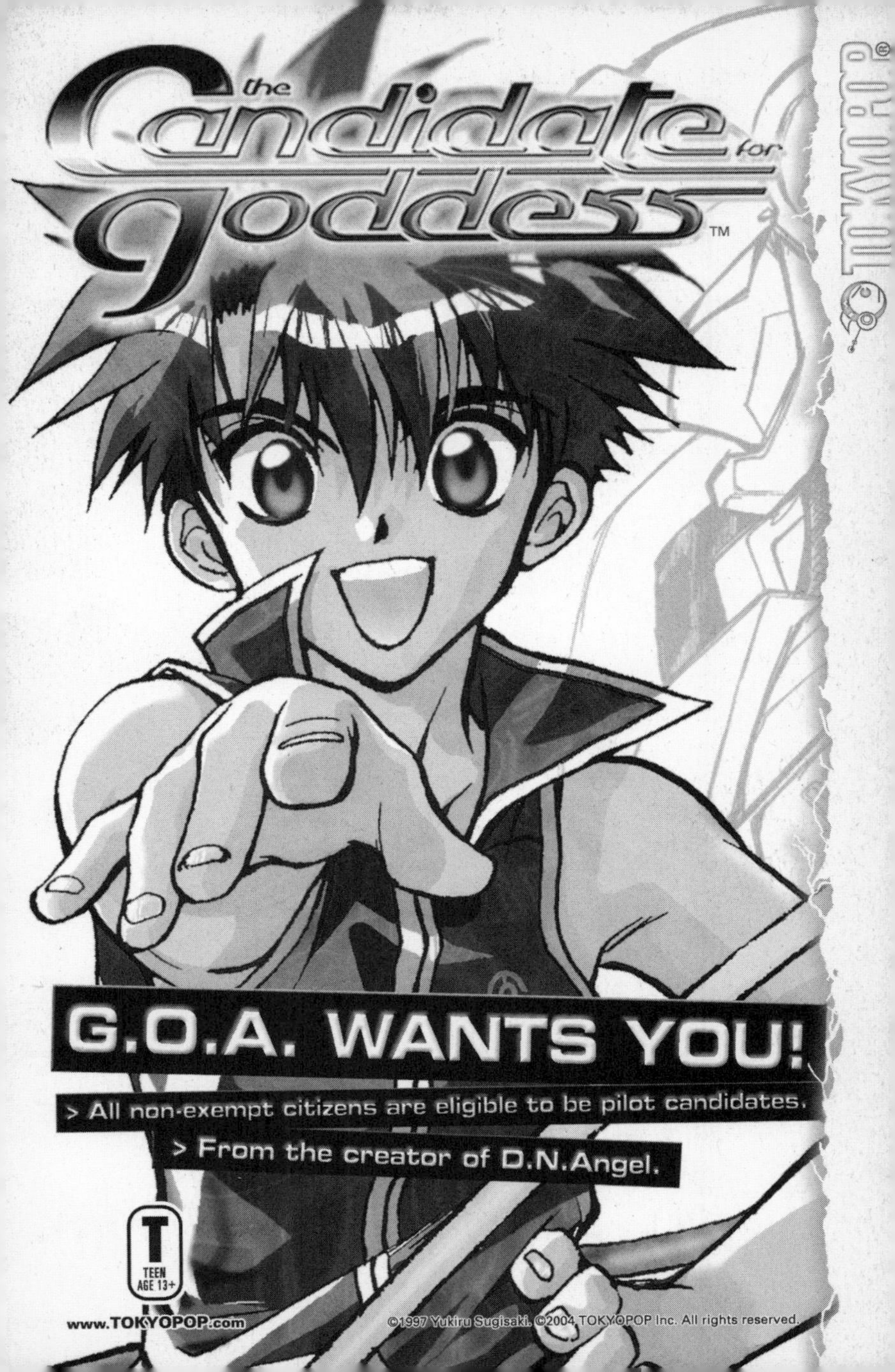
the Candidate for Goddess™
TOKYOPOP®
G.O.A. WANTS YOU!
> All non-exempt citizens are eligible to be pilot candidates.
> From the creator of D.N.Angel.
T
TEEN
AGE 13+
www.TOKYOPOP.com
©1997 Yukiru Sugisaki. ©2004 TOKYOPOP Inc. All rights reserved.

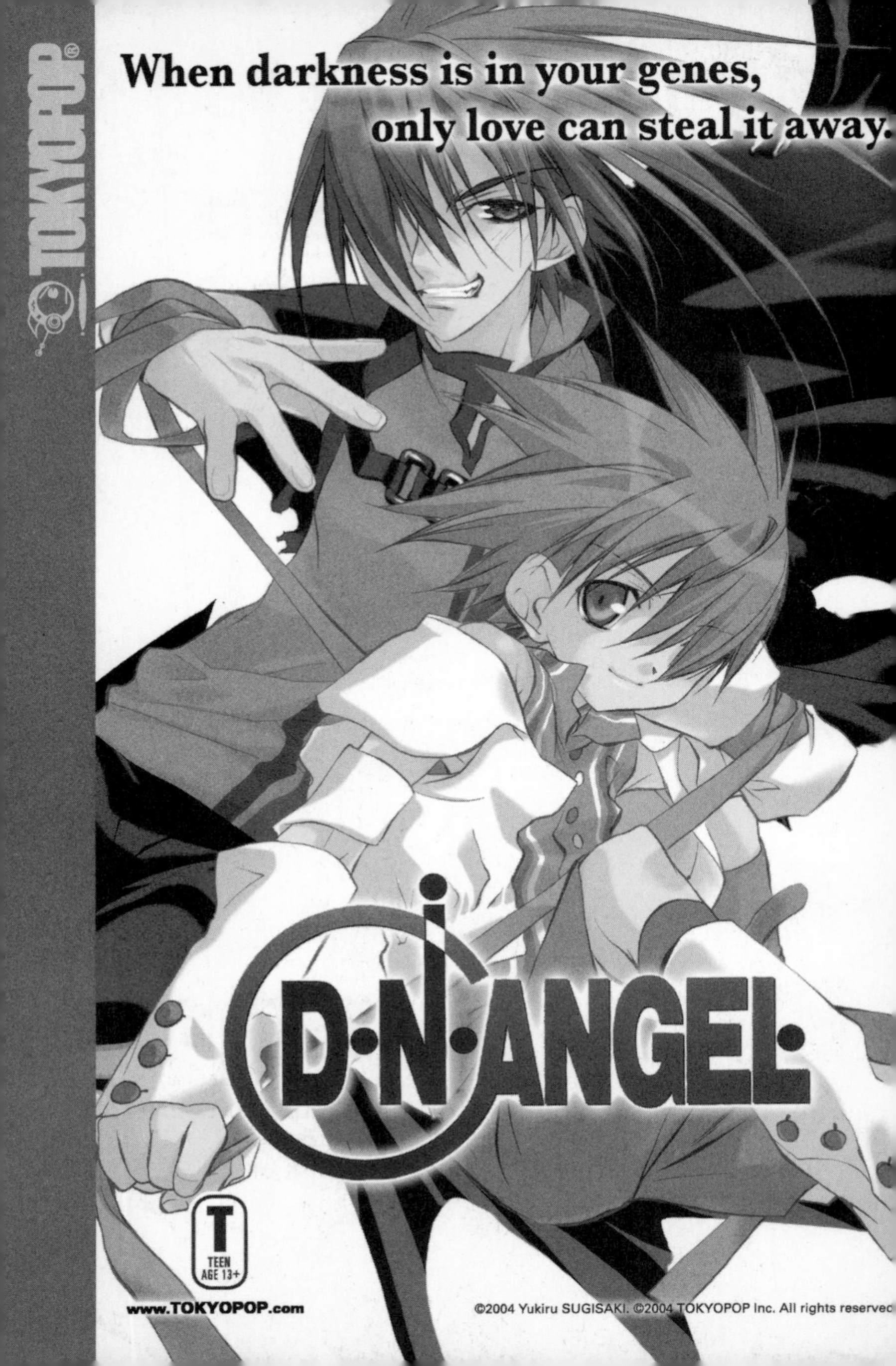

TOKYOPOP
When darkness is in your genes,
only love can steal it away.
D·N·ANGEL
T
TEEN
AGE 13+
www.TOKYOPOP.com
©2004 Yukiru SUGISAKI. ©2004 TOKYOPOP Inc. All rights reserved

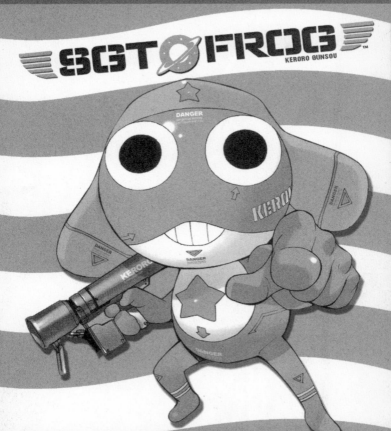

SGT FROG WANTS YOU!

SGT FROG
KERORO GUNSOU

A WACKY MANGA OF ALIEN FROGS & WORLD DOMINATION BY MINE YOSHIZAKI

BASED ON THE HIT VIDEO GAME SERIES

Suikoden III

幻想水滸伝

A legendary hero.
A war with no future.
An epic for today.

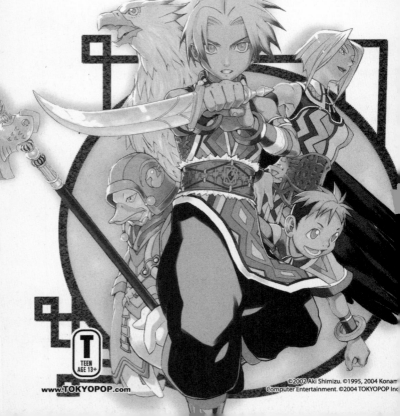

ALSO AVAILABLE FROM 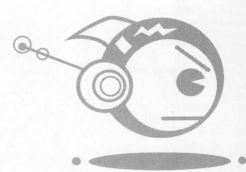 TOKYOPOP®

NORTHWEST

07.15.04Y

This is the back of the book.
You wouldn't want to spoil a great ending!

This book is printed "manga-style," in the authentic Japanese right-to-left format. Since none of the artwork has been flipped or altered, readers get to experience the story just as the creator intended. You've been asking for it, so TOKYOPOP® delivered: authentic, hot-off-the-press, and far more fun!

DIRECTIONS

If this is your first time reading manga-style, here's a quick guide to help you understand how it works.

It's easy... just start in the top right panel and follow the numbers. Have fun, and look for more 100% authentic manga from TOKYOPOP®!

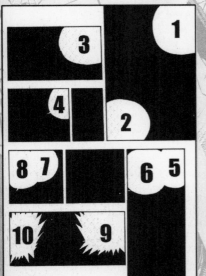

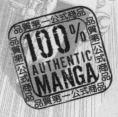